The Lean Business Guidebook

The Lean Business Guidebook

How to Satisfy Your Customers and Maximize Your Profit

MJS Bindra & Ekroop Kaur

Routledge
Taylor & Francis Group

A PRODUCTIVITY PRESS BOOK

First published 2022
by Routledge
605 Third Avenue, New York, NY 10158

and by Routledge
2 Park Square, Milton Park, Abingdon, Oxon, OX14 4RN

Routledge is an imprint of the Taylor & Francis Group, an informa business

ISBN: 978-1-032-11834-5 (hbk)
ISBN: 978-1-032-11825-3 (pbk)
ISBN: 978-1-003-22174-6 (ebk)

DOI: 10.4324/9781003221746

Typeset in Garamond
by Apex CoVantage, LLC

Contents

Foreword

I have known MJS Bindra since the 1990s when we were spearheading the different verticals of a large corporate group. He has always been passionate about machines and their optimum output. On the plant floor, he was always the first one to detect and solve the challenges. He has been on a journey to do things in a different way with a better yield. His zest to streamline tedious daily processes has helped so many companies. The author is a technical person with a strong financial background and exposure to large technology companies across the world. He has mastered lean and kaizen methodologies at Toyota and Komatsu in Japan and lean accounting concepts in America and successfully implemented these across 50 companies in India, Africa and Russia.

The author has created a successful system as to how to run a company with a happy customer base and continuously enhance revenues and profits. How to continuously evolve company products? How to make profits surge faster than revenues? This will determine the success for any company in the future because business transformation involves making fundamental changes in how business is conducted in order to help cope with shifts in market environment.

This is what this book is about. Why is there constant firefighting? Why are managers always busy? Over the years I have seen many approaches to continuously improve the workplace and do things in a better way, but companies are rarely able to sustain the gains they achieve. Kaizen and lean are simple tools that are reasonably easy to understand and grasp. It has been implemented in hundreds of companies across industries, and in the majority of the companies it couldn't go as deep as it did in Toyota. What are the reasons? This book identifies the 'missing link' of why most companies abandon the lean and kaizen implementation half way or a quarter way in. The 'missing link' is to implement 'lean production system, daily management and lean accounting' together as a single package in a company for sustenance. This book explains briefly in simple words the lean production system and daily management concepts but amply elaborates on the lean accounting system – the main missing link of the failure in many companies.

This is almost the first comprehensive book that also details the short-comings of the current standard cost accounting practices and advantages of the lean accounting system and why this should be implemented without delay. This book presents a model that is deep, practical and comprehensive.

The implementation of the lean production system, daily management system and lean accounting system will result in operational benefits and make room for more production. The central message of this book is the finance relevance of value adding and non-value adding activities. Most managers are unaware of the true capacity of their company. What is eating the capacity of the company? How much capacity is being used by the non-value adding activities? How to identify these? How to eliminate or reduce these?

Why don't managers have the financial bent of mind? This book has the answer. The challenge is how both the operational people in different functions understand their daily work linkage with the profit and loss statement and the finance people understand the operational equally well so that they can help operational people identify where the financial losses are happening and together as a team identify what action plan can be adopted to bridge this gap. Why are finance people always glued to the ledgers in their department? Why are they not out there on the field assisting the operational people and being the part of the transformation journey?

Lean accounting has picked up acceptance slower than expected as there are too few books available and too few specialists who understand the kaizen and lean concept thoroughly and have mastered the financial accountancy. I especially like the book's emphasis on operations managers knowing the financial aspect of the business and finance people having the operational focus.

This book explains the concept of the corporate scorecard, which says everything about a company's financial, operational and capacity usage performance for the month. Its introduction is emphasized. Everyone in a company is covered under the performance management system, either in the functional scorecards, performance scorecards or workers skill matrix, which are updated monthly. How to prepare the business plan for a company? How to conduct a one-hour operational and financial performance review meeting every month? How to save managers valuable time that is wasted in performing unnecessary transactions? Every month use the lean assessment audit and know the lean score. The assessment audit will enable a company to monitor the course of its lean journey.

This book breathes hope and it unfolds that it is not difficult to implement, and it will bring in enthusiasm and optimism and inspiration that it is possible to achieve the operational and financial results that the authors could achieve in many companies.

Another key point is emphasis on people: that makes or breaks a company. People have to be carefully selected and continuously trained on the processes and sustenance methodology and financial aspect of everything they do as a team with their combined skill, spirit and fervor. Developing people in such way is the only way to success.

I am convinced that if you follow the recommended methodology in this book, you will not look back.

I hope all of you will enjoy the book. I did.

PY Rajput
CEO, Avon Ispat and Power Ltd.

Preface

A commercial passenger aircraft is a highly complicated piece of machinery. It is assembled using a million components made from complex metals engineered with precision and close tolerances. This deftly created machine can fly more than 300 passengers for more than 16 hours nonstop for more than 15,000 kilometers across continents, crossing different weather zones and providing five-star luxury in comfort, food and beverages, which may not be available in similar variety in a single restaurant on the ground. It stops for a couple of hours and is ready to take off again. This cycle continues flawlessly. It has taken more than a hundred years from 1903 when the Wright brothers took to sky for the first time for teams of aviation engineers to bring the aviation industry to this stable stage.

Almost at the same time in 1903, Henry Ford founded the Ford Motor Company, the first organized company to produce automobiles. What happened on the ground is entirely different from what strides have been made in the aviation sector since then.

Why did most of the manufacturing industries not come up to the standards of the aviation industry? Although automobile, electronics, pharmaceutical and space industries have reached world-class status, most companies in the manufacturing field still function with glitches evading the control of the management. In spite of the fact that Toyota started practicing its 'Toyota Production System' in 1950s, 'daily management' came only in the early 1990s along with 'lean accounting' in mid-1990s. Why so? This is the starting point of my book. As the head of manufacturing plants in various large corporations, I was invariably uncertain about my monthly journey of meeting the budget targets and trying to get solutions for the crucial issues that posed hurdles in my way. I started my career as a management trainee in 1973. Fresh from college I entered the industrial world, and it took me 30 years to rise to the top level in the multinational corporate. I learned by taking instructions from my seniors and executing the same with total acceptance. I was made to understand that in the manufacturing industry regular hurdles like breakdowns, long changeover time, internal rejections, poor yield, large time frame required for new product development, customer complaints regarding quality and associated firefighting are inevitable. As I rose in my career, I felt that there should be a solution to all these impediments.

During my working years I luckily had abundant opportunities for long tenure technical trainings in America, Germany and Japan, which reformed my outlook for solving complex technical problems. I was still far away from discovering solutions to my challenges in running the company as a profit center head. Many things were not in my control. Every month was still a battle to achieve my targets. The turning point came during my training on the 'Toyota Production System' at Komatsu Career Creation Ltd., Tokyo, Japan, at the turn of the century in year 2000 and my visits to many Japanese companies including Toyota, Komatsu, Nippon and Sumitomo Corporation that transformed my perspective toward the manufacturing plants. I later practiced using the 'daily management' tool and devoted considerable time and effort in learning and practicing 'lean accounting'. I had the opportunity of being trained by Brian Maskell in the United States who was at the forefront of inventing the concept of lean accounting. The knowledge of 'Toyota Production System', 'daily management' and 'lean accounting' helped me understand why most companies abandon the lean and kaizen implementation half way.

There are solutions available for breakdowns, long changeover times, quality problems, low yield, customer complaints and non-conformity. But what is required to imbibe lean and kaizen in a company forever as a culture? What is the right way to run a company with control over its operations and business to increase revenues and profits? How to proactively keep the operations under control and in great stride? The solution was implementation of lean production system, daily management and lean accounting simultaneously as an integrated system in a company. In which function should they be implemented first and why? Who should direct the lean implementation in a company? Who should lead it? This book answers all the questions and carves a way for smooth lean journey.

In the last 20 years I have had the opportunity to implement these tools in more than 50 companies across industries in India, Nepal, East Africa, UAE, Taiwan, Russia, Brazil and Japan. The 'Toyota Production System', 'daily management' and 'lean accounting' implementation took me to one of the world's largest textile machinery manufacturers in India to implement cellular manufacturing, reduce throughput time to one third, implement flow and pull and reduce their inventories to one fourth, resulting in tremendous increase in cash flow. I also worked in a large capital machine building industry in India, some of the largest steel companies in east Africa in their cold rolled, aluminum, zinc and color coated lines and several mini steel plants and electric resistance welded tube mills in India, Nepal and East Africa.

I have also worked in diverse industries like a chicken farm in Zambia; agricultural, rose farms, footwear, confectionaries, lead acid batteries, paint resins, plastic packaging plants in Kenya and Uganda; a large corporation in Russia that pioneers in municipal machines like road sweeping, vacuum sucking, washing, mud sucking and snow clearing machines; in Dubai port in UAE; and a Tanzanian gold mine near Lake Victoria where the workplace for kaizen implementation was 5 kilometers below the ground level. Lean accounting was successfully implemented in the paint resin plant, a mini steel plant in Kenya and a capital machinery manufacturer in India.

There are two important motivations for writing this book. First, I had read that if you want to be remembered even after leaving this world, write a book, write a good book and leave it for the progeny to use your expertise and grow. Second, I do not want young people to struggle the way I did but to move forward. I learned from my peers and superiors. I followed what they told me. It was like knowledge being passed around from one generation to the other. I was hardly doing anything proactively. It was like facing the challenges to the best of my abilities. If you continue to do what you have been doing, then you will continue to get the same outcomes. This is what was happening to me. Everyone in the company thinks they are doing their best, yet the targets and improvements are not achieved. A sense of job satisfaction eludes the young, enthusiastic engineers. I would not want our young future leaders to waste their early years. I would like to give them a jump start. This book is a step in that direction.

When I met Ekroop, now my daughter-in-law, she had just begun working for a manufacturing company but had been using snippets of lean in her day-to-day role since the inception of her career unbeknownst to her. I helped her realize the value of lean and how she had been using it. Being a quick learner, she grasped the concepts of lean quickly and started building on that knowledge in a way I had never seen before. After that I asked her if she would like to help me co-author this book to highlight the aspects of traditional accounting methods where lean concepts can be useful to which she happily obliged.

I'd been traveling far and wide throughout my career and suddenly I found myself confined to my home due to the COVID-19 pandemic. This gave me ample time to compile my experiences and my knowledge in this book. My time was thus gainfully spent. I would like this book to be in the hands of every young leader across the industries. This is a must-have book for all promoters, CXOs, CAs, lean and kaizen consultants, managers, shop floor leaders, HODs, engineers, finance and accounts personnel and across all functions. This book is not meant to impart theoretical knowledge of the lean production system, daily management and lean accounting as there are many books already available on the subject but there are very few books available on lean accounting. The benefits of lean accounting still have not been harvested by businesses as it is not well understood or it challenges traditional accounting. Its knowledge is still limited. The purpose of writing this book is to fill that gap. Lean accounting and its implementation process are dealt with in detail in this book in simple language so that finance and non-finance people can understand the subject well.

This book will guide you step by step where to start, what to do with your people, your machines, your overheads. Who should lead the implementation? This book will empower people in a company at all levels and show them what to do on day-to-day basis to achieve the strategy of the company along with their career goals. These are challenging times for companies and only the tough ones that have the determination to control their costs and spending while having clear vision of the customer's changing needs will survive.

I advise all companies to embrace 'lean production system, daily management and lean accounting' together as guided in this book. I assure you that your company will stand out and achieve the values and benefits not available to your competitors. I am confident that this book will guide professionals toward establishing a smooth growth road map for companies. Certainly, the future will be more exciting.

I would appreciate receiving critique, assessment, corrections and forthright reviews from my readers to improve this book. I may be contacted at lean.kaizen.acc@gmail.com.

MJS Bindra
Readers can also get in touch at
ekroop.kaur04@gmail.com

Acknowledgements

A book is an intellectual object that takes a considerable investment of time to compose and a still considerable investment of time to read. While writing this book I have tried to make it simple so that it is easier for readers to understand and implement the concepts.

First and the foremost, praises and thanks to God, the Almighty, for His blessings that He has showered upon me throughout this endeavor.

I would like to express special gratitude to Mr. R. Marwaha who was my guide, mentor and confidante in my career journey and made me who I am today.

I would like to thank Mr. VK Grover, Director, Kaizen Institute who gave me tremendous invaluable guidance and exposure to lean and kaizen knowledge by opening up his books and digital library for me to grab whatever I could. I have found in him the Guru and a knowledge bank of lean and kaizen concepts.

I have been fortunate to be in touch with a network of lean practitioners and blog writers across the globe. They have helped me in understanding the deeper meaning of lean and kaizen concepts and comprehending lean accounting in depth. This book would not have been possible without the corporate groups and companies with whom I worked on the kaizen and lean projects, workshops and consulting engagements and as an executive trainer and assessor over the last 20 years. I thank those young teams, managers and top management executives who were associated with me in the kaizen implementation journey across India, Nepal, Kenya, Zambia, Uganda, Tanzania, UAE, Taiwan, Brazil, Russia and Japan. It was a prized and valuable opportunity for me to understand diverse industries and witness commitment and enthusiasm among the young budding leaders to achieve success in the lean journeys. These 'new school' millennials worked positively, proactively and confidently with me to steer these companies up on the success ladder with increase in profits and revenues and a thousand steps ahead of their competitors. I also remained young in health, vigor and spirit mingling with these millennials.

Finally, I want to thank my wife, Bittu Bindra, for tolerating me so long and putting up with me throughout the arduous process of writing this book and helping me in final proof reading. A lifelong partner makes both the journey and destination worthwhile.

Exceptional thanks to my son Sayyam Jeet Singh Bindra, a civil engineer by profession settled in Melbourne, Australia, and my daughter-in-law Ekroop Kaur, a chartered accountant (ICAI) and certified public accountant (Australia), who has co-authored this book with me. They were the right people in giving me ideas on 'what not to do'. Their commitment, persistent support and drive for perfection were essential in realizing this book. I feel blessed by their presence.

I would also like to thank young man Sahib Preet Singh Rooprai, an architect who is at present pursuing construction management in Canada, for doing the artwork for this book.

MJS Bindra

About the Authors

MJS Bindra is a turnaround specialist who is uniquely qualified to transform multinational or regional companies, large, medium or small, into lean enterprises. He is a professional engineer with an MBA in marketing and finance from BITS Mesra and advanced management from IIM Ahmedabad. He has more than 45 years of experience working with global organizations and thought leaders from diverse industries and fields. In his formative days, he underwent long tenure technical trainings in the world's leading companies like Wean United USA, Muller Weingarten Germany, Schloemann Siemag Germany and Sumitomo Corporation Japan. He developed his skills in the Toyota Production System at Komatsu Career Creation Ltd., Japan, in 2000 and visited many Japanese companies including Toyota, Komatsu, Nippon and Sumitomo Corporation. The concept of daily management was matured during his tenure with Kaizen Institute. The lean accounting principles were adapted after being trained under Brian Maskell in the United States who was at the forefront of inventing the concept of lean accounting.

He has held director level positions in sectors as diverse as capital machine building, steel industry, electric resistance welded (ERW) tubes and cold drawn tube industry. He has supported and implemented lean and kaizen implementation in these companies as well as managing 450+ kaizen workshops in a variety of industries like textiles, machine building, steel mills, flower farms, industrial chemicals, gold mine, edible oil refinery, roofing sheets, ports, automotive, meat processing, jute mill and sugar mill and conducted 250+ training sessions on operational excellence tools with a focus on training of executives and leaders at all levels during the consulting stage. He developed expertise and specialization in total productive maintenance (TPM) all pillars, total flow management (layout design, cellular manufacturing, just-in-time, kanban), policy deployment and lean accounting. Some of the results achieved during implementation in industry with overall equipment effectiveness (OEE) were 30% to 35% improvement at most of clients served, material wastage and rejection reduction by 40% to 50%, inventory reduction by 40% to 50%, throughput time reduction by 20% to 30% and so forth.

Ekroop Kaur is an accomplished chartered accountant (ICAI) and certified public accountant (Australia). She started her corporate career with Vodafone and has also worked with Bharti Infratel Ltd. and Avery Dennison India Ltd. While commencing her stint in Avery Dennison, a renowned manufacturing company that mostly uses traditional standard cost accounting methods, she came across MJS Bindra, her father-in-law and co-author of this book, as her lean mentor. After meeting him, she realized that she had already been using snippets of lean in her previous roles and was curious to learn more. Her learnings from the corporate world about the value of customer experience, challenges in dynamic industry environments, role of finance in major investment decisions and importance of immaculate internal procedures and operational processes are what shaped her perspective.

Chapter 1

Why Is Lean Accounting Vital for a Company?

Perfection is not attainable. But if we chase perfection, we can catch excellence.

– Vince Lombardi

In the last three decades, a number of large companies have transformed their manufacturing processes by implementing lean business strategy and kaizen[1]. These initiatives, known as 'point kaizen', made their manufacturing systems efficient and cost effective. However, the companies have not been able to sustain the benefits achieved through point kaizen. Even today plant teams are unable to compute the financial benefits from kaizen implementation and struggle to correlate them with their day-to-day activities or their influence on the company's financial statements.

Plant executives are equipped with technical and operational skills, but they are not financially savvy. They cannot comprehend the financial statements or how initiatives for improvement in manufacturing processes on the plant floor are reflected in the profit and loss (P&L) statement or how profits are driven by their day-to-day activities. They are unable to identify opportunities to increase profits within the company. Financial statements exhibiting lower profits in a month when they worked hard and higher profits in a relaxed month leave them perplexed.

DOI: 10.4324/9781003221746-1

1

If you are a functional manager in your company, can you spontaneously respond to the following business performance indicators?

- Monetary value of average monthly dispatch
- Current energy consumption by the function
- Current cost of raw materials and consumables
- Current yield percentage and its absolute value
- Updated count of managers, engineers, supervisors, staff and workmen in their function
- Updated manpower cost and overtime value for their function
- Reasons for internal rejections on the plant floor, average monthly internal rejections per million and its monetary value
- Average customer complaint count and customer returns in a month and its monetary value
- Month end inventories of raw material, work in progress and finished goods in volume and monetary value
- Slow moving inventory (not used in the last 60 days) in volume and monetary value
- Non-moving inventory (not used in the last 180 days) in volume and monetary value
- Skill set of the supervisors and workmen
- Training hours utilized for skill improvement of workforce

How many could you answer? Functional managers struggle to answer questions that go beyond their immediate work responsibilities but are critical to deliver results in alignment with the company's goals like those mentioned earlier. Functional managers attend review meetings every month where operational and financial performance is discussed. However, it is often witnessed that functional managers are not well versed with their department's costs per unit or struggle to interpret the financial performance of their function from the P&L statement even though it is shared with them each month. They implement lean tools in their functions but are unable to translate financial gains from the plant floor into the P&L statement. Thus, they fail to adequately address the queries raised by finance executives.

Even if functional managers can calculate the financial gains from their lean and kaizen projects, they are unable to crack the complexity of the P&L statement. They cannot rationalize why higher profits are generated in leaner months when higher volumes were dispatched and lower profits in the months when they exerted overtime on the plant floor.

Finance executives prepare financial statements for all stakeholders, but functional managers, who add tangible value on the shop floor, work toward continual improvement[2] and are responsible for profitability of their functions or value streams, cannot interpolate the numbers in the P&L statement. On the other hand, finance executives lack the knowledge of key business drivers that drive each line item in the P&L statement since they are traditionally book-keepers and lack technical knowledge of processes on the plant floor.

1.1 How Do We Bring the Change We Expect?

Our main motive is to break the complexity of the P&L statement to make it more useful to functional managers and stakeholders. Hence, we need a better approach to construct the P&L statement that gives a true as well as relevant representation of financial performance of the company. The P&L statement prepared with lean accounting addresses the aforementioned issues. It makes comprehension of financial jargon easy for functional teams while complying with the rules and regulations of the statutory authorities.

Lean principles promote the concept of 'value streams' over 'departments'[3]. In lean manufacturing, several mini companies run within a company. To form a mini company, all the managers, executives, supervisors and workmen in a company are grouped into a value stream based on a product family instead of functional departments and are therefore best suited to serve customers. Lean accounting helps to run these mini companies profitably by bringing in more clarity for functional managers. A P&L statement is prepared for each value stream with a different statement for each different product family. The P&L statement is prepared in a way to reflect the performance for the month as well as the output of lean and kaizen initiatives on the plant floor.

Lean accounting[4] is ideal for companies that have a diverse product portfolio. It helps to understand the adverse impact of inventory on a company. It illustrates the potential gains from lower inventory level, lead-time reduction and better customer service without any stock unavailability. Lean accounting promotes monthly preparation of the P&L statement so that opportunity for improvement can be explored every month because quicker action and higher benefits can be reaped only if improvements are made at the right time.

Lean accounting breaks corporate stereotypes and myths like business control through detailed tracking, profit realization through complete utilization of resources, consideration of direct labor as a critical conversion cost and excess capacity as harmful. Rather, lean accounting advocates that some of the important responsibilities of functional managers are timely delivery of the material, lower throughput time, higher inventory turnover and first time right approach to work and not accountability for machine utilization and cost variances from budget or labor efficiency.

Lean accounting makes the marketing department focus on value added product selling. It ensures that new product development will be a healthy figure as a percentage of total products. It helps to monitor cost structure of new product development as an independent value stream without any revenue till the product is market ready. Until then, only provisions for expenses are made which are borne by other value streams.

Lean accounting promotes that value stream managers must understand the monetary value of their business activities. This requires them to have knowledge of cost per minute of downtime due to breakdowns, changeover time, defects, rework, poor yield and waiting. They should be aware of excessive transport cost due to poor layout and value of slow and non-moving inventory. Lean accounting insists that finance managers should collaborate with functional managers to understand these monetary values and work as a team toward cost reduction and to improve the bottom line.

1.2 Operational Excellence for Business Excellence

For any company to prosper, it is important to serve the customers with timely delivery of quality products. But in order to survive, it is imperative to produce and deliver the products at low cost, which can be made possible by reduction or elimination of wastages in the company[5]. These wastages are something that occupy 70% to 80% of manpower's and machines' available time. These wastages consist of downtime, defects, machines working at lower capacity due to lower speed and lesser loads, excessive changeover times, poor yields, unwanted produce, excess inventories in the system and warehouses choked with slow and non-moving inventory. There are lean and kaizen tools that aid in reduction of wastes within a reasonable time through existing teams. Companies should aim to internally develop expertise for reduction or elimination of wastes. Initially, assistance from external experts may be required but eventually an in-house team for internal training, monitoring and audit of the continuous improvement lean and kaizen tools should be developed.

With lean manufacturing, daily management, lean accounting and lean ERP, companies can implement a cost strategy that captures real-time product-wise report to analyze profitable and unprofitable products. The profit can be captured for each value stream separately and can be used for company-wide profit analysis. The focus of previous activities is to enhance customer satisfaction by improvements in quality, delivery and cost. The objective is to provide best quality product, on time and at lowest cost to the customer.

Lean production system, daily management and lean accounting can improve the operational and financial health of a company significantly. On an average, companies adopting lean principles may witness the following results on their current state in a reasonable period of time:

- Increase in profit by 30%
- Increase in sales by 20%
- Increase in productivity by 40%
- Decline in defects by 50%
- Decline in throughput time by 30%
- Free floor space by 30%
- Inventory reduction by 50%
- Overall cost reduction by 30%

CASE STUDY

- A company, one of the top three global players, manufactures textile machineries for the cotton industry right from blow room to spinning. The manufactured machines have state-of-the-art technology that makes these machines ultra-reliable. This company implemented the lean production system. After the first phase of journey, which lasted for 18 months, the following results were achieved:

- Value adding ratio increased from 6.6% to 20%.

- Machine under assembly decreased from 86 to 20.

- Space utilized declined by 50%.

- Throughput time for assembly declined more than four times.

- In stores, the inventories decreased from 39 days to nine days of sales.

- Kaizen assessment score grew from 25% to 60%.
- There was a corresponding surge in profits and cash flows.

A company will have to adopt the mantra of *eliminate, combine, reduce and simplify* **(ECRS)** techniques to get rid of wastage, which would mean eliminate unnecessary processes, combine or reduce what cannot be eliminated and simplify processes to reduce time. This can be done through the following:

- Optimization of cost of production by reduction in 'lead time' (throughput time) of the manufacturing process from order to dispatch or collection from customers
- Standardization of processes to speed up and stabilize output at all work centers
- Getting the work done 'first time right'
- Reduction in breakdowns on the manufacturing machines, internal and external defects, rejection and excessive changeover times
- Identification of machines running at low capacity (i.e., production per hour is less than capacity or keeps fluctuating).
- Reduction or elimination of excess, slow moving and non-moving inventories in the stores and shop floor

ECRS can be achieved by implementation of lean and kaizen tools to the initiatives mentioned earlier like:

- The *kanban system*[6,7] can be deployed in the production flows to enhance continuous and pull flow. This system ensures inventory control and no stockouts because this system is used as a scheduling system that articulates what to produce, when to produce and how much to produce (see Chapter 2 for more details).
- However, it is paramount that a sustenance tool like the *daily management system*[8] is implemented so that operational improvements achieved are sustained (see Chapter 3 for more details).
- A *performance measurement system* should be in place for employees to evaluate their monthly performance against the targets. Employees have a clear understanding of their responsibilities (see Chapter 10 for more details).

- Additionally, by implementing *lean accounting* and *lean ERP*, a company can monitor product pricing to track profitability of each product, each customer, every month (see Chapter 5 and Chapter 15 for more details).
- *Focused improvement projects* are implemented in each value stream with regular assessment audits and review of the results.

Key Takeaways

1. Functional managers are not financially savvy.
2. Financial executives lack operational knowledge of processes on the plant floor.
3. Departments are out. Value streams are in.
4. Value streams are mini companies run by value stream managers.
5. Every value stream should make profit for the company. Each product should make profit for the company.
6. Lean production system, daily management and lean accounting should be implemented together.

Recommended List for Further Reading

1. Imai, M. (1991). *Kaizen (Ky'zen): The key to Japan's competitive success*. Singapore: McGraw-Hill.
2. Imai, M. (2001). *Gemba Kaizen: A commonsense, low-cost approach to management*, International edition. Singapore: McGraw-Hill.
3. Rother, M. and Shook, J. (1999). *Learning to see: Value-stream mapping to create value and eliminate muda*. Brookline, Massachusetts: Lean Enterprise Institute.
4. Maskell, B.H., Baggaley, B. and Grasso, L. (2012). *Practical lean accounting: A proven system for measuring and managing the lean enterprise*. Boca Raton, FL: CRC Press.
5. Womack, J.P. and Jones, D.T. (2003). *Lean thinking: Banish waste and create wealth in your corporation*. New York: Free Press.
6. David, J.L. (1986). *Kanban just-in-time at Toyota: Management begins at the workplace*. Cambridge, MA: Productivity Press.
7. Gross, J. (2012). *Kanban made simple*. Broadway, New York: AMACON.
8. Mann, D. (2005). *Creating a lean culture-tools to sustain lean conversions*. New York: Productivity Press.

Chapter 2

Revolutionizing Manufacturing Operations: Toyota Production System

---

Ask 'why' five times about every matter.

– Taiichi Ohno

The current market scenario is different from what it was when Henry Ford introduced the first reliable car on the market in 1908. The demand was huge, and products sold were few. There was only one Model T car in only one color – black – which was sold for many years. That was the time when whatever you produced would be sold anyway. General Motors (GM) joined the same race shortly after since the demand was high. The industry had this boom for many decades till it encountered the 1973 oil crisis that deteriorated the demands of all products across industries. It was at this time that Ford, GM and Chrysler started losing business to Japanese companies. Ford and GM cars were for the masses, but the times were changing.

A new wave embarked that shifted the focus to differentiated products with unique features. Toyota founders along with Taiichi Ohno[1] visited the United States and admired the Ford and GM cars, but they were not exhilarated by the idea of mass production. They found Ford and GM models were not futuristic in an era of incessantly evolving technology, continuous innovation in product features and dynamic consumer demand. Hence, their mind was fiddling with the idea to establish a system that was capable of

DOI: 10.4324/9781003221746-2

9

producing diverse products in low quantity while simultaneously eliminating wastage in the processes to achieve low cost. They were captivated by American supermarkets where everything was available, the customer could pick whatever he liked and the shelves were replenished just in time to maintain continuous supply. This stimulated the idea in their mind to come up with a manufacturing system that works on pull and flow, that is, the moment a car (product) is picked up by dealers from the warehouse (supermarket), they will manufacture and replenish it. Next they thought why not implement this in the raw material procurement stage and also during the production stage? It was at this moment in 1950 that the 'Toyota Production System' was born.

The Toyota Production System has now ventured beyond automobile companies into diverse industries in the last 70 years and is considered the benchmark for world-class manufacturing. It established that application of lean principles cannot be restricted to manufacturing functions on the plant floor but must be applied across functions. By the 1980s companies from the West started touring Toyota and other companies in Japan, intrigued by the marvels unfolding there. As if they landed in a utopia of manufacturing, they were amazed to witness sparkling clean companies efficiently delivering diverse products at a rapid pace. In this book 'Toyota Production System' and 'lean production system' will be used interchangeably. It will be assumed one and the same.

Revolution in Manufacturing Systems and Business Environment

The manufacturing industry has transformed extensively over the last five decades. Product features are constantly evolving due to advancement in technology and introduction of artificial intelligence (AI). This has led to automation in processes through robotics like auto-defect detection, remote-controlled maintenance, IT software development and data analytics in the last two decades. Therefore, it is time that functional processes should be made compatible with the latest technology.

The markets need diverse products in each industry at all times due to ever-changing demands and preferences of the consumer. Companies need to have manufacturing systems that cater to erratic consumer demands and outshine competitive products to survive in tough business environments. This entails that products should be available when the customer needs, as per the customer needs and as per the quality the customer needs. For example, the customer may not buy in bulk and ask for frequent deliveries instead, maybe three times a day directly to be delivered at the assembly line in the auto sector. The customer may also pick up the small quantity needed for the next two to three days from the company plant during the milk run. Therefore, the industry must employ a manufacturing system that is flexible and reliable with quick changeovers and short lead times. The industry needs to control the costs while providing this variability. Wastage in processes needs to be reduced, minimized or eliminated and high throughput time should be unacceptable.

Shigeo Shingo revolutionized manufacturing in 1985 with his book on single-minute exchange of dies (SMED) wherein he introduced the concept of reduction in changeover time. Toyota, a leading automobile multinational corporation, reduced the downtime of the machines and made layout changes to suit process flow. Taiichi Ohno, father of the Toyota Production System, introduced the concept of kanban and supermarket and reduced the batch size. These initiatives resulted in delivery of diverse products with short delivery schedules fetching more profits for the companies. These practices were accepted by the industries as they were sustainable in the long run and resulted in collapse of the forecast-based material resource planning (MRP). Data collection for manpower, machine, material and overheads on the plant floor for MRP was discontinued. The tedious effort and time involved in collection, monitoring, reporting, variance analysis and lengthy review meetings were bid farewell.

Globalization and rapid advancement in technology have created a tough competitive environment that offers customers abundant alternatives at cheap prices. Market determines the product price. A company does not need to set the price because the customer will not pay the selling price decided by the company. The concept of cost-plus-profit margin is antiquated. Sales and marketing teams require internal manufacturing costs to monitor contribution from the product, but a company can demand superfluous prices only if the features or brand command that value. Knowledge of internal costs is essential for cost reduction because low costs play significant role in profitability, but it is immaterial to the customer. Therefore, since the market determines the price based on value created in the product or services for the customer, pricing requires thorough understanding of the market, customer requirements and the competitors and assessment of how much value is being created for the customer.

To conclude, profits can be maintained only through the reduction of internal cost because market prices and product costs are not connected. The real issue is how to reduce the cost of manufacturing and services.

What Has Been Changing in the Companies?

Traditional companies build control through a company information system. In lean companies, control is built into operations. A lean company strives for simplicity and transparency. Value stream and functional managers do not understand the financial numbers presented by the finance team in the P&L statement, and the finance team that prepares this summary of business performance does not understand what is happening inside the plant. How can a company improve its operations, diversify, expand or reduce its costs under these circumstances? This is why businesses are now embracing lean. A business adopting lean principles tries to eliminate wastes in its organization in order to increase efficiency and focus on creating value for customers.

2.1 Journey of Lean Production System Implementation

The journey starts once management is convinced that embarking on a lean journey through lean production system and lean accounting is the only way to improve customer satisfaction, deliver products in a timely manner and fulfill stakeholder expectations of a healthy margin. Lean accounting introduces a company to a completely new perspective of the business processes. The company switches to pull system by use of kanban to reduce variances. Planning through MRP is replaced by actual market pull of the products.

The operations are transformed by implementation of the following lean and kaizen tools across value streams as a part of a lean production system (discussed in detail later in this chapter):

- Safety
- 5S
- Creation of Value Stream
- Throughput Time Measurement
- Total Productive Maintenance (TPM) implementation through autonomous and planned maintenance
- Single-Minute Exchange of Dies (SMED)
- Flow and Pull System and Supermarket concept through Kanban
- Cost of Poor Quality
- Standardization
- Visual Management
- Daily Management System

Key Measurements in the Value Stream

The old measures of standard cost accounting are substituted by the following measures:

- Cycle Time
- Throughput Time
- First Time Right Quality
- Inventory Management
- On Time In Full and Error Free (OTIFEF) Delivery

All businesses have their own set of irritants that prevent them from reaching their targets. It is the same story each month with a new challenge. It can be non-availability of raw materials that hampers the flow of the process, quality issues or equipment breakdown that prevents the finished products from reaching the customer in time. Lean production system implementation offers the solution to these problems. It increases the 'flow' in the processes from raw material to finished products by eliminating the obstructions. However, it is imperative that the company pledges its resources, time and effort in the continuous improvement projects as per lean to achieve the finest outcomes.

Manage the Change

A company decides to commence a lean journey in the first place probably because it observes that there is room for process improvement. But if it keeps repeating those flawed procedures, it won't get results that are any better than what it had before. The real progress will come if the company is ready for continual improvement, or kaizen. The first step in a lean journey is to change the present paradigms in the company. As quoted by Henry Ford, "If you always do what you always did, you'll always get what you've always got." But most of the time it is wise to assume that there will be a resistance to change because change is not easily welcomed by all. However, transparency and communication play a key role in setting the right expectations from lean implementation that would make it easier to adapt to the change.

Communication of pros and cons of changing to each and every employee is essential. It is also important to ascertain how much dissatisfaction or pain there is in the company regarding the present state. The higher the pain, the greater the dissatisfaction will be and the easier it will be to accept the change.

Four things will happen:

■ Dissatisfaction without vision and first steps of improvements will lead to frustration.
■ Vision without dissatisfaction and first steps of improvements will be wishful thinking.
■ First steps of improvement without dissatisfaction or vision will be a failed start.
■ The tipping point will come when dissatisfaction, vision of the company and first steps that the company is taking for improvements have more acceptance than resistance to change.

Therefore, these four factors – understanding of pros and cons of changing, the level of dissatisfaction, vision and first steps of improvements – will have to dwarf the resistance to change. With these efforts ultimately the environment for change comes within a reasonable period of time in any company.

2.2 Kaizen

Kaizen is a Japanese business term that translates into 'continuous improvement' or 'continuous continuous (continual) improvement', or 'change for better'. It is not a suggestion but rather a well thought out strategy to achieve improvement with a target in mind. It is a set of initiatives to improve the delivery time to customers, reduce downtime of machines, reduce change-over times, reduce minor stoppages and restore original speed of the machines to enable a company to release free capacity that can be utilized to increase production and profits for it. Kaizen aspires to extract benefits from the facilities without demand for fresh investment so that contribution earned intensifies existing profit margins. But kaizen has to be practiced every day by everyone everywhere in the company.

Levels of Kaizen

There are three levels of kaizen:

■ *System or Flow Kaizen* – This focuses on the total value stream. This is kaizen for management. It is always linked with the goals. For example, overall lead-time reduction covering lean projects on layout improvement, line balancing, daily work schedule, changeover time reduction, pull system for production planning and inventory management and so forth.

■ *Process Kaizen* – This focuses on individual processes. This is kaizen for work teams and team leaders. It is always linked with the business goals. For example, a team takes up reduction in rejections in a particular process.

■ *Point² Kaizen* – This is small improvement without a bigger focus or link with any goal. For example, teams are taking up projects on 5S improvements, operator movement reduction, closing leakage on machines and so forth.

Improvement in a single operation or improvement in efficiencies and effectiveness of some departments does not warranty the benefits to the company. The company and the customers will benefit only when all functions in the company improve as a whole through kaizen (continual improvement in the value stream concept). Only when the entire manufacturing system as a whole is improved as per lean principles, will the operational and financial benefits be derived. Hence, system or flow kaizen has to be implemented in all value streams in the company.

In kaizen, real data are sacrosanct. The opinion of a few people does not dictate commencement of work on a continual improvement project. Eight steps are observed in problem-solving for continuous improvement:

■ Define the problem – Go to the workplace and study the actual problem and the desired state as to what it should be and identify this gap. A well-defined problem is half solved.
■ Observe the workplace on facts and collect data – Collect data using the five senses (i.e., sight, hearing, smell, touch and taste).
■ Analyze the data as to find out what can be the root cause – What is the true reason that has contributed to the creation of the problem, defect or non-conformance? Do Pareto analysis to reach the true cause or top three causes. Create a fishbone diagram of selected causes. Validate the data of selected causes whether the causes are significant or non-significant. For the significant causes analyze whether the frequency of occurrence will be high or low and whether the impact of these causes will be high or low. Do why-why analysis of validated causes.
■ Outline the countermeasures in three categories – First is what corrective action should be done immediately to maintain continuity of

operations or services. Second is attending to root cause corrective action if it involves procurement of spares or outsource help. Third is to put preventive measures in place so that problem never repeats again.
■ Attend to the countermeasures.
■ Check the results regarding whether the problem has been minimized or eliminated. Observe at least for three months. If progress is noticeable, then kaizen is efficacious; otherwise, retrace steps back to workplace and start again.
■ Standardize the action plan and train all concerned persons.
■ Deploy it horizontally across the value streams.

In large companies, the focus is on results and not how they are achieved. This philosophy is called 'management by results' where the management in the company focuses on the results without assessing how these results are achieved each month and which best practices in their process contribute to these results. As a result, the company fails to generate consistent outcomes or maintain reliable processes. The company operates in a firefighting mode to tackle issues that obstruct the desired results and the executives in the company refuse to get involved in the structured way of running the company. In general, 'firefighting' is a safety issue when the fire brigade is called to douse a fire. But in business, firefighting refers to constant non-value adding issues or activities in the company that occupy the productive time of the workforce. This transpires when there is delay or shortage in a customer's order fulfillment or a dissatisfied customer complains about quality and faulty shipments but the spark lights up due to unstructured plant operations, minor and major breakdowns on critical machines, long changeover times or slow speed of machines due to wait for materials or decisions from the management. The operations team's emphasis is on full plant and labor utilization, optimizing the department's efficiencies and full overhead absorption to achieve low cost per unit to adhere to the standard cost accounting system in traditional companies. Thus, when a customer moans, the entire company starts extinguishing the fire that ignited due to mismanagement and unstructured processes wasting their valuable time that could have been used to identify new business opportunities.

However, kaizen focuses on 'management by process' because if the company's processes are structured, then consistent results can be accomplished each month. It is a challenging route where the managers begin by listing specification of the products and customer needs and preferences and then frame the standard operating procedures (SOPs) outlining how the existing facilities on the functional floor should be utilized to achieve the desired outcomes. If the processes are right and the company goes through 'plan-do-check-act' and 'standardize-do-check-act' routes, the desired results will be achieved.

Lean is where the company wants to reach, and kaizen is the way to reach there. Lean means using less material, machine and man-hours and standardizing methods and measurements. This book unfolds what needs to be done and how it is to be done. Improvement initiatives and sustainability go hand in hand. Improvement without sustenance is inoperable, but sustenance without further improvement is being shortsighted because nothing remains static – either it will improve, or it will deteriorate. Tools for improvement and sustenance together bring better results, and kaizen tools have stood the test of time. Everyone in the company has to work as a team once the course of action is decided. The whole team will implement it as a common goal. If the desired results are not achieved, the team will analyze where it has gone wrong in implementation of kaizen tools and not question the competence of kaizen tools.

Kaizen is implemented without expending money, that is, existing resources (material, machine, method, manpower, and measurement) are improved upon. Additional balancing resources, if required, must be added.

All kaizen happens at gemba. The more you are away from gemba, the more it weakens the gemba. Gemba is a Japanese word meaning 'real place' or 'workplace' where the value addition is done and in manufacturing industries where raw material is converted to finish product of acceptable quality and on time supply to customers. When management does not appreciate gemba, the weakening of the workplace will take place.

2.3 Total Productive Maintenance (TPM)[3]

Western companies practiced many preventive maintenance techniques, but they could not control downtime of the manufacturing machines due to breakdown and minor stoppages that wrecked productivity and quality. Preventive maintenance practices did not help to bring the operations under complete control.

The Journey at Nippon Denso

TPM was invented and perfected by Nippon Denso of the Toyota Group in Japan. They managed to bring control over the downtime of the machines (reduce it to zero), increase capacity utilization and reduce rejections on the machines. But how did Nippon Denso achieve this?

Nippon Denso compared its current situation with that of a mother who takes care of her child with utmost attention to help him or her grow. Whenever the situation goes beyond her control, she consults a doctor. Nippon Denso's improvement teams realized it is the operations team that is the mother of the machines in the company. They are always near the machines and can touch, hear and feel the machine closely during the whole shift. The people most likely to first notice equipment abnormalities or other strange symptoms are not the maintenance staff but the operators who work with the equipment day in and day out. Hence, they came up with the idea to include the operations team in simple things like cleaning, lubricating, inspecting and tightening of the machines. The experiment began in which the operators became mother of their machines and maintenance workers were doctors who were required only if the operator is unable to handle the situation.

This was the epiphany that led to birth of total productive maintenance (TPM) techniques. Then, Nippon Denso added autonomous maintenance by operators. Maintenance workers were responsible for maintaining the natural wear and tear and focused on the scheduled monthly, quarterly or yearly maintenance. This is known as planned maintenance. The learning earned from scheduled maintenance went into crafting changes to the new machinery brought in. This led to maintenance prevention. The preventive maintenance along with maintenance prevention and maintenance improvement gave birth to productive maintenance.

Nippon Denso had made quality circles, involving all employees to achieve zero defects, zero breakdown and zero accidents in all functional areas of the organization. The productive maintenance became total productive maintenance where total means the company as a whole. Nippon Denso of the Toyota Group became the first company to get the TPM certification in 1971 by the Japan Institute of Plant Engineers.

TPM Has Eight Pillars for Plant-Wide Implementation

TPM eight pillars (Figure 2.1) implementation plant wide enables the companies to achieve zero goals like zero breakdown and losses, zero defects and zero accidents, hazards and pollution. It enables reduction of chronic losses and avoidance of the sporadic losses. It enables the plants to achieve its basic conditions. Basic conditions are the sum of two categories, necessary

Figure 2.1   **Eight Pillars of Total Productive Maintenance (TPM).**

1. Focused Improvement	2. Autonomous Maintenance	3. Planned Maintenance	4. Quality Maintenance	5. Education and Training	6. Safety Health and Environment	7. Early Equipment Management	8. Office TPM

and desirable. Necessary conditions are minimum required to support the equipment operations and desirable conditions are not essential for operation but these are needed to prevent breakdowns and defects.

Focused improvement pillar establishes OEE loss calculation, minimize OEE losses through root cause analysis. Autonomous maintenance pillar implementation reduces forced deterioration of equipment. Planned maintenance pillar implementation enhances natural life and reliability of equipment. Education and training pillar improves technical skills and capabilities of maintenance and production teams. Early equipment management minimize design weakness and make improvement to have better equipment with minimum losses. Quality maintenance pillar reduce defects relation to man, machine, material, methods by deep understanding of phenomenon and causes. Safety, health and environment pillar enforces activities to prevent hazards & manage safely. TPM in office pillar improves processes, reduce errors and improve productivity of the workplace.

Benefits of TPM

Companies can double their productivity, overall plant efficiency (OPE) and overall equipment effectiveness (OEE) of critical machines in a short period of time. Increase in OEE will result in reduction or elimination of customer complaints and reduce the overall manufacturing cost by 30%. The goal of achieving 100% OTIFEF, that is, delivering the right quantity at the right time, of the right quality comes within close range. Implementation of TPM also helps to reduce the incidents and accidents by 100%.

Elimination of 16 Losses in a Company

There are 16 losses that are generated in plants and offices. These losses reduce the availability, performance and quality of the products. These are the losses that reduce productivity, effect timely delivery of the products to the customers and hamper the quality. Internally for a company, these are the losses that result in reduced profit margins. They can be broken down into five categories:

- Availability loss
- Performance loss
- Defects and rework loss
- Manpower related loss
- Cost loss

Figure 2.2 shows which pillar will focus on which type of defect for its reduction and elimination. Double tick against the pillar means this pillar will have a main focus on this defect and single tick means this pillar has a secondary focus on this defect.

The Autonomous and Planned Maintenance pillars focus on reduction in breakdown losses and improvement in the OEE of the machines. The Planned Maintenance pillar also takes care of minor stoppage loss, reduced speed loss and energy loss. The Quality Maintenance pillar focuses on defects and rework losses. The Focus Improvement pillar focuses on setup loss, tool change loss, management loss, operating motion loss, adjustment and measurement loss, line organization loss and start up loss. The Office TPM pillar focuses on logistic loss.

The TPM sensei (external expert) works on the shop floor with the plant teams on the 'manager model machines' and implements the TPM. These 'manager model machines' become the archetype for the changes to be brought throughout the plant on all the machines. TPM activities should not stop the flow in lean companies. There should be a scheduled time for autonomous and planned maintenance activities. The maintenance team should be part of the value streams and report to the value stream manager so that practice of maintenance work order and waiting for the maintenance team are discontinued going forward.

S.N.	Losses	Autonomous Maintenance	Planned Maintenance	Quality Maintenance	Focus Improvement	Safety Health and Environment	Education and Training	Office TPM	Early Equipment Management
Availability Losses									
1	Breakdown Loss	✓✓	✓✓				✓		✓
2	Planned Maintenance Time Loss	✓	✓✓				✓		✓
3	Setup Loss	✓			✓✓				
4	Tool Change Loss	✓			✓✓				
5	Start Up Loss		✓		✓✓				
Performance Losses									
6	Minor Stoppage Loss		✓✓		✓				
7	Reduced Speed Loss		✓✓		✓				
Defect and Rework Loss									
8	Defect and Rework Loss	✓		✓✓			✓		
Human Efficiency Related Losses									
9	Management Loss				✓✓				
10	Operating Motion Loss	✓			✓✓				
11	Adjustment and Measurement Loss			✓	✓✓				
12	Line Organization Loss	✓			✓✓				
13	Logistic Loss							✓✓	
Cost Losses									
14	Yield Loss				✓				
15	Energy Loss				✓				
16	Die, Tool and FOS Loss	✓		✓	✓				

✓✓ = Pillar Main focus

✓ = Secondary focus

Figure 2.2 Linking the Eight Pillars of TPM with the 16 Losses.

2.4 Total Quality Maintenance (TQM)[4]

Quality Begins and Ends with the Customer.

– Joel Ross

Quality is remembered long after the price is forgotten. According to the definitive text *Total Quality: A User's Guide for Implementation*, total quality management (TQM) is a management technique based on the idea that all "employees continuously improve their ability to provide on-demand products and services that customers will find of particular value". TQM consists of organization-wide efforts to install and make permanent a climate in which an organization continuously improves its ability to deliver high-quality products and services to customers. It focuses on efforts of employees as a team to continuously improve the systems, processes, services and culture of the company to attain long-term customer satisfaction.

W. Edwards Deming (1900–1993) was the early pioneer of quality control and is the father of the world-famous 'Deming Prize for Quality'. Deming developed the 'Deming Chain Reaction' that says as the quality improves, the cost will decrease and productivity will rise, resulting in more jobs, greater market share and long-term survival.

There are eight principles of TQM:

- Customer focus
- Total employee commitment
- Process approach
- Integrated system
- Strategic and systematic approach
- Continual improvement
- Fact-based decision-making
- Communication

Where Is Your Company on the Quality Journey?

The objective of TQM is to do the right thing the first time and every subsequent time so that resources are not wasted in fixing mistakes or processes. The driving force for TQM is continuous improvement. It integrates all function to attain the highest level of customer satisfaction.

Quality Levels	Defect Status
Level 0	• Defects reach customers
Level 1	• Defects are stopped at plant gate
Level 2	• Defects are reduced in plant
Level 3	• Defects are reduced in the upstream processes
Level 4	• Zero defects in the process

Figure 2.3   Company's TQM Level Assessment.

The cost of a dissatisfied customer, which also includes the next in line process customer, due to undesirable quality received is an avoidable loss if the company embraces principles of TQM.

Figure 2.3 helps to determine at which level the company is on its quality journey. If the company defects are reaching the customers, it is at level 0 of the TQM. The company has a grave problem on the quality front that should be addressed urgently. If the company is at level 1, it should alert quality inspectors who detect defects inside the plant and do not allow them to reach the customers. Level 2 means the company has started improving; its quality and defects are being detected in the processes and the company has a mechanism to address it. Further corrective and preventive actions are proactively done to reduce it further to take the company to level 3. At level 4 the company has reduced the defects in all its processes to zero and it has become a Six Sigma company.

Six Sigma[5]

This is a quality management technique that improves business processes by eliminating defects. It identifies poor processes by using standard methods for recognizing, defining, measuring, analyzing, improving, controlling, standardizing and integrating the changes to make the processes robust, repeatable and perfect. Six Sigma can be applied to all functions, and it can be safely assumed that all processes generate wastage and that a company can make production more efficient, improve product quality, upgrade service quality, improve delivery times and reduce billing cycles. Six Sigma has a clear set of tools that can be used by companies to identify defects, find the root cause and improve the process to get accurate results consistently.

Assess the Company's Quality Level in Parts per Million (PPM)

Cost of Quality or Cost of Poor Quality

Quality has a cost and poor quality adds to this cost since it disrupts the flow of production, and resources like material, labor and machine utilized in that production are wasted because it could have been sold as a finished product. The quality control function does not ensure the quality of a product. It only assesses the quality at various phases of production of a product. Therefore, quality has to be ensured at the source of production. Every operator has to understand his role in manufacturing and should be skilled in his work so that excellent quality products are manufactured at each cell and function.

The present cost of the quality is calculated by the following equation:

$$Cost\ of\ Quality = A + P + IF + EF$$

where,

A = Appraisal Costs – This is the fixed cost of the quality control/quality assurance function.

P = Prevention Costs – This is the cost incurred in preventing poor quality (i.e., the money spent on vendor management system, training and expenses toward new product development).

IF = Internal Failure – This is the result of rework, rejections and non-conformity in the company.

EF = External Failure – These costs are a result of customer complaints, material returns from customers, discounts to customers and warranty and guarantee costs.

Contribution of Quality in Profitability

TQM is designed to improve the quality of the product and to ensure higher customer satisfaction and a better working environment for employees. The most dramatic impact of TQM is reduction of cost of quality directly affecting the profitability. The company can determine its quality cost as a percentage of the sales value depending on its present sigma level. The company can convert this cost value into profits if it focuses on quality of products and processes and improves the quality levels. Figure 2.4 can be used to ascertain the current sigma level of the company to compute cost of quality failure in the company.

Sigma Level	PPM	Accuracy Level	Inaccuracy Level
Sigma 1	690000	31%	69%
Sigma 2	308537	69%	31%
Sigma 3	66807	93.30%	6.70%
Sigma 4	6210	99.40%	0.60%
Sigma 5	233	99.98%	0.02%
Sigma 6	3.4	100.00%	0.00%

Figure 2.4   Assess the Company's PPM Level.

Cost of Quality	
Quality Sigma Level	Quality Costs as % of Sales
3	25
4	15
5	10
6	5

Figure 2.5   Company's Cost of Quality.

When the product acceptance level in a company is at 93.3%, the company is at sigma level 3. If it implements the lean production system, daily management and lean accounting with focus on TQM, it can reach level 4 with product acceptance level of 99.4% and save 10% on costs (see Figure 2.5, 25–15). A 6.1% increase in product quality level acceptance gives 10% increase in profits. These numbers help the company to understand where it is on the journey of lean production system and lean accounting and keeps the company's employees motivated to continue on the journey. The action plan to improve the quality must begin with the reduction of external and internal failures, improvement measures in place for prevention and appraisal.

2.5 Toyota Production System (TPS)[6]

The terms 'lean manufacturing', 'Toyota way', 'Toyota Production System', 'kaizen' and 'continuous improvement' are often used interchangeably. Toyota, with its Toyota Production System, revolutionized manufacturing systems in the 1950s and pioneered the concept of lean production. It became a radical embodiment of efficiency and productivity in manufacturing industries. TPS is an incredible breakthrough owed to Sakichi Toyoda (1867–1930), his son Kiichiro Toyoda (1894–1952), Eiji Toyoda (1913–2013). Taiichi Ohno (1912–1990) with strong backing from Eiji Toyoda helped establish the Toyota Production System. It is a production system developed based on the philosophy of achieving complete elimination of wastes by using efficient methods to enable companies to produce just-in-time to satisfy customers' diverse demands.

The Toyota system was adopted by many industries in Japan after the oil shock in the 1970s. The goal of companies using TPS is to provide the exact quantity, of exact quality, exactly when the customer wants it. There are two pillars of TPS:

- *Jidoka* – Automation with a human touch (i.e., machine stops safely, as soon as the normal processing is completed)
- *Just-In-Time* – Making only what is needed, only when it is needed, and only in the amount that is needed

The Toyota Production System is an effective tool for achieving the ultimate goal – profit – which is achieved by reducing the costs in the value stream. Also, it quickly adjusts to changes in the market demand without wasteful slack time. TPS demands and ensures no operator will accept defective goods, will not produce defective products and will not pass defective goods to the next process. Also, Toyota cultivates and ensures respect for human dignity.

The Toyota Production System is the mother of all production systems. Now all major companies in the world have their own production systems, which are nothing but an imitation of the Toyota Production System. Following are some examples:

- ANAND Production System (APS)
- Production System BEHR
- DaimlerChrysler Production System
- Electrolux Production System
- Production System FAG
- Genoa-LPS
- LuK Process Optimization System (Fahrzeug Hydraulik)
- Beispiel: Produktionssystem Osram

- Stanley Production System
- Rolls-Royce Production system
- Boeing lean + journey

How Can a Company Improve Its Bottom Line (Profits)?

There can be two ways in which a company can increase its profits:

Addition Route (This Is Not Lean)

Companies spend millions of dollars in buying machines, material handling equipment and store materials and then build a number of warehouses to store them. They invest in quality control instruments and build additional sheds. But this is not kaizen. This may be innovation where the company is bringing in new technology. If the company is not innovating but buying additional machines and resources to increase the volume, then it is a serious predicament. The company is catering to a workforce that is demanding more resources to produce more instead of focusing on its performance to improve upon the current performance level because this is a complex route. The company will never become a lean company with consistent healthy profit margins and comfortable cash flow through this scheme.

Deletion Route (This Is Lean)

If companies deliberate why employees cannot accomplish healthy margin without a plea for additional investment, they will fathom that it is because of inability of the employees to identify wastes in the processes and its impact on the product's cost. Kiichiro Toyoda, Eiji Toyoda and Shoichiro Toyoda, founders of Toyota, explained waste ("muda" in Japanese) as *anything other than the* minimum *amount of equipment, materials, parts, space, and worker's time, which are absolutely essential to* add value *to the product.*

What Are These Wastes?

The main goal of TPS is to address and eliminate three main issues:

- Overburden (Muri)
- Inconsistency (Mura)
- Waste (Muda)

TPS aims to bring consistency in process to eliminate burden on employees, which reduces the stress on them resulting in fewer errors or wastage.

There are eight types of wastes (muda), which can be coined as an acronym: *D.O.W.N.T.I.M.E.*

D – Defects

Muda due to defects, rejections and generation of scrap is an outcome of deteriorated machine conditions, inconsistency, poor material quality, unskilled employees, poor design or misunderstanding customer needs. It results in loss of material, high conversion costs, loss of customers and cost of rework. The key tools that can be used to reduce these losses are poka yoke (mistake proofing), jidoka (automation with human touch), standard work, root cause analysis, TQM and Six Sigma.

O – Overproduction

Muda of overproduction is producing earlier than the customer's requirement. This is the worst kind of muda because it ties up the working capital in the company and results in excessive finished good inventory that adds to storage cost and degrades quality. Overproduction may be due to fear of stockout due to defects, machine breakdown, high changeover time, poor forecast and maximum capacity utilization. TPS contradicts this just-in-case production philosophy by adopting just-in-time production philosophy where every item is made only when it is needed. The way to prevent overproduction is to implement the 'pull' system through kanban.

W – Waiting

The muda of waiting happens when manpower, machine and material wait for each other. It is caused by workload imbalance, poor layout, unorganized workplace, high inventory and poorly scheduled processes. It results in delays, lower capacity usage and lower manpower productivity and higher throughput time The tools required to reduce this loss are workload balancing, flow layout and cellular manufacturing.

N – Not Utilizing Human Potential

The muda of underutilized talent of people is the whole company struggling with the current production when it is the job of the first line of manager, supervisors and workmen to produce the current products. This is caused by lack of people involvement and criticism and blaming. This results in underutilized mental capacity of people, thus lost opportunity. The key tools used for eliminating this loss are involvement of people in kaizen projects and rewards and recognition.

T – Transport (Poor Layout)

The muda of transportation is transporting the material from one place to another or unnecessary movement of manpower. This takes place mainly due to poor layout. It increases the logistic costs, product damage, searching and waiting and investments in logistics equipment. This loss can be reduced by workload balance, flow layout, cellular manufacturing and mizusumashi (water spider or trained material handler).

I – Inventory (Slow Moving and Non-Moving)

The muda of inventory is bulk of inventory in raw material, work in progress (WIP) and finished goods, packaging materials and spare parts inventory. This happens due to fear of stockout, poor performance of suppliers, transport delays, poor layout and rejection in production processes. This results in high holding costs, immediate storage needs and people to move them. The inventory can get damaged or become obsolete. The key tools required to reduce inventory are implementation of the pull system through kanban.

M – Motion

The muda of motion is movement of people within the area of operation, stretched hand movements. This loss happens due to lack of standard work, poor layout, unbalanced workload and poor machine design. This results in poor manpower productivity due to wasted time in excess motions. The key tools to reduce these losses are workload balance and flow layout through cellular manufacturing.

E – Extra Processes

The muda of overprocessing is adding more value to the product than required by the customer. This results in taking extra time and material usages thus excess costs. The example is grinding operation where machining is good enough, finishing painting certain areas that are not necessary.

What Happens in Traditional Companies Where Kaizen and Lean Techniques Are Not Practiced?

In traditional companies, most of the functions are oblivious to customer requirements. Traditional companies suffer machine breakdowns, multiple minor stoppages and machines run at slow speeds. The changeover to produce another product that the customer immediately requires is difficult because the changeover takes forever. The defect rate in products keeps rising, some defective products are reworked and sold while balance defective products are sold as scrap. Counterfactual measures are used to calculate yield by considering scrap sold in computation.

Companies manufacture few products in excessive quantities because it is easier to produce them and also reflects better utilization of machine and manpower for absorption of overheads, but it leaves the company with unsold inventory at the end of the month, which piles up and is sold later at discount.

The company has an abominable layout that is not highlighted unless the lean teams draw a spaghetti diagram to show movement of material and the manpower in the plant. The concepts of throughput time, flow rate, value and standardization are unheard of.

Eliminating Waste

The different types of wastes as described earlier disrupt production flow. Through implementation of various kaizen and lean tools as described, the wastes can be reduced or eliminated. Various other tools are also put in place so that the sustenance is achieved and the organization does not fall back to its original position. Zero tolerance for waste helps in achieving and sustaining the overall objective of reduction in cost and delivery time by systematic working on standardization of the processes.

The flow can be measured in time unit, and elimination of the wastes reduce the throughput time and increases total output. The reduction of seven wastes is called deletion of the non-value adding activities. This deletion of the wastes from company processes will be achieved by implementation of lean production system, daily management and lean accounting.

When wastes are eliminated from the company, the company gets extra capacity to produce more in the form of manpower free time, machine free time, reduced inventory and free space in the premises. This free capacity is coming to the company without spending any money. Companies taking up waste removal as their business strategy can enhance their capacity by 10% to 15% every year.

Toyota's Five Strategies to Become Number One in the Industry[7]

Managers remain under pressure to deliver material in time and acceptable quality to customers. Toyota ensures that if following strategies are followed, there will not be any pressure of quality and delivery and the company will manufacture the lowest cost:

Kaizen Is the Most Powerful Strategy in the World

Shut down the machine when a quality issue is noticed. Rectify and only then start the machine.

Tell down the line to the last man whatever is known about the product that they are making. The heart of the kaizen is information. Acknowledge that there will be a continuing existence of the defects and problems. Don't blame. Accept problems and solve it together.

True excellence comes when two things are done well. First, get our hands dirty, and second, to put our stomachs on the floor means the operation and maintenance personnel should be ready to lie down below the machine to see the defective areas.

Just-In-Time

There should not be large storages of inventories in the company. The stores will be like supermarkets where a designed quantity will be kept for each item, and it will be replenished when it will be consumed with the same quantity. The company will produce 'just-in-time'. The company will produce to pull from the customers. Whatever is produced must be dispatched. Work on pull from customer requires intense concentration and exacting focus on every detail to maintain just-in-time.

Suggestion System

Base your kaizen journey on the attention to details of every employee and every work team. Employees should be encouraged to share their ideas for improvements.

Kanban System

The production must work on pull from the next process and the customer. Use kanban to trigger replenishment. Use supermarket. No other authorization is required.

Ask Your Customers

Be in touch with the customers and address their changing needs promptly.

Toyota Production System Implementation

To implement previous strategies, the Toyota Production System envisages the implementation of the following systems and methods as per Figure 2.6:

5S[8]

5S is the foundation of TPS and is the first step toward establishing a culture of continual improvement. It is a system of organizing the workplace so that work can be done efficiently, effectively and safely because a messy and unorganized workplace will lead to oversight of opportunities for improvements that lie in the workplace. Without 5S, it will be difficult to execute continual improvement for removal or reduction in the non-value adding activities. 5S has to be implemented by everyone in the workplace from workmen, supervisors and managers to the top management. 5S has to be implemented in office spaces as well as the plant floor. It is believed that if

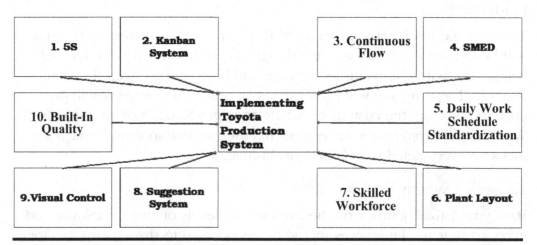

Figure 2.6   Elements of the Toyota Production System.

a company cannot implement 5S, it should not proceed further in the lean and kaizen journey. 5S cleanses the mind so that one can think of moving to implement next level of lean tools. The 5S are as follows:

- *Seiri (Sort)* – Clear the litter and throw things out that are not needed.
- *Seiton (Set in Order)* – Keep the things systematically that are required so that it can be reached in less than 30 seconds.
- *Seiso (Shine)* – Self-clean the workplace and shine it.
- *Seiketsu (Standardize)* – Divide the workplace into zones and fix responsibility of 5S.
- *Shitsuke (Sustain)* – Maintain the discipline. Keep it going. Audit and celebrate.

There is a *sixth S – Safety* as per lean principles. The plant has to be incident free so that every employee goes back home safely at the end of the shift. Detailed safety practices must be enforced with the help of safety specialists.

Heinrich's law outlines relationship between near miss, minor and major accidents at workplace. It states that in a group of 330 incidents, there will be 300 near miss incidents, 29 minor injury incidents and one major injury incident. Near miss is the event when the incident that was about to happen was missed due to quick response. If a company controls the near miss incidents, the plant can be made incident free. The concept gives importance to every 'near miss' incident. Record and analyze the root so that preventive measures for near miss incidents can be put in place to avoid minor or major accidents.

Kanban System[9]

Kanban is a scheduling system that originated from the Toyota Production System's philosophy of just-in-time manufacturing or the 'pull' approach. A company wants to manufacture what the customer wants to avoid excessive inventory.

Traditional companies use the *'push system'* in which production is based on demand forecast that drives the material resource planning (MRP)[10] software to produce sufficient quantity ahead of time. The MRP software also generates the plan for design, material, machine, their schedule, assembly and logistics and so forth based on the demand forecast to ensure lowest possible inventory. However, a company can end with excessive inventory if the forecast for the month is inaccurate or does not cater to the customer's actual demand. It will rouse firefighting, mid-month plan change, sales loss and customer dissatisfaction along with waste, cost of inventory handling and storage and poor inter-department relations. Detailed data tracking by the finance team to analyze variances based on forecast will add to non-value adding time.

Toyota adopted the *'pull system'* based on its philosophy of just-in-time production. Toyota started operating on the same model used by super-markets where the shelves are stocked with enough units to meet customer demand. In a lean company with a pull system, there are mini supermarkets on the plant floors, in between the processes and a finished goods supermarket in the warehouse that contains calculated quantities of finished products. When a customer pulls the material, immediately a signal through the kan-ban system is sent to the production shop and the same product in quantity equivalent to kanban is produced and sent to finished goods supermarket for replenishment. The finished products are always available and there are no stockouts. This not only prevents the loss of sales but also helps in the inventory management. The quantity of raw material, WIP and finished goods in supermarkets cater to 30% to 40% volume upswing of market demand. Pull strategy eliminates the need for detailed tracking of labor and material.

Efficient inventory management ensures that there is no stockout of any item and there is just enough material in stock to maintain low cost of inventory. A company has to decide what to keep in stock, how much to keep in stock, volume of maximum stock, what to purchase and when to purchase. Pareto analysis is done to determine who are runner, repeater and stranger items. Frequency of purchases in a year along with purchase quantities will be the criteria for categorization. Runners are A-class items responsible for 80% of the purchased quantities. These are normally 10% to 20% of all products. Repeaters are B-class items, responsible for 15% of the quantities procured (20% to 30% of all items). Strangers are C-class items responsible for 5% of items in quantities (50% to 70% of all items).

It can be decided now which items should be 'make to stock (MTS)' or 'make to order (MTO)'. Class A and Class B can be 'make to stock' and Class C can be 'make to order'.

Two methods are used for inventory management:

■ *Fixed Time Variable Quantity Method (FTVQ)* – This is used for procurement of items that are used regularly. These are runner and repeater items in the Pareto analysis (Class A and Class B). In this method, pitch time for procurement is fixed and quantity is decided based on maximum stock and the current stock. The kanban system is introduced to track the inventory and follow up. Thus, the kanban system helps to maintain the just-in-time procurement. When material is used, it should be immediately replenished by kanban command. Kanban implementation is further implemented at all stages of production and storage.

■ *Fixed Quantity Variable Time Method (FQVT)* – This is used for procurement of items that are not used regularly. These are stranger items in the Pareto analysis (Class C). In this method, the reorder level and standard order quantity is decided. A fixed quantity is replenished when the inventory level drops lower than the standard order point.

A company is able to adapt to demand changes quickly and also reduce its inventory. The company, when on a lean journey, starts becoming stable. The teams have to adopt a rigid and consistent work routine to achieve something like the 'pull' system. The corrective actions are initiated in real time so that problems are fixed immediately. The whole system in the company is vigilant. The company functions on value stream concept and each value stream manager is aware of his customer's changing needs. Value stream managers have marketing, purchase and finance personnel reporting functionally to them. This allows the flexibility to make a decisive action plan in real time to address the customer's needs.

Continuous Flow[11]

This approach creates a system of stirring material through the manufacturing processes in a way that 'one-piece flow' or 'small batch of product' is produced at a time as opposed to batch manufacturing in which a large batch of products is produced at a given time. The batch size is decided based on kanban freed at the supermarket. Lean follows 'pull and flow' ideology in which as soon as the customer picks a product (pull), the supermarket shelf is replenished by manufacturing in equivalent quantity (kanban quantity).

Single-Minute Exchange of Dies (SMED)[12]

Changeover time is a non-value adding activity that can at times consume 20% of the total time available for production. The time saved is directly available for production. A fast, frequent and rudimental changeover allows production of what the customers want on time. A company should not live with long changeover time. The changeover time can be reduced by 60% 70% in a three- to four-month duration. Short changeover reduces the product throughput time. The SMED (single-minute exchange of dies tool) is used for the changeover time reduction. The SMED is a method, developed by Shigeo Shingo of the Toyota Group in the year 1958, that is used in analysis and improvement of the time lost in change from one product to another. With this tool Toyota could reduce changeover time on a large 3000-ton mechanical press from four hours to three minutes in 1970.

SMED reduces the batch size, reduces the stocks, enlarges the capacities of the machine and thus reduces the capital expenditure and production costs. SMED also helps in timely supply of material to the customers.

Standardization of the Daily Work Schedule[13]

Taiichi Ohno said, "Where there is no standard, there can be no Kaizen." Standardization means finding, documenting and applying the best, safest and easiest way to do something so that consistent results can be accomplished. In lean manufacturing, there are three elements of standardization:

- *Takt Time* – Takt is a German word that translates to 'beat or pulse' or, in this case, a customer's pulse. Takt time refers to the maximum acceptable time to fulfill a customer's demand. The company must synchronize its operations to the customer's heartbeat (i.e., customer's demand). This means its capacity to produce should be at least 20% more than the customer demand to prevent stockout.
- *Work Sequence* – This refers to the sequence in which operations must be carried out to remain within the takt time.
- *Standard Inventory* – It refers to the quantity of raw materials and machinery required to maintain undisrupted flow of operations.

However, standardization of the processes does not mean culmination of scope for further improvement. Nothing is static in this world; things are either improving or deteriorating. If the process standards for man, machine, material, method and measurement stop improving at the workplace, these will start dwindling. When kaizen is implemented, it calls for continuous improvement by *PDCA-SDCA*. A continuous evaluation tool of management processes is plan-do-check-act (PDCA) to identify the problem in current processes for improvement. The problem is the gap between the actual situation and the desired results. PDCA works in the following manner:

- *Plan* – The first step is to identify the problem in current processes by collecting and analyzing the data to reveal 'why' the problem is arising and decide 'who' is responsible and 'when', 'where', and 'how' the problem will be solved. A well-defined problem is half solved.
- *Do* – The improvement measures to solve the problem decided in the previous stage are implemented in this stage.
- *Check* – The next step is to audit the result of implementation of planned improvement measures to check if problem persists or has been solved. This is the most important stage of PDCA to eliminate the problem entirely.
- *Act* – If the plan has been successfully implemented and checked, then it is time to act (i.e., go ahead with 'standardization' and 'horizontal deployment'). If not, analyze the data again till the root cause of the problem is identified.

There are several tools that can be used for PDCA like 'problem-solving methodology' and 'root cause analysis' to solve non-complex problems and sporadic losses. Root cause analysis involves five steps:

- Pareto analysis (pick from stratification)
- Cause-and-effect analysis
- Validation – significant/non-significant
- Why-why analysis
- Countermeasures – corrective/preventive/high impact/medium impact/ low impact

Immediate preventive action prevents adverse impact on customer satisfaction, and fixing the root cause prevents manifestation of the problem.

Complex hitches may have many causes that need advanced data analysis tools like phenomenon analysis, design of experiment and so forth to solve these problems. Preventive root cause action put a stop to the error from recurring on any process or products.

Once PDCA (plan-do-check-act) has been successfully completed, the next step is to standardize the process with SDCA(standardize-do- check-act).

SDCA follows PDCA (see Figure 2.7), which depicts that when a company brings improvements in its operation by PDCA, then there is a need

Figure 2.7 PDCA-SDCA Linkage.

for standardization. PDCA begins with "P", that is, planning for improvement and ends with 'A', which refers to standardization. SDCA starts with 'S,' that is, denotes standardization. SDCA ensures sustenance.

'A' and 'S' stand for *standardization*

'D' means to work as per standard

'C' means to check as per standard

'A' means to revise the standard if further improvement in the process is required

The methodology ensures a continuous improvement cycle in the workplace. SDCA is an important concept of standardization to prevent deterioration:

- *Standardize* – To determine a standard, find the best, easiest and safest way of doing a process known within the company. This requires brainstorming from all stakeholders including employees who will actually execute the process.
- *Do* – Once a standard has been agreed upon, training should be provided on roles and responsibilities and the standard should be tested in a controlled environment.
- *Check* – At this stage, check the impact of change in the standard on the process and business environment to ascertain if it is an accurate standard.
- *Act* – Once the standard has been checked, it becomes the new benchmark. It should be documented and shared with relevant stakeholders for implementation and continued improvement.

Standardize 5M for Every Process

Every process has input(s) and output. Process is a sequence of operations that follow one after another to convert the raw material to finished products or in a service industry a series of operation(s) to give the required service to the client. Output is the result of a process. If a company wants constant output, it must provide consistent inputs. If the inputs are managed well, the output will be unblemished in quality, quantity and time.

The 5Ms are inputs related to manpower, machine, material, method and measurement. If the company manages consistency of the 5Ms, the output will be consistent.

The employees are the principal asset because they create value, solve problems and improve the organization, and the lean management system substantiates this. This first M drives all the other Ms. Focus should be on the following parameters for each M to increase the productivity of 5Ms:

■ *Manpower* – Skill, performance and multitasking
■ *Machine* – Downtime, capability and defects
■ *Material* – Yield (less material usage), right specifications and less variation. Material has the largest value in the profit and loss statement.
■ *Methods* – Daily work schedule, SOPs, work instruction and typical checklists, daily performance board, action plan board
■ *Measurement* – Cost of poor quality (COPQ), measurement system analysis (MSA) and process capability

Lean accounting unveils the opportunities for profits within the company. When the company has deep pockets, 5Ms are not scrutinized, but during adversity, management starts with elimination of the first M – manpower – to reduce the overhead costs. But Toyota realized that human wisdom and ingenuity is indispensable to delivering ever-better cars to customers. It uses the downturn of the economy to provide better training and enhance the skills of its employees to enable them to monetize opportunities when they arise next.

Why is there more rejection? Why is there less production? This happens when management is by crisis. A company must have standards for each 'M' to manage the business by standards.

M1 – Manpower Standardization – Manpower is standardized by skill sets. Technical and functional training is imparted to manpower at all levels each month. Respect for manpower has a deep meaning. Instead of skill-set standardization, standard cost accounting uses measures like manpower utilization without focus on productivity. In the lean production system, processes are standardized with daily, shift-wise and hourly tracking of the "process" by the employees. Also focus is on attendance and leave planning, skills development, performance scorecard and reward and recognition scheme (see Chapter 9 and Chapter 10).

M2 – Machine Standardization – Standardization of processes ensures consistent quality every time a product is manufactured. This can be done by standardization of temperature, pressure, speed and feed or similar controlling parameters.

M3 – Material Standardization – Standard output will not be achieved if input specifications keep fluctuating. Therefore, material specifications and its quality should be standardized. To achieve material cost reduction, a lean company measures the yield and breaks down the product cost into its components to study how much material is lost in the process through scrap, rework and quality rejection. Material chemical standards as per ASMT, DIN, BS, IS, GOST, physical specifications and heat treatment requirements should be standardized.

M4 – Method Standardization – The methodology of processes is to be standardized, which means the work-station layout, work in progress, sequence of work, cycle time of work, materials and tools used, machines and other process parameters, quality parameters, method of measurements, standard operation chart, line balancing and so forth have to be standardized. A new type of culture is to be created wherein everyone starts working within a certain set of parameters as defined in the standard methodology. The results will come if the process is correct and it is followed correctly. The lean culture has to be followed every hour every day to achieve consistent results.

M5 – Measurement Standardization – The methodology of measurement has to standardized by crafting quality standards and quality checklists for each process on the plant floor and in all functions. Seven quality control tools, measurement system analysis and process capability assessment can be used to standardize measurement.

Plant Layout

The goal of lean principles is to maximize value by elimination of waste. This requires seamless and standardized processes to avoid overproduction that leads to excess inventory and unnecessary movement of materials and workforce in a plant that does not add any value. In lean, plant layout should allow seamless flow for material, minimize handling time and effort, save floor space and shorten lead times. Flow should be unidirectional. No spaghetti shall be formed. There shall be no return travel of the material. Transportation index is to be the lowest (tons × meters). Number of touches should be minimized. Loading and unloading of material should be from the front side, operator side. Layout should identify places for input, output and work in progress, well defined and marked. Provide supermarket showing standard inventory in terms of calculated hours/days of raw materials, work in progress and finished goods on the layout. Pay attention to the logistics of wastes – waste handling and disposal. Preferably waste should also drop to the front so the quick disposal can be done. Tools, tackles and consumables shall be kept in easy access and nearest to operators in front of the machine.

Skilled Workforce

One of the major principles of TPS is to 'develop exceptional people and teams who follow the company's philosophy'. It is important that the people who work in a company share its values and beliefs. A highly competent workforce is indispensable to a company's success. A company should invest in training its employees, enhance their skills cross functionally and empower them within the company. This will improve productivity and create a smooth flow in operations by solving difficult technical problems. A culture of working as teams together toward common company goals must be fostered among the employees.

Suggestion System

A successful suggestion system starts with a culture committed to building collaboration, teamwork and worker empowerment by focusing people on continuous improvement. The person who actually performs the job is the true expert in that job. The suggestion system is a key driver of continuous improvement, and a successful suggestion system engages and empowers the employees at all levels of the organization to take ownership and improve their processes to maximize productivity and attain common company goals. The suggestion system should be simple and accessible with a quick evaluation and response time to get the best out of opportunities highlighted by the workforce.

Visual Controls for All Standards

Visual control is a technique employed where information is communicated by using visual signals instead of texts or other written instructions. Humans collect information 83% visually and only 11% by ear. Visual controls aim to make problems, abnormalities or deviation from standard visible to everyone. Computerized systems manage the process while being disconnected from the actual production area. When the company adopts lean, managers must be adjacent to the processes because visual control brings focus on the process. The lean management system's three-part prescription for focusing on the processes is 'go to the place', 'look at the process' and 'talk with the people'. Visual controls help to identify problems swiftly to reduce waste and production costs resulting in shorter lead time, reduced inventory and a safe work environment with higher profits.

Built-In Quality

It is a functional management system to promote company-wide quality control. The quality is to be ensured in all phases of manufacturing. Quality is to be built into the product by operators/workers on the plant floor. Quality assurance, as defined in this rule of Toyota, is to ensure that the quality of the product promotes satisfaction, reliability and economy for the customer.

Lean Production System Brings a Paradigm Shift that Forces You to Rethink

The lean production system brings drastic transformation in manufacturing operations/services to enable you to become a world-class company. The principles and philosophy of the lean production system are to eliminate waste and create value at each step. But to identify waste and opportunities to maximize value in business operation, the lean production system forces you to reconsider the following questions:

Why Do We Have Defects?

Toyota forces the company to rethink that when the company can produce more than 99.5% products of good quality, then why can it not produce 100% products of good quality? What is the reason that 0.5% of the products produced are of poor quality?

Why Do We Have Breakdowns?

The company's breakdowns are roughly 2% to 5% of the total time. When the company can run its machines for 95% of time smoothly, what happens 5% of the time when the operators, materials and tools remain unchanged? This means machines are not maintained properly or operators do not clean, lubricate or inspect the machine and ignore warnings from the machine. Toyota forces the company to rethink benefits of proper maintenance practices to reduce breakdowns to zero.

Why Do We Need Quality Control?

The company needs to rethink that when the production department knows what to produce, then why do we need a quality department and quality inspectors around?

Why Can't We Have SMED?

The changeover time can run into several hours. What methods can operators use to reduce it to half or one fourth of the time?

Why Is Inventory Piling Up?

Why does the company have inventory piled in a warehouse but there are still stockouts? The workmen are afraid of breakdowns and high changeover time, so they do not halt production to give machines for maintenance. They produce more of products that are easier to meet internal targets but at the end of the month, the company is saddled with sales loss for some products and excess inventory for other products. Why are the machines unstable and the company unable to produce and dispatch what is required?

Why Does Hourly Production Vary?

Why do the processes produce variable quantity per hour every hour of the shift when everything from raw material, manpower, machine and methodology are same? Why are there some good hours where production is more than 150% of the bad hours where the production is low? How can we achieve a consistent production rate every hour?

Why Are Operators Watching the Machines?

Why can the machine operators not run more than one machine and multitask? Why do they have to stand and watch?

Why Not Pull?

Why does the company not have a designed finished good products super-market as one sees in the grocery stores? Whatever is withdrawn from the finished goods supermarket can be replenished from the production shop. There will be no sales loss or excess inventory.

Why Not Involve Operators in Standardization and Daily Management?

People in production or operation are often bewildered by computer-generated reports of performance problems in graphic or table format. However, it is a different story when the operators themselves have been involved in recording the data while working on the process in the start-up meetings led by their team leader. When the plant floor workmen write something with their own hand and in their own language then that is considered as the best standard. Visual meeting around the boards that are updated by hand always produce better results. The real point is the human interaction and sense of loyalty that goes with it. Standing meetings around handwritten boards always work better than the sophisticated computer boards hooked up with the ERP (Enterprise resource planning) system.

Why Is Throughput Time Always Large in Traditional Companies?

One of the most important principles of lean is timely delivery to the cus-tomer. The idea is to reduce the throughput time to customers. Therefore, a company should prioritize throughput time over procurement cost per unit. The traditional companies run on material resource/requirement planning (MRP) invented by Joseph Orlicky and Oliver Wright in the early 1950s. MRP was appropriate for large batch size production when economic order quan-tity (EOQ) and economies of scale were practiced for a low cost per unit. But this led to higher throughput time because traditional companies check demand forecast, compute capital resources required for production through capital resource planning (CRP), create financial budgets for manpower and material and manufacture large batches for higher utilization of machine and manpower. In addition to this, breakdowns, short stoppages and long changeover times add to throughput time.

Hence, throughput time and ad hoc inventory costs like storage, space occupied, and obsolescence should be considered before resorting to bulk buying.

Key Takeaways

1. The lean management system is a system that is capable of producing diverse products in low quantities while simultaneously eliminating wastage in the processes to achieve low cost.
2. The industry must employ a manufacturing system that is flexible and reliable with quick changeovers and short lead times.
3. Market determines the product price. Market prices and product costs are not connected. The real issue is how to reduce the cost of manufacturing and services to maintain and enhance profits.
4. Lean is where the company wants to reach, and kaizen is the way to reach there.
5. Quality has to be ensured at the source of production.
6. In traditional companies, most of the functions are oblivious to customer requirements.
7. Nothing is static in this world. Everything is either improving or deteriorating. If the processes stop improving at the workplace, processes standards will start dwindling with respect to man, machine, material, method and methodology.
8. If the company manages consistency of the 5Ms, the output will be consistent.
9. Employees are the principal assets because they create value, solve problems and improve the organization, and lean management system substantiates this. This first M drives all the other Ms. A highly competent workforce is indispensable to a company's success.
10. A company should prioritize throughput time over procurement cost per unit in the initial lean journey.

Recommended List for Further Reading

1. Taiichi Ohno[1]
Ōhno, T. and Miller, J. (1993). *Workplace management*, 1st Indian edition. Madras India: Productivity Press.
Ohno, T. and Mito, S. (1992). *Just-in-time for today and tomorrow*, 1st Indian edition. Madras India: Productivity Press.
Ohno, T. (2002). *Toyota production system-beyond large-scale production*, Indian edition. Madras India: Productivity Press.
2. Point[2] Kaizen
Maskell.com. Blog- *Planes, Lanes and Value Stream Flow. What's the point of "Point Kaizen"*.
3. Total Productive Maintenance (TPM)[3]
Total Productive Maintenance® is the registered trademark of J.I.P.M
Author: Productivity Press Development Team (1999). *OEE for operators overall equipment effectiveness*. Portland, OR: Productivity Press.

Kunio Shirose and Productivity Press (1992). *TPM for operators.* Cambridge, MA: Productivity Press.

Seiichi Nakajima, E O'shima and Nihon Puranto Mentenansu Kyōkai (1996). *TPM: Total productive maintenance encyclopedia.* Tokyo, Japan and Atlanta, GA: Japan Institute of Plant Maintenance (JIPM).

Shirose, Kunio, Kaneda, M. and Kimura, Y. (2004). *P-M Analysis an advanced step in TPM implementation.* Portland, OR: Productivity Press.

Japan Institute of Plant Maintenance – *JIPM Deployment Guide-Manual-TPM[R] Sample formats for the 12 steps of TPM.* www.jipm.or.jp

4. Total Quality Maintenance (TQM)[4]

Omachonu, V.K. and Ross, J.E. (2005). *Principles of total quality.* Florida: CRC Press and Taylor and Francis e-Library.

Mohanty, R.P. and Lakhe, R.R. (2006). *TQM in the service sector.* Mumbai: Jaico Publishing House.

5. Six Sigma[5]

Michalski, W.J. and King, D.G. (2003). *Six sigma tool navigator: The master guide for teams.* New York: Productivity Press.

Harry, M.J. and Schroeder, R. (2000). *Six sigma: The breakthrough management strategy revolutionizing the world's top corporations.* New York: Random House.

6. Toyota Production System (TPS)[6]

Cusumano, M.A. and Kentarō, Nobeoka (2010). *Thinking beyond lean: How multi-project management is transforming product development at Toyota and other companies.* New York, NY: Free Press.

Dennis, P. (2007). *Lean production simplified: A plain-language guide to the world's most powerful production system.* Boca Raton, FL: CRC Press and Taylor & Francis Group.

Dyer, C.E. and Nihon Nōritsu, Kyōkai (1993). *Canon production system: Creative involvement of the total workforce,* 1st Indian edition. Cambridge, MA: Productivity Press. Madras, India.

Hiroyuki, Hirano (1990). *JIT implementation manual. 5: The complete guide to just-in-time manufacturing: Standardized operations: Jidoka and maintenance/safety.* Boca Raton, FL: Productivity Press.

Hutchins, D. (1990). *Just in time.* Madras, India: Productivity Press.

Yasuhiro, Monden (1998). *Toyota production system.* Norcross, GA: Institute of Industrial Engineers.

Global.Toyota.company. Production System

7. Toyota's five strategies to become number one in the industry

Dennis, Chambers K. (2012). *How Toyota changed the world.* Ahmedabad: Jaico Publishing House.

Liker, J.K. (2004). *The Toyota way: 14 management principles from the world's greatest manufacturer.* New York: McGraw-Hill.

8. 5S[8]

Takashi, Osada (2003). *The 5 S's: Five keys to a total quality environment.* Chiyoda-ku, Tokyo, Japan: Asian Productivity Organization.

Debashis, Sarkar (2006). *5S for service organizations and offices: A lean look at improvements.* Milwaukee, WI: Asq Quality Press.

9. Kanban System[9]

Gross, J. (2012). *Kanban made simple.* Broadway, New York, NY: AMACON, a division of American Management Association.

Louis, R.S. (2017). *Integrating kanban with MRP II: Automating a pull system for enhanced jit inventory management.* Portland, OR: Productivity Press.

10. MRP[10]

Waddell, Bill (2006). *MRP R.I.P* – www.superfactory.com

11. Continuous Flow[11]

Coimbra, E.A. and Kaizen Institute (2009). *Total flow management: Achieving excellence with Kaizen and lean supply chains.* Howick, NZ: Kaizen Institute.

Productivity Development Team (1999). *Cellular manufacturing: One-piece flow for work teams learning package.* Portland, OR: Productivity Press.

Rother, M. and Harris, R. (2001). *Creating continuous flow: An action guide for managers, engineers and production associates.* Brookline: Lean Enterprise Institute.

Smalley, A. (2009). *Creating level pull: A lean production system improvement guide for production-control, operations, and engineering professionals.* Cambridge, MA: Lean Enterprise Institute.

12. Single-Minute Exchange of Dies (SMED)

Shigeo, Shingō (2000). *A revolution in manufacturing: The SMED system.* Portland, OR: Productivity Press.

Sekine, K. and Arai, K. (2011). *Kaizen for quick changeover: Going beyond SMED.* Cambridge, MA: Productivity Press.

13. Standardization of the Daily Work Schedule

Niederstadt, J. (2017). *Standardized work for noncyclical processes.* New York: Productivity Press.

Shigehiro, Nakamura (1993). *The new standardization: Keystone of continuous improvement in manufacturing.* Portland, OR: Productivity Press.

Chapter 3

The Lean Way of Doing Business

Lean thinking defines value as providing benefit to the customer; anything else is waste.

– Eric Ries

Lean manufacturing, or lean production, is a production methodology derived from Toyota's operating model. The term 'lean' was coined by John Krafcik in 1988 in his article 'Triumph of the Lean Production System'. Lean is production of 'good quality' products 'in the required' quantity that the customer wants 'on time'. In a lean company, the product or service has to be produced or given with the least material, least time, least man and machine hours, least piling of inventory and with least efforts. It all sums up as 'least cost to company'.

A lean company is a company that imbibes lean principles derived from the Toyota Production System in its manufacturing processes to deliver maximum value to its customers by reduction in throughput time through elimination of waste in processes. In simple words, a lean company maximizes value while minimizing waste. Lean methodologies help companies to achieve their goals in a smart and sustainable way. The lean business model originated in manufacturing industries, but it can be applied to almost any business. A lean company connotes that all functions in the company are lean like lean production, lean purchase, lean design, lean IT, lean administration and so forth. A lean company produces in small quantities at regular

DOI: 10.4324/9781003221746-3

49

intervals (pull and flow) and focuses on cost reduction to maintain profit margins or pass on the price reduction to customers to gain competitive edge and market share.

3.1 Lean Culture

It is imperative to work on the culture of the company to befit it to the lean philosophy. Operations are reassessed to evaluate how they should be run. Employees should run the operations and not vice versa. Running an operation is like driving a car. All employees have to work in real time with real and current data. The car can't be run on the road with the rearview mirror.

Top management has to ensure that the daily management process is implemented and reviewed for a continuous 40 days for sustenance and habit formation for all team members. The ultimate goal is to have an internally managed and process-oriented company with a priority for improvement environment so that lean culture takes the root in the organization and it becomes a habit of the employees to do everything the kaizen way, the standardized way. Sustenance is the key. It will be possible only if education and training is the central focus of the organization and becomes as important as the final product dispatches from the plants or providing services to the clients.

James Womack and Daniel Jones defined the five principles of lean manufacturing in their book *Lean Thinking: Banish Waste and Create Wealth in Your Corporation*[1] as per Figure 3.1.

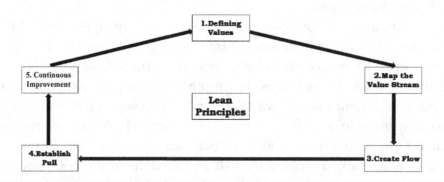

Figure 3.1   Lean Principles as Defined by Womack and Jones in *Lean Thinking: Banish Waste and Create Wealth in Your Corporation*.

Defining Value, That Is, What Does 'Value to the Customer' Mean?

Publilius Syrus quotes, "Everything is worth what its purchaser will pay for it." Customers are the lifeline of the company. Each product manufactured or service provided has a value that is an equivalent to what a customer would be willing to pay for it. The value may lie in the quality provided, delivery speed or quantity among may other things. While several companies may manufacture same product, it is the experience that the customer encounters while interacting with the company that defines his loyalty, differentiates the company from its competitors and determines the price of the product. Therefore, lean companies focus on low-cost manufacturing by elimination of waste because each value stream and each business process contains waste, and this is what prevents companies from creating 'value for the customers'. They create value at each step by waste elimination and let the market determine the price of the product.

Map the Value Streams

Before we discuss about value streams, let us understand the following:

What Is a Value Adding Activity? (This Is Lean)

Value adding activities are business processes for which the customer is willing to pay (i.e., activities that manufacture the product by converting raw materials into finished goods). These activities add value only if they are completed with minimum resources correctly the first time and help the business to deliver the product or service while fully conforming to customer requirements or specifications.

What Is a Non-Value Adding Activity? (This Is Not Lean)

Non-value adding activities are business processes for which the customer is 'not' willing to pay. For example, customers will not pay for rework or quality checks. These activities add to the cost of doing business but do not add value to the product or process or are unnecessary. These activities should be eliminated, simplified, reduced or integrated.

On an average, a company has only 20% value adding and 80% non-value adding activities. These percentages might vary from industry to industry but often, for one value adding activity, the company has four non-value adding activities for which the customer does not pay. The company has to focus on the non-value adding activities for its improvement strategy because lean thinking is all about continuous waste elimination. Lean requires total employee involvement tools and a no-blame culture.

What Is a Value Stream?

The organizational structure in a traditional company is based on function and is divided into several departments (cost centers) through which the customer orders are received; raw materials are procured, processed and converted into finished product and delivered to the customer; and payments are collected. The decision-making authority lies with the department's head whose sole objective is to run his or her department efficiently. He or she is the face of the department and all communication flows through him or her. This structure leads to slower decision-making, inter-departmental conflicts, prioritizing individual department objectives over company goals and customer-centricity and increase in non-value adding activities.

In lean companies, departments are replaced by value stream. Value stream can be defined as a 'set of processes' to manufacture a product or provide a service for which the customer is willing to pay. All the steps and processes involved in taking a specific product from raw materials and delivering the final product to the customer make a value stream. Understanding value stream is critical for a company when it starts with the lean journey because it helps to create a link between the processes that create value for the customer and allow for a productive analysis to identify waste and non-value adding activities. To form the value streams, the company is rearranged in such a way that products that require similar process steps or production flow, irrespective of the end user, are grouped into a family. Value streams represent product or service families in the company, serve a set of customers and involve processes that are required from the start of value creation till the end product reaches the customer.

Each value stream is made up of several functions and is headed by a value stream manager. 'Functions' consist of sales, marketing, design, R&D, production planning and control, procurement, production, maintenance, manufacturing engineering, quality assurance, projects, customer service, logistics, after sales support and so forth. Each function is headed by a functional manager who reports to the value stream manager. The value stream manager is in direct touch with the customer and is responsible for running the value stream as a profit center or a mini company within the company.

In many companies there can be a single value stream and a single value stream manager who can be at general manager or vice president level.

How to Map a Value Stream

Once the value streams have been identified, the next step is to map the value stream. *Value stream mapping (VSM)*[2], as defined by the Lean Enterprise Institute, is a simple diagram of every step involved in the material and information flows needed to bring a product from order to delivery. In a lean company, the productivity of the value stream is paramount. The work centers are brought closer to each other, and their output is balanced for smoother flow. The slowest work center determines the output of the value stream and impacts the flow and throughput time, that is, the path from the first process to delivery to the customer.

To formulate a value stream, first create a production flow matrix with machines or work centers on the X-axis and product families on the Y-axis. Each value stream should generate significant business revenue. The value stream map is generated based on product family or products families or services that are bringing in the significant proportion of the total business. The next step is to draw a spaghetti diagram that outlines the path of an item or activity or a person through a process using a continuous path line. These continuous path lines display the current status of the process flow on which the kaizen teams work to identify value adding and non-value adding movements in the operations. The main purpose of value stream map is to visualize the path a product or service takes to reach a customer so that this can be done in the fastest, easiest and most cost-effective way. Value stream map shows the throughput time, which is the time taken to procure and process raw material into a finished product and dispatch to the customer. The whole lean and kaizen exercise is just to reduce this throughput time to as low as possible.

Value stream map is the actual picture of the layout as to how the manufacturing process is laid out on the shop floor. It shows how the final product develops from raw material stores after being processed in the plant, lands in the finished goods supermarket and reaches the final customer. The value stream map helps to draw the detailed operations on paper for calculating the actual value adding time for which the customer pays and the total non-value adding time which is being used to manufacture the products which the customers does not pay for. The next step is to map data boxes for the current value stream. For each function, identify the cycle time of each sub-process; changeover times; scrap generation rate; number of operators, supervisors and executives; space occupied (square meters footage); and the machine uptime.

Therefore, when a company draws the value stream maps, it is then realized where the opportunities for improvements lie. Let us take an example to study how value stream mapping is done to study current position of the company. Perfect Gear Company is a capital machine builder group with three divisions for capital machinery – hot rolling mills, cold rolling mills and gearbox division. These three divisions can be called as three value streams. Gearbox division (value stream III) is the promising value stream where the company has recently gone in for foreign collaboration for new technology and is eyeing the potential export market in Europe and America. *The work on the lean production system is taken up in all the three value streams but for the purpose of this book, we will focus on gearbox division (value stream III) only.*

The value stream map of the Perfect Gear Company was prepared at the end of March 2018 as shown in Figure 3.2.

Calculate Value Adding Ratio and Throughput Time at the End of March 2018

There can be multiple routes to process a product. For the purpose of value stream mapping, the longest route to process the product is taken and value adding ratio and throughput time are calculated. See Figure 3.3 for calculation of value adding ratios and throughput time. The value adding ratio is 0.4%, which indicates the plant is being run inefficiently.

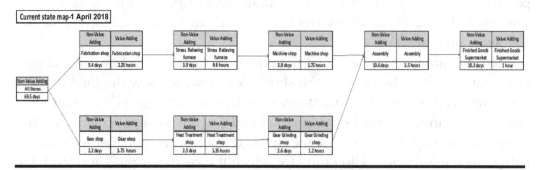

Figure 3.2 Current Value Stream Map of Gearbox Division of Perfect Gear Company.

Flow route from stores to fabrication shop to stress relieving to machine shop to assembly shop and finished goods supermarket is a longer route. Hence, we calculate the value adding and non-value adding hours for this route only.
Top route value adding hours = 2.25 + 0.6 + 1.75 +3.5 + 1 = 9.1 hours
Top route non-value adding hours = (69.5 + 9.4 + 3.9 +3.8 +10.6 + 10.2) × 23.5 = 2523.9 hours
Value adding ratio in % = [value adding hours/(value adding + non-value adding hours)] × 100 = [9.1/(9.1 + 2523.9)] × 100 = 0.4%
Throughput time is sum of value adding and non-value adding hours (i.e., 2533 hours, which is the time taken for raw materials to dispatch from the company as finished goods).
The raw material takes 2533/23.5 = 108 days to dispatch. The lower the throughput time, the better for the company.

Figure 3.3   Value Adding Ratio and Throughput Time.

Role of a Value Stream Manager

Value streams are *profit centers* in a lean enterprise and value stream managers are responsible for the production, sale, delivery and profitability of the products and services under them. Most companies carry a false notion that value stream manager is a production manager. But in reality, he is a business manager who is responsible for the whole chain from sales to after sales service to customers. He should have a clear understanding of customer needs and changing preferences of the customer. The value stream manager reports to the customers first before reporting to the company management.

As lean matures, it becomes increasingly necessary to dismantle the departments and manage the company by value streams. A value stream has its own sales, own inventories, own purchasing and its own accounting. Growth and improvement strategies revolve around the value stream. The company needs a team of people within each value stream whose focus is on growth of value stream, increase in customer value, elimination of waste and increase in profitability. When there are empowered teams in the value stream, the decision-making improves at the middle and bottom level. The value stream manager's job is to lead the team operating the process, not just in manufacturing on the plant floor but also in all business functions and to take the responsibility for productivity, cost, deliveries and quality of the value stream.

Developing a lean value stream exposes sources of waste in all the process, both operating and non-operating, that lead up to final delivery of the product. The value stream manager has to spend considerable time on the plant floor as well as in functional areas to set up the value stream, create the process layout, identify waste to reduce throughput time and increase productivity and profitability of the value stream. The value stream manager takes full control of and accountability for this mini company within the company. Once value streams are formed, all financial analysis is performed at value stream level and finance teams provide information required for taking decisions, but they do not make the decision for the value streams. The value stream manager works closely with the CFO to drop the old measures as per standard cost accounting and bring in new lean measures as per the lean accounting. The finance team assists a value stream in implementing the lean production system and lean accounting by being part of each continuous improvement team. The value stream manager has a firm conviction that lean principles can be adopted to work in value stream setting, coupled with a willingness to try, fail and learn. He or she ensures that all functional managers in the value stream prioritize improved flow in the value stream.

Challenges in Setting Up a Value Stream Organization

Value stream setup breaks the traditional function-based setup in a company by forming several mini-companies within the company based on product families that function with autonomy. However, implementation of this change can come with following challenges:

Change in Role of Functional Heads

Functional heads might be apprehensive about the change because they will become part of something instead of leading their function. On the contrary, as a functional manager in a value stream they will start having a clear vision of what the customer needs and customer satisfaction will become the fundamental goal of the company.

Manpower Costs Will Increase

Manpower costs will increase when the workforce is divided to represent each function in the value stream. A company may have to hire more people in the long run, but extra hiring can be avoided initially by sharing some personnel among different functions. However, in the long term, people will be in their own functions.

Need for Machines and Space

A company will need capital funds to invest in more machines as resources are divided among the functions. But as far as possible, no new facility is bought except for some balancing resources that would have been required anyway. Under lean, extra resources bring flexibility. But the company might have a monster machine that will have to be shared initially based on the time it is used by the value streams. Lean production system does not recommend monster machines and avoids it as far as technically possible. The company will not need more space unless volumes increase drastically.

Large Numbers of Products and Variety

Lean production system and lean accounting tools are designed to best serve companies with a huge portfolio of products. Value streams bring management control over the portfolio by grouping products into families so that maximum value can be delivered to customers. Processes are made flexible to customize products as per customer preferences and to avoid overproduction.

The Sales Team Is Often Divided by Geography

The sales team continues to be divided in the same way and is not rearranged as per value streams. The marketing team takes take the central role of the voice of customer to the value streams.

Create Flow[3]

Once the value streams have been identified, the next step is to ensure a smooth flow of each activity in the value stream. This requires removal of obstacles and bottleneck processes so that the time taken in the value stream is as low as possible. The bottleneck process is that process in the value stream that has minimum production capacity per hour and determines the output rate of the value stream. The bottleneck processes can be like waiting for decisions, review of work done or queuing of material from a faster process. The bottlenecks should be scrutinized to identify the issues so that corrective action can be taken to increase the output.

The bottleneck cells or processes are the one that have the lowest production capacity. This is the process that determines the output of the value stream. The lean and kaizen activities are first focused on this process so that a smooth "flow" without waste can be created.

In the current value stream map in Figure 3.2, gear shop (3.75 tons per hour) is the bottleneck operation with the lowest production capacity and highest cycle time. Next, we need to reflect on which process steps are non-value adding and can be eliminated or replaced, where distance can be reduced from one process to next and where there is production loss from changeover time, scrap, rework or breakdowns that prevents the value stream from serving customer needs. This is covered in detail in Chapter 8.

Establish Pull[4]

As discussed under the Toyota Production System, establishing a 'pull system' is an important step toward elimination of waste and avoiding excessive inventory in warehouses. Instead of forecasting demand, tools like kanban and supermarket allow companies to produce as per customer demand or pull, which reduces wastage, avoids overproduction, allows flexibility in catering to dynamic customer preference and ensures inventory pile-up.

Continuous Improvement

The importance of continuous improvement (Kaizen) in a company cannot be emphasized enough. There is always a scope to be better. Tools like PDCA and SDCA discussed in the previous chapter help the company to continuously evaluate its processes and bring improvement.

What Happens When the Lean Production System Is Implemented?

The lean production system focuses on increasing productivity, reducing cost of production and providing faster service and delivery to the customers. The lean production system results in the following benefits as highlighted in Figure 3.4.

Figure 3.4   Benefits of the Lean Production System.

Productivity

The lean business model is a value-based approach that focuses on increasing productivity of the business processes. The vertical organization structure is replaced by value streams for faster decision-making, shorter delivery time, better financial governance and reduced wastage. Machine downtime, production below capacity, material and quality issues add to cost and are unacceptable in lean companies.

Product input cost constitutes of material, labor, consumables, maintenance, changeover time and cost of quality. Output is the actual demand by customers that they pull or buy and is what the company will be able to produce and dispatch. The lean production system will have the following impact on these factors:

■ *Raw materials* – They are replenished through kanban system. The material comes just-in-time (JIT) in quantity that will actually be consumed, and standard supermarket controls the maximum stock of each item, which leads to reduction in slow and non-moving inventory. Refer to the kanban system in Chapter 2. The scrap generated is monitored and yield is recorded for continuous improvement in productivity. Routine items are procured from certified suppliers using long-term purchase orders through e-kanban trigger.

■ *Labor* – The kanban system allows for production of only what is required by the customers through the pull system. Workmen follow standard operating procedures (SOPs) for production and follow the 'first time right' approach to reduce the need for rework. They monitor the hourly or shift-wise production and target to achieve the planned per hour production. This improves labor productivity, and reduces rework and time lost due to wait for decisions.

■ *Consumables* –Consumables should be managed within or below the budget. If a company spends beyond budget, identify the reasons along with why-why analysis.

■ *Maintenance and Changeover Times* – Breakdowns decrease, and maintenance is done as per scheduled shutdowns. Total productive maintenance, annual maintenance and preventive maintenance are implemented on machines to reduce downtime and changeover time and maintain speeds. Even time taken for annual and preventive maintenance is targeted for reduction. It releases more time for production, so productivity improves due to better machine performance and reduction in setup time of machines.

- *Quality* – Quality is implemented at source that reduces cost of poor quality and improves productivity due to good quality.
- *Transportation* – Layout changes smoothen the flow with minimum travel of manpower and material and milk runs are planned for both vendors and customers. This results in the reduction of transportation costs and decrease in throughput time.
- *Space Requirement* – Reduction in inventory and changes in layout create free space for expansion.

Cost

Fewer people and less equipment go into the processes. The previous productivity measures result in lowest average cost for the value stream and the profit margins increase. There is no such thing as cost of products. It depends what happens during the day in the value stream. How much is produced?

Delivery

Throughput time is less as batch sizes reduce. Logistics is under control as processes are under control and no premium freight is being spent now in airfreight of the delayed deliveries earlier.

The Start of the Lean and Kaizen Journey

Once the current state map is documented, a company starts understanding the need for lean operations in the company. The management should take the services of a lean sensei (lean production system expert) to assist the functional teams in identification of opportunities for improvement and draw up the future state map, a road map and the benefit sheet. The teams identify the non-value adding activities that can be reduced to free the capacity. This surplus capacity can be used for more production runs and to increase revenue and earnings. They will result in an increase in value adding ratio and a decrease in throughput time.

3.2 Daily Management System (DMS)[5]

Most companies implement the lean and kaizen tools sincerely and vigorously, but the results fizzle out in few months because companies are unable to sustain the improvements that were brought in and which started giving returns both operationally and financially with satisfied customers who were happy to get quality products on time.

To address this issue, David Mann developed the "lean management system" in 1995 and that became the game changing tool for *sustenance*. In most organizations, managers are aware of the challenges they face on a daily basis, but they do not know how to address them and sustain the gains from lean implementation.

Daily management systems (DMS) described here and implemented in many companies including Perfect Gear Company is a set of processes through which team members check their progress of the daily tasks to evaluate whether they are achieving the improved results from their efforts in continual improvement projects by reducing the non-value adding activities. Daily management ensures that the workmen, supervisors and managers have knowledge of their operations on an hourly basis and know how to address the issues that may arise. They should also know what they are supposed to do in a day on an hourly basis and what parameters they have to monitor on regular basis.

Companies started realizing that the real reasons for non-sustenance was due to new tools being imposed on employees without working on the existing culture in the company which continues to be traditional. Only the operations team was involved in kaizen movement and other functions were not sensitized. Two things were required to rectify this: first, a new lean culture building exercise across all the functions in the value stream including the most important function – finance – and second, inclusion at every level of the organization so that each employee knows what he is expected to do on the production floor in a day and the daily checklist against which they have to ensure the operations.

To implement a DMS at the workplace, the following tools are used:

■ A *daily work schedule* outlining how a manager and supervisor are going to spend their time in a day
■ A *typical checklist* against which they will have to monitor their workplace
■ A daily performance board on the workplace
■ A *set meeting module* to communicate the day's challenges
■ An *attendance board* to maintain discipline

Daily Work Schedules for Managers and Supervisors

A schedule of activities that managers and supervisors are expected to perform in a day on an hourly, daily, monthly, quarterly or yearly basis and shift-wise is prepared. For supervisors, almost 80% of the day is covered by daily repeat activities. The rest of the time is reserved for improvement practices. More than 40% of manager time is reserved for kaizen practices and analysis of the previous day's missed opportunities to take corrective and preventive actions. If managers and supervisors know what they are expected to do and what key measures they will be judged on as per the performance measurement system, it will bring clarity and transparency to the system. Some work schedule formats are given in Figure 3.5 through Figure 3.9:

Time	Daily task	Month	Quarterly	Checklist	
7.05–7.10	Kaizen pledge				
7.10–7.20	Workstation housekeeping	April, July	Board report compilation	Confirm all posting by	
7.20–7.30	Review previous day's checklist	October, January	FAC committee meeting		
7.30–7.45	Meeting with finance team	March	Yearly tasks	Confirm all posting by	
7.45–8.00	Gap analysis	March	Preparation of draft accounts		
8.00–8.20	Meeting with functional head	March	Attending to audit queries	Match the control accounts to lists	
8.20–10.00	Various activities related to accounting – signing checks LPOs indents, petty cash				
10.00–11.00	Attending value stream manager-functional head meeting			Confirm system availability and WIP control with	

Figure 3.5   Daily Work Schedule for Finance Manager.

Time	Daily task	Month	Quarterly	Checklist		
11.00–12.00		September	Budget preparation			
12.00–1.00				Bank position		
1.00–2.00	Lunch break			Overdue debtors		
2.00–4.00	Value adding activities			Overdue creditors		
Day	Weekly tasks			Errors on system		
Mon	Issues arising from the weekend and the HOD morning meeting					
Tue	Policy deployment meeting in afternoon					
Wed	Inventory check and supply chain discussion					
Thu	Check signing					
Fri	Meeting with MD for update					
Day	Monthly task					
4th	Management report checking and analysis					
5th	Check DCT-DST-DPT reports for accuracy and further forwarding to MD					
7th	Meeting with production to discuss DPT performance					
8th	Meeting with sales to discuss DCT performance.					
22nd	Payroll approval and checking					

Figure 3.5   (Continued)

Time	Daily task	Note	Month	Quarterly tasks
7.05–7.10	Kaizen pledge			
7.10–7.20	Workstation housekeeping		April, July, October, January	Prepare ratios for board report and other assigned duties
7.20–7.30	Sorting previous day's receipts and invoices		March	Yearly tasks
7.30–7.45	Meeting with finance head		Feb	Preparation of assigned audit schedules
7.45–8.45	Identify creditors to be paid and overdue creditors		Feb	Audit queries, creditors circularization and reconciliation
8.45–9.00	Match supplier invoices, post import indents and payment			
9.00–9.30	Post all matched LPOs and indents			
9.00–10.00	6K filing of all documents posted (i.e., invoices payments unmatched LPOs receipts)		September	Budget preparation
10.00–10.30	Petty cash reconciliation			
10.30–12.00				
12.00–1.00	Petty cash issue			
1.00–2.00	Lunch break			
2.00–4.00	Value adding activities			
	Weekly tasks			
Mon	Confirm export entries returned, box score data			
Tues	Prepare box score			
Wed	Prepare dept OEE, attend HK meeting			
Thu	Creditors' reconciliations against supplier statements			
Fri	Post petty cash transactions			
Sat	Casuals payment			

Figure 3.6   Daily Work Schedule for Accountant.

Time	Daily task	Note	Month	Quarterly tasks
Day	**Monthly task**			
4th	Data repeat run and correctional posting			
5th	Prepare payment analysis for import agent			
5th	Prepare vehicle fuel consumption analysis			
4th Wk	Participate in monthly stock take			
10th	Post check payments, make remittance			
15th	Prepare VAT returns for filing			
15th	Prepare KBS levy returns for payment and filing			
3rd	Post journals-prepayment, barclay card, sales rebate			
5th	Prepare business ratios and submit to FM			

Figure 3.6 (Continued)

Time	Daily task	Notes	Month	Quarterly tasks
7.05–7.10	Kaizen pledge		By 8th of every quarter	Quarterly pay returns
7.10–7.20	Workstation housekeeping		Month	Yearly tasks
7.20–7.30	Confirm payments and bankings on the bank			Participate in budget preparation
7.30–7.45	Meeting with finance head			Any end year adjustments
7.45–8.00	Bank position			Pay returns for the year
8.00–8.20	Writing checks and remittance			
8.20–9.20	Post debtors payments and identify overdue debtors			

Figure 3.7 Daily Work Schedule for Accounts Assistant.

Time	Daily task	Notes	Month	Quarterly tasks
9.20–10.30	Posting cash book direct payments			
10.30–12.00				
12.00–1.00				
1.00–2.00	Lunch break			
2.00–4.00	Value adding activities			
Day	**Monthly task**			
10th of the month	Writing checks			
1st of every month	Imprest reconciliations			
1st of every month	Passing journals for salaries and imprest			
By 5th every month	Statutory returns (NSSF, DIT, HELB, NHIF, PAYE)			
By 20th every month	Withholding tax			
On receipt of bank statement	Cashbook reconciliation			
4th day every month	Sending statements			
5th day every month	DCT and DST reports			
End of the month	Making adjustments for bank charges for both local and export debtors			
End of the month	Reconciling statutory accounts			
End of the month	Printing debtors' reports to sales team			
End of the month	Any other report required			

Figure 3.7   (Continued)

Time		Tasks
7.00	7.05	Workstation housekeeping
7.05	7.15	Meeting with supervisor with operators (communication)
7.15	8.00	Update all visuals, re-check shift planning and adjustments
8.00	8.15	Hourly monitoring and catchup countermeasures
8.15	9.00	Problem-solving
9.00	9.30	Meeting with functional supervisors
9.30	10.00	Check – skill related (every day – every process)
10.00	10.15	Hourly monitoring and catch-up countermeasures
10.30	11.00	Lunch break
11.00	11.15	Hourly monitoring and catch-up countermeasures
11.15	12.00	Check – skill related (every day – every process)
12.00	12.15	Hourly monitoring and catch-up countermeasures
12.15	1.00	Problem-solving
1.00	1.15	Hourly monitoring and catch-up countermeasures
1.15	2.00	
2.00	2.15	Hourly monitoring and catch-up countermeasures
2.15	3.00	Planning for next shift
3.00	3.15	Hourly monitoring and catch-up countermeasures
3.15	3.30	Visuals updation (safety, quality, productivity, cost, human development)

Figure 3.8   Daily Work Schedule for Plant Floor Team Supervisor in a Steel Company in East Africa.

Time		Tasks
8.30	8.35	Work area housekeeping
8.35	9.00	Management of critical issues
9.00	9.30	Gemba walk with team supervisor of 1st shift, assign tasks
9.30	10.00	Participate in meeting with value stream manager, supervisors and supporting department representatives
10.00	11.00	Abnormality management (resolve issues with other departments)
11.00	11.30	Gemba walk – with checklist and gemba walk route, assign tasks
10.30	11.00	Check – focus on improvement (every day – one process)
11.00	12.30	
12.30	1.00	Lunch break

Figure 3.9   Daily Work Schedule for Plant Floor Senior Supervisor in a Steel Company in East Africa.

Time		Tasks
1.00	1.30	Gemba walk – with checklist and gemba walk route, assign tasks
1.30	3.00	
3.00	3.30	Planning for second shift
3.30	4.00	Management of critical issues
4.00	4.30	Gemba walk with team supervisors of 2nd shift, assign tasks
4.30	5.00	Abnormality management
Note. Senior Supervisor to have one-to-one communication with operator (daily one) during gemba walk		

Figure 3.9 (Continued)

Time		Tasks
8.30	8.35	Work area housekeeping
8.35	9.00	Management of critical issues
9.00	9.30	Gemba walk – with checklist and gemba walk route, assign tasks
9.30	10.00	
10.00	11.00	Participate in meeting with supervisors and supporting department representatives
11.00	11.30	Abnormality management
10.30	11.00	
11.00	12.30	
12.30	1.00	Lunch break
1.00	1.30	
1.30	3.00	
3.00	3.30	
3.30	4.00	Gemba walk with checklist and gemba walk route, assign tasks
4.00	4.30	
4.30	5.00	

Figure 3.10 Daily Work Schedule for Production Manager in a Steel Company in East Africa.

Figure 3.10 shows the daily work schedule for a production manager of a steel company in East Africa. Many hours during the day are kept blank because this is the time that the production manager has to utilize for the kaizen and lean activities. The manager has to put in corrective and preventive action for the issues and non-conformities that is cropping up on daily basis in the plant. The manager has to work on the elimination of all seven wastes.

Typical Checklists

When the managers and supervisors go to the workplace, they have the checklists with them. These checklists are procedures that are to be practiced by workmen and supervisors. These are used for evaluating the working on the plant floor to check whether the working is in line with the targets in the SOP's. This has to be done every hour and every day. The supervisor's checklist for stores (Figure 3.11) is appended in the following for guidance.

Figure 3.12 is a sample of the plant floor team supervisor typical checklist in a steel company in East Africa. It shows what the team supervisor has to check on the plant floor when he or she goes for the round. This brings in standardization. It does not kill individual initiative. These typical checklists can be revised if there is a better suggestion to improve these.

A number of typical checklists are shown here so that all levels of employees will get a clear idea of how to prepare one for their company. Figure 3.13 is a sample of the plant floor supervisor's typical checklist in a steel company in East Africa.

Supervisor's Typical Checklist		Name:						
Date:		Gemba:						
No.	Once a day check points	1	2	3	4	Notes:	Daily assignments:	
1	Manpower availability							
2	Is the gemba clean?							
3	Is peep (Place for everything and everything in place) observed in the whole store?							
4	Are the weighed materials clearly leveled?							
5	Is the packing clean?							
6	Is there spillage of material at the gemba?							
7	Are the weighing tools clean?							
8	Are the pumps clean?							
9	Are the operators in the rights PPEs?							

Figure 3.11 Sample Supervisor Typical Checklist for Stores.

Team Supervisor Typical Checklist			Name:					
Date:			Gemba:					
No.	Once a day check points	1	Notes:					Daily assignments:
1	Manpower availability							
2	Allocation of manpower							
3	Leave plan updation							
4	Check and update visual charts							
5	Conduct meeting with workmen							
No.	Multiple times a day check points	1	2	3	4	6	7	
6	Check plan vs. actual							
7	Countermeasures taken on problems observed							
8	Critical m/c speed-feed, temp, pressure							
9	Check quality of product randomly							
10	Overall 5S condition							
11	Operator work schedule (every day – every process)							
12	Self standard work							

Figure 3.12   Sample Plant Floor Team Supervisor Typical Checklist in a Steel Company in East Africa.

Supervisor's Typical Checklist					Name:		
Date:				Gemba:			
No.	Once a day check points	1	2	3	4	Notes:	Daily assignments:
1	Gemba walk						
2	Manpower availability						
3	Check operator training plan (multiskilling)						
4	Output: plan vs. actual: line -1, evaluate countermeasures taken by team supervisor						
5	Output: plan vs. actual: line -2, evaluate countermeasures taken by team supervisor						
6	Output: plan vs. actual: line -3, evaluate countermeasures taken by team supervisor						
7	Overall 5s condition on all lines						

Figure 3.13   Sample Plant Floor Supervisor Typical Checklist in a Steel Company in East Africa.

Supervisor's Typical Checklist		Name:					
8	Follow-up of kaizen project status/tasks assigned						
9	Operator standard work (every day – one process) focus on improvement						
10	Attend meeting with functional head and value stream manager						
11	Check and assess overtime need						
12	Self daily work schedule						

Figure 3.13 (Continued)

Manager's Typical Checklist			Name:			
Date:			Gemba:			
No.	Check points	1	2	Notes:	Daily assignments:	
1	R M stock status					
2	Section-wise production status analysis					
3	Check daily performance trend					
4	Overall 5S condition on all gembas					
5	Follow-up of kaizen project status/tasks assigned					
6	F G stock status					
7	Attend meeting with value stream manager					
8	Manpower planning for week and change management					
9	Check and approve overtime needs					
10	Follow-up for new projects, new initiatives, etc.					
11	Self daily work schedule					

Figure 3.14. Sample Manager Typical Checklist in a Steel Company in East Africa.

Figure 3.14 is a sample of the manager's typical checklist for a steel company in East Africa.

Daily Performance Boards of the Operations

Control on any business process is a manual activity to be performed by human beings. They are expected to collect data, understand the processes and eliminate the confusion and the waste from them.

A lean company typically uses more performance boards spread across the functions to depict current status of operations. They are managed by the supervisors and first line of executives and can be compared to sports activities like cricket, baseball, badminton volleyball and so forth where everyone's eyes are on visual screens to check the scores and cheer the players.

Daily performance boards augment focus and employee engagement. Every supervisor, at the end of the shift, updates the hourly production board for the production, downtime, quality rejection, first time right and so forth during the shift. Most of the data recording is done by hand. The supervisors also update the data in the ERP system through the computer available near the workplace or handheld gadget or through the mobile. Workmen can see their performance of the day on the board right at the workplace. The functional manager on the morning shift round can see the workplace performance on these boards for the last three shifts. These visual plans and charts help to monitor the processes in each shift, identify the problems and help in taking timely remedial action after root cause analysis. Some visual boards are highlighted in Figure 3.15 through Figure 3.17.

Figure 3.15 Daily Performance Board Maintained by Shift Supervisors at Workplace at an ERW Tube Mill in Western India.

Figure 3.16 Daily Performance Board Maintained by Shift Supervisors at Workplace at an ERW Tube Mill in North India.

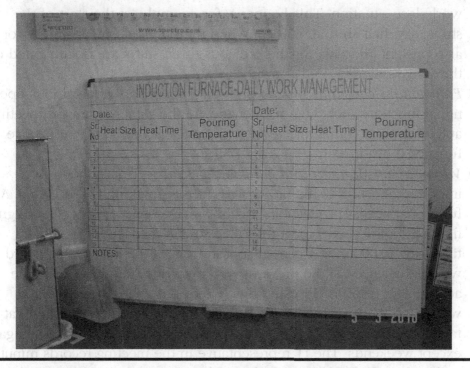

Figure 3.17 Daily Performance Board Maintained by Shift Supervisors at Workplace at a Mini Steel Plant in East Africa.

Daily performance boards embed the goals in workmen's mind. The workmen watch the outcomes on display boards the whole day and become concerned if the numbers are not being achieved. This is a revolution that is taking place where workmen know exactly what is happening. This is what brings the total involvement and improvements. When the CEO, CFO, value stream manager and other functional managers take a walk through the plant they should be able to see the progress of the previous day as well as cumulative progress. They should be able to congratulate the cell staff for their good performance without consulting anyone else. Since the performance is evident, standing meetings take place for improvements and decision on the action plan. The workplace becomes a live company where real-time decisions take place.

Daily Meetings Module on the Plant Floor

There should be the following meetings every day on the plant floor:

- *Supervisors and Workmen* – Supervisors or team leaders of all functions should read the logs books and have a short standing meeting with the workmen for five minutes to apprise themselves of the real workplace situation. This happens, for example, at the start of the shifts, say, first shift at 6.00 am when the previous shift's supervisor is also present and data for the previous three shifts are documented on the visual boards.
- *Functional Heads and Supervisors* – All supervisors from various operational functions including maintenance in the value stream get together at 8.00 am and communicate the challenges faced to their respective functional head.
- *Value Stream Manager and Functional Heads* – This is the most important meeting of the day where decision-making will be done. All functional heads (productions, quality, maintenance, purchase, design, finance, logistics, etc.) meet the value stream manager at a prefixed time, say, 10.00 am at a central spot in front of the action plan board where challenges of the previous day are written on the board. The action plan, responsibility and timeline of action are discussed and written on the board. This can be a 20-minute standing meeting that takes place every day at the same time and same spot without any gap except weekends. The IT representative in the meeting records minutes and updates ERP. The action plan with countermeasures, responsibilities

and timelines on the 'action plan board' is conveyed to top management through an ERP-run dashboard by IT personnel where they are apprised of any decisions or sanctions required from them.

Figure 3.18 through Figure 3.20 show the setup of the value stream manager meeting with functional heads in different plants. All functional managers take their place in the yellow circles and the value stream manager stands in the front yellow circle. The challenges are discussed and action plan with countermeasure, responsibility and timeline on the action plan are decided. During the meeting, final decisions are written on the action plan board.

Figure 3.21 shows a sample of an action plan board at a plant in East Africa. The challenges faced, immediate countermeasure to be taken, by

Figure 3.18   Manager Level Meeting at a Plant in Capital Machine Building Company in India.

Figure 3.19   Manager Level Meeting at a Chemical Plant in East Africa.

Figure 3.20   Manager Level Meeting at a Cold Rolling Mill Plant in East Africa.

Sl. No	Problem description	Why-why?	Countermeasure	Who?	When?

Figure 3.21 Sample of Action Plan Board for Value Stream Meeting at a Plant in East Africa.

whom and the timeline are decided. This is updated on the board. When the action plan is implemented successfully, it is erased.

Figure 3.22 shows a sample of an action plan board for maintenance function.

An Attendance Board to Maintain Discipline

There is a meeting attendance board where the attendance is marked after the manager level meeting is over. It is mandatory for every functional head to attend this meeting. Figure 3.23 and Figure 3.24 show an attendance board on the plant floor near the daily meeting place.

Obeya Corner

This can be called as a mission control or a war room also. It is at the most prominent place in the company, which is accessible to workmen, supervisors, executives, managers, senior managers and top management. This room or display area has the current status report of all continual improvement projects under execution in the company. The plant floor level obeya

Sl. No	Problem description	Reason	Temporary counter measure	Who?	When?	Counter-measure against root cause	Who?	When?

Figure 3.22   Action Plan Board for Maintenance Function at a Mini Steel Plant in East Africa.

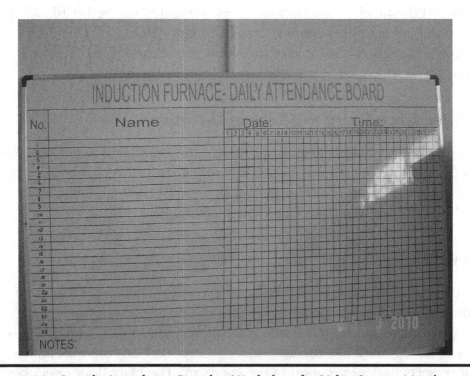

Figure 3.23   Sample Attendance Board at Workplace for Value Stream Meeting at a Mini Steel Plant in East Africa.

SNo.	Name	Month:															Date:							Meeting time:							
		1	2	3	4	5	6	7	8	9	10	11	12	13	14	15	16	17	18	19	20	21	22	23	24	25	26	27	28	29	30	31

Figure 3.24 Sample Attendance Board for Value Stream Meeting.

Figure 3.25 Plant Floor Level Obeya Corner.

corner is accessible to all to see the progress of continual projects under implementation. These displays are based on PDCA as:

PLAN – Value stream maps
DO – Action plan
CHECK – Current results
ACT – SOPs

A sample of the obeya concept is shown in Figure 3.25.

3.3 Lean Accounting

The companies that implement lean and kaizen tools along with the daily management system find themselves in a crisis if the finance function does not recognize lean implementation in the company. Earlier, accountants did not adapt to the change brought by lean and convinced management that consumption of resources for implementation of lean and kaizen tools was not financially feasible and led to decline in profits. This resulted in discontinuation of the lean journey in many companies.

A few promoters of lean and kaizen tools who had financial background and were championing the implementation of lean production and daily management system were encouraged by this to get together, mostly in the United States in the early 2000s to analyze why finance function could not see improvement in bottom line in the companies when inventory was reducing, wastes were declining, throughput time was coming down, customers were getting quality products on time and cash flow of the company was improving. They found that companies continued using traditional management accounting that concealed problems as well as improvements. The traditional accounting system is complex and can create adverse financial numbers despite improvement in operations in the company. This is why it is important to bid goodbye to standard cost accounting. This will be discussed in detail in subsequent chapters.

Companies need an accounting system that supports the lean production system so that profits reflect the decrease in inventory and downtime of the machines and improvement in productivity. It plays a vital role in boosting the morale of the workforce. The lean accounting system was thus conceptualized in the early 2000s by these lean advocates. It has been successfully implemented and now profoundly accepted in many large corporations in the United States. However, lean accounting is still not as popular as it should have been across the world. Art Byrne, CEO of The Wiremold Company, says in his book *The Lean Turnaround:*[6] *How Business Leaders Use Lean Principles to Create Value and Transform Their Company*, "Of all the excess baggage that traditional companies carry, the most intractable is standard cost accounting. This system encourages much of the bad behavior you will be working hard to eliminate. It is the number one thing you DO NOT NEED, and I strongly recommend that you convert to Lean Accounting methods as soon as possible."

Implementation of the Lean Production System, Daily Management System and Lean Accounting in One Road Map

In order to extract maximum benefit the lean production system, daily management system and lean accounting should be implemented together when a company embarks on its lean journey. The lean production system brings large operational improvements in the company. These operational improvements are sustained through daily management system. Lean accounting convinces all that these operational improvements are resulting in financial results and visibility in profit and loss statement, cash flow statement and balance sheet.

Through lean assessment, the current status of the company is ascertained, and a plan is devised to commence the company's lean journey. This ensures that the low hanging fruits are plucked, and initial time and resource allocation are meaningful and motivating for everyone. Companies where the top management participates with appropriate contribution of their time, financial resources and regular reviews undeniably succeed in lean and kaizen implementation.

3.4 Successful Implementation of Lean Tools

Figure 3.26 shows the step-by-step process of implementation of the lean production system, daily management and lean accounting in the company and who is responsible for implementation of each process.

The lean principles are easier to explain and understand because they sound logical, but they are difficult to implement and sustain because they command perseverance, consistency and discipline. Many companies lose patience in the early stages due to lack of support from top management and finance function. Companies have to amend their current practices to bring in the lean culture. But there are also companies that are quick to adopt and implement lean production system, daily management and lean accounting because it makes sense to them to do something that enables them to maximize profits using fewer resources.

Lean thinking has to be applied to each function, including support functions, so that lean thinking and lean culture is developed in the entire company. Everyone in the company from the CEO to the store manager has to rethink how they perform their tasks because lean impacts everyone. Every process should be analyzed for wastes once new tools and techniques are implemented. Creating value for customer, who could be the ultimate customer or the next process, should be everyone's principal goal in the company. Everyone should have conviction in benefits of the lean production system, daily management and lean accounting. Everyone at all levels in the company shall adopt this after proper training and recognizing its usefulness rather than it being forced upon the organization.

Sl. No	Description	Refer to chapter	Responsibility					
			CEOs	CFOs	Lean sensei	Kaizen promotion champion	Value stream managers **	Functional managers*
1	Training on lean production system	Chapter 2, 3, 4	✓✓	✓✓	✓	✓	✓	✓
2	Start implementing lean production system		✓✓	✓✓	✓	✓	✓	✓
3	Lean accounting assessment audit	Chapter 17	✓✓	✓✓	✓	✓	✓	✓
4	Training on lean accounting	Chapter 5	✓	✓✓	✓	✓	✓	✓
5	Start implementing lean accounting system	Chapter 5 and Chapter 7	✓	✓✓	✓	✓	✓	✓
6	Identification of cells and value streams	Chapter 5	✓	✓✓	✓	✓	✓	✓
7	Implementation of cell measures	Chapter 6	✓	✓✓	✓	✓	✓	✓
8	Implementation of value stream measures	Chapter 6	✓	✓✓	✓	✓	✓	✓
9	Calculations of financial benefits of lean improvements	Chapter 6	✓	✓✓	✓	✓	✓	✓
10	Elimination/reduction of transactions in the accounting and operations and other support system	Chapter 16	✓✓	✓✓	✓	✓	✓	✓
11	Implementation of value stream costing in parallel	Chapter 7	✓	✓✓	✓	✓	✓	✓
12	Implementation of value stream cost analysis	Chapter 7	✓	✓✓	✓	✓	✓	✓
13	Implementation of capacity analysis	Chapter 8	✓✓	✓✓	✓	✓	✓	✓
14	Implementation of corporate scorecard	Chapter 9	✓✓	✓✓	✓	✓	✓	✓
15	Celebrate at every step		✓✓	✓✓	✓	✓	✓	✓

* Head of functions of fabrication, machining, gear cutting, heat treatment, gear grinding, assembly, logistics, quality, maintenance, purchase, finance, HRD, design and R&D.
** Only one value stream is referred to in detail in this book.
✓ = Direct responsibility to implement and sustain
✓✓ = Ultimate responsibility

Figure 3.26 Step-By-Step Implementation Process and Responsibility of Lean Production System and Lean Accounting at Perfect Gear Company.

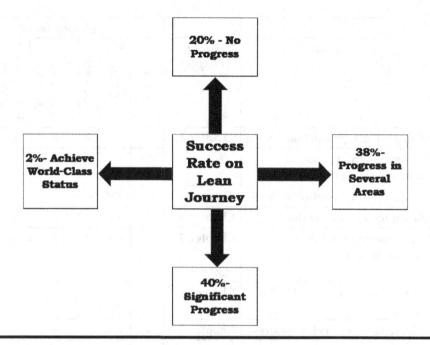

Figure 3.27 Success Rate of Lean Journey.

Figure 3.27 shows our experience in the success rate of the companies that started implementing the lean production system.

■ In 20% of companies, there is no progress, and the kaizen movement fizzles out. These are the companies where kaizen is implemented in spurts and no serious efforts are put out. There is no role of top management.
■ In 38% of companies, point kaizens (local improvements) are successful. These are the companies where daily management is also brought in. The lean and kaizen is not implemented across the company. The lean culture building is missing across all functions. The top management is happy with the improved housekeeping and localized improvements.
■ In 40% of companies, significant improvements materialize and are sustained and a lean culture is visible with an environment of continual improvement. Here the lean production system is implemented across the company at all levels in all functions. Daily management and lean accounting is simultaneously implemented. The budgeting process is dynamic and monthly reviews are done and corrective steps are taken in time. The CEO and the CFO work in tandem. The CFO anchors the continual improvement mission.

■ Two percent of companies from the previous category move to world-class status.

Companies must strive hard to be among the 40% of companies that achieved significant progress and the 2% that became world-class companies. There have been companies who were once world leaders but did not survive when they refused to adapt to the changes in customer behavior and environment or were not ready to embrace new technologies and became vulnerable to competitive forces. Some of the prominent ones among them are Polaroid, Pan-Am, Compaq, GM, Kodak, HMV, Westinghouse, Minolta, SmithCorona, Eastern Airlines, Pullman Company, TWA, Nokia, Xerox, Yahoo, Segway, BlackBerry, Radio Shack, Palm and Hummer.

3.5 Why Do We Need External Expertise to Implement Continuous Improvement Tools?

The managers of a company are well versed with the company's product technology and are expert in their fields. But the plant heads, head of functions and internal change agent teams face issues at the time of implementation of the lean production system, daily management and lean accounting tools because their priority lies in production and they remain occupied with daily firefighting to tackle operational issues.

The change agents need to commence the process of implementation, and an external expert can play a significant role in assisting with this by inculcating confidence that it can be done, and it is possible while simultaneously laying out a road map to show how it is to be done. He or she will be able to share success stories from his or her past domestic and international experiences in the industry to gain trust of top management and functional teams.

An external expert will have experience in the implementation process and be aware of challenges and obstacles that could obstruct the implementation and the solution to deal with them to lift up demotivated employees to continue on the lean journey. He or she will be able to give full attention to improvement activities and bring in a culture of "change management". The external expert will give proper guidance and make the transition and overall lean implementation journey smooth for the company.

Hence, it is advisable to use the services of an external expert for faster implementation of the lean production system, daily management and lean accounting tools in the company. The lean production system, daily management and lean accounting tools together in one comprehensive 'road map' is must. This strategy will bring pre-eminent contribution in a company's journey to be a low cost, high quality producer.

Key Takeaways

1. Lean makes a company a '*least cost producer*'.
2. A value stream map for a manufacturing plant shows the throughput time as the time elapsed from receipt of order to procurement and process of raw materials into a finished product, dispatch to the customer and collection of money. The whole lean and kaizen exercise is just to reduce this throughput time to as low as possible.
3. A value stream manager is in direct touch with the customer and is responsible for running the value stream as a profit center or a mini company within the company. All functional managers including marketing, after sales, design, procurement and finance report to him or her.
4. The 'bottleneck cells or processes' are the ones that have the lowest production capacity. This is the process that determines the output of the value stream.
5. A 'pull system' is one of the important steps toward elimination of waste.
6. Teams identify the 'non-value adding' activities that can be reduced to free the capacity. This surplus capacity can be used for more production runs and to increase revenue and earnings.
7. The daily management system ensures that the workmen, supervisors and managers have knowledge of their operations on an hourly basis and know how to address the issues that may arise.
8. In order to extract maximum benefit the lean production system, daily management and lean accounting should be implemented together when the company embarks on its lean journey.
9. Everyone should have conviction in the benefits of lean production system, daily management and lean accounting. Everyone at all levels in the company shall adopt this after proper training and recognizing its usefulness rather than it being forced upon the organization.
10. Sustenance is the key. It will be possible only if education and training is the central focus of the organization and becomes as important as the final product dispatches from the plant or providing services to the clients.

Recommended List for Further Reading

1. **"The Lean Thinking"**[1]
   Womack, J.P. and Jones, D.T. (2003). *Lean thinking: Banish waste and create wealth in your corporation*. New York: Free Press.

Womack, J.P. and Jones, D.T. (2015). *Lean solutions: How companies and customers can create value and wealth together.* New York: Free Press.

Womack, J.P., Jones, D.T. and Roos, D. (2007). *The machine that changed the world.* London: Simon & Schuster.

2. **Value Stream Mapping (VSM)[2]**

Rother, M. and Shook, J. (1999). *Learning to see: Value-stream mapping to create value and eliminate muda.* Brookline, MA: Lean Enterprise Institute.

Jones, D.T. and Womack, J.P. (2011). *Seeing the whole value stream.* Cambridge, MA: Lean Enterprise Institute.

Keyte, B. and Locher, D. (2004). *The complete lean enterprise value stream mapping for administrative and office processes.* New York, NY: Productivity Press.

Maskell.com. Blog- *'Role of Value stream manager'.*

Maskell.com. Blog- *'Value Stream Management'.*

3. **Create Flow[3]**

Harris, R., Harris, C., Wilson, E., Rother, M. and Lean Enterprise Institute (2003). *Making materials flow: A lean material-handling guide for operations, production-control, and engineering professionals.* Brookline, MA: Lean Enterprise Institute, ©, Reprinted.

Rother, M. and Harris, R. (2001). *Creating continuous flow: An action guide for managers, engineers and production associates.* Brookline: Lean Enterprise Institute.

4. **Establish Pull[4]**

Smalley, A. (2004). *Creating level pull: A lean production-system improvement guide for production-control, operations, and engineering professionals.* Cambridge, MA: Lean Enterprise Institute.

Jones, D.T. and Womack, J.P. (2011). *Seeing the whole value stream.* Cambridge, MA: Lean Enterprise Institute.

5. **Daily Management System[5]**

Mann, David (2005). *Creating a lean culture-tools to sustain lean conversions.* New York: Productivity Press.

6. **'The Lean Turnaround"[6]**

Byrne, Art (2012). *The lean turnaround: How business leaders use lean principles to create value and transform their company.* New York, NY: McGraw-Hill Education.

Henderson, B.A. and Larco, J.L. (2003). *Lean transformation: How to change your business into a lean enterprise.* Richmond: Oaklea Press.

Chapter 4

Who Should Lead the Implementation of Lean Strategy?

A pessimist sees the difficulty in every opportunity; an optimist sees the opportunity in every difficulty.

– Sir Winston Churchill

The role of an external expert in guiding the lean journey of a company is discussed in the previous chapter. But there has to be someone within a company also who leads the implementation process. Lean commands a major overhaul of a company's philosophy and culture. There is going to be disruption in routine business, remodeling of processes and uprooting of traditional methods before the outcome of lean journey becomes visible. Therefore, patience, discipline and conviction in the lean strategy are prerequisites of this process.

Art Byrne[1], CEO of The Wiremold Company and author of *The Lean Turnaround: How Business Leaders Use Lean Principles to Create Value and Transform Their Companies*, says, "You cannot just drop lean on a traditional structure and hope it to be successful. You will need to make a fundamental change to a value stream structure. Determine the new roles for value stream leaders or managers, and then announce this to your organization before you begin your first serious kaizen effort." He then adds, "The biggest and most common mistake that I see companies make is thinking they can

DOI: 10.4324/9781003221746-4

somehow move to a Lean Strategy while preserving their traditional organizational structure."

The major challenge for a company is to keep running the business smoothly to fulfill customer requirements when the change is happening. Lean does not require an immediate switch to a new way of working, but rather it is a step-by-step approach to bring a gradual change in the business operations. All employees are trained on and are informed about what is being done, how it will serve customers better and what the benefits are to the company. They are educated about how this strategy upholds the company when the external factors are unfavorable, how it decreases the break-even points and how it helps when the company faces an adverse situation. It builds confidence in employees by explaining how this strategy secures everyone's jobs. The teams are formed for each aspect of the strategy and changes are gradually introduced under the supervision of a sensei, a lean expert who has rich experience in transformation of companies.

Implementation of the lean production system, daily management and lean accounting tools is the core responsibility of the top management in the company. The top management is not only responsible for taking strategic business decisions. This is why lean has to be not only a business strategy, but rather the 'only' strategy followed by top management to run the business and use as guidance for defining key responsibilities in the company.

4.1 Who Will Lead Lean Strategy Implementation – the CEO, the CFO or Both?

The answer is simple. The implementation has to be led by both the CEO and the CFO. There will be certain aspects of the strategy that will have to be handled by the CEO while others will have to be handled by the CFO, but there will be many aspects where both the CEO and the CFO have to function as a team to ensure that the lean production system, daily management and lean accounting tools are implemented together smoothly.

The lean journey should commence with a *top management conclave* administered by a sensei, an expert in lean production system, daily management and lean accounting tools. All value stream managers, functional managers, senior champions and project leaders should be part of this conclave with the agenda to share thoughts on future vision and mission of the company, reflect on performance for previous years and plan the current year along with how lean production system, daily management and lean accounting tools are going to help in achieving customer satisfaction and profits growth. The lean sensei will address queries on what to expect during the implementation of lean strategy, expected operational and financial gains and step-by-step implementation of the road map and prepare the company for cultural change.

The support of the promoters for the success of the lean production system, daily management and lean accounting tools is of utmost importance. The sensei will prepare them for the impact on present operations once the company sets out on its lean journey so that customers remain unaffected. Promoters may also have doubts about layoffs but lean makes the company so agile that it not only increases its market share in the present segment but also diversifies into new products such that the situation of layoffs never arises.

A lean journey takes a minimum two years to transform a company into a lean company that has controlled operations, motivated employees and quick response time to customers. Therefore, the confidence, support and trust of the management in lean strategy are imperative to its success. It requires patience, dedication and consistency from everyone involved in its implementation. Only dedicated companies with unfailing support from the management become lean companies that are not only lean and mean but also have a healthy cash flow and significant growth in bottom line each month.

"Do it your way." "Do it my way." The old dictator says, "Follow me . . . let's figure this out together." This is the lean way. CEOs and CFOs might struggle initially with lean implementation as their way of working undergoes a major transformation with new expectations from the lean company. A new business perspective is introduced that has no hierarchies, no cozy offices and no long meetings. The first step is to get trained on the principles of the lean production system, daily management and lean accounting tools using a sensei who is a lean expert. It is recommended to visit companies that have implemented lean and lean accounting to witness the success stories in person and gain confidence in possibilities of its success within your own company.

4.2 Barriers in Lean Implementation

Companies that initiate implementation combat initial teething issues like poor commitment from management because of poor knowledge and understanding of lean strategy, lack of confidence in its benefits or inability to adapt to the changes. Similarly, there are initial issues with functional teams because of inadequate knowledge and understanding, improper communication about changes from top management, fear of loss of job, problem in quantifying the benefits from lean initiatives and distractions or slow-downs due to firefighting on other projects.

4.3 How Can the CEO and the CFO Ensure a Smooth Lean Implementation Journey?

Lean is a holistic approach to management that produces exemplary results. The lean strategy aims at eliminating non-value adding processes to ensure optimum utilization of resources like money, manpower and equipment in a company. *A company's lean journey starts with a vision to be a company that excels in customer satisfaction, elimination of waste and value creation.* But this journey commences with a comprehensive revamp of the existing culture and processes of the company. Thus, the CEO and the CFO have to lead by example on how to embrace the change.

First, *the CEO and CFO should communicate the vision of the lean journey with conviction to explain why the organization has selected the lean management path and what specific outcomes are expected over a period of time.* The CEO and the CFO should be at the forefront to adopt the new culture and new way of doing things and inspire others to join in the transformation of the organization. Lean transformation brings a substantial shift in company's culture and the CEO and the CFO need to participate and *lead the change* process. They need to create the urgency for this change, start incorporating new processes and work toward getting the team on board with new ways of working. Once a company embarks on the lean journey, the lean strategy becomes the core business strategy. The fundamentals of the lean production system, daily management and lean accounting tools have to be complied with diligently to get the desired results. The CEO and the CFO should develop a good understanding of benefits of lean and translate the language of lean to the language of money so that it is visible to everyone why lean is indispensable.

There will be some people in the company who would be enthusiastic to implement the changes and willing to learn and experiment. The lean leaders should *provide an 'air cover' for these early adopters* so that they can experiment with methods, materials and technology. These early adopters are in the minority (may be 20% of the total employees) and a leader should protect them till a critical mass builds up in the company. There is the majority of people who are not drivers but followers. They observe their surroundings to verify what is safe and acceptable and join in when they start seeing results. However, there may be some reluctant employees who do not support changing the status quo. They are threatened by change, try to undermine lean transformation, coax others to join them and oppose the changes being brought in. These concrete heads might try to convince others that this is just another "flavor of the month" and the company has taken such initiatives earlier but failed. A leader should not hesitate to eliminate these concrete heads from the company. By doing this, the CEO and the CFO will send a strong message to the company about their resolution to implement the lean production system, daily management and lean accounting Tools.

One of the fundamental philosophies of lean management is *'gemba walks'*. Taiichi Ohno[2] developed the concept of gemba walks. It denotes the action of overseeing actual process, understanding the work, asking questions and learning. It is an opportunity for the staff to stand back from their day-to-day tasks and walk their workplace floor to identify wasteful activities. The objective is to understand a value stream and its entire process. Along with *Genchi Genbutsu* (go, look, see), gemba walk is one of key principles of kaizen, or continuous improvement. Both the CEO and the CFO should actively participate in the real work arena of the company, proactively engage with employees to understand their challenges, identify opportunities for improvement and enhance the productivity at the workplace by being a confident *problem-solver*. When a leader immerses himself in the business operations in this manner, he creates a work environment that keeps the employees motivated, engaged and aligned with the company's goals.

A lean organization thrives on continuous learning and process improvement. It substitutes traditional hierarchal systems with lean governance that reduces bureaucracy and empowers employees. This requires an inclusive work culture with open communication that encourages ideas and opinions to float freely. Having a good idea is not enough till it is implemented. The CEO and the CFO should motivate employees to bring their best set of skills to the table by *trusting and respecting the inputs shared by employees*[3] since they are the ones who essentially do the work and handle the machines. To implement lean strategy successfully, the CEO and the CFO should set stretched goals for the employees, but they have to discover innovative approaches for problem-solving rather than working unproductive long hours.

A leader has to *mentor the employees* to be committed, dedicated and motivated during the entire transformation process. Rewarding the people for small achievements, calling out the best and celebrating each milestone boosts the confidence in the employees that they are headed in the right direction. However, a leader also makes it safe for the teams to fail. Instead of creating a fear of consequences in case of failure, the CEO and the CFO should act as an *empathetic coach* who patiently reflects with the teams to understand what went wrong and to find the solution to rectify it. They should inculcate a mindset that it is okay to fail sometimes and gain more knowledge and experience out of mistakes in order to encourage employees to take ownership and responsibility for their work.

It is important to infuse confidence and trust in employees that lean implementation will *not result in layoffs*. Substantial gains can be achieved from implementation of the lean production system, daily management and lean accounting tools, but it will not be possible without its workforce. The lean implementation drive will slow down and stutter to a stop unless a commitment is made to employees that they will not lose jobs due to increase in productivity. They should be assured that company is working toward diversification and expansion to increase current product sales and focus on new product developments. This might sound like asking too much of a CEO and a CFO but reluctance to give commitment can become a major hindrance in the journey of lean implementation. It is rather a failure of the management if they are uncertain about bringing in extra business or venturing into diversification.

A lean company is a *customer-centric company*. Customer satisfaction and loyalty become the values that drive the processes and employees in the company. The CEO and the CFO have to inculcate a customer-focused culture in the company by developing company goals and aligning business strategies that exceed customer expectations. Customer service excellence should not be limited to frontline but rather ooze out from each process and every employee of the company. The CEO and the CFO should ensure that each employee has a clear understanding of how an activity performed by him contributes to augmentation of customer experience.

Toyota leaders are driven by the following five values:

■ Continuously challenging traditional approaches
■ Strive to constantly improve performance (kaizen)

- Knowledge-based operations (genchi genbutsu)
- Enable and promote teamwork
- Promote mutual respect

The CEO and the CFO have to *communicate* and convince all the stakeholders – top management, board of directors, shareholders, unions, banks, auditors, suppliers and customers to join in the company's lean transformation journey because lean will be implemented across the company, not only in the manufacturing area but also in all the functions since they are all interdependent. But the CEO and the CFO do not have to be lean experts. They can establish a 'kaizen promotion office', appoint a person as the company's lean champion and *hire a lean expert* to guide them and the teams.

Once the implementation of the lean production system starts, the company cannot continue using the standard cost accounting method to analyze business performance. A lean company requires business performance indicators in line with lean accounting principles because standard costing does not reflect the value of lean improvements in financial statements. The CEO and the CFO should sensitize the functional managers, mainly finance, to *adapt to reporting as per lean accounting* so that the monetary impact of reduction in waste, value creation and 'pull and flow' can be reflected in financial statements and employees can witness the outcomes of their efforts. This is vital for keeping the workforce motivated. An effective lean performance measurement system should be able to achieve operational improvements and translate it into financial projections.

Last, every small improvement, every small milestone achieved should be celebrated and employees should be encouraged and motivated with *reward and recognition*. The lean journey is expected to gain sustainable productivity improvement of 10% to 20% every year. Even if 8% improvement in productivity is achieved against target of 10% to 20%, it still calls for celebration.

4.4 The CFO's Role in Implementation of Lean Accounting[4]

The CFO and his team are the enterprise behind the funds in a company, and they grind at their job to ensure that business operations do not surpass budget and keep different regulators at bay through timely compliances. They engineer the management reporting, financial analysis and statutory reporting in the company. But the CFO's role is no longer circumscribed to financial planning; instead, it has evolved into that of a key strategic player.

The finance team is the catalyst to bring a culture change and warrant successful implementation of '*lean business strategy*'. The management, board of directors or shareholders will never foster conviction in lean strategy if the operational improvements don't reflect in the financial health of the company.

The change has to begin by '*discontinuation of standard costing*' and a switch to value stream-based costing. Inventory is where the evil of standard costing exists along with time wasted in computing standard costs, collecting and reporting actual costs, analyzing variances and holding budget review meetings. Despite all this, standard costing does not help managers to understand the root cause of problem in their processes. The lean CFO must swiftly steer the company away from traditional standard costing-based measurement systems and induct new measures as per the lean business strategy. This is key to the success of the lean strategy. The CFO must explain to the operations managers that instead of machines and manpower utilization, it is more important to focus on '*flow*', which means customers get the products in required quantity as fast as possible without overproduction or sales loss. If the machines or manpower is idle, it is the responsibility of sales and marketing to procure more business or expedite new product development. The lean CFO must prepare the stakeholders about decline in profits in the initial journey of lean due to reduction in inventory and explain how it will be beneficial in the long run.

The CFO should *develop an in-depth understanding of the 'lean business strategy'* so that he can communicate it to other departments to identify what value is created by their department for the customers and how to formulate the value streams. He will need to partner with value stream managers to design the value stream map and identify waste and non-value adding activities. Since the CFO has expertise in developing performance measurements, he will be responsible for '*creation of a performance measurement system*' that measures and manages flow of the value stream with focus on economic drivers of financial success in a lean company. The current pricing mechanism for product costs should be replaced with the new cost structure as per value stream costing.

The CFO and his team should 'embrace new technology' to bring in automation in book-keeping, data collection and use of lean ERP platforms. This will release their non-value adding time for business partnering and gemba walk and give better insights into business problems and improvement opportunities. The *lean CFO* must take control of the ERP system and modify it to suit the lean production system, daily management and lean accounting tools (see Chapter 15). The data collection system and measurement system should be validated by him to *maintain sanctity of data quality* because all business decisions will be based on these data. The ERP system under standard costing obstructs the flow of material, information and funds because of unnecessary transactions like review, approvals and reporting. The lean CFO should use the '*Lean ERP*' platform to *reduce transactions* that will make analysis and flow of work easier.

The lean CFO has to *lead the way for a lean CEO*, not only in the financial field but also in the operational and support functions. He will monitor the progress of continuous improvements and their impact on operational processes. The new reporting structure designed by the CFO on basis of lean tools should give adequate insights to the CEO for strategic decision-making. Initially, the CFO may release *traditional P&L statement* along with *lean accounting-based P&L statement* every month till the time the management adapts to the simple, clear and value stream-based P&L generated under lean accounting. The CFO has to impart knowledge regarding interpretation of the new P&L to the management as well as value stream and functional managers so that it can be made useful for taking significant business decisions.

Everyone thinks the right place to start implementation of the lean production system in the company is on the plant floor but the right place to start is the finance function with CFO as the team leader. It will be explained in this book why it should be so.

Key Takeaways

1. A lean company is a '*customer-centric company*'.
2. Having a good idea is not enough till it is implemented.
3. Lean has to be not only a business strategy, but rather the 'only' strategy, followed by top management to run the business and use as guidance for defining key responsibilities in the company.
4. The CEO and the CFO should communicate the vision of the lean journey with conviction to explain why the organization has selected the lean management path and what specific outcomes are expected over a period of time.
5. The CEO and the CFO need to participate and lead the change process. They need to create the urgency for this change, start incorporating new processes and work toward getting the team on board with new ways of working

6. Everyone thinks the right place to start implementation of the *'lean production system, daily management and lean accounting tools'* in the company is on plant floor but the right place to start is the *'finance function with the CFO as the team leader'*.
7. The management, board of directors or shareholders will never foster conviction in lean strategy if the operational improvements don't reflect in the financial health of the company.

Recommended List for Further Reading

1. **Art Byrne[1], the CEO of The Wiremold Company and co-author**
"The Lean Turnaround: How Business Leaders Use Lean Principles to Create Value and Transform Their Companies".
2. **Taiichi Ohno[2]**
Dennis Chambers, K. (2012). *How Toyota changed the world*. Ahmedabad: Jaico Publishing House.
3. **Trusting and Respecting the Inputs Shared by Employees**
Big Think Edge (2018). *What does it mean to have a growth mind-set?* [online] Big Think Edge. Available at: www.bigthinkedge.com/what-does-it-mean-to-have-a-growth-mindset/.
Eurich, T. (2018). *What self-awareness really is (and how to cultivate it)*. [online] Harvard Business Review. Available at: https://hbr.org/2018/01/what-self-awareness-really-is-and-how-to-cultivate-it.
facebook.com/CenterforCreativeLeadership (2010). *The best ways to communicate your organization's vision*. [online] Center for Creative Leadership. Available at: www.ccl.org/multimedia/podcast/communicating-the-vision/.
Genever, H. (2017). *Why risk-takers are winners (and why all entrepreneurs should take risks) | LivePlan Blog*. [online] LivePlan Blog. Available at: www.liveplan.com/blog/why-risk-takers-are-winners-and-why-all-entrepreneurs-should-take-risks/
Kramp, J. (2014). *5 reasons to lead with high expectations*. [online] The Riverstone Group. Available at: www.theriverstonegroup.com/5-reasons-to-lead-with-high-expectations/#:~:text=The%20most%20effective%20leaders%20set [Accessed 18 Dec. 2020].
McNamara, C. (2019). *Employee training and development: Reasons and benefits*. [online] Managementhelp.org. Available at: https://managementhelp.org/training/basics/reasons-for-training.htm.
Michael Page Team (2018). *What is integrity in the workplace? | Michael Page*. [online] Michael Page. Available at: www.michaelpage.com.au/advice/career-advice/productivity-and-performance/what-integrity-workplace
4. **CFO's Role in Implementation of Lean Accounting[3]**
Katko, N.S. (2014). *The lean CFO: Architect of the lean management system*. Boca Raton, FL: CRC Press and Taylor & Francis Group.

Maskell.com. Blog- *"Economics of Lean"*.
Maskell.com. Blog- *"The Lean CFO" by Nick Katco.*
Stenzel, J. (2007). *Orest Fiume; Lean accounting: Best practices for sustainable integration- lean strategy and accounting: The role of the CEO and CFO.* Hoboken, NJ: John Wiley & Sons.

Chapter 5

Bid Adieu to Standard Cost Accounting, Welcome Lean Accounting

Be ready to revise any system, scrap any method, abandon any theory, if the success of the job requires it.

– Henry Ford

There has been a surge in number of companies that employ the lean manufacturing system in their plant processes. But these companies continue to use standard cost accounting for financial control and decision-making. It is important to understand the difference in the fundamental philosophy of *traditional companies – companies that have not yet embraced lean principles or kaizen tools –* and *lean companies*. Traditional companies have a cost-based approach while lean companies have a value-based approach.

Standard costing hinders successful lean implementation because it was designed for mass manufacturing companies to achieve the '*lowest cost per unit*'. Mass manufacturing was popularized in the late 1910s and 1920s by Henry Ford's Ford Motor Company, which introduced the first moving assembly line for mass production of an entire automobile. But this can result in alarming waste for companies with a diverse product portfolio. In a dynamic environment where customer preferences are rapidly changing, standard cost accounting will not support diligent business decision-making or control.

DOI: 10.4324/9781003221746-5

5.1 What Is Standard Costing?

Standard costing[1] is an accounting method in which standard or 'pre-determined' costs for raw materials, labor and overheads are calculated for each part of the product that is designed to be processed till the finished product is manufactured. The actual cost is captured for each part as it moves from one process to another. The standard cost and actual costs are then compared, and the variance is reported.

Actual cost < standard cost = Favorable variance
Actual cost > standard cost = Unfavorable variance

Standard costing encourages business practices that prevent deviation from standard costs irrespective of their impact on company's operational or financial performance.

There are three main components of standard costing. Let's analyze their impact on company performance when this cost-focused approach is followed.

Direct Material

The price and quantity of raw material used in manufacturing a product is a key driver of its cost. Therefore, procuring the raw material at an optimal price and sufficient quantity are important factors in product costing. Will this not impact how a procurement manager in a company fulfills his responsibilities? The key performance indicator of a procurement manager is lowest procurement price per unit. To achieve this, he searches for vendors with the lowest selling price and negotiates bulk deals to avail further discounts which, at times, might necessitate compromise on quality. This will give a favorable purchase price variance and lowest cost per unit, but the rejection rate will increase at the time of quality assessment. Instead of the procurement team, the manufacturing team will be held accountable for poor yield because the customers will not receive quality product. Bulk purchase may lead to shortages and stockouts in other items that are required to complete the final product. Customer satisfaction will start dwindling due to poor quality and insufficient production. This is an example of how lowering cost prioritized over creating value for customers in traditional companies impacts overall business performance. Throughput time and ad hoc inventory costs like storage, space occupied and obsolescence are usually not considered before resorting to bulk buying.

Direct Labor

Direct labor is the work done by workmen who actually make the product on the product line. The efficiency of workers is a key driver of this cost. In standard cost accounting, direct labor is considered as an important conversion cost and is thus used as the basis for allocation of all other costs. Standard costing encourages full utilization of resources to lower cost per unit. The labor is kept occupied on production of large batches that results in accumulation of inventory, higher manpower cost and poor quality products. Overloading workmen leads to unstable and variable processes that lead to waste (muda in Japanese).

In earlier times, when industries were labor intensive, the manpower costs were a significant proportion of overall costs. Detailed manpower tracking was required to analyze labor hours expended in the production of each unit and department heads were held accountable for unfavorable variance in the labor costs from the plan. This is not relevant in lean accounting where value stream costs are tracked and manpower costs are directly allocated to the value stream.

Overhead Absorption

The traditional cost accounting approach is to allocate manufacturing overhead costs to the products manufactured. This can be done on the basis of volume such as number of units produced, direct labor hours or production machine hours. The criteria selected by a company for allocation becomes the underlying cause of manufacturing overheads. This might be viable for cost allocation in financial statements but there are many factors that drive manufacturing overheads. For example, a customer may demand additional manufacturing operations for a customized product while other customers may demand more quantities of uniform products.

The overhead absorption variance encourages large batches and large runs resulting in overproduction, long lead time and high inventories. This is a classic example of accumulating wastes. This method compels managers to produce in excess due to which higher inventories are created in the company.

5.2 Why Is Standard Cost Accounting Not Suitable for Lean Companies?

Standard costing is an effective tool for budgeting and may help to establish ideal costs in a given scenario but the very fact that it revolves around assumptions and guesswork is what makes it unsuitable for lean companies where real-time accurate information is needed for quick decision-making. Accountants feel comfortable in using standard cost system, but this method does not bring business or improve its performance. Standard cost accounting supports mass production or production based on the push system where production targets are based on forecasting. Production in large batches lowers cost per unit, keeps employees occupied to absorb overheads and results in economies of scale. Several factors like duplication of costs, inaccurate data capturing on the plant floor and approximation of timing on labor and machines are some major drawbacks of this method since all operators do not have the same efficiency and it is assumed that irrespective of the level of production, the costs will remain the same.

Product Costing

Standard costing is designed for repetitive manufacturing processes with homogeneous outcomes. The standard costs calculated during budgeting are based on assumptions about the business environment, customer demand and standard product costs. Sales and marketing function use standard costs with standard margins for product pricing. This is the price at which products are sold and all the costs are allocated.

But in order to assess the correct cost of 'manufacturing' a 'specific product' for 'a customer', the traditional approach may not be suitable because price based on standard costs will not support accurate decision-making since there could be variance in purchase price of raw material, quantity of material used, labor rate, labor efficiency, consumption of overheads and volume variation. Instead of using a single cost driver such as machine hours for allocation, several cost drivers require consideration like the number of machine setups, the quantity of material purchased or used, the number of changeovers, the number of machine hours and so forth. Therefore, a single cost driver cannot govern the cost allocation of a diverse product and customer portfolio. The traditional approach does not take into consideration the intricacy of processes in manufacturing diverse products and one average rate is applied to all processes.

Accountability for delivering a quality product and customer satisfaction lies with the manufacturing teams. They have to explain about deliveries and quality to the customers and they also have to explain the variances in the financial parameters to management. This creates a chaos in the minds of operations managers and companies are left with dissatisfied customers who did not receive products on time or had quality issues along with sales loss and superfluous inventory.

Lean companies use direct cost. Instead of allocation as done in standard cost accounting, the actual cost of direct material, direct labor and manufacturing overheads are added up to compute the average cost of the product of the value stream in lean accounting because it gives a true picture of the cost structure.

Inventory Accumulation

The major reason why standard costing hinders successful lean implementation is that standard costing encourages inventory accumulation. Lean starts with elimination of waste, and waste due to overproduction and piling of inventory are some of the first wastes lean intends to eliminate. In standard costing, costs are allocated using a cost driver. This emboldens workmen to overproduce because higher production quantity will lower average product cost since costs will be apportioned over higher number of units. Consequently, inventory starts piling up, which will require additional handling and storage cost.

The department heads are held accountable for their department's manpower, machine and overhead utilization. Since the operations team understands that labor hours absorb overheads, they monitor it closely to maintain costs within budget. If they are lagging behind during the month, they create more labor hours by the third and fourth week of the month so that overhead per hour remains within the budget even if they produce more than what is required. At the end of the month there is excess unsold inventory because there was no synchronization between demand and production. The managers have easily beaten the system by producing more to meet their operating targets and satisfy the accountants. This happens every month and later the company will have a special sales campaign to sell these products at a discount.

Also, since production is not aligned with customer demand, that is, there is no 'pull and flow', the slow moving and non-moving inventory proliferates. This is why lean emphasizes the importance of pull and flow in production so that the conundrum of excess inventory is resolved and waste is eliminated.

Full Utilization of Resources and Capacity

Standard costs are estimates computed in an idyllic scenario. Traditional companies focus on full utilization of resources and capacity to absorb overheads and lower cost per unit as explained earlier. Excess capacity is treated as loss of business opportunity. Standard costing does not capture true meaning of capacity. Underutilized capacity is presented as a reason for loss in revenue in income statement and inventory is considered as an asset. It is believed that higher inventory of finished goods generates higher profits and production in large batches lowers standard product cost. We will discuss later in the book in Chapter 8 what is the true meaning of capacity for a company.

In lean companies it is encouraged to have excess capacity (at least 20%) to bring flexibility in operations. Faster product delivery to customer is more important than full utilization of manpower and machines. Low throughput time gives more profits than full utilization of resources and issues associated with it.

Lack of Cost Visibility

Standard costs are pre-determined costs calculated using complex assumptions about industry environment, customer demand, labor efficiency and machine performance for each product. While other departments contribute to this construct, only the finance team understands the computation. The standard costs decided at the beginning of the year may change due to changes in economic factors, market environment or technological advancements. It may become difficult to explain that the variance from budget is a result of flaw in operations or assumptions.

There is no clear visibility to aid prudent decision-making. Variance analysis, review meetings and decisions on remedial actions consume a company's resources and become a costly affair without adding any value to the overall business performance. Lean accounting organizes the company into value streams based on product families, and the cost of labor and material for the products made in the value stream are assigned to that value stream. Overheads are not allocated in lean accounting because each product family has a different process. They are accounted for each value stream as per actual expenditure.

Transaction Heavy

In a company that follows standard cost accounting, standard cost is set for each part of each product. There is a detailed system of recording each and every transaction to track the flow of product through each and every process in the course of production. This is a futile and cumbersome activity that generates thousands and thousands of transactions to track labor and material costs. In a company with a diverse product portfolio, standard costing may produce variances in huge volumes that not only will be difficult to analyze but also will be without any meaningful information to exercise control.

As per the accounting principles of financial reporting, popularly known as generally accepted accounting principles (GAAP), the inventory should be recorded at actual cost. If a company follows standard costing, it will have to adjust the cost of inventory, including work in progress, and cost of goods sold to reflect actual cost. Can you grasp how many transactions will be generated in a company that manufactures hundreds of different products? Do you think it is possible to efficiently analyze and spawn control over the volume of transactions that will be generated? To collect the actual data, millions of transactions are done in a month which are wasteful, and time expended in collection in itself is a wasteful activity.

Not Understood by the Operations Team

The financial performance in P&L statement highlighting deviations from the budget is shared with operations managers, but they struggle to decipher the corrective measures required on plant floor. These operations managers do not understand the intricacies of standard costing and P&L statement. For example, a divisional manager does not find cost and profitability for his division in traditional company P&L because it does not provide a clear picture for products manufactured in his division. If operations managers are going to be held accountable for the deviations, then the P&L should offer some valuable information about performance of their division.

Look at this from another viewpoint on how theoretical measures lead to exploitation of processes by people. Operations managers use their limited knowledge of maintaining costs within budget to run operations, which results in excessive production and inventory. Once they understand how allocation of costs can be manipulated, they use it consistently to meet their targets without regard for the overall company goal and profitability. This is what happened to Ford, GM and Chrysler during the financial crisis of 2008 when they ran out of cash and did the same thing to appease the unions to protect the workmen's bonuses. The accountants who prepare the P&L statement are oblivious to processes and workings on the plant floor. They do not have a thorough knowledge of how the product is manufactured in the company. It is inexplicable why a company has inventory but is still running into losses.

In lean companies, all financial analysis is done at value stream level and value stream managers are provided with real-time information for quick decision-making so that flow of the processes is maintained and production is strictly as per pull.

No Clear Root Cause Analysis

Production people dread the monthly financials statements being presented by the accountants in the review meetings. The functional managers feel they have worked so hard during the month by putting in extra hours and overtime along with their teams and management accountants still blame the losses due to deviation from the standard costs on them asking for explanation of the variances.

The company could have made the loss because it operates on the forecasting model and the team produced the product mix and quantities based on this model, but the marketing team was unable to sell these because customer requirements were different during the month. The unsold products have landed up in stores as inventory. The company suffered a sale loss as well as increase in inventory. Now, there will be long meetings, and everyone will discuss trivial issues with no outcome for corrective or preventive action because the root cause is still not clear.

It might also be possible that there are multiple holidays in a month due to which the operation team could not meet the production target, but the P&L statement still shows good profit, and the finance review meeting goes smoothly. This leaves operations managers in production, procurement, assembly, quality and so forth bamboozled. It happened due to higher sale of finished goods from the warehouses and low procurement of the raw material from the market. Functional managers are perplexed about the financial picture generated by the accounting system. It becomes a challenge each month to interpret the root cause of profit or loss and missing link with the operational measures to identify where the scope for improvement actually lies.

This is how standard costing provokes firefighting because no one is able to identify the root cause of the problems and is busy extinguishing the fire of current problems in the company without ensuring they do not reoccur. In standard costing, only material cost is real, whereas labor and overhead are allocated. Individual machines and manpower utilization are strictly monitored, and the operations team is accountable for variances. Therefore, they manipulate production in order to meet their targets without regard for the bigger company goal.

5.3 Variance Analysis

Under standard cost accounting, once the actual costs are recorded, the next step is to calculate labor utilization, machine utilization and overhead costs followed by calculation of variances with respect to the budget. In the monthly review, the operations managers will have to explain the variances in volume, labor and machine utilization and overhead absorption along with loss in sales and increase in inventories. Why are there these inexplicable variances in the operating and financial measures? There could be three possible reasons.

The first reason is the company works on MRP software. It operates on a push system based on budget to forecast demand. Operations managers are given a planning schedule to produce a certain product mix for the month. However, in real time, customers ask for different products in fluctuating quantities. This results in course correction in the product mix during the month. This will surely lead to stockout situation for some products and excess inventories for other products. Operations managers will have to explain underutilization of production capacity and variance in labor and overhead absorption. Due to lower sales of many products, cost per unit will increase.

Also, operations managers could target products that are easier to make and require less changeovers to increase production. Machines will skip scheduled maintenance but capacity utilization, labor variance and overhead absorption variance will decrease considerably, and the managers will not struggle to explain the variance in the next review meeting. But what will happen to the customers? They will not get the material they want. The company will be saddled with unsold products, sales loss of other products and increase in inventories. Neither the company profits nor the customers are happy, and the operating managers are no wiser as to what they are supposed to do take the company out of this mess.

The second reason is, from 1920 to 1950, the labor and overheads used to be allocated, which was almost 60% to 70% of the total costs that used to bring the variance when the true data were not available from the operation. A little variation in data used to generate a large variation in profit and loss. In the present time labor and overheads have decreased to 30% to 40%, and in lean accounting where the labor and overheads are charged directly to the value stream, the variation will be less or none at all.

The third reason is that the traditional companies carry four to six months' worth of inventories. They monitor it very closely because any small difference creates a large variation in balance sheet and P&L statements. A lean company carries 15 days to a month of inventory, so the variance is less. Stock taking is done every month. In lean accounting, direct cost for most of the material is assigned to the cost centers for which it is received in the plant.

5.4 Profit and Loss Statements Based on Standard Cost Accounting System

In earlier times companies used to keep their financials undisclosed. As the companies became public, the financial data also became available publicly. Hence, companies resorted to complex financial statements that are difficult to understand. This served the company's purpose of withholding financial clarity from public but if the managers working inside the company do not understand business performance, then how will they contribute to the improvement of business operations? In traditional companies, a P&L statement is understandable to finance professionals only.

Let us continue with an example of the Perfect Gear Company that is a capital machine-building group. *The company's lean journey will be used in this book to understand how it has been transformed in two years with tremendous gains achieved at all fronts. This example could become the true North Star to follow for the lean practicing companies.* From the P&L statement in Table 5.1 made with standard cost accounting, plant managers will understand only the division's return on sales (ROS). They will not gain any perspective on the internal functional cost structure that is paramount for cost control.

Profit and Loss Statement as per Standard Costing Based on Variance Reporting

We will now take up only value stream III – gearbox division of Perfect Gear Company as an example for our discussion in this book. In Table 5.2

Table 5.1 P&L Statement for All the Value Streams of Perfect Gear Company in USD'000 for the Year Ending March 2018 (Current Year).

Description	Value stream I – hot rolling mill division	Valuestream II– cold rolling mill division	Value stream III– gearbox division	New product develop-ment	Division P&L
Revenue	45000	21300	40000	0	106300
Material costs	21234	10967	17780	8166	58147
Conversion costs	7345	3543	6778	2876	20542
Value streams profits	16421	6790	15442		38653
Value stream ROS	0	0	0		0
Employee costs	6638	6638	6638		19915
Corporate expenses	3569	1100	3333		8002
Prior period inventory	6700	3422	5765		15887
Current inventory	8900	5000	6265		20165
Inventory change	−2200	−1578	−500		−4278
Division gross profit	8414	630	5971		15014
Division ROS	19%	3%	15%		14%

Table 5.2 P&L Statement Based on the Standard Cost Accounting- Variance Reporting Method for Perfect Gear Company in USD'000 for the Year Ending March 2018 (Current Year).

Sales revenue	40000
Cost of sales	
Standard cost	32000
Purchase price variance	2659.0
Material usage variance	1640.2
Labor efficiency variance	−999.8
Labor rate variance	3129.4
Overhead volume variance	−2530.0
Overhead spending variance	−1870.0
Total cost of sales	34028.8
Gross profits	5971.2
Less depreciation, interest	3947.2
Profit before tax	2024.0
Profit before tax %	5%

the plant floor managers cannot understand anything except that they have made a profit of 5%. It fails to communicate meaningful information about performance of the company. It is a plain statement and does not mention the costs of the operations, and operations managers are not able to co-relate their daily activities and their financial contribution. The marketing manager struggles to explain why profits did not increase when sales increased.

Let us look at another way of making financial statements.

Profit and Loss Statement as per Standard Cost Accounting Based on Cost Categories

The P&L statement in Table 5.3 is better as it gives details of the variable and fixed cost, but it still does not break up cost in broad categories. The functional managers still don't understand the cost of their function to identify the scope for improvement. Also, they are not able to see the benefits of lean implementation or continual improvement projects.

Both the previously prepared statements do not enlighten operations managers about elements of the costs that may be meaningful for them to take measures for improvement in business performance.

Let us analyze once again what are the few things that are correct but still make the P&L statement confusing for operations managers.

Analysis of a Profit and Loss Statement of a Traditional Company

Let us again look at the traditional scenario and analyze the P&L statement in Figure 5.3.

Sales value is the amount of revenue for the 'all' items dispatched this month. The dispatch (sales) may be lower or much more than what has actually been produced on the shop floor that month. Also, some of the dispatched items could belong to inventory that was manufactured a few weeks or a few months back. (There is a great possibility when you are on MRP mode.)

Material cost in the P&L statement is the sum of opening inventory and material bought in during the month minus the closing inventory. Materials procured this month might be in lower quantity or in bulk quantity, if the company scored a good discount, compared with previous months. The 'material cost' in the P&L statement has only a partial correlation with the products that have been sold this month. The 'sales value' in the P&L

Table 5.3 **P&L Statement Based on the Standard Cost Accounting Cost Categories for Perfect Gear Company in USD'000 for the Year Ending March 2018 (Current Year).**

Sales	40000
Cost of sales	
Purchases	7947
Inventory material – opening/closing (increase/decrease)	9333
Total material costs	17280
Variable costs	
Stores consumables	3211
Power and fuels	2019
Outside job works	1547
Fixed costs	
Company wages	3038
Company salaries	3600
Corporate overheads	3333
Total cost of sales	16749
Gross profits	5971
Less depreciation, interest	3947
Profit before tax	2024
Profit before tax %	5%

account is the sales value of the products that have been dispatched this month but may have been partially manufactured this month and partially sold from the warehouse. The opening inventory may have a component of labor, machine and overhead attached to it from previous months.

This means the material costs is 'not' the true material costs of the products that have been dispatched this month, the contribution achieved for the month is not the 'true' contribution of this month, even 'net profit' is not a true reflection of this month's true net profit.

This means net profit in the P&L statement will not reflect the true picture of business performance for the month and no one will know what happened on the plant floor and in all the functions in that month. There will be perplexity in the company if workers work hard but produce more and dispatches are less and also dispatch more of low-value products and there is shortage in dispatch of high-margin products that will result in lower gross profit.

Also, when the company has a month of smooth operations on the plant floor with no stress and overtime, but dispatches are higher (mainly from the warehouse) with favorable product mix (high margin products) resulting in higher contribution and higher gross profit, the workmen and operations managers will still be baffled and will wonder from where so much gross profit has come.

There will also be months with almost the same revenue but different profit in the P&L statement. Why does this happen? This is unfathomable by operations managers as well as the finance team in the company.

This is why a profit and loss statement synchronized with the operational reality of the month, exhibiting a true picture of business performance and providing meaningful information to both management and operations teams, is essential.

How a Profit and Loss Statement Can Be Manipulated Under the Standard Cost Accounting System

Companies have to comply with the GAAP while finalizing the balance sheet and P&L statements as per the regulatory authorities. These complex accounting principles govern the preparation and presentation of financial statements. Apart from displaying financial performance of the business, financial statements are also prepared to comply with statutory, government and regulatory requirements like taxation, audit and financial disclosures. As a result, they often contain complex financial data that are not useful or relevant to business performance.

GAAP requires inventory to be valued at actual cost based on where it is lying – if it in raw material stage, it will be cost of raw material, if it is work in progress, labor and overhead incurred will be added to the cost and if it is finished goods, then actual value of inventory is calculated as per all the costs gone into transforming raw material into finished goods. In a traditional company, the inventory is normally doing two to four turns in a year. This means the company carries inventory for three to six months.

In a standard cost accounting system, production costs are collected product-wise using labor and overheads rates as the product traverses from raw material to finished good in various production centers. The profit or the loss from the current month can be postponed to the future by accounting jugglery. The means unsold inventory can be capitalized *(recorded as an asset in balance sheet rather than as an expense in P&L)* at the month end.

For capitalization of inventory, the cost of material can be assigned using any of the following methods:

- Weighted average method
- FIFO – first in first out
- LIFO – last in first out
- Actual costs by tracking individual items

Current month's labor and overheads cost can be built into the inventory for capitalization and this cost can be moved from the P&L statement to the balance sheet. This increases profits by reducing current month expenses and inventory is shown as an asset in balance sheet. This is why in standard cost accounting the reported profits may not be authentic but still look good. But this is a flawed P&L statement that has consumed more cash, leaving the company with a poor cash flow. The inventories will occupy more space and the company may have to provide for future write-offs and obsolescence. Why is the company able to do this and get away with it?

This explains why standard cost accounting system cannot work with the simple requirements of lean management system.

5.5 Lean Accounting[2] – Cleaning Up the Mess!

Lean production system, daily management system and lean accounting are pre-requisites to creating a world-class company. Companies started implementing kaizen tools as early as the 1950s and achieved localized improvements with overwhelming success, but they failed to sustain the gains and kaizen activities slowed down. In some companies, it fizzled out till the dedicated daily management tools were evolved and implemented. These tools helped in sustenance of continual improvement activities *but still the accountants still refused to acknowledge financial gains even though the customers were happy with timely deliveries and significant improvements in the quality.*

Around 1998, a group of like-minded kaizen experts with strong technical and financial background, some having CA or MBA degrees, collaborated to search for the missing link in successful implementation of the lean production system and daily management system. The spotlight was directed toward finance function, and it was concluded that the lean production system must start in the company with the finance department. Finance function should play a substantial role in implementation of lean throughout the company with the help of cross-functional teams and this is why the role of the CFO in implementation of lean tools is noteworthy.

Companies that adopt the lean production system and daily management system resort to lean accounting in an attempt to operate business resourcefully by complimenting initiatives like just-in-time inventory, efficient manufacturing processes and faster delivery methods with a robust financial system because standard cost accounting fails to capture the efficiencies of lean management techniques accurately. Lean accounting is designed to allow companies to gain insight into performance of value streams rather than monitoring cost per unit. Value streams allow companies to view and report the benefits of the lean management methods by displaying product profitability and savings from waste elimination clearly. Standard cost accounting is not suitable for the businesses of the future where a variety of products has to be manufactured in small quantities and regular supplies are to be given to the customers at the lower prices.

More transactions happen during the lean journey due to more orders, more tracking, more labor reporting and increased job order costing. The ERP system only 'preserves' and 'automates' this waste, whereas SOPs in traditional companies standardize these wastes.

Standard costing system tends to reward people and departments that get the work done without regard for quality, quantity and product mix. Traditional management by objective (MOB) rewards personal targets of the employee rather than the team. This practice breeds competition rather than cooperation among employees. This produces heroes and firefighters, and companies start thinking that when these people are on duty on the plant floor, the production output will be better. This is management by results and not management by process.

Figure 5.4 illustrates that a company must embrace the lean production system, daily management system and lean accounting to become a world-class company. All three systems must be implemented as per one road map to achieve phenomenal results. There will be a gradual acceptance of change as the benefits starts becoming visible in customer satisfaction, operational measures and financial measures of the company.

The importance of lean accounting in a company that has implemented lean manufacturing systems should be clear by now. Lean accounting is a process to run the business by making not only the finance team, but also each employee fully aware and customer focused (not only on the needs of ultimate customer but also to follow the concept of 'next process is my

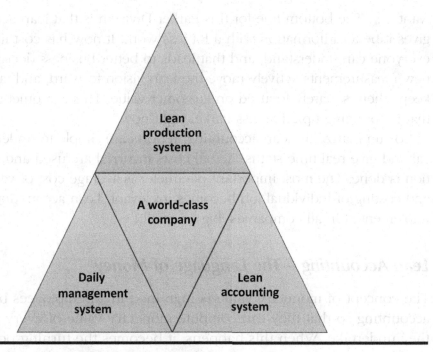

Figure 5.4   Journey of a World-Class Company.

customer'). The lean teams take a vow that no one will accept defect in process material, no one will produce defective material and no one will transfer defective material to the next process.

Lean accounting is also known as value stream costing. It gives clearcut, up-to-date meaningful financial information and establishes a clear link between money and operations. Lean accounting evolved through trial and error. The standard accounting measures proved to be disastrous for lean companies because they still chastened the managers for machine and manpower utilization and overhead absorption when managers were busy reducing throughput time and increasing on time in full and error free (OTIFEF) supply of products to customers.

Bruce Baggaley[3] quotes in 'Creating the Course and Tools for a Lean Accounting System' about Parker Hannifin Corporation's Director of Corporate Accounting Fred Garbinski's beliefs that a lean accounting system must ultimately play a pervasive role in a company trying to grow the business and advance the lean transformation while maintaining control. He says, "It simplifies what we do, it's a better match with what we're doing on the shop floor, it's more accurate, and it's consistent with the behavior you want. . . . The bottom line for this Parker Division is that lean accounting gives it better information with a lot less work. It now has cost information everyone can understand, and that leads to better business decisions. The new measurements actively move the lean vision forward, and target costing keeps them squarely focused on customer value. This is a quiet revolution that is springing up all across Parker right now."

To summarize, in lean accounting, reports are simple to understand, logical and give real-time status. Actual costs incurred are used and no allocation is done. The most important parameter is average cost of value stream and costing of individual job becomes irrelevant. Lean accounting can be implemented in all companies, big or small.

Lean Accounting – The Language of Money

The concept of monetary value is ingrained in all employees by lean accounting so that they can compute monetary value of every activity they undertake. When this happens, it becomes the turning point for the company because then the lean production system, daily management system and lean accounting become permanently instilled in their operations.

Lean accounting gives clear and understandable financial reporting for the company by efficiently measuring the execution of the lean business strategy of the company, that is, the language of lean is translated into the language of money. Lean accounting assigns monetary value to each activity in the company such as the following:

- Cost of breakdown per minute
- Cost of small stoppages per minute
- Cost of changeover total and per minute
- Cost of running the machine slow per minute
- Cost of yield loss per unit
- Cost of machinery stoppages per minute due to waiting for decisions
- Consumable costs per unit
- Fixed cost per unit
- Variable costs per unit
- Cost of quality/cost of poor quality

Thus, lean accounting brings in cost awareness by sensitizing employees that every activity in the company has a cost and the cost is expended before any revenue comes in.

5.6 Features of Lean Accounting

Strategy, Not a Short-Term Improvement Project

Lean is a business strategy – rather, lean is the only strategy. It is not something that happens in one corner of the company but everything that happens in the company will happen around lean. The lean production system, daily management system and lean accounting ensures that all employees are customer-centric and maintain a clear line of sight with them.

Lean accounting helps to understand the lean production system, daily management system more clearly. It is simple, transparent and explicable. The lean management system is not cost reduction, but the idea is to release more available capacity by reducing non-productive activities so that more products can be made and sold in the free time made available to grow revenue and profit. Lean accounting gives visibility into the outcome of lean production system implementation and helps to reduce the resistance to new lean initiatives to a great extent.

Changes Basic Composition of the Company

Lean transforms the basic structure of the company into value stream structure with new performance measures that link the company's strategy and strategic measures to value stream and cells. Lean accounting helps in rapid construction of a lean horizontal company to replace the existing top-down chain of command, and the bottom-line employees are empowered to run the company through comprehensible insights provided by lean accounting into performance of the company along with patronage of top management.

Under the value stream concept, lean accounting logically regroups the workmen, supervisors, executives and managers into value streams instead of functional departments. This results in formation of mini companies within the company that are product based and best suited to provide service to the customers. Lean accounting helps to run these mini companies profitably as it is understood by the functional managers clearly and enhances business acumen at all levels. Business planning is done at value stream level by sales and marketing, operations and finance functions as a team instead of production planning and control team and processes are standardized to bring consistency in operations. A P&L statement is prepared separately for each value stream and a separate statement is prepared for different product family groups, making it ideal for companies with a diverse products portfolio. Lean accounting propels the company in the right direction for long-term benefits.

Focuses on Monetary Value and Spending

Lean accounting assigns monetary value to each process or activity in the company. More than for finance, lean accounting is for each functional manager, irrespective nature of their functions, to enable him to link all value adding and non-value adding activities to their monetary value. This helps the manager understand the implications of their job well done or under-performed. Only when each manager, executive, supervisor and workman in the value stream understands the value of money, informed and inventive decisions can be taken.

Lean accounting narrates the losses by using parameters like value per minute or value per unit or per kilogram so that teams understand the value of each minute and each unit. It enables the employees to understand the concept of 'time' by preaching the value of contribution per minute and value loss per minute of downtime. Once everyone starts seeing loss incurred through monetary value of the wastes in the company, they will know where the opportunity for improvement lies.

Lean tools focus on highlighting activities where funds are consumed in order to reduce such activities. It reduces expenditure by encouraging continual improvement lean projects to control costs and reduce spending. P&L statements are prepared once in a month in traditional companies, which allow improvement opportunity once in a month per year, whereas in lean accounting, weekly corporate scorecards are prepared, which provide an opportunity for corrective action 52 times a year.

Lean accounting nudges marketing to focus on value added product selling. The only control the company has is the control on its internal operations because market determines the price. The company can control cost of production and sell the product at or below the market price line. The more it controls overall costs, the more surety it has for continuity of its business. Therefore, the lower the costs, the higher will be the profits.

Capacity Utilization

Other than the existing capacity, more capacity is created when eight wastes are eliminated, which calls for more orders from current markets and new product development. Lean uses available capacity to increase revenue without need for any additional investment. It enables the company to understand its current capacity to deliver value to customers and how much of it is productive, non-productive or available.

Inventory Reduction

Inventory reduction is the biggest opportunity in a lean journey. Inventory is considered as an asset in standard cost accounting but in reality, unsold inventory is a liability. Standard cost accounting magnifies profits by allocating labor and overhead cost to inventory and showing it as an asset in balance sheet rather than an expense in P&L.

Banks grant working capital against a high amount of inventory. But why do you need this inventory in the first place? Lean brings flow that eradicates the need for stocking inventory and gradually, high working capital.

Lean strives for lower inventory by bringing flow and pull in the value streams along with supermarket concept in the finished goods warehouse, raw material and main stores. The kanban system is used to trigger manufacturing and purchase so that only that material is purchased which is to be replenished. Once inventory comes under control, standard levels are maintained from raw material stores to finished warehouse. Certified vendors replenish the stocks in the company's stores directly. These vendors have long-term contracts, and they get e-kanban to trigger the dispatch.

Lean accounting helps to understand the negative role of inventory in a company. It makes gains from lower inventory level visible in throughput time or lead time and customer service. Cost of a product is related to the speed with which it flows through the plant and reaches the customer. The procurement team's primary function is to ensure the material is available at the most reasonable price from a quality source so that the flow is not disrupted. Their secondary function is to buy at the cheapest price per unit. Their function is never to buy the products in bulk to get cheaper prices for the items, which are not runner. They have to follow the rules of the supermarket. Instead of making stock taking sacrosanct, why not have calculated level of stocks for all runner and repeater items? Why do you need to stock items that are readily available off the shelf with the suppliers? Functional managers and their teams in lean company do the stock taking monthly in three days without halting plant operations so that they know what inventories are lying in their jurisdiction.

Focus Away from Standard Costs

Standard cost accounting micromanages processes and standardizes wasteful practices. There is no business rule that requires detailed tracking and scrutiny of everything in order to control the business. Proactive control and studying and perfecting every process to eliminate root cause is the recipe for smooth operations and less waste. Lean accounting quickly disperses standard cost accounting to eliminate the negative impact of its performance measures that sway the company in an anti-lean direction. Lower labor rate per unit or high machine utilization is not important. What is important is quick changeovers and maintaining the 'flow'.

A value stream manager has to adapt to thinking in terms of value stream cost for decisions on products, external purchase or outsourcing of production. He may decrease prices to sell more products in a month and increase market share when spare capacity increases due to reduction in eight wastes. The pricing decisions should be based on 'basket full of products' and not individual products. Also, price increase can be negotiated with the customer once more value can be added to products.

Real-Time Data Analysis Instead of Tedious Data Collection

One of the major goals of lean accounting is to reduce wasteful transactions by identifying and eliminating non-value adding data collection. Lean accounting releases time of managers by reducing heavy transaction volume generated under standard cost accounting regime. The number of transactions generated in a value stream and functions within it are reviewed to eliminate non-value adding transactions. Non-value adding transactions can be reduced by taking the following steps: issue open purchase orders, use actual costs, drop allocations, make use of kanban system, vendor certification authorizing supplier to dispatch without quality check, voucher on receipt there by eliminating three-way matching of price (MRN-PO-Invoice).

Lean accounting provides live information that allows for proactive action. Controls are gradually transferred to operations on the plant floor and unnecessary entries are reduced to permit data tracking without loss of control. Since finance, sales and marketing personnel report to value stream managers, customer insights are easily available. Also, since frequency of reporting decreases to monthly and weekly reporting and progressively reports are generated hour-wise, shift-wise or daily as per the need of the company, prompt decision-making becomes possible.

Performance Measurement System

Lean accounting links key performance indicators to monetary value so that all functional managers, executives and supervisors in the value streams understand the value of 'time'. They have to ensure that throughput time or lead time is minimum. Lean accounting provides clarity on skills available and skills required for development of employees at each level and training programs are deployed accordingly. Lean accounting ensures long-term improvements through new performance measures.

Better and Faster Decision-Making

Lean accounting encourages faster decision-making by ensuring reports are available on a daily basis monthly, if not weekly, instead of quarterly or yearly reports. Weekly reports keep the issue on top of the mind of functional managers, which makes it easier to recall the events and relate the profit numbers with the actual work happening on the plant floor. Decision-making becomes easier and is focused on the value stream's profits and contribution.

Lean accounting helps in better decision-making when companies are booking more orders, purchasing from outside the company, developing new products and making capital investment.

Role of Accountants

In lean accounting, the accountants collaborate with each function and start understanding the company's processes to appreciate what drives the financial numbers displayed in a P&L statement.

Value stream as a team, and not only the finance or operations team, is responsible for profit and loss. Lean accounting makes financial statements useful for functional managers to enable them to use the data therein for improvement in business performance.[4]

5.7 Implementation of Lean Accounting

Lean accounting brings a paradigm shift in how a company functions. Since conversion of raw materials into finished goods and other operational improvements take place on the plant floor, most of the value additions takes place on the plant floor. Therefore, a robust accounting system that addresses the needs of internal as well as external stakeholders and provides a clear picture of the company's financial performance that is comprehensible by functional managers in sales and marketing, finance and accounts, design and R&D, PPC, procurement, production, assembly, quality control and logistics and so forth. With a few journal entries, the finance department can prepare a P&L statement as per GAAP for external use by banks and compliance with statutory authorities.

What is being stressed here is that finance and accounts should shift their focus to internal processes to become familiar with them and to collaborate with the functional managers to jointly bring internal improvements through implementation of lean production system and lean accounting. If a company starts following the pull system for each customer and establishes supermarket for finished products and kanban system for replenishment, it will start seeing decline in inventory and improvements in the operational parameters resulting in higher more profits and better cash flow. The P&L statement prepared for value streams under lean accounting presents a true reflection of performance for the month and is clearly understood by all functional managers. This P&L statement can also be called value stream income statement.

Preparation of Profit and Loss Statement Based on Lean Accounting

Let us understand how the P&L statement is prepared when lean accounting is implemented. In order to understand the function or value stream's performance so that timely corrective action can be taken, all functional managers and value stream managers need the same information in a simplified yet elaborate format. There is a way in which the company can comply with the regulatory and statutory requirements while making the internal P&L statement comprehensible for the plant managers.

The P&L statement in Figure 5.5 is prepared as per lean accounting for a value stream. This statement, which is made available to functional managers by first of the next month, narrates the actual position of the operations for the preceding month on the plant floor. The variable and fixed costs are detailed in this statement and all costs in each function are added up to derive the company's variable and fixed costs. The actual costs for each month are also updated in the functional scorecards for the functional managers and performance scorecards for the first line of executives and supervisors.

Now look at the following P&L statement prepared as per lean accounting for a value stream. Can the internal teams correlate it with the actual performance of the operations and dispatches that happened on the plant floor during the month if they get this statement on the first day of the next month?

Key parameters	Current state March 2018		
	Annual P&L	*Monthly average*	*% of sales*
Monthly quantity dispatched	**1000 tons**		
Sales price	**$3.33 per kg**		
Sales revenue	40000	3333	
Material cost	17280	1440	**43.2%**
Contribution 1 (A)	**22720**	**1893**	**56.8%**
Total variable expenses (B)	**6778**	**563**	**16.9%**
Consumables and stores	1093	91	
Oil and lubricants	208	17	
Inserts	160	13	
Accessories	80	7	
Grinding wheels	88	7	
Cutting oil	120	10	
Tool cutter	101	8	
Gas	53	4	
Paints	82	7	
Grease	27	2	
Others	480	40	
Power and fuels	2019	168	
Job works	1547	129	
Other plant misc. expenses	720	60	
Contribution 2 (C) = (A-B)	**15942**	**1329**	**39.9%**
Total fixed expenses (D)	**9972**	**831**	**24.9%**
Wages – workers	1893	158	
Wages – fabrication	373	31	
Overtime	773	64	
Salary – executives	3600	300	
Other corporate overheads	3333	278	
Net profits-EBITDA (E) = (C-D)	**5971**	**498**	**14.9%**
Depreciation and amortization	2107	176	
EBIT	**3864**	**322**	**9.7%**
Bank interest	933	78	
Interest on term loans	907	76	
Net earnings before tax (EBT)	**2024**	**169**	**5.1%**

Figure 5.5   Profit and Loss Statement Based on Lean Accounting for Perfect Gear Company in USD'000.

Once the company starts its lean journey and kaizen tools, like the pull and flow system, are in place using kanban system to trigger manufacturing in the plant, the company starts producing, on a pull basis, products required by the customers and dispatches them. The company has an ERP system that is used by all functions for their daily activities. An ERP system displays live information for material ready for dispatch after it is duly cleared by the quality control department.

The P&L statement will be made only for the items/products that are manufactured, finished, packed and ready for dispatch plus already dispatched during the month. Sales values will represent only items/products those are manufactured, finished, packed and ready for dispatch plus already dispatched. An ERP system will compute actual cost of material used for manufacturing these items/products through the bill of material pertaining to those products that are manufactured, finished, packed and ready for dispatch plus already dispatched during the month. Accountants will consider only the material cost of previous items/products and not all the items that were procured that month and received in the stores.

Contribution 1 is difference in sales value of this month's production and its material costs and Contribution 2 is derived by deducting actual variable costs incurred that month. EBITDA or net profit is what is left after deducting actual fixed costs and corporate office expenses. Corporate office expenses should be shared in proportion of sales value of value streams if there is more than one value stream in the company. No ad hoc allocation is done. *Allocation is a bad word in lean accounting.* The variable and fixed costs are the sum of all costs in each function to build the total costs for the value stream. The 'functional scorecards' for the functional managers and performance score cards for the first line of executives and supervisors will have costs for respective function (see Chapter 10). Deduct depreciation and interest for the month, both short term and long term to derive EBT (Earnings Before Tax). This is how the P&L statement for a value stream is made using lean accounting. The P&L statement for the company is sum of the P&L statements of all value streams.

The previous statements can be made swiftly in a day after the month end since the teams work on this throughout the month. The simplified statements make contribution and profit figures meaningful for all functional managers. The correlation between production and profit becomes evident and the root cause of losses that could be due to material shortage, breakdown, performance issues, quality issues and waiting times is easily highlighted. This intelligibility increases pace of improvement in the company and the consequent upswing in the business.

Every month this internal P&L statement can be made suitable for external use through few journal entries using the ERP system. The sales value will be equivalent to dispatch value and material costs and net inventory will be computed with opening and closing figure. The remaining cost items in the P&L statement will be the same. This GAAP-compliant P&L statement can be shared with the top management and outside agencies as per the statutory requirements or for any other external use.

Lean P&L statement describes which value stream is profitable, which value stream is pulling down the company and which value streams are subsidizing other value streams. A similar exercise can be done for all products also through the bill of material using ERP costing through the bill of material for the product to determine which products are making losses or are being subsided by other products. For once the companies, top management and marketing function are usually bamboozled when they witness that the customers, who they thought were their biggest profit buckets, are actually negative contribution clients.

But the biggest challenge in lean accounting lies in convincing the finance team in the company about the meaningful information lean accounting enables them to share. They feel that they are asked to do something illegal when they change the format of P&L. But how would a P&L statement that still uses true data without manipulation lose its integrity? *The accountants under lean accounting simply make two P&L statements, one for internal use and one for external use, or one production based and other sales based, both serving their purpose to respective stakeholders by sharing relevant and comprehensible information.*

Each team in the company must be sensitized about internal costs, and the numbers in a P&L statement should be interpretable by teams so that cost reduction and capacity generation opportunities can be recognized. The company does not have control on market prices, but the marketing team can make efforts to solicit price increase for the negative contribution products as per the new knowledge gained from lean accounting, and decrease in cost of production will leverage negotiations for veering in the business from competition.

Financial parameters get better if operational parameters get better. If operational scorecard is achieved, financial scorecard will definitely be achieved. In subsequent chapters, the lean accounting implementation process will be explained step by step, tailor-made to suit the company.

5.8 Lean Accounting Ensures Improved Results

The outcome of implementation of lean accounting along with the lean production system and daily management will be visible in the following measures:

■ Increased cash flow
■ Improved profit margins
■ Simpler planning and scheduling
■ Short cycle times
■ Lower inventories
■ Higher quality
■ On time delivery
■ Less machine downtime

Improvement in operational parameters will be noticeable in reduction of non-value adding use of capacity and reflect in the corporate scorecard once they are implemented (see Chapter 8 and Chapter 9).

5.9 What Happens When a Company Starts Implementing Lean Accounting?

Lean accounting brings transparency. When a company practices lean, it first pursues the inventory. Initially, the inventory will start declining because old inventory has labor, machine and overhead components attached to it. Since current month expenses along with previous month expenses are tied to inventory, there will be loss every month till the inventory drops to 30 days or less. If inventory starts doing 12 to 24 turns a year, it means the inventory stock is 15 days to one month. If the company is able to produce and sell the products in the same month in which it buys the raw materials, it does not have to keep any inventory with labor and overheads attached to it in the balance sheet. The company can still match expense with the revenue, and there will be no need to capitalize. Even if it is higher and needs to be capitalized, it will still be of lesser value as compared with standard cost accounting system.

Inventory cost is average cost of the products. Any of the four methods can be used for valuation since it will not make a big dent in the P&L. The following method is used to calculate the cost of inventory in lean accounting –

- *Raw Material* – Purchase price as per either of the four methodologies as elaborated earlier in the chapter
- *Work in Progress* – Inventory in hand × average cost per unit × average % completion
- *Finished Goods* – Inventory in hand × average cost per unit

This practice complies with GAAP's requirement of recording inventory at actual cost.

Lean companies do not carry substantial inventory, which helps to reduce receivables, generating more cash and less dependence on banks. Lean accounting ensures that the value stream managers and functional managers have to work to serve the customers and not for finance function to generate more profits.

Key Takeaways

1. Standard cost accounting is not suitable for the businesses of the future where variety of products have to be manufactured in small quantities and regular supplies are to be given to the customers at the lower prices.
2. Traditional companies have a cost-based approach ('lowest cost per unit') while lean companies have a value-based approach (supply of quality products or services on time in full quantities to customers).
3. Standard costing encourages inventory accumulation. Bulk purchase of some items will definitely lead to shortages and stockouts in other items that are required to complete the final product.
4. Higher manpower and machine utilization is not important. What is important is quick changeovers and maintaining the 'flow' of products or services to the customers.
5. Low throughput time gives more profits than full utilization of resources.
6. The accountants who prepare the P&L statement are oblivious to processes and workings on the plant floor. On the other hand, the operational and other functional managers are not able to co-relate their daily activities with their financial contribution to the company.
7. A lean accounting P&L statement describes which value stream is profitable, which value stream is pulling down the company and which value streams are subsidizing other value streams.

8. With lean accounting, the language of lean is translated into the language of money. The correlation between production and profit becomes evident and the root cause of losses that could be due to material shortage, breakdown, performance issues, quality issues and waiting times gets highlighted. This intelligibility increases pace of improvement in the company and the consequent upswing in the business.

Recommended List for Further Reading

1. Standard Costing[1]
2. Lean Accounting[2]
   Cunningham, J.E. (2017). *Real numbers: Management accounting in a lean organization.* Evanston, IL: JCC Press.
   Maskell.com. Blog- *"Standard Costing Debunked".*
   Maskell, B.H. (2009). *Making the numbers count: The accountant as change agent on the world class team.* Boca Raton, FL: CRC Press.
   Maskell, B.H., Baggaley, B. and Grasso, L. (2012). *Practical lean accounting: A proven system for measuring and managing the lean enterprise.* Boca Raton, FL: CRC Press.
   Stenzel, J. (2007). *Lean accounting: Best practices for sustainable integration.* Hoboken, NJ: John Wiley & Sons.
3. Bruce Baggaley[3] quotes
   Baggaley, Bruce (2003). *Lean accounting series – creating the course and tools for a lean accounting system.* (Originally published in 2003 on Lean Enterprise Institute website, www.lean.org)
4. General
   Katzenbach, J.R. and Smith, D.K. (2015). *The wisdom of teams: Creating the high-performance organization.* Boston: Harvard Business Review Press.

Chapter 6

Lean Measures for a Lean Company

For the system to work, everyone must agree we all work for the front line instead of for the front office.

– Jim Lancaster

In a company that follows standard cost accounting, the company is divided into departments and each department head focuses on improving its efficiency without concern for the customer or the company as a whole. The work floor managers control operations and interaction with customers and focus on their requirements is limited to sales and marketing and customer service department. Traditional companies use a forecast model (MRP system) for planning their production, so there is always a difference between production planned as per forecast and actual requirement of the customer, which results in a pile of unsold inventory as well as sales loss at the end of the month because dispatches are limited to the products demanded by the customers. The remaining items produced as per forecast are left behind in the warehouse for months to come. The financial control of the company lies with the finance department that prepares the P&L statement using information from the ERP system. *All the department heads meet once in a month two or three weeks after month end to discuss and analyze business performance in previous month, but by this time the company is in the middle of current month and too late for corrective actions.*

DOI: 10.4324/9781003221746-6

Some of the measures used to track performance on the work floor in a traditional company are as follows:

■ Labor rate, hours put in, labor efficiency and utilization
■ Machine efficiency and utilization
■ Overhead absorption
■ Purchase price and volume variance

In traditional companies, when the performance is measured using the previous parameters, large batches are produced to comply with these measures that result in increase in inventory. Overproduction is a major waste that happens in most companies. Traditional companies have a misconception that large batches and immense inventory volumes enable better customer service. But the antithesis prevails. Overproduction prevents smooth flow of work, increases storage costs and lead time and results in production beyond the customer's requirements. It becomes difficult to detect defects in time because they keep accumulating and once detected, the rework consumes copious volume of resources and time. Companies do not appreciate idle labor or machinery but are happy with capital expenditure to fund the production process even if it is not driven by increase in customer demand. Overproduction can lead to shortage and stockout of items that may be critical to the customer.

What happens in an overproduction prone environment? First, managers, executives and supervisors waste their time chasing materials to complete a product and dispatch, and then they waste their time in gathering information and explaining the variances, that is, crisis management and firefighting. Data collection for the previous traditional measures further increases as the companies move on to the lean journey.

This is what happened to GM, Ford and Chrysler in 2008. They were working on these parameters to satisfy their accountants and unions to produce cars in bulk and ensure the workers get their production bonuses. These huge numbers of cars that they produced could not be sold as there were no buyers for them, and cheaper Japanese cars became more popular. Ultimately, they ran out of funds because all the money was tied in inventories and bulk raw material purchases. GM, Ford and Chrysler had to resort to aid from the government.

Lean companies have a different philosophy. They deploy lean measures that illustrate achievement of strategic goals. Measures used provide meaningful information to employees in each function in order to empower them to assess present situation and make future plans using continuously improvement projects. During the initial journey, the CEO and the CFO contemplate which measures are to be used, removed or are critical to success. The CEO, CFO and value stream managers must take note of requirements of employees to determine which lean measures should be employed. Since each company is unique, its measures should also be unique. The right measures will be the one through which the value streams deliver value to the customers. If the customer is satisfied and the financial measures meet stakeholders' expectations, then the company has been successful in its choice of measures.

A lean company runs operations through kanban, pull system, standard work, performance measurement and business plan review. It operates in real time and discussions on budget control and variance are replaced with discussions on customer satisfaction and waste elimination. The finance function plays a pivotal role in assisting continual improvement project teams to implement lean tools in all functions as well as complying with regulatory and government requirements. Improvement in operational scorecard is driven by increase in sales, decrease in throughput time and increase in capacity due to reduction in non-value adding use of capacity. If operational scorecard is achieved, financial scorecard will definitely be achieved. Thus, lean accounting puts high performance pressure on functional teams.

6.1 How a Traditional Company and a Lean Company Differ in Organizational Setup

Traditional companies have top-down management control where the decisions emerge from the top management and trickle down to managers on the plant floor with no clear understanding of 'why' to the first line of supervisors and workmen. This is a vertical organization. The traditional company setup is shown in Figure 6.1. In a traditional company, visions, strategy, goals and ideas percolate from top to bottom. The CEO and the CFO decide the vision and strategy, give ideas and set goals for managers and executives. The command emanates from the top management and senior managers and employees down the line are expected to abide by it. The department heads are not expected to snoop into the other departments of the company. The outcome of this constricted organization depends on individuals without any motivation or loyalty down the line.

Figure 6.1 Command and Control in a Traditional Company.

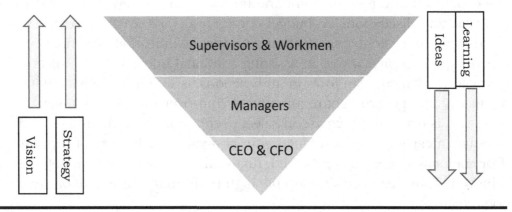

Figure 6.2 Command and Control in a Lean Company.

A lean company is a horizontal organization in which workmen are trained to understand what they are doing as per their skill matrix so that they can perform their job based on standardized processes and achieve expected results that are then exhibited by measurement system. Please note that standardized processes in lean companies does not mean that there is no scope for further improvement because PDCA and SDCA cycles ensure continuous improvement. The lean production system, daily management system and lean accounting implementation takes two to three years.

The lean company does not give orders from top but empowers the first line with support and guidance from higher level. The lean company operations setup is shown in Figure 6.2 along with the changes over time. In a lean company the workplace takes precedence. The people at the workplace such as supervisors, team leaders and workmen are expected to run the plant floor as per the SOPs, standard work, standard checklists and three level meetings as described in Chapter 3. The workplace staff and workmen understand the needs of the current products and the challenges in current operations. They will share ideas and finalize cell (workplace) measures and goals with their functional managers. Functional managers and the management help them to achieve their goals by providing resources.

The traditional company transforms to a lean company as shown in Figure 6.2 when lean is built into the culture and the lean production system, daily management system and lean accounting is implemented and practiced vigorously by everyone.

"The teams at Goodyear are now telling the boss how to run things. And I must say, I'm not doing a half-bad job because of it."

– Stanley Gault[1], Chairman (quoted in
Principles of Total Quality, p. 82)

6.2 Performance Measurement in a Lean Company

There is a saying that "you get what you measure." Therefore, the measures should be simple, actionable and promote positive behavior among workmen. The measures mentioned next are a broad guideline but companies must select measures suitable for their products and industry. There are two key lean measurements:

- *Takt Time* – This denotes customer demand of each product.
- *Flow Rate* – This denotes rate of production of each product.

The motive of a lean production system journey is to keep flow rate a little ahead of takt time.

Selection of Performance Measures[2]

The measures at each level should be designed to monitor and improve the flow rate of products to the customers. The measures for the top management are based on the company's current strategy. Each value stream in a company is treated as a mini company and each mini company can have its own unique measures. The measures for value stream managers and functional managers have to be decided at value stream level and the cell measures for plant floor supervisors, team leaders and workmen should be decided after discussion with them. If the measures are mutually consented by workmen, team leaders and supervisors, there is a better chance of faster implementation than the one imposed from the top. If measures improve at cell level, they will enhance performance of the value stream and achievement of measures at value stream level will ensure improvement in the overall company's performance. Usually, once the measures start displaying improvement monthly, many companies switch to weekly measurement for some parameters, especially on the plant floor.

The performance measurement selection should support execution of the company's strategy. It should primarily be non-financial so that it can be easily measured on the plant floor and in functional areas. It should induce the right behavior to upkeep lean initiatives and customer service and measure processes, not people. Trends and targets should be established against which actual results can be measured over time. The frequency of measurements should also be set – hourly, shift-wise or daily – and be visible to everyone in the workplace. Supervisors and workmen should be able to relate their work with the measures and record these on the visual boards and in ERP. Last, measures should be clear and easy to calculate by respective users themselves.

The measures should be linked to work processes of every employee, from the CEO to the workmen. There are three levels of performance measurements in a lean company:

Plant or Corporate Level Measurement

These monthly measurements enable senior managers to monitor the achievement of strategic goals and initiate strategic changes. The promoters or top management should aim for the following:

■ Healthy profit margin
■ Increase in cash flow
■ Increase in market share
■ Customer value
■ Continuous improvement culture
■ Happy people

Value Stream Level Measurement

Value stream measures guide the continuous improvement teams monthly or weekly in their 'pursuit of perfection' in their processes. These measures determine the progress of value streams in achievement of their performance goals. Value stream measures identify critical success factors, reduce waste, increase flow and drive higher profitability along with safety and training. Key measures at the value stream level to achieve the top management objectives are as follows:

- Customer satisfaction measured by OTIFEF (on time in full and error free delivery to customers)
- Throughput time or lead time
- First time right
- Inventory days
- Sales per employee

Cell (Workplace) Level Measurement

Cell or workplace refers to a group of machines or workstations physically and geographically linked and staffed by a consistent team of operators who manufacture products or parts of product within a product family. The cell level measures bring each process within the value stream under control and enable cell teams to monitor their daily production activities. Cell level performance is measured by the hour, by the day or whenever required. Lean cell measurements should be few in number and focused on lean. The data for lean measures are collated by workmen, team leaders or supervisors and is displayed in the workplace. The supervisors and workmen write on the board, but the lean measures are also systematically updated in the ERP system by end of shift or day by team leaders. These measures are linked with the functional head's balance scorecard to support the company in achieving its strategy. The cell level measures focus on the following:

- Near miss incidents (safety)
- Production per hour
- Work in progress inventory with respect to standard work in progress inventory (WIP to SWIP)
- First time right
- OEE of critical and bottleneck machines
- Mean time between failure (MTBF)/Mean time to repair (MTTR).
- Machine charge rate
- Loss per minute due to stoppages
- Cost per minute of downtime due to changeover

■ Sales per person
■ On time in full error free (OTIFEF)
■ Throughput time or lead time
■ Stock level in stores (slow moving and non-moving inventory)
■ Average cost of per unit shipped
■ Cost of quality
■ Accounts receivable (in days and value)
■ Accounts payable (in days and value)
■ Value stream gross profit percentage (PBIT or EBIT)

Each level has its own focus and measures, but they are interlinked. If the measures at the work floor level or cell levels improve, the value stream and company goals will be accomplished.

The measures are implemented after drawing out a suitable strategy wherein priority is given to the individual company's requirements. The company should avoid complex measures and use these time-tested measures to bring success to the company. Let's discuss these cell measures in detail:

Near Miss Incidents (Safety)

Near miss incidents are recorded as per the Heinrich principle (see Chapter 2 for details). Incidents are defects that create waste, increase labor hours, incur loss of production and generate additional medical expenditure. Reporting near miss incidents allows timely remedial action to prevent major incidents. The shift supervisor shall use a set format to record incidents and the functional head should conduct an inquiry and deploy countermeasures. The inquiry report should be signed by the value stream manager and shared with HR for record and follow up.

Production per Hour or Hourly Production

Ideally, there should be no fluctuation in production per hour in any hour of the shift or the day. Toyota questions why the same weight or numbers per hour cannot be produced every hour of the shift when everything from raw material, manpower, machine and methodology remains same? Why is production in some hours more than 150% of the worst hours? Therefore, a check on production per hour for critical machines, especially bottleneck machines, is necessary. To find reasons of fluctuations, lean production system tools can be used for root cause analysis and for taking corrective and preventive measures.

Compare the average hourly production to takt time (customer requirement per hour).

Average production per hour in the shift = Production for eight hours/ (Number of hours in a shift − breaks allowed − planned shutdown)

Record *minimum production per hour* and how many times in the last 24 hours this quantity was produced. Record *maximum production per hour* and how many times it was achieved in the last 24 hours and investigate why it is not repeated maximum times in the shift. Analyze the root cause with plant teams consisting of cross-functional employees and implement corrective and preventive action.

Work in Progress Inventory with Respect to Standard Work in Progress Inventory (WIP to SWIP)

Measure the amount of inventory within the cell compared with the amount of inventory designed to be in the cell as per work cell design for standard work and the 'pull' principle. Only when there is a kanban or some other pull signal should the product be manufactured. This increases the rate of material flow through the value stream.

WIP/SWIP = Work in progress inventory/Standard work in progress inventory

If,

- WIP/SWIP = 1 − The production cell is in control of its inventory and throughput time will be as per designed value.
- WIP/SWIP > 1 − The inventory is more in the production cell. Throughput time will be more. There are chances that even stockouts of some other items will take place.
- WIP/SWIP < 1 − The inventory is less in the production cell. The stockout of some items will take place and actual throughput time can be more. Some other challenges of line stoppage can take place.

It is always preferable to keep all the materials required equal to or little more than the SWIP near the machine.

First Time Right

This is the percentage of acceptable products that are produced in the cell right first time without rework, repair or scrap. The lean principle of 'standardized work' helps to bring in this consistency in processes. This is also called first time yield. This is one of the areas where the maximum opportunity for savings lies in a company.

First time yield (by numbers or by weight) = (Saleable production – rework – rejected material – process scrap)/(Total raw material used in percentage)

The first time right should be calculated for each product or family of products and unit of measures must be same for numerator and denominator. First time right measure gives us true value of the quality. The root cause analysis is done to assess the reason for quality issues. This should be measured for every shift or day since it is the most valuable quality information about the cell and the value stream that you can derive. The value stream manager must follow up on the implementation of the corrective actions. There lies a huge savings opportunity for the company.

Overall Equipment Effectiveness (OEE) of Critical and Bottleneck Machines

A machine has to be stable and available when required except for the planned shutdown. OEE measures the effectiveness and ability of a machine to manufacture at intended rate and manufacture products of acceptable quality. Lean principles require the company to manufacture at a flow rate that meets the takt time (customer required rate) for a bottleneck or constraint machine so that continuous flow of material is maintained from the value stream.

OEE = Availability × Performance × Quality

Where,

- *Availability* = (Planned machine production time – all breakdowns or minor stoppages)/(Time for which the machine is available for production – planned shutdown)
- *Performance* = Rate of actual production per hour/Planned production per hour in the available time
- *Quality or yield* = (Production – rejections, scrap, rework, etc.)/(Material taken in for production – planned or expected loss)

OEE should be calculated for all critical machines in the value stream, especially the bottleneck machines (all 'A' category machines as per TPM-PM Pillar because OEE explains how effectively the company uses its production capacity. In most traditional companies where TPM implementation is commenced, it is noticed that the OEE ratio is never more than 30% to 40% initially. For example, a company has a machine downtime of 40%, that is, availability – 60%, performance ratio – 60% and quality ratio – 93%, which results in OEE of this machine at 33%.

In this company if the demand for the products rises, then the operations team will demand new machines to cater to the customer demand, but a lean company will work internally on all the three factors – availability, performance and quality to improve OEE to, say 65% in few weeks, by implementing autonomous maintenance, planned maintenance pillars and other total productive maintenance (TPM) pillars. The company fulfilled increased customer demand without additional investment.

CASE STUDY

Calculation of OEE for a Continuous Casting Machine in a Mini Steel Plant in East Africa

To compute availability, the time for planned shutdown due to preventive maintenance and shift change, shutdown due to material not available, unplanned shutdown due to breakdowns, minor stoppages due to machine or material and time for changeover are noted every day.

- Availability ratio (A) is 68%.
- Theoretical speed is the speed at which the machine should run, and actual speed is the speed it actually ran during production. This gives performance. The performance ratio (P) is 79%.

■ The first time right quantity as well as rejections are noted daily. The quality ratio (Q) is 93%.

$$OEE = 0.68 \times 0.79 \times 0.93 = 0.50 \text{ or } 50\%$$

The overall equipment effectiveness of the continuous casting machine for the month is 50%. Table 6.1. shows detailed calculation. Note the variation in the last column where it shows the day-wise OEE calculation. It fluctuates between 19% and 66%. Thus, a huge opportunity lies to improve average OEE because it will increase capacity without any investment. Only the continuous improvement team's time and efforts will be required to implement TPM-AM-PM.

No new machine is bought, no new operator is hired and no additional space is required in the layout to almost doubled the output. This is the benefit of TPM implementation under lean production system.

Mean Time between Failure (MTBF) and Mean Time to Repair (MTTR)

These measures are also calculated for all critical machines in the value stream, especially the bottleneck machine (All 'A' category machines as per TPM-PM Pillar). Mean time between failure (MTBF) is an indicator of *reliability* of a machine. It is the average time for which a machine performs without any breakdown. When the company implements TPM, the MTBF should continuously rise and number of breakdowns should decline.

MTBF = Total available time/Nos. of breakdowns

Mean time to repair (MTTR) is an indicator of *maintainability* of equipment. MTTR is the average time the machine was down during the month. When we implement TPM, MTTR should continuously go down with decline in breakdowns and better maintenance techniques.

MTTR = Total downtime/Nos. of breakdowns

Table 6.1 OEE Calculation for a Continuous Casting Machine at a Mini Steel Plant.

			13/08	14/08	15/08	16/08	17/08	18/08	19/08	20/08	21/08	22/08	23/08	24/08	25/08	26/08	29/08	30/08	31/08	Total
OEE	%	$OEE=Av*P*Q$	42%	44%	19%	41%	66%	41%	46%	41%	60%	36%	38%	16%	54%	34%	49%	26%	45%	39%
Quality	%	$Q=H/D$	97%	90%	89%	95%	95%	94%	95%	95%	97%	92%	92%	75%	95%	92%	94%	96%	91%	93%
Performance	%	$P=F/E$	75%	60%	58%	96%	91%	52%	62%	63%	74%	52%	51%	56%	62%	50%	55%	52%	53%	61%
Availability	%	$Av=(A-B-C)/(A-B)$	58%	81%	37%	45%	76%	84%	78%	69%	84%	75%	80%	39%	92%	74%	94%	52%	93%	68%
Actual machine Speed	Units per min	$F=D/(A-B-C)$	0.56	0.45	0.43	0.72	0.68	0.39	0.46	0.48	0.56	0.39	0.39	0.42	0.47	0.37	0.42	0.39	0.40	0.46
Theoritical machine speed	Units per min	E	0.75	0.75	0.75	0.75	0.75	0.75	0.75	0.75	0.75	0.75	0.75	0.75	0.75	0.75	0.75	0.75	0.75	
Production (No. of units)	Total	D	247	176	207	252	242	380	377	326	247	207	212	143	243	182	266	137	106	3950
	Reject	G	7	18	22	12	11	24	20	15	7	16	17	36	13	14	15	6	10	263
	Good	H	240	158	185	240	231	356	357	311	240	191	195	107	230	168	251	131	96	3687
Total machine up-time	mins	$J=(A-B-C)$	440	390	480	350	355	970	815	685	445	530	550	340	520	490	640	350	265	8615
Unplanned downtime (mins)	Total	C	315	90	825	430	110	180	225	315	85	180	140	540	45	175	40	320	20	4035
	Mold changeover time		0	0	0	0	0	135	65	60	35	50	90	0	0	0	0	0	0	435
	Minor stoppages (material related)		270	70	75	180	30	0	0	0	0	0	0	440	0	0	0	0	0	1065
	Minor stoppages (machine related)		45	0	120	0	30	0	110	85	0	95	0	60	15	90	0	40	55	745
	Break downs		0	20	630	250	50	45	50	170	50	35	50	40	30	85	0	265	20	1790
Planned downtime (mins)	Total	B	685	960	135	660	975	290	400	440	910	730	840	545	840	735	760	750	1215	11870
	Material not available		485	225	105	630	945	260	370	410	880	700	810	515	810	705	730	720	1185	10485
	Shift change over		30	30	30	30	30	30	30	30	30	30	30	30	30	30	30	30	30	510
	Breaks		0	0	0	0	0	0	0	0	0	0	0	0	0	0	0	0	0	0
	Not scheduled		170	705	0	0	0	0	0	0	0	0	0	0	0	0	0	0	0	875
	Prev. maint.		0	0	0	0	0	0	0	0	0	0	0	0	0	0	0	0	0	0
Total time available	mins	A	1440	1440	1440	1440	1440	1440	1440	1440	1440	1440	1530	1425	1405	1400	1440	1420	1500	24520
Operator A/B/C																				
Date			13/08	14/08	15/08	16/08	17/08	18/08	19/08	20/08	21/08	22/08	23/08	24/08	25/08	26/08	29/08	30/08	31/08	Total

Table 6.2 Mean Time Between Failure Trend.

In minutes	Oct-15	Nov-15	Dec-15	Jan-16	Feb-16
Total running time	30475	32768	33937	34295	35298
Number of breakdowns	40	38	36	34	30
In minutes	762	862	943	1009	1177

Table 6.3 Mean Time to Repair Trend.

MTTR	Mean time to repair				
In minutes	Oct-15	Nov-15	Dec-15	Jan-16	Feb-16
Total downtime due to breakdowns	8405	6112	4943	4585	3582
Total number of breakdowns	40	38	36	34	30
In minutes	210	161	137	135	119

In the example in Table 6.2, the number of breakdowns comes down from October 2015 to February 201" and MTBF increases from 762 to 1177, minutes which indicates the condition of the machine is improving since it runs for an average 1177 minutes between each breakdown.

In the next example in Table 6.3, the number of breakdowns decreases from October 2015 to February 2016 and MTTR decreases from 210 to 119 minutes, which indicates improvement in the machine as it breaks down, on an average, for 119 minutes in a month.

Machine Charge Rate

The machine charge rate calculates loss per minute from machine downtime, especially from the bottleneck machine. This downtime can occur due to breakdown, changeover, waiting time for material, design or any other reason. It is a very important step to sensitize functional managers about the cost of downtime for each machine when the company implements TPM and the lean accounting system because it makes them aware about the loss borne by the company every hour when the machine is down. The machine charge rate can also be useful while calculating the offloading costs of the job work to vendors or paid work to customers. This should be seen in broader concept of the lean accounting system.

Table 6.4 shows calculation of machine charge rate for a company in India. The values shown are in US$.

Table 6.4   Machine Charge Rate Calculations for CNC Gear Grinding Machines in US$.

S. NO.	Description	GGM1	US$	GGM2	US$	GGM3	US$	GGM4	US$	GGM5	US$	GGM6	US$
1	Value of machine		188000		34960		30138		27727		27727		110545
2	Cost of accessories												
3	Value of machine		188000		34960		30138		27727		27727		110545
4	Depreciation %	13	24440	13	4370	13	3767	13	3466	13	3466	13	13818
5	Interest@ %P.A.	13	24440	13	4545	13	3918	13	3605	13	3605	13	14371
6	Power cost per hour		4.0		2		2		2		2		4
7	Worker salary and number of worker PM	1	900	1	700	1	700	1	700	1	700	1	900
8	Helper salary & number of worker PM	1	700	1	600	1	600	1	600	1	600	1	700
9	Number of shifts		3		3		3		3		3		3
10	Labor costs (US$)/year		57600		46800		46800		46800		46800		57600
11	Charge rate per year 4+5+6+10	26	141520	26	73235	26	69461	26	68846	26	68846	26	120829
12	Number of working days per year		365		365		312		312		312		365
13	Charge rate per days		388		201		223		221		221		331
14	Number of working hours per day		24		24		24		24		24		24
15	Charge rate per hour		20		10		11		11		11		18

Loss per Minute Due to Stoppages

This refers to the loss borne by company for each minute a machine breaks down.

Loss per minute due to stoppages = Total loss/Total minutes of breakdown

---

Breakdowns should be recorded daily against the breakdown codes and at month end, the data should be analyzed to identify reasons for breakdowns. This can be done using tools like Pareto analysis. This exercise is helpful when the company is implementing autonomous maintenance, planned maintenance and focus improvement pillars in the plant. It guides from where improvements can be initiated to reduce non-value adding use of capacity and release it to increase productivity. The TPM activities should focus on issues that cause 60% of breakdown, then next 20% breakdown and then reduction or elimination of breakdown.

Table 6.5 shows record of stoppages and breakdowns in a tube mill in a processing plant. The Pareto analysis was done and light grey shade area shows the specific stoppages and breakdowns which adds upto 61.5% of the total stoppages and breakdown time. The corrective and preventive counter-measures are to be implemented to eliminate these losses on first priority. The second priority will be to implement countermeasure for specific stoppages and breakdowns in the dark grey shade are that accounts for further losses from 61.5% to 80.7%.

Table 6.6 shows calculation of loss due to stoppages and breakdowns.

For every 10% reduction in stoppages and breakdown, financial benefits earned by the company are calculated. There is a loss of $86,077 in the current month. After three months when the stoppages and breakdowns decreased by 10%, the loss came down to $77,384, which indicates a saving of of $8,693. After the next three months when the breakdown decreased by another 10%, the loss came down to $69,644, which indicates a saving of $16,413 from the current month. Therefore, loss per minute due to stoppage = 86077/10865 = $7.9 per minute.

Cost per Minute of Downtime Due to Changeover

Changeover refers to time wasted in the plant when machines switch from manufacturing of one product to another. Sometimes, there is a small

Table 6.5   Monthly Stoppages/Breakdowns Times for 3″ Tube Mill.

		Monthly stoppage			Month	Mar-18
Breakdown ERP code	Description		Nos. of breakdowns	Total break-down time in minutes	% breakdown of total break-down time	% breakdown of total breakdown – Cumulative
RC01	Roll change		12	2055	18.9%	18.9%
OT003	Starting delay		47	925	8.5%	27.4%
OT011	Lunch		29	870	8.0%	35.4%
OT010	Thickness/punch/length change		64	865	8.0%	43.4%
RM003	Material not shifted		13	470	4.3%	47.7%
PR004	Impeder problem/change		23	430	4.0%	51.7%
PR016	Strip fold in RLA		7	365	3.4%	55.0%
M016	Run out conveyor (ROT problem)		13	355	3.3%	58.3%
P001	Power failure (MSEB)		6	345	3.2%	61.5%
OT006	Blade change (cutter broken/change)		19	310	2.9%	64.3%
PR001	Size problem/setting		9	295	2.7%	67.1%
RM001	Material not available		5	285	2.6%	69.7%
RM002	Material not slitted		5	200	1.8%	71.5%
RC02	Setup		4	200	1.8%	73.4%
PR017	Strip fold/joint broken in FF		10	185	1.7%	75.1%
PR011	TH bearing		6	165	1.5%	76.6%
M049	Propeller shaft bolt broken		3	165	1.5%	78.1%
PR014	Pocket full		12	145	1.3%	79.4%
M005	Propeller shaft		5	135	1.2%	80.7%
E013	Mill trip		4	120	1.1%	81.8%
M028	RLA problem		1	120	1.1%	82.9%
M010	Weld roll assembly replacement/work		1	115	1.1%	83.9%
OT016	Joint delay		7	115	1.1%	85.0%
PR003	Bend problem/cutting problem		3	105	1.0%	86.0%
PR008	Edge press fin pass		2	100	0.9%	86.9%
E008	Welder problem (H.F trip)		5	100	0.9%	87.8%
M051	Lead screw/tool post problem		2	100	0.9%	88.7%
M054	Shear and welder desk/shear cutter		3	100	0.9%	89.6%
PR010	Tool change/broken		18	90	0.8%	90.5%
U007	Crane problem electrical		3	90	0.8%	91.3%
U006	Coolant problem mechanical		3	85	0.8%	92.1%

(Continued)

Table 6.5   (Continued)

Breakdown ERP code	Description	Nos. of breakdowns	Total break-down time in minutes	% breakdown of total break-down time	% breakdown of total breakdown – Cumulative
	Monthly stoppage			Month	Mar-18
M037	Choke bearing sizing top 3	2	80	0.7%	92.8%
OT012	Misc. others	2	75	0.7%	93.5%
PR015	Misc. production	2	70	0.6%	94.2%
OT004	Tool change/bearing broken	9	65	0.6%	94.8%
M048	Dumping problem	1	60	0.6%	95.3%
OT008	Scheduled maintenance	1	60	0.6%	95.9%
OT001	Cranes not available	2	45	0.4%	96.3%
OT014	Other roll change/problem	1	40	0.4%	96.6%
PR007	Fin replacement	2	35	0.3%	97.0%
E006	Cut-off problem (COC trip)	2	35	0.3%	97.3%
E015	Dumping problem	4	35	0.3%	97.6%
M002	Pinch roll (pin broken)	1	35	0.3%	97.9%
M015	COC problem	1	30	0.3%	98.2%
M043	Seam guide bearing broken	1	30	0.3%	98.5%
M046	Air problem	1	30	0.3%	98.8%
OT002	Manpower (shift change)	1	30	0.3%	99.0%
OT005	Clamps change	1	30	0.3%	99.3%
E007	Run out motor	2	20	0.2%	99.5%
M050	Impeder line bolt broken/HF trip	1	20	0.2%	99.7%
M031	Choke bearing fin pass top 3	1	15	0.1%	99.8%
PR002	Welding problem (wrinkle, overlap)	1	10	0.1%	99.9%
PR009	Weld joint broken (joint delay)	1	10	0.1%	100.0%
			384	10865	100.0%

changeover where only a few items on the machine are changed but there are 'long' changeover times when a large number of parts are changed on the machine for manufacturing of some other product.

Single-minute exchange of dies (SMED), a lean tool developed by Shigeo Shingo, is an effective lean tool to reduce the changeover time by 50% in a

Table 6.6 Calculations of Loss for an ERW Tube Mill in US$.

Description	Current state	After three months of TPM implement ation – breakdown decreased by 10%	After six months of TPM implementation – breakdown decreased by further 10%
Total breakdown time including changeover in minutes	10865	9778	8800
Total time available for production in minutes. 26 days × 22.5 hours × 60	35100	35100	35100
Total time actual mill is run in minutes	24235	25322	26300
Production in the month in metric tons	3200	3340	3470
Production per minute achieved in metric ton	0.13	0.13	0.13
Production loss due to breakdown in metric ton	1435	1290	1161
Profit US$ per ton	60	60	60
Loss of profit due to breakdown in value – in US$	86077	77384	69664
Savings due to TPM implementation from the current per month – in US$		8693	16413

short span of three to four months. There is scope of further reduction of 25%. This 50% to 75% reduction liberates non-value adding capacity for productive use to grow the topline and bottom line.

Cost per minute of downtime due to changeover = (Total minutes lost due to changeover time) × (Loss per minute due to downtime in the value stream [use loss per minute from previous section])

In Table 6.5, the roll change on RC01 (first row) in 3″ ERW tube mill happens 12 times a month, consuming 2055 minutes i.e., almost 18.9% of the total time. This means the company is losing 2055 × $7.9 = $16234/per month. The company can save 50% ($8117 every month) of it with SMED tool implementation and start becoming profitable.

Sale per Employee

It measures the productivity of the company.

> *Sales per employee* = (Total sales – discounts)/(Average number of full-time equivalent employees)

Full-time equivalent employee = Total hours worked by full- and part-time workers (including overtime)/Number of available straight-time hours per employee during the period.

The hours include working hours of all employees in a value stream, from workmen to value stream manager.

On Time, In Full, Error Free (OTIFEF)

OTIFEF percentage measures customer satisfaction. It measures the shipment of the right products in the right quantity to the customer without any quality problems. It shows the effectiveness of the company's functional processes in manufacturing the products as per schedule. It can be measured daily, weekly and monthly but a company that is implementing it for the first time should measure it monthly. The orders that are not fully supplied will not be considered.

> *OTIFEF for the month* = (Quantity dispatched in full on time error free – customer returns) × 100/(Scheduled quantity which was planned to be dispatched in that month)

Delivering good quality in sufficient quantity and as per customer schedule sets a company apart in the industry. The company can seize the competition business in the process and generate more revenue and profit. Table 6.7 demonstrates how OTIFEF is calculated.

Throughput Time or Lead Time

The company often has excess inventory, quality issues, long lead time for procurement, delayed deliveries, out of stock items and unaccomplished sales targets. This happens due to the company's oversight of a vital

Table 6.7   OTIFEF Calculation.

	OTIFEF- by quantity							
	Oct-09				Nov-09			
	Ordered quantity	OT-On time	IF-In full	EF-Error free	Ordered quantity	OT-On time	IF-In full	EF-Error free
Local dispatch	1,08,946	78,212	72,096	71,096	88,803	74,189	71,649	71,549
Export dispatch	1,37,430	1,07,430	97,430	90,430	1,52,720	1,30,880	1,28,880	1,20,880
Total Dispatch	2,46,376	1,85,642	1,69,526	1,61,526	2,41,523	2,05,069	2,00,529	1,92,429
OTIFEF								
Local				65.26%				80.57%
Export				65.80%				79.15%
Total				65.56%				79.67%

aspect – throughput time. Throughput time is the time required by a product to pass through the entire manufacturing process for being converted from raw materials into finished goods, including inspection and quality assessment time. The customer must get the product on time. Therefore, a company should prioritize throughput time over procurement cost per unit.

Throughput time or lead time measures the flow of products from receipt of raw materials or customer orders to the shipment of finished goods. Flow is related to the inventory velocity, that is, how fast it is flowing in the company. Throughput time is a major indicator of success or failure of the lean production system and lean accounting implementation in the company for the CEO and the CFO. It is an excellent performance measure for a value stream to remove the bottlenecks and wastes in all functions and smoothen the flow of material. It reflects the speed of conversion of raw materials or customer orders to finished product expressed in hours or days

> *Throughput time (in hours or days)* = (Raw material + work in progress + finished goods)/Products shipped in one hour or one day

For example, if a product is produced in a large batch size with seven processes involved and each process takes three days, then the finished product will take 21 days to manufacture. The throughput time, 21 days, is the time this product will take to be manufactured and delivered to customer. Therefore, if throughput time decreases, the flow of the product increases, which increases cash flow and company profitability.

Consumables and Spare Parts Consumption

The consumption of frequently used consumables and spare parts should be monitored monthly on the basis of their value, volume and increase in consumption with respect to previous periods. Pareto analysis can help to determine which items constitute, in the given order, 80% of the value, volume and last, variation in usage with respect to previous periods. Using this, opportunities for improvement can be discovered through problem-solving techniques like what corrective or preventive action can be taken to optimize the consumption and what are the reasons for high consumption, high value and high quantities?

The actual consumption of consumables and spare parts should be studied against standard consumption. There may be cases where even the standard set can be questioned for the items. Several approaches can be used for this. First, compare the quantity consumed with cost and product life to identify substitutes with better product specification and source. Second, assess whether a compromise with the specifications is being made. Third, look at the environment wherein the consumption is high due to contamination or wrong fitting practices. Last, determine whether there is any negligence in the operations. Root cause analysis will help to define the problem so that countermeasure can be derived and suitable corrective and preventive action can be put in place.

Stock Level in Stores (Slow Moving and Non-Moving Inventory)

At every month end, the items that have not moved for 90 days are categorized as 'slow moving' items and the items that have not moved for 180 days are categorized as 'non-moving' items. These items will be minimized and reduced to zero once the supermarket concept starts coming up in the plant. These items must be discussed during monthly review meeting for devising an action plan for their disposal.

Average Cost of Per Unit Shipped

Value stream profitability is crucial. Knowing the cost of each product is not important but it can still be computed once in a while to review which product is subsidizing which within the value stream. In a lean company, average product cost is used to evaluate the profits of the company. It includes all value stream costs – production, labor, materials, production support, operation support, facilities, maintenance and all other value stream costs.

> *Average cost per unit in a month* = Total value stream costs/Total units dispatched in the month

Total value stream costs are material costs plus variable costs plus fixed costs including corporate overheads.

Cost of Quality and Rejection Loss per Unit

Poor quality disrupts flow as it puts brakes on the flow. There is loss in productivity because the material, labor and machine costs utilized are wasted because the product could not be sold as a finished product. Quality control function cannot ensure the quality of the products; quality has to be produced at the source. Every operator must be able to read the drawings and bill of materials and should be suitably skilled and understand his role in manufacturing so that quality products come out of each cell and function. The present cost of the quality is calculated in the following way.

> *Cost of quality* = A + P + I + E

Where,

- *Appraisal Cost (A)* = Fixed cost of quality control department + checking and testing of purchased goods + calibration costs + traveling costs + field testing
- *Prevention Costs (P)* = Supplier evaluation + new product development + quality training

- *Internal Failure (IF)* = Rework + rejection + non-conformity internal failure
- *External Failure (EF)* = Customer complaints + customer material return + discounts given to customer due to poor quality or delivery + warranty and guaranty costs.

Table 6.8 shows the format for computation of cost of poor quality. It can be filled up monthly and should reflect a downward trend.

Table 6.8   Format for Cost of Poor Quality for Perfect Gear Company.

	Oct-18	Nov-18	Dec-18	Jan-19	Feb-19	Mar-19
(A) Appraisal costs						
Cost of audit of suppliers						
Customer entertainment						
Cost of communication						
Cost of tour						
Cost of QC equipment purchased						
Cost of NCR/rework/reject						
Total cost						
(B) Prevention cost						
Cost of training						
Cost of audit (internal/external)						
Cost of consultancy						
Cost of calibration						
Total cost						
(C) IF (internal failure)						
Rework						
Rejection						
Non-conformity internal						
Total cost						
(D) EF (external failure)						
Customer complaints						
Customer material return						
Discounts given to customer due to poor quality or delivery						
Warranty and guaranty costs						
Total cost						
Grand total (A + B + C + D)						
Prepared by:				Checked by:		

> *Value of loss due to rejection per unit* = Cost of quality per month/Total units dispatched in the month

Accounts Receivable (AR) Days Outstanding

A company believes revenue is made when invoice is generated but the real revenue is earned when each penny is collected against that invoice. Cost is incurred upfront when the product is manufactured but the revenue is earned when the money is received from the customers. This measure assesses the average time required to collect money after shipment. Downward trend of accounts receivable in outstanding days indicates an increase in the rate of cash flow through the value stream. To compute AR days outstanding, calculate the monetary value of average sales per day and divide it by the period end accounts receivable balance.

> *Average sales per day* = Average monthly sales/Working days in a month

> *Accounts receivable days outstanding* = Accounts receivable balance/ Average sales per day

Accounts Payable (AP) Days Outstanding

Like accounts receivable, it is important to pay the suppliers on time to maintain a healthy relation with suppliers and ensure timely supply of materials. This measure calculates the average time taken to pay after shipment. Lean companies consider vendors as part of their family. Toyota's vendor management department implements relevant lean tools at the plants of their vendors so that they are also lean and are able to supply the material on time and at low costs.

The accounts payable process is a non-value adding activity. This process should not only be standardized but also should be simplified so that the transaction cost per voucher is minimum.

The company must know how much accounts payable (in days) is with respect to the sales and purchase. The payable days with respect to sales will enable the company to compare this figure with the amount receivable.

> *Average purchases per day* = Average monthly purchase/Working days in month

> *Accounts payable days outstanding (w.r.t. purchase)* = Accounts payable balance/Average purchases per day

> *Accounts payable days outstanding days (w.r.t. sales)* = Accounts payable balance/Average sales per day

Value Stream Net Profit % – EBITDA

It measures the profitability of the value stream during the period.

It includes the sales value and costs (variables and fixed costs) of all shipments from the value stream during the period. Costs include production labor, production materials, production support, operation support, facilities and maintenance and any other actual cost spent.

Table 6.9. shows how the EBITDA and EBIT are arrived at.

> *Value stream net profit %* = (Value stream revenue – value stream costs) × 100/Value Stream Revenue

The value stream manager, functional managers, supervisors and workmen must use these measurements to monitor the progress on the shop floors and all other measures should be eliminated. The measures must be easy for people to compute and directly related to the company's business strategy. If people at all levels have clearly understood what these measures are and what is the linkage with each other and how the effect of cell measures enhances the value streams and the company's strategic goals, then there is no reason why this lean company will not continuously improve its business growth and profits.

6.3 Scorecards for Lean Measures

All the previous measures are consolidated in different scorecards that are appropriately made to suit employees at each level. Corporate scorecards are

Table 6.9 Profit and Loss Statement for Computing EBITDA of A Value Stream for Perfect Gear Company in USD'000.

Key parameters	Mar-18			Mar-19		
	Annual P&L	Monthly average	% of sales	Annual P&L	Monthly average	% of sales
Monthly quantity dispatched	1000 tons			1500 tons		
Sales price	$3.33 per kg			$3.67 per kg		
Sales revenue	40000	3333		66000	5500	
Material cost	17280	1440	43.2%	31200	2600	47.3%
Contribution 1 (A)	22720	1893	56.8%	34800	2900	52.7%
Total variable expenses (B)	6778	565	16.9%	9794	816	14.8%
Consumables and stores	1093	91		1640	137	
Oil and lubricants	208	17		312	26	
Inserts	160	13		240	20	
Accessories	80	7		64	5	
Grinding wheels	88	7		144	12	
Cutting oil	120	10		208	17	
Tool cutter	101	8		144	12	
Gas	53	4		80	7	
Paints	82	7		122	10	
Grease	27	2		56	5	
Others	480	40		800	67	
Power and fuels	2019	168		3040	253	
Job works	1547	129		2384	199	
Other plant misc. expenses	720	60		560	47	
Contribution 2 (C) = (A-B)	15942	1329	39.9%	25006	2084	37.9%
Total fixed expenses (D)	9971	831	24.9%	9213	768	14.0%
Wages – workers	1893	158		2240	187	
Wages – fabrication	373	31		312	26	
Overtime	773	64		736	61	
Salary – executives	3600	300		2885	240	
Net profits-EBITDA (E) = (C-D)	5971	498	14.9%	15794	1316	23.9%
Depreciation and amortization	2107	176		2400	200	
EBIT	3864	322	9.7%	13394	1116	20.3%
Bank interest	933	78		960	80	
Interest on term loans	907	76		1120	93	
Net earnings before tax (EBT)	2024	169	5.1%	11314	943	17.1%

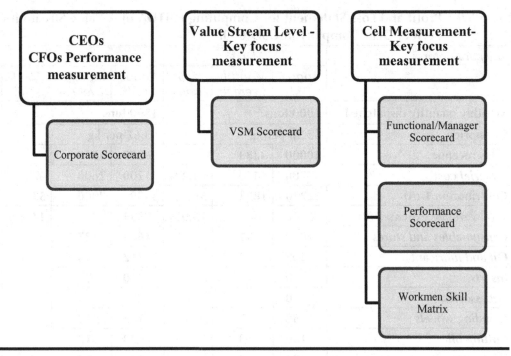

Figure 6.3   Different Scorecards Measuring Performance at Various Levels.

for top management. Value stream managers have functional scorecards as well as corporate scorecards. Each functional manager will have a functional scorecard. All executives and supervisors will have a performance scorecard. All team leaders and workmen will have skill matrix scorecard.

Each level will have its own performance measurement system. If the cell measures do not benefit the value stream measures and company measures, then there is a flaw in selection of the cell measures and it should be looked into immediately. If the measures as per above lean methodology are selected than there will be marked improvement in value stream and company measures and lean implementation will be successful. Figure 6.3 summarizes scorecards for employees at different level.

Key Takeaways

1. There is a saying 'You get what you measure.' Therefore, the measures should be simple, actionable and promote positive behavior among workmen.
2. The measures at each level should be designed to monitor and improve the flow rate of products to the customers. Throughput time reflects the speed of

conversion of raw materials to finished product expressed in hours or days. It is a major indicator of success or failure of the lean production system and lean accounting implementation in the company for the CEO and the CFO.

3. The measures must be easy for people to compute and directly related to the company's business strategy. If people at top level, value stream level and cell level have clearly understood the measures, then there is no reason why this lean company will not continuously improve its business growth and profits.

4. If operational measures are achieved, financial measures will definitely be achieved. Thus, lean accounting puts high performance pressure on functional teams.

5. Delivering good quality in sufficient quantity and as per customer schedule sets a company apart in the industry. The company can seize the competition business in the process and generate more revenue and profit.

6. Companies believe revenue is made when invoice is generated but the real revenue is earned when each penny is collected against that invoice.

Recommended List for Further Reading

1. **Priciples of Total Quality**
   Omachonu, V.K. and Ross, J.E. (2005). *Principles of total quality*. Boca Raton, FL: CRC Press and Taylor & Francis e-Library.[1]
2. **Performance Measures**
   Maskell.com. Blog- *"The best performance measure for the manufacturing CEO"*.
   Maskell.com. Blog- *"Why lean performance measurements?"*.
   Maskell, B.H. (2009). *Making the numbers count: The accountant as change agent on the world class team*. Boca Raton, FL: CRC Press.
   Maskell, B.H., Baggaley, B. and Grasso, L. (2012). *Practical lean accounting: A proven system for measuring and managing the lean enterprise*. Boca Raton, FL: CRC Press.

Chapter 7

Value Stream Costing

The most dangerous kind of waste is the waste we do not recognize.

– Shigeo Shingo

Importance of Value Stream Costing in Better Decision-Making

If a customer wants to buy a 'true' US-made car in the United States, he or she will have to choose between Honda or Toyota because these companies manufacture and buy their parts only from within the United States. Ford and GM cars are manufactured using parts procured from overseas countries such as China and India. This is because Honda and Toyota adopted lean production system and lean accounting and understood how parts produced in-house are more economically viable with additional advantage of swift availability, just-in-time production and better quality control. Ford and GM use standard cost accounting that induces the decision to procure parts at lowest cost, even if it means buying from offshore countries. They are misled into believing they are procuring parts at low cost, but it is not so.

If a part is produced in-house, standard cost accounting companies meticulously calculate material costs, allocate production costs and overheads and then add a standard margin of profit set by the management to finalize price of the product. This approach is not recognized under lean cost accounting. Lean accounting companies calculate the cost of products based on value stream. The product price is calculated as a basket of products being manufactured by the value stream and not individually for each product. It takes

DOI: 10.4324/9781003221746-7

into account the material costs and incremental conversion costs, but the conversion costs shrink when productivity increases due to capacity released by reduction in non-value adding use of capacity. The overall cost of products decreases, and it becomes cheaper to produce in-house with the auxiliary benefit of quick availability and better quality. This is a major advantage that value stream cost accounting brings to the table.

Components of Cost in a Value Stream

All direct costs like labor, machine, materials, maintenance, support services and facilities incurred within a value stream construct the total cost of a value stream. Value adding and non-value adding costs from all functions, auxiliary and support services, as per current and future state map which pertains to a value stream, are included.

The cost of each material consumed by a value stream is assigned to the value stream when it enters the plant or when it is issued to the value stream. Manpower is allocated to the value streams and respective function. All costs are allocated to their respective function and the respective value stream. If any large equipment is shared, its manpower costs will be shared based on the time that it is used for by the value stream. Machine costs like maintenance, tooling, utilities and depreciation are divided as per the relevant machine for each value stream and function. Support like tooling and spare parts for machines are assigned to value stream as soon as they enter the plant. Facility and warehouse costs consisting of rent, interest, utilities, repair, maintenance and depreciation are allocated to the value streams based on their revenue. Square footage area is allocated with the prevailing rate to the value streams. All other supports costs of all functions are to be calculated and posted. Corporate overheads costs are allocated based on their sales revenues of each value stream. Average cost is used as a primary value stream performance measurement.

Don't introduce a complex tracking system in order to be precise. Keep it simple. During a lean journey, reporting is done for functions under each value stream and not by departments. Therefore, people in the company are assigned to functions in the value stream with little or no overlap. As far as possible, there should no shared resources within value streams. The costs of the large equipment are to be shared by value streams. Production processes in the value streams start coming under control with the implementation of a lean production system and daily management system and value stream costing shows the results financially.

Table 7.1 P&L Statement for Year Ending March 2018 for Perfect Gear Company in USD'000 for the Year Ending March 2018.

Description	Value stream I – hot rolling mill division	Value stream II – cold rolling mill division	Value stream III – gearbox division	New product develop- ment	Division P & L
Revenue	45000	21300	40000	0	106300
Material costs	21234	10967	17780	8166	58147
Conversion costs	7345	3543	6778	2876	20542
Value streams profits	16421	6790	15442		38653
Value stream ROS	36%	32%	39%		36%
Employee costs	6638	6638	6638		19915
Corporate expenses	3569	1100	3333		8002
Prior period inventory	6700	3422	5765		15887
Current inventory	8900	5000	6265		20165
Inventory change	−2200	−1578	−500		−4278
Division gross profit	8414	630	5971		15014
Division ROS	19%	3%	15%		14%

Let's use the example of Perfect Gear Company to outline the process of value stream costing. There might be some repetition from the previous chapters to understand the full context. Table 7.1 shows the value stream-wise P&L statement for the company. Value stream III – gearbox division is taken up for analysis in this book. Perfect Gear Company implemented the lean production system, daily management system rigorously and their lean journey was fruitful. They have also implemented lean accounting in the same road map.

The company's value stream III's annual turnover saw a steep rise of 50% and profits shot from 5% to 17% of sales. Table 7.2 summarizes financial numbers for March 2018 and March 2019 for the gearbox division.

The improvements in the operational and financial measures are a result of lean initiatives implemented across the value stream on the plant floor and consequently in the P&L statement. The capacity of each function and overall company is documented monthly. Finance employees are part of operational improvement teams, and they help them in achieving the targets. Hence, the line of action is clear.

These improvements happened due to implementation of lean produc-tion system and daily management along with clarity provided by lean

Table 7.2   Key Financial Results for Perfect Gear Company for Year 2018 and Year 2019 for the Gearbox Division (value stream III).

Key parameters	UOM	Current state March 2018	Future state March 2019
Average dispatch per day	Tons	40	58
Average monthly dispatch	Tons	1000	1500
Average sales price	USD per kg	3.33	3.67
Monthly dispatch	USD (in Mn)	3.33	5.50
Annual turnover	USD (in Mn)	40	66

accounting to each function in the value stream. They understood the concept of lean accounting and its importance in decision-making and came onboard when they started witnessing a new world of opportunities opened by surplus capacity that was made available by reduction in non-value adding use of capacity.

7.1 Value Stream Costing Process[1]

The journey of lean accounting was initiated in the month of March 2018 in Perfect Gear Company and value stream mapping for current state of the company as on 31 March 2018 was done. The lean accounting measures were recorded on a monthly basis and value stream mapping was again done for future state on 31 March 2019. Value stream costing is an 11-step process as follows:

Collect Operational Data for All Functions

Operational data like number of personnel, operators, fitters, total shifts, working hours, available time, downtime (due to breakdown, rework, changeover and waiting), cycle time of each machine and machine performance rates are collected for all functions and recorded in data boxes to prepare current state map. This is done for all direct functions in the value stream:

■ Raw material that goes through fabrication, stress relieving furnace shop, machine shop, gear cutting shop, heat treatment and gear grinding shop

- Work in progress material that reaches the assembly shop and is assembled, tested, cleared by quality assurance department and handed over to logistics for dispatch

Data are collected by the finance team along with the operations team and duly verified for its accuracy. The accuracy of the data is important because future course of action will be governed by these numbers.

Data Boxes for Support Functions

The data boxes are an integral part of the value stream map. Value stream map captures the flow of a product from receipt of customer order to delivery of final product and collection of money from the customer. For a large company, a value steam map can occupy a whole wall in the conference room due to the volume of operational information captured in one place. Data boxes are prepared for all operations as well as support functions like marketing, design, purchase, finance and accounts, maintenance, quality, information technology and HRD. They list down each activity performed by each function during the process of running the business. The time spent by machine and manpower, the downtime due to breakdown, scrap generation, rework, waiting for materials or waiting for inspection, changeover time and number of changeovers per shift or per day are recorded in the data boxes. A typical data box is shown in Table 7.3.

Current Manpower Costs

All employees of the company work in their functional areas in the value streams without any ambiguity. The functional managers are the custodians of their employees and they check and countersign the manpower list for their respective functions. The functional managers capture the responsibility, reporting, skill level, training requirements, skill up-gradation and performance level of each employee. The finance department, in coordination with HRD, prepares the salaries, wages, overtime, bonuses and cost to company for each employee. This will be checked and countersigned by the functional head because they are going to drive their resources to achieve the functional results and hence, should be aware of the manpower costs on monthly basis. These data are not used for manpower reduction in the function but to be fully conscious of manpower costs. Support functions are also mapped for number of employees, their pay structures and other parameters

Table 7.3 Typical Data Box for a Machine Shop.

Machine name – Machine shop	
Number of operators per shift per machine	1
Total employees other than operators	15
Total shifts	3
Total shift hours	8
5s and PM hours per shift	0.5
Available time (hours per day)	22.5
Average downtime:	
On each machine per day in hours	3.00
Due to scrap per day on each machine	0.50
Due to rework per day on each machine	1.00
Due to wait for materials, inspections, etc. per day	1.50
Cycle time (hours per ton)	1.75
Change over time (hours)	3.00
Number of changeover per day on each machine	3
Number of machines	15
Machine performance:	70%
Total machine available time (hours per day)	338
Net machine available time (hours per day)	113
Net flow rate (tons per day)	45
Number of working days in a month	26
Average monthly production in tons	1170
Running time during lunch and tea break of 30 minutes	0.5

as detailed in Table 7.4. It is important to include not only those people and processes that are directly in the flow but also all the processes that support the value stream.

Capture the Current Level of Inventory in All Functional Areas

Stock checking (stock taking) is undertaken in the entire company and all functional areas are covered to assess how much inventory they are carrying. Though this information is readily available in many companies where an elaborate ERP system is used, stock checking is still done manually again regularly at the beginning of each month. There can be variation between ERP and physical stock. One-time correction for stock in the ERP system can

Table 7.4 Manpower Costs for March 2018 for the Gearbox Division (Value Stream III) of Perfect Gear Company.

Value stream cost centers	Current state March 2018		
	Number of employees	Average salary (in USD)	Total manpower costs (in USD'000)
Corporate	21	5333	112
Marketing	23	2667	61
Design	50	933	47
Purchase, subcontracting and stores	50	933	47
Finance and accounts	31	933	29
Fabrication	46	667	31
Stress relieving shop	9	533	5
Machine shop and tool room.	60	667	40
Gear cutting shop	55	653	36
Heat treatment shop	29	667	19
Gear grinding shop	29	800	23
Maintenance function- Mechanical and electrical	42	600	25
Assembly and testing shop	50	667	33
Finished good supermarket and logistics	9	667	6
Quality assurance	25	667	17
Information technology system	17	800	14
HRD	15	600	9
Total	561		554

be made in consultation with management. It is possible to do stock taking every month by including the functional teams. Once the inventory level comes down, it becomes easier to take stock.

While stock checking, prepare a list of slow moving stock (stock that has not moved in the last three months) and non-moving or dead stock (stock that has not moved in the last six months) and separately maintain a machinery insurance spare list. Look in each nook and corner of the company, on the roof, inside all cabinets, operators and lockers, all hidden stores, material lying outside – under the grass or partially buried. Table 7.5 shows the total inventory costs for the month of March 2018 for the gearbox division (value stream III).

Table 7.5 Total Inventory Costs for March 2018 for the Gearbox Division (Value Stream III) of Perfect Gear Company.

Inventory status			
Particulars	*Current state*		
Average dispatch per day in tons	40		
Average monthly dispatch in tons	1000		
Average sales price (USD/kg)	0.00		
Monthly dispatch (USD Mn)	3.33		
Annual turnover (USD Mn)	40		
Category	*Current state*		
	RM cost USD/kg	*Weight (in tons)*	*Value (USD'000)*
Raw materials	0.67	2210	1473
Job work with suppliers	1.60	95	152
Stores	4.00	466	1864
WIP – fabrication	0.67	510	340
WIP – machine shop	1.60	147	235
WIP – gear shop	1.60	84	134
WIP – gear-grinding shop	1.60	100	160
Assembly shop	1.47	409	600
Finished goods	3.33	392	1307
Total inventory		4413	6265

Material Used and Its Cost in a Month

Material cost for each item is the direct cost from the invoices. This information is available in the ERP system. The company has to decide which method of costing it wants to follow from among the four options available as per the GAAP – weighted average method, FIFO, LIFO or actual cost by tracking individual items. Once selected, it has to consistently followed each year.

Calculate the Functions-Wise Current Conversion Costs

This is a very important milestone. The material, manpower, plant floor costs, consumables and so forth of all functions are calculated and updated every month. Function-wise conversion costs for the month of March 2018 for the gearbox division (value stream III) is appended in Table 7.6. This is

Table 7.6   Function-Wise Conversion Costs for the Gearbox Division (Value Stream III) of Perfect Gear Company in USD'000 for March 2018.

Value streams	Material costs	Employee costs	Outside process costs	Fabrication costs	Stress relieving costs	Machining costs	Other consumables and tooling costs	Other corporate misc expenses	Total costs
Corporate	-	112	-	-	-	-	-	278	390
Marketing	-	61	-	-	-	-	-	-	61
Design	-	47	-	-	-	-	-	-	47
Purchase, subcontracting and stores	-	47	-	-	-	-	-	-	47
Finance and accounts	-	29	-	-	-	-	-	-	29
Fabrication	200	31	-	79	-	-	4	-	314
Stress relieving department	30	5	-	-	13	-	-	-	48
Machine shop and tool room	864	40	052	-	-	99	9	-	1064
Gear cutting shop	-	36	-	-	-	073	9	-	118
Heat treatment shop	-	19	77	-	-	-	-	-	96
Gear grinding shop	-	23	-	-	-	83	13	-	119
Maintenance function – mechanical and electrical	-	25	-	-	-	-	37	-	62
Assembly, testing and rework shop	346	33	-	9	-	5	2	-	395
Logistics and dispatch	-	6	-	-	-	-	-	-	6
Quality assurance	-	17	-	-	-	-	-	-	17
Information system	-	14	-	-	-	-	-	-	14
HRD	-	9	-	-	-	-	-	-	9
Total	1440	554	129	88	13	260	74	278	2836
Average material costs USD/kg	1.44								
Average manpower costs USD/kg	0.55								
Average conversion costs USD/kg	0.84								

done by the finance team with the help of functional managers under the leadership of the value stream manager. ERP helps in collection of data, but the data are checked for accuracy. This regular exercise enables functional managers to understand the cost of their function and remember it on their fingertips.

Prepare Current Value Stream Map

This map lays out the manufacturing process on the shop floor. It shows how the material moves from left to right, from raw material stores through the plant to the finished good supermarket, ready for dispatch. The value stream map helps to draw the operations details on paper to identify value adding time that the client is paying for and non-value adding time that the company uses for manufacturing the products, but the customers do not pay for. A value stream map also shows the throughput time, which is the time gap between the raw material coming into the plant till it goes out as finished product and is dispatched to the customer. The less the throughput time, the better will be the earnings for the company. The whole lean and kaizen exercise is just to reduce this throughput time.

When the current value stream mapping (see Figure 7.1) is done, it reveals the opportunities for improvements available in the current setup to guide the improvement projects in order to reach the desired future state.

Current Value-Adding Ratio and Current Throughput Time

As discussed in the previous chapter, the longer route is always taken up for calculations of throughput time. In the following example found in Figure 7.2, value adding time is 9.1 hours and non-value adding and value adding time together are 2523.9 hours. This is throughput time. The value adding ratio is 0.4%. It is very poor. It indicates the plant is being run inefficiently.

Current Average Product Family Cost of the Value Stream

Table 7.6 shows the total costs derived from the individual functional costs. The total cost is $2,835,870 and dispatch for the month of March 2018 is

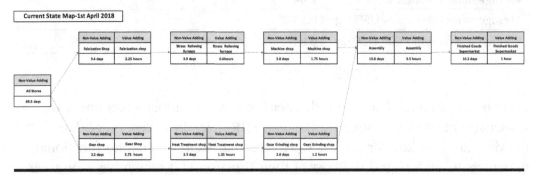

Figure 7.1   Current State Map and Value Adding Ratio.

Flow route from stores to fabrication shop to stress relieving to machine shop to assembly shop and finished good supermarket is a longer route. Hence, calculation the value adding and non-value adding hours is done for this route only.

Top route value adding hours = 2.25 + 0.6 + 1.75 +3.5 + 1 = 9.1 hours

Top route non-value adding hours = (69.5 + 9.4 + 3.9 +3.8 +10.6 + 10.2) × 23.5 = 2523.9 hours

Value adding ratio = Value adding hours/(Value adding + Non-value adding hours) = 9.1 / (9.1 + 2523.9) = 0.4%

Throughput time is sum of value adding and non-value adding hours (i.e., 2533 hours which is the time taken for raw materials to dispatch from the company as finished goods)

The raw material takes 2533 / 23.5 = 108 days to dispatch. The lower the throughput time, the better for the company.

Figure 7.2   Value Adding Ratio and Throughput Time.

1000 tons. The average product cost for the value stream is $2.84 per kg. The average product cost can be broken down into average material cost – $1.44 per kg, average manpower costs – $0.55 per kg and average conversion costs – $0.84 per kg.

Identify the Primary Bottleneck Machine or Machines that Become the Pacemaker for the Company

The bottleneck cell is the one that has lowest production capabilities. This is the process that determines the output of the value stream. Lean and kaizen activities are first focused on this process. All improvement projects focus on these areas to get positive results. There can be more than one process where cycle time is largest or approximately the same. In the current value stream map, the bottleneck operation with the least production capacity and largest cycle time is gear shop (3.75 hours per ton) as shown in Figure 7.1.

Prepare Current Profit and Loss Statement for the Value Stream

It is important to understand the profit and loss statement as per lean accounting. It should be prepared in the given format only so that value stream managers can drive the P&L statement and all other functional managers understand it. The P&L statement for the year ending March 2018 is shown in Table 7.7.

Table 7.7   P &L Statement for Perfect Gear Company in USD'000 for the Year Ending March 2018.

Key parameters	Current state March 2018		
	Annual P&L	Monthly average	% of sales
Monthly quantity dispatched	1000 tons		
Sales price	$3.33 per kg		
Sales revenue	40000	3333	
Material cost	17280	1440	43.2%
Contribution 1 (A)	22720	1893	56.8%
Total variable expenses (B)	6778	565	16.9%
Consumables and stores	1093	91	
Oil and lubricants	208	17	
Inserts	160	13	
Accessories	80	7	
Grinding wheels	88	7	
Cutting oil	120	10	
Tool cutter	101	8	
Gas	53	4	
Paints	82	7	
Grease	27	2	
Others	480	40	
Power and fuels	2019	168	
Job works	1547	129	
Other plant misc. expenses	720	60	
Contribution 2 (C) = (A-B)	15942	1329	39.9%
Total fixed expenses (D)	9971	831	24.9%
Wages – workers	1893	158	
Wages – fabrication	373	31	
Overtime	773	64	
Salary – executives	3600	300	
Other corporate overheads	3333	278	
Net profits-EBITDA (E) = (C-D)	5971	498	14.9%
Depreciation and amortization	2107	176	
EBIT	3864	322	9.7%
Bank interest	933	78	
Interest on term loans	907	76	
Net earnings before tax (EBT)	2024	169	5.1%

7.2 The Start of the Lean and Kaizen Journey

Once the company successfully assesses its current status the top management should take the services of a lean sensei, (lean production system expert) to assist the functional teams in the lean and kaizen improvement journey as per the road map for future state for which operational teething issues are to be addressed, non-value adding activities are to be reduced and more free capacity is to be created which is to be used to increase the throughput to bring in more productivity, more production, increased revenues and earnings. There will be increase in value adding ratio and throughput time will reduce once lean tools are implemented.

Tentative lean and kaizen implementation road map was created in three phases to achieve future state map that was possible in next two years. The opportunities to be realized function-wise are finalized. This methodology is discussed in detail in Chapter 18.

Value stream cost analysis exercise is done for each function to compute the numbers of hours that can be liberated for both employees and machines during the lean and kaizen journey. The current state value stream map was created in the month of March 2018. The value stream map is again prepared for the month of March 2019. The calculation procedure for each function is explained in detail in the next chapter.

Future State Value Stream Costing

The improvements in the operational and financial measures during the 12-month period of the lean and kaizen journey are consolidated. Each step for the current state is now recorded for future state as on 31 March 2019.

Collect Operational Data for All Functions

Update Data Boxes for Support Functions

Current Manpower Costs

Function-wise salary and wages are updated at the end of March 2019 as per Table 7.8.

Capture the Current Levels of Inventory in All Functional Areas

Capture the level of inventory in raw material stores and main stores, WIP and finished goods at the end of March 2019. It is consolidated in Table 7.9.

Table 7.8 Manpower Costs for Future State for March 2019 of the Gearbox Division (Value Stream III) of Perfect Gear Company.

Value stream cost centers	Current state March 2018			Future state March 2019		
	Number of employees	Average salary in US$	Total manpower costs (in USD'000)	Number of employees	Average salary (10% increase)	Total manpower costs (in USD'000)
Corporate	21	5333	112	21	4140	87
Marketing	23	2667	61	17	2933	50
Design	50	933	47	42	1027	43
Purchase, subcontracting and stores	50	933	47	44	1027	45
Finance and accounts	31	933	29	25	1027	26
Fabrication	46	667	31	42	733	31
Stress relieving shop	9	533	5	9	587	5
Machine shop and tool room	60	667	40	60	733	44
Gear cutting shop	55	653	36	52	719	37
Heat treatment shop	29	667	19	27	733	20
Gear grinding shop	29	800	23	28	880	25
Maintenance function – mechanical and electrical	42	600	25	38	660	25
Assembly and testing shop	50	667	33	50	733	37
Finished good supermarket and logistics	9	667	6	9	733	7
Quality assurance	25	667	17	22	733	16
Information technology system	17	800	14	12	880	11
HRD	15		9	10	660	7
Total	561		554	508		516

Table 7.9 Total Inventory Costs as of End of March 2019 for Perfect Gear Company.

Inventory status		
Particulars	Current state	Future state
Average dispatch per day in tons	40	58
Average monthly dispatch in tons	1000	1500
Average sales price (USD/kg)	0.00	0.00
Monthly dispatch (USD Mn)	3.33	0.00
Annual turnover (USD Mn)	40	66

Category	Current state			Future state		
	RM cost USD/kg	Weight (in tons)	Value (USD'000)	RM cost USD/ kg (5% increase)	Weight (in tons)	Value (USD'000)
Raw materials	0.67	2210	1473	0.70	750	525
Job work with suppliers	1.60	95	152	1.68	100	168
Stores	4.00	466	1864	4.20	200	840
WIP – fabrication	0.67	510	340	0.70	200	140
WIP – machine shop	1.60	147	235	1.68	100	168
WIP – gear shop	1.60	84	134	1.68	50	84
WIP – gear-grinding shop	1.60	100	160	1.68	50	84
Assembly shop	1.47	409	600	1.54	200	308
Finished goods	3.33	392	1307	3.50	75	263
Total inventory		4413	6265		1725	2580

Material Costs Used in a Month – It Is Consolidated in Table 7.9.

Calculate the Functions-Wise Current Conversion Costs

This is a very important milestone. The costs –materials, manpower, plant floor costs, consumables and so forth – of all functions are calculated to the last dollar as per Table 7.10. This has to be updated every month by finance

Table 7.10   Function-Wise Conversion Costs.

Value streams	Material costs	Employee costs	Outside process costs	Fabrication costs	Stress relieving costs	Machining costs	Other consumables and tooling costs	Other corporate misc expenses	Total costs
Functional costs in the value stream per month (in USD'000) Future state as of March 2019 (Dispatch per month – 1500 tons)									
Corporate	-	100	-	-	-	-	-	253	353
Marketing	-	50	-	-	-	-	-	-	50
Design	-	43	-	-	-	-	-	-	43
Purchase, subcontracting and stores	-	40	-	-	-	-	-	-	40
Finance and accounts	-	26	-	-	-	-	-	-	26
Fabrication	360	31	-	118	-	-	5	-	514
Stress relieving department	59	5	-	-	19	-	-	-	83
Machine shop and tool room	1587	40	80	-	-	134	013	-	1853
Gear cutting shop	-	37	-	-	-	103	13	-	154
Heat treatment shop	-	20	119	-	-	-	-	-	138
Gear grinding shop	-	25	-	-	-	117	19	-	161
Maintenance function – mechanical and electrical	-	23	-	-	-	-	52	-	75
Assembly and testing and rework shop	595	37	-	13	-	10	2	-	657
Logistics and dispatch	-	7	-	-	-	-	-	-	7
Quality assurance	-	14	-	-	-	-	-	-	14
Information system	-	11	-	-	-	-	-	-	11
HRD	-	7	-	-	-	-	-	-	7
Total	2601	516	199	131	19	364	104	253	4186
Average material costs USD/kg	1.73								
Average manpower costs USD/kg	0.34								
Average conversion costs USD/kg	0.71								
Average total costs USD/kg	2.79								

with the help of functional managers under the leadership of value stream manager. ERP helps in the collection of data.

This regular monthly exercise of calculating the costs makes the functional managers well acquainted with their function's costs. In the future state, these individual costs are now at the functional manager's fingertips. It now becomes easier to control and monitor as any cost increase is quickly seen and analyzed for taking corrective action.

Prepare the Value Stream Map for March 2019

Future state value stream map of the Perfect Gear Company is prepared at the end of March 2019. The future value stream map is shown in Figure 7.3.

Value Adding Ratio and Current Throughput Time as of March 2019

In the month of March 2018 the throughput time was 2523.9 hours. Now, the value adding time is 9.1 hours and the sum of non-value adding and value adding time added together is 674.45 hours as shown in Figure 7.4. There is a reduction in non-value adding time to the extent of 1850 hours. This means the company has reduced wasteful activities by 79 days (108 days – 29 days) in a 12-month lean and kaizen journey. This leads to huge savings. The value adding ratio improved to 1.3% from 0.4% by the end of March 2019. The operations and financial measures have improved. It indicates that the plant is successful in its lean journey and on path to become the least cost producer.

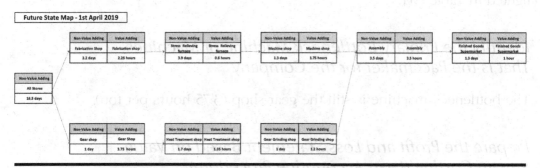

Figure 7.3 Value Stream Map and Value Adding Ratio for Year Ending March 2019.

Flow route from stores to fabrication shop to stress relieving to machine shop to assembly shop and finished good supermarket is a longer route. Hence, calculation of the value adding and non-value adding hours is done for this route only.
Top route value adding hours = 2.25 + 0.6 + 1.75 + 3.5 + 1 = 9.1 hours
Top route non–value adding hours = (16.5 + 2.2 + 3.9 + 1.3 + 3.5 + 1.3) × 23.5 = 674.45 hours
Value adding ratio = value adding hours/(value adding + non-value adding hours) = 9.1 / (9.1 + 674.45) = 1.3%
Throughput time is sum of value adding and non-value adding hours (i.e., 683.5 hours which is the time taken for raw materials to dispatch from the company as finished goods)
The raw material takes 683.5 / 23.5 = 29 days to dispatch. The lower the throughput time, the better for the company.

Figure 7.4   Value Adding Ratio and Throughput Time for the Month of March 2019.

Average Product Family Cost of the Value Stream

Table 7.10 shows the total cost derived from individual functional cost. The total costs are $4,183,840 and dispatch for the month of March 2018 is 1500 tons. So the average product cost for the value stream is $2.79 per kg. The breakdown of the average product cost is average material costs – $1.73 per kg, average manpower costs $0.34 per kg and average conversion costs as $0.71 per kg. The average product costs cost decreased by $0.05 per kg despite an increase in the raw material cost. The dispatches have increased from 1000 tons per month to 1500 tons per month in the span of 12 months. The average product sales price is $3.67 per kg, up from $3.33 per kg.

Improvements in operational and financial parameters for Perfect Gear Company in the 12-month journey from March 2018 to March 2019 are highlighted in Table 7.11.

Identify the Primary Bottleneck Machine or Machines That Is the Pacemaker for the Company

The bottleneck machine is still the gear shop (3.75 hours per ton).

Prepare the Profit and Loss Statement Based on Value Stream Costing (Lean Accounting Procedure)

It is very important to understand how lean accounting makes the P&L statement and why it should be done this way. Value stream managers and

Table 7.11 Improvement in Operational and Financial Parameters in the 12-Month Lean Journey for Perfect Gear Company.

Key parameters	UOM	Current state March 2018	Future state March 2019	Improvements in one year
Average material costs	USD per kg	1.44	1.73	Please note: a 20% increase in raw material costs has taken place as of March2019
Average manpower costs	USD per kg	0.55	0.34	40% drop in manpower costs
Average conversion costs	USD per kg	0.84	0.71	16% drop in conversion costs
Average total costs	USD per kg	2.84	2.79	2% drop in average costs despite 20% increase in raw material costs
Average sales price	USD per kg	3.33	3.67	10% increase in sales price
Average dispatch per day	Tons	40	58	1.5 times
Average monthly dispatch	Tons	1000	1500	1.5 times
Annual turnover	USD (in Mn)	40	66	65% increase
Annual net profit	%	5.10%	17.10%	3.35 times

functional managers should be able to see the financial outcome of their operational efforts in their value stream in the P&L statement clearly. This is the core of lean accounting. The following process is beneficial for functional managers to understand the events of the month and subsequent profit earned.

Finance prepares an internal P&L statement that shows the financial performance of the month with sales value of the products that have been 'manufactured' that month and 'materials used for this production'. The actual variable costs and fixed costs expenditures will be used. This P&L statement will be called 'Value Stream P&L Statement'.

Finance will simultaneously prepare a second P&L statement with sales value of dispatched products and material bought that month and that takes account of changes in the inventories. Values for variable cost, fixed costs, depreciation and interests remain the same in both the P&L statements. The difference between the first P&L statement and the second P&L statement is in the aforementioned three values only.

The top management and the CFO of the company should be convinced about this methodology. With a few clicks on computer, the *'internal P&L statement'* can be converted to *'external P&L statement'*. Both statements reflect the *'true financial state'* of operations of the plant for the month. The ERP system is profoundly helpful in this.

The second P&L statement will meet the guidelines of (GAAP) for statutory and regulatory reporting. Please refer to Chapter 5 for more details on how the lean accounting complies with all the requirements of GAAP.

Contribution 1 is the difference between sales value of the month's production and cost of material used in this production. Contribution 2 is derived by reducing actual variable costs incurred that month from contribution 1. If fixed costs, including corporate office expenses, are reduced from contribution 2, EBITDA (Earnings Before interest, Taxation, Depreciation and Amortization) is derived and deduct depreciation for the month to derive EBIT (Earnings Before Interest and Taxation) and interest (short term and long term) to derive EBT (Earnings Before Tax) or PBT (Profit Before Tax).

This exercise is done for all value streams individually and added up to obtain the company's P&L statement. If the company's product profile falls in one value stream, this statement is sufficient, but if the company has several product families that can be divided into value streams, then division can be done whenever the company is ready. If the company has several plants with different family of products or value stream, it can be added up following the same sequence. This will be the P&L statement for the group.

The P&L statements can be made quickly in a day or so after the month is over. The simplified contribution and P&L statements are understandable to all functional managers. In the internal value stream P&L statement, when the production is high, the profit will be higher. If the production is less due to material availability, breakdowns, performance issues or quality issues, everyone will see the repercussions in lower profits. If the product mix is favorable, the profits will be higher or vice versa. Operations managers will be able to correlate this with the month's performance easily.

The external P&L statement is the responsibility of finance to bring the profit number in line with the GAAP reporting requirements.

This will give tremendous boost to the pace of improvements in the company and bring the desired upswing in business results.

Improvements in Operations After a Lean and Kaizen Journey

Table 7.11 shows the improvement in the cost structure in 12 months.

The financial improvements are the consequences of operational improvements across functions in the last 12 months. The net profit (EBIDTA) was 14.9% and net earnings before tax (EBT) was 5% as of end of March 2018. The net profit (EBIDTA) improved to 23.9% and net earnings before tax (EBT) to 17.1% by end of March end 2019. See Table 7.12.

There is a 9% improvement in net (EBIDTA) and 12.1% improvement in net earnings before tax (EBT).

At this stage, the operations managers along with the finance and account managers become well aware of the internal costs as well as the requirements of the customers. These improvement initiatives are now built into the company culture through revisions of the SOPs across the functions and regular trainings for sustenance. The company is now capable of providing more value added services to the customers.

7.3 What Is "Value Stream Costing" Used For?

Value stream costing helps in making the value stream P&L statement on monthly basis, to start with. Once the working is understood by functional managers and first line of supervisors, then the company can move on to formulating it on weekly basis. The company will be more vigilant now. If the company generates reports 12 times a year, it will have the opportunity to take corrective action 12 times, or if the reports can be generated every week, the opportunity increases to 52 times a year. Based on the monthly and weekly P&L statement, the corporate scorecard is created on a monthly or weekly basis and the company implements the performance measurement system for all managers, executives, supervisors and workmen.

In a typical P&L statement the material, labor and machine costs add up to approximately 80%. That means the company should concentrate carefully on these three costs for root cause analysis to find the wastes. Average value stream cost per product can be calculated and this value can be used for making decisions on pricing of the current products, outsourcing, new product pricing and so forth.

7.4 Advantages of Value Stream Costing

The value stream P&L statement and cost reports are created in real time in a simple, meaningful and candid format. Profitability is driven by creating

Table 7.12 P &L Statement for Perfect Gear Company in USD'000 for Year Ending 2018 and 2019.

Key parameters	Current state March 2018			Future state March 2019		
	Annual P&L	Monthly average	% of sales	Annual P&L	Monthly average	% of sales
Monthly quantity dispatched	1000 tons			1500 tons		
Sales price	$3.33 per kg			$3.67 per kg		
Sales revenue	40000	3333		66000	5500	
Material cost	17280	1440	43.2%	31200	2600	47.3%
Contribution 1 (A)	22720	1893	56.8%	34800	2900	52.7%
Total variable expenses (B)	6778	565	16.9%	9794	816	14.8%
Consumables and stores	1093	91		1640	137	
Oil and lubricants	208	17		312	26	
Inserts	160	13		240	20	
Accessories	80	7		64	5	
Grinding wheels	88	7		144	12	
Cutting oil	120	10		208	17	
Tool cutter	101	8		144	12	
Gas	53	4		80	7	
Paints	82	7		122	10	
Grease	27	2		56	5	
Others	480	40		800	67	
Power and fuels	2019	168		3040	253	
Job works	1547	129		2384	199	
Other plant misc. expenses	720	60		560	47	
Contribution 2 (C) = (A-B)	15942	1329	39.9%	25006	2084	37.9%
Total fixed expenses (D)	9971	831	24.9%	9213	768	14.0%
Wages – workers	1893	158		2240	187	
Wages – fabrication	373	31		312	26	
Overtime	773	64		736	61	
Salary – executives	3600	300		2885	240	
Other corporate overheads	3333	278		3040	253	
Net profits-EBITDA (E) = (C-D)	5971	498	14.9%	15794	1316	23.9%
Depreciation and amortization	2107	176		2400	200	
EBIT	3864	322	9.7%	13394	1116	20.3%
Bank interest	933	78		960	80	
Interest on term loans	907	76		1120	93	
Net earnings before tax (EBT)	2024	169	5.1%	11314	943	17.1%

maximum flow of product through the value stream at the pull of the customer. The cost of any particular product depends primarily on how quickly it flows through the value stream, mainly through the bottleneck operations within the value stream. Rate of flow through the value stream is more important than utilization of machines and resources, efficiency of individuals or overhead allocation. Maximum flow is possible only if non-value adding activities reduce. It means the waste in the value stream like breakdown, excess scrap generation, rework, poor quality, excessive changeover times and slow speeds are reduced. The cost of the product varies according to volume and product mix because overheads costs are allocated to the value stream as a whole and not as per labor time. Revenue is directly proportional to volume of products dispatched. With the value stream costs under control, the profits from the value stream rise faster than the revenue. This is what is portrayed in the example of Perfect Gear Company in Table 7.11 and Table 7.12.

Value stream costing provides easy-to-calculate value stream performance measurement parameters. These enable long-term improvements and focus attention on value stream issues, challenges and opportunities. Value stream costing helps value stream managers to take responsibility of financial performance of the value stream. It brings in accountability, teamwork and ownership. It highlights unnecessary transactions in the value stream system and helps the value stream manager understand that all costs are fixed in the short term but variable in the long term.

When value stream costing is done across the company, it highlights which plant or value stream is profitable and which plant or value stream is subsidizing other plants and value streams. If this exercise is done for all products too, the company can determine which products are unprofitable or are being subsidized by other products. Value stream costing provides meaningful information that adds value to lean improvement initiatives being implemented so that corrective actions can be taken in real time. One can imagine how much would one enjoy their job if the data provide relevant information to help them overcome obstacles and create a smooth flow that allows more time to enhance quality of their work.

The finance team partners with production, design, R&D, quality, purchase and marketing functions to fillip the growth of the company. Value stream costing displays a true picture of costs to help managers make decisions on product part pricing, new product profitability, capital investment and target pricing. It helps in computing cost of the product that varies according to volume and product mix since overhead costs are allocated to the value stream as a whole and not as per labor time to the products. It is not necessary to know the cost of the individual products to make decisions. Pricing decisions for a lean organization are never made with reference to the cost of a product. Market decides the price. The company can command the premium only if it is delivering more value to the customer because it is the value to the customer that determines the price. Is the company making a profit on this product if it is sold at this price? The right approach is to look at the potential order and work out its impact on the value stream profitability.

When companies produce more products in the same value streams, then the company spends extra on material costs with a little increase in variable cost because machine depreciation, fixed costs, overheads and facilities is already borne by the quantities already being produced. Material, some variable cost and maybe overtime would be the only incremental expenditure. The product cost varies at various levels of production and value stream costing brings about this clarity.

Key Takeaways

1. Lean accounting companies calculate the cost of products based on value stream. The product price is calculated as a basket of products being manufactured by the value stream and not individually for each product.
2. Don't introduce a complex tracking system in order to be precise. Keep it simple.
3. All employees of the company work in their functional areas in the value streams without any ambiguity. The functional managers are the custodians of their employees.
4. It is possible to do stock taking every month by including the functional teams in this exercise. Once the inventory level comes down, it becomes easier to do stock taking without the need to stop the production.
5. The less the throughput time, the better will be the earnings for the company. The whole lean and kaizen exercise is just to reduce this throughput time.
6. The bottleneck cell is the one that has lowest production capabilities. This is the process that determines the output of the value stream. Lean and kaizen activities are first focused on this process to get positive results.
7. The regular monthly exercise of calculating the costs for all functions of each value stream – materials, manpower, plant floor costs, consumables and so forth – are done to the last dollar under value stream costing. These costs are now at the functional manager's fingertips. It now becomes easier to control and monitor as any cost increase is quickly seen and analyzed for taking corrective action.

8. *Value stream costing* brings clarity about product cost and how it reduces with increased levels of production.
9. With the value stream costs under control, the profits from the value stream rise faster than the revenue.
10. Value stream managers and functional managers should be able to see the financial outcome of their operational efforts in their value stream in the *Value Stream P&L Statement. This is the core of lean accounting.*

Recommended List for Further Reading

1. **Value Stream Costing**
   Bill Waddel.pdf – (2009). *"The obstacle to lean accounting"*.
   Bill Waddel.pdf – (2010). *"The advancement of lean accounting"*.
   Cunningham, J.E. (2017). *Real numbers: Management accounting in a lean organization.* Evanston, IL: JCC Press.
   Maskell.com. Blog- *"The fundamentals of value stream costing"*.
   Maskell.com. Blog- *"Untangling complexity with lean accounting by Eldad Coppens"*.
   Maskell, B.H. (2009). *Making the numbers count: The accountant as change agent on the world class team.* Boca Raton, FL: CRC Press.
   Maskell, B.H., Baggaley, B. and Grasso, L. (2012). *Practical lean accounting: A proven system for measuring and managing the lean enterprise.* Boca Raton, FL: CRC Press.
   Maskell, B.H., Baggaley, B., Katko, N. and Pruno, D. (2007). *The lean business management system. Lean accounting: Principles & practice toolkit.* Cherry Hill, NJ: BMA Press.
   Stenzel, J. (2007). *Lean accounting: Best practices for sustainable integration.* Hoboken, NJ: John Wiley & Sons.

Chapter 8

Plant Capacity Assessment

> *The essential question is not, "How busy are you?' but 'What are you busy at?'*
>
> **– Oprah Winfrey**

8.1 What Is Capacity?

Capacity may be defined as an internal benchmark for maximum production possible of a particular product in a plant. The capacity of a plant is the production allowed by a company's functional capabilities. In standard costing, a company measures utilization of manpower, machines and overheads absorption to assess the capacity available and utilized. However, this methodology prompts the company to produce more for better utilization of manpower and machine and absorption of overheads, which results in unsold inventories, stockouts and dissatisfied customers.

Lean looks at the capacity from the customer's perspective, that is, whether the capacity is used for value adding or non-value adding activities. If the company's use of capacity for non-value adding activities decreases, then the capacity increases. Lean focuses not only on cost cutting exercise but also on releasing the capacity from non-value adding activities. With this surplus capacity, the company can produce more products to generate additional revenue and profits. In doing so, revenue increases faster than the costs without investment in additional resources. However, the missing link

DOI: 10.4324/9781003221746-8

between lean operational improvements and visible financial improvements is data about capacity of a value stream.

There are two types of capacities in a company – manpower capacity and machine capacity. In a lean company, machine and manpower utilization measures are not encouraged since they are calculated and allocated based on assumptions. Lean promotes factual data based on value stream mapping and actual cycle time. Hence, to derive the true capacity, the current value stream map of the plant with accurate information in data boxes and an established system for observation of shop floor by operation and finance teams should be in place.

The maximum reiterative cycle time is taken as the production rate of the machine. The machine with longest cycle time (in minutes or hours per unit) is the bottleneck machine that is the key factor that determines the output of a value stream. This is called the 'pacemaker' process. The faster machine piles up material behind this bottleneck machine, but the faster machine will not have material piled behind it.

Traditional companies run their material resource planning (MRP) software with the capacity resources planning (CRP) software. Capacities of resources are captured in ERP under standard costing to generate the production plan that is used for procurement and resource planning. At the month end, higher production, higher manpower efficiency and better machine utilization than the standard reflect a good performance and profitability. Lower production, efficiency and utilization reflect poor performance and lower profits. Lean accounting disapproves it.

Lean accounting expels the use of efficiency of manpower and utilization of machines in the company. It uses real-time parameters to manage the processes.

8.2 Plant Capacity Assessment[1]

To assess capacity of a plant, start recording the activities of the two resources in a plant – machines and manpower – in all the functions during a day and analyze and bifurcate the activities into value adding and non-value adding activities.

Value Adding Capacity Usage

The activities that transform raw materials into finished products are value adding activities because this is what the customer actually pays for. The machine and manpower used for these activities is value adding capacity usage. If the company is reworking on a product for a second or third time, then it becomes non-value adding use of capacity.

Non-Value Adding Capacity Usage

The primary cause of low productivity is that wasteful activities consume too many resources. The hours spent on all activities which slow down or halt processes like breakdown, minor or major stoppages, scrapping, reworking, waiting for material, decisions, changeover times, poor performance rate and so forth constitute non-value adding use of capacity because customers do not pay for these activities. Time utilized in support functions and activities like assembly, quality, logistics, purchase, design, marketing, HRD, IT and maintenance functions that are required to run the company are also part of non-value adding capacity usage, but these activities are essential because they prevent delay in delivery and quality complaints.

Total Capacity

It is the '*total time available for production or service*' during the month for machine and manpower. Roughly, one shift plant runs for 7.5 hours (30 minutes break for lunch and tea), which means 22.5 hours in a day for three shifts.

Available or Free Capacity

It is the difference between total time available and sum of value adding and non-value adding capacity usage (d = c − a − b). This available free time can be easily utilized for increasing the production and more time can be made available if the non-value adding use of capacity is reduced through implementation of lean and kaizen tools.

What Is a Target Benchmark?

In a lean company, there are no industry or external benchmarks to be achieved in future. The company learns itself where it stands currently with its unique product lines, machines and manpower skillset. Accordingly, it identifies the target benchmark it aspires to achieve in the future.

How to Calculate Capacity

Let us use an example of a value stream that has only an assembly cell and calculate total capacity, productive capacity and non-productive capacity in the assembly cell to assess free and available capacity.

An assembly cell assembles 45,000 pieces in a month. Currently, the total productive capacity used is 42%. Unproductive capacity is 41% and available surplus capacity is 17%.

Manpower and Machine Capacity Calculation

Key parameters for capacity for current and future state map are given in Table 8.1 and Table 8.2.

- *Total Manpower Available Time* = (Number of shifts × Shift duration) − Preventive maintenance per shift
- *Average Downtime* is the sum of:
  - *Scrap and Rework Time (in hours)* = (Quantity produced in a month × [scrap % + rework %] × Cycle time
  - *Downtime (in hours)* = Downtime % × Total manpower available time
  - *Inspection Time (in hours)* = Total quantity produced in a month × Inspection % × Inspection time (in hours)
- *Changeover Time* = (Quantity per month/Average batch size) × Change over time
- *Total Machine Available Time* = ([Number of operators in each shift × Number of machines] + Number of other employees) × Total manpower available time
- *Net Machine Available Time* = Total machine available time − (Average downtime + [Changeover time × Number of changeover days on each machine]) × Number of machines × Number of operators
- *Net Flow Rate* = (Net machine available time × Assembly performance %)/Cycle time (hours per ton)
- *Average Monthly Dispatch* = Net flow rate × Number of days in a month
- *Manpower Value Adding Capacity Usage (Hours)* = Cycle time × Number of units produced in a month
- *Manpower Non-Value Adding Capacity or Manpower Unproductive Capacity Usage (in hours)* = Changeover time + Average downtime + 5S + Meeting time + Desk time for reporting

Table 8.1   Assembly Cell Capacity Assessment.

Number of fitters per shift per station	4	4	
Total employees other than operators	5	5	
Total shifts	2	2	
Total shift hours	8	8	
PM hours per shift	0.5	0.5	
Available time (hours per day)	15.0	15.0	
Average downtime	2.5	1.25	
On each workstation per day in hours	0.00	0.00	
Due to scrap per day on each workstation	0.00	0.00	
Due to rework per day on each workstation	0.50	0.25	Rework reduced from 30 minutes to 15 minutes
Due to wait for materials, inspections, etc. per day on each workstation	2.00	1.00	Wait for material, inspection, etc. reduced from two hours to one hour
Cycle time (hours per ton)	3.50	3.50	
Changeover time (hours per changeover)	0.50	0.25	Changeover time reduced from 30 minutes to 15 minutes
Number of change per days on each workstation	1.0	1.0	
Number of assembly workstation	5	5	
Assembly performance	60%	85%	Assembly performance improved to 85% from 60%
Total manpower available time (hours per day)	375	375	
Net manpower available time (hours per day)	315	360	
Net flow rate (tons per day)	54	87	
Number of working days in a month	26	26	
Average monthly capacity in tons	1404	2273	Assembly capability per month increased from 1404 tons to 2273 tons"

- *Manpower Productive Capacity* = Manpower value adding capacity usage + time spent on focused improvement
- *Manpower Productive Capacity Usage %* = Manpower productive capacity/Total available manpower time × 100
- *Manpower Unproductive Capacity Usage %* = Manpower non-value adding capacity usage/Total available manpower time × 100
- *Available Surplus Capacity %* = 100% – Manpower unproductive capacity usage % – Manpower productive capacity usage %

In the *first stage of improvement (future state I)*, the assembly line team implemented improvement projects for *changeover time reduction by using single-minute exchange of dies (SMED)* and successfully reduced the changeover time to three hours.

The team dwindled downtime, scrap and rework rate. After the team deployed improvement project in the assembly line, manpower non-productive capacity reduced to 26% and surplus capacity available increased to 32%, which can be utilized for additional production. Additional revenue and profits can be generated from the same infrastructure without any additional investment in machinery or manpower. Marketing needs to source new orders and next phase of improvement can be planned.

In the *next stage of improvement (future state II)*, productive, non-productive and available time changed after the team brought further improvement in the assembly line. Sales and marketing are required to bring more orders and assembly line executes these orders. Expansion in the productive capacity from 42% to 54% is evident in increase in production by 30% as more components are assembled in a month. Non-productive capacity remains more or less the same as these are indispensable activities which necessary for conducting business.

In the *last stage of improvement (future state III)*, there is more focus on operational improvement. The teams continue with the lean and kaizen initiatives and further reduce changeover time, downtime, scrap and rework rate. Unproductive capacity declines, making surplus capacity available. The teams can plan for increase in sales of current product portfolio or bring in new products. This will boost both the top and bottom line. These results are achieved without additional investment or hiring of new personnel.

These simple calculations mentioned in Table 8.2 for an automobile assembly showcases how well the teams can start understanding the production processes and become aware of the use of value adding capacity,

Table 8.2   Assembly Cell Capacity Improvement Outcome.

Description	Current state	Bringing improvement in the assembly cell	Future state I	Future state II increase sales by 30%.	Bring improvement by	Future state III
Manpower productive capacity	42%		42%	54%		54%
Manpower non-productive capacity	41%		26%	31%		15%
Manpower available capacity	17%		32%	15%		31%
Quantity per month	45000		45000	58500		58500
Assembly cycle time – minutes	1.5		1.5	1.5		1.5
Changeover time – hours	6	Reduce changeover time by 50%	3	3	Reduce changeover time by 50%	1.5
Shift working hours	7		7	7		7
Shifts per day	3		3	3		3
Average batch size	2000		2000	2000		2000
Scrap rate %	12	40% improvement	7	7	Further 50% improvement. Us e standard work, DWM	3.5
Rework rate%	15	40% improvement	9	9	Further 50% improvement reduction	4.5
Downtime %	15	50% improvement	7.5	7.5	Further 60% improvement	3
Inspection %	9		9	9	Drop to 5	5
Inspection time – minutes	3		3	3	Drop to two using DWM	2
Assembly team (number of employees)	5		5	5		5
Days per month	26		26	26		26
Total available manpower time – hours	2730		2730	2730		2730
Mfg productive time – hours	1125		1125	1463		1463

(*Continued*)

Table 8.2   (Continued)

Description	Current state	Bringing improvement in the assembly cell	Future state I	Future state II increase sales by 30%.	Bring improvement by	Future state III
Changeover time – hours	135		67.5	88		44
Scrap and rework time hours	304		180	234		117
Downtime hours	410		205	205		82
Inspection time hours	203		203	263		98
5S time for the month hours	26		26	26		26
Meetings hours	26		26	26		26
Desk time for reporting	13		13	13		13
Focused improvement projects	13		13	13		13
Total productive time including focused improvement projects time in hours	1138		1138	1475.5		1476
Total non-productive time in hours	1116		720	855		405

non-value adding capacity and available free capacity and get clarity about their plant assembly operations.

Understanding the Process for Capacity Calculations for a Larger Company[2]

The journey of lean accounting for gearbox division of Perfect Gear Company with other initiatives is mapped in Table 8.3 and Table 8.4 for year 2018 and 2019. Its annual turnover witnessed a steep rise of 50% with profits leaping from 5% to 17%. This was the outcome of improvements and clarity provided by the lean accounting to the operational people in all functions including finance and accounting. Functional managers shifted their focus to the plant floor in understanding the operational details to identify where the opportunities lie.

Table 8.3 P&L Statement for the Gearbox Division (Value Stream III) of Perfect Gear Company in USD'000 for Year Ending 2018 and 2019.

Key parameters	Current state March 2018			Future state March 2019		
	Annual P&L	Monthly average	% of sales	Annual P&L	Monthly average	% of sales
Monthly quantity dispatched	1000 tons			1500 tons		
Sales price	$3.33 per kg			$3.67 per kg		
Sales revenue	40000	3333		66000	5500	
Material cost	17280	1440	43.2%	31200	2600	47.3%
Contribution 1 (A)	22720	1893	56.8%	34800	2900	52.7%
Total variable expenses (B)	6778	565	16.9%	9794	816	14.8%
Consumables and stores	1093	91		1640	137	
Oil and lubricants	208	17		312	26	
Inserts	160	13		240	20	
Accessories	80	7		64	5	
Grinding wheels	88	7		144	12	
Cutting oil	120	10		208	17	
Tool cutter	101	8		144	12	
Gas	53	4		80	7	
Paints	82	7		122	10	
Grease	27	2		56	5	
Others	480	40		800	67	
Power and fuels	2019	168		3040	253	
Job works	1547	129		2384	199	
Other plant misc. expenses	720	60		560	47	
Contribution 2 (C) = (A-B)	15942	1329	39.9%	25006	2084	37.9%
Total fixed expenses (D)	9971	831	24.9%	9213	768	14.0%
Wages – workers	1893	158		2240	187	
Wages – fabrication	373	31		312	26	
Overtime	773	64		736	61	
Salary – executives	3600	300		2885	240	
Other corporate overheads	3333	278		3040	253	
Net Profits-EBITDA (E) = (C-D)	5971	498	14.9%	15794	1316	23.9%
Depreciation and amortization	2107	176		2400	200	
EBIT	3864	322	9.7%	13394	1116	20.3%
Bank interest	933	78		960	80	
Interest on term loans	907	76		1120	93	
Net earnings before tax (EBT)	2024	169	5.1%	11314	943	17.1%

Table 8.4 Key Financial Results for Perfect Gear Company for
Year 2018 and Year 2019.

Key parameters	UOM	Current state March 2018	Future state March 2019
Average dispatch per day	Tons	40	58
Average monthly dispatch	Tons	1000	1500
Average sales price	USD per kg	3.33	3.67
Monthly dispatch	USD (in Mn)	3.33	5.50
Annual turnover	USD (in Mn)	40	66

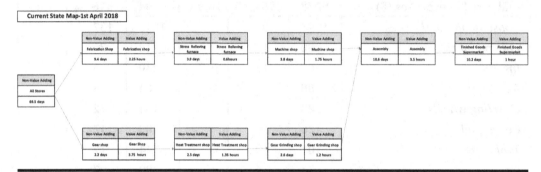

Figure 8.1 Current State Map for Year Ending 31 March 2018.

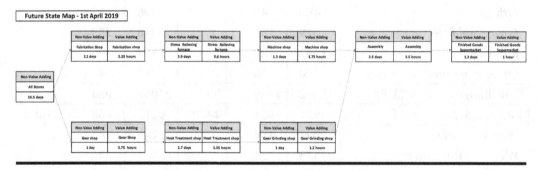

Figure 8.2 Future State Map for Year Ending 31 March 2019.

Value stream mapping is the starting point of the capacity calculations as shown in Figure 8.1 and Figure 8.2. The data collection and preparation of value stream maps are discussed in previous chapters.

As discussed previously, there are three types of uses of *capacity – value adding capacity usage, non-value adding capacity usage* and *free capacity available.* The capacity calculation for machines and manpower is done separately for computing capacity of each function on the plant floor as well as all other support functions. This is explained in upcoming tables that answer the following questions:

■ What are the activities involved in the functioning of the people in a particular function? Determine whether these activities are value adding or non-value adding.
■ What is the total time consumed in value adding and non-value adding activities?
■ What is the total time and free available time in each function?

There are two tables for each function of the value stream. One is for current state (for the month of March 2018) and the second is for the future state (for the month of March 2019).

■ Total downtime hours, scrap generated in a month, rework taken up, time taken for waiting for material and inspection and time consumed in changeovers during the month are the hours spent on non-value adding activities
■ Productive hours = Net available time available during the day × Number of days available in a month
■ Total available time = Number of shifts working during the day × Total shift hours × Number of machines × Number of working days in a month

Free time available = Total available hours − Productive hours − the Non-productive hours

Based on this data the percentage of value-adding capacity usage, non-value adding capacity usage and free capacity available is arrived. This exercise can be seen in the spreadsheets from Table 8.5 to Table 8.33. Now armed with this knowledge of how much non-productive hours are there due to downtime, scrap generated, rework taken up, time wasted waiting for material and inspection and time consumed in changeovers, the lean project teams are formed with finance accountants as part of the team and lean projects are implemented with the target to reduce the non-productive time.

This exercise should be done every month and again these data were consolidated for future state to arrive at the value adding capacity usage, non-value adding capacity usage and free capacity available for future state and see the improvements.

8.3 Kaizen and Lean Tools for Reduction in Non-Productive Hours[3]

Figure 8.3 shows kaizen and lean tools that are available for implementation to reduce non-productive hours. If the total non-productive hours in a month start declining, there will be ensured improvement in dispatch volume and revenue and profits will increase in greater proportion than increase in revenue.

All the functions should be mapped for their current and future status as shown charts appended from Table 8.5 through Table 8.33. *In each example, first current state map for March 2018 is shown and then future state map for March 2019 is shown followed by the improvements that have been achieved. As stated earlier the value stream mapping was done on March 2019 after*

Sl. no.	Hours wasted in manpower and machine due to the following losses	Kaizen and lean tools available for improvements (refer to chapter 5 and chapter 7)	Benefits achieved
1	Breakdowns	TPM (AM, PM)	Hours saved for increased production
2	Long changeovers	SMED	Hours saved for increased production
3	Quality issues like defects, rework and scrap generation	TQM, COPQ, MSA, Six Sigma, poka yoke, jidoka, standard work, root cause analysis	Higher yield, increased productivity, reduced variations
4	Waiting for material and inspection	Workload balance, flow layout, problem-solving methodology, PDCA, SDCA, data stratification, root cause analysis	Hours saved for increased production
5	High inventory levels	Inventory management, pull system, supermarket, kanban system	Reduced lead time/ throughput time, reduced inventory, increased cash flows
6	Logistic losses due to excess transportation and poor layout	Workload balancing, flow layout and cellular manufacturing, mizusumashi	Hourly production achievement, increase in productivity of man and machine

Figure 8.3 Main Losses at Perfect Gear Company Resulting in Generation of Non-Productive Hours and Kaizen and Lean Tools Available to Reduce/Eliminate These Losses.

Sl. no.	Hours wasted in manpower and machine due to the following losses	Kaizen and lean tools available for improvements (refer to chapter 5 and chapter 7)	Benefits achieved
7	Low sustenance of improvements brought in	Standard work, SOPs, daily management tools like leader standard work, leader checklists, accountability and attendance boards	Hourly production achievement, increase in productivity of man and machine
8	Change paradigm to accept the changes being brought in. Cluttered workplace	Kaizen mindset, kaizen principles and mudas understanding, 6S tool	Understand wastages in the company, build kaizen thinking. Clutter-free and well-kept workplace.

Figure 8.3   (Continued)

12 months of lean journey and actual capacity usage status of the plant is reflected here as on March 2019. For the namesake the 'future' state is used to reflect the improvements brought in.

Improvements in the Fabrication Shop from Lean Implementation

- Average downtime on each machine reduced by two hours and 45 minutes, which is a result of 45 minutes reduction in downtime, 30 minutes scrap downtime, 30 minutes reduction rework and one hour reduction in wait time for material and inspection
- Changeover time reduced from 30 minutes to 15 minutes
- Machine performance improved to 70% from 65%, which increased production by 300 tons
- Movement of material reduced from one hour to 30 minutes
- Four executive level positions relocated to other value streams

Improvements in the Stress Relieving Shop from Lean Implementation

- Average downtime on each furnace reduced by two hours and 15 minutes, which is a result of 30 minutes reduction in downtime, 15 minutes scrap downtime, 30 minutes reduction rework and one hour reduction in wait time for material and inspection
- Changeover time reduced from ten to eight hours

Table 8.5 Current State Map and Data Box for Fabrication Shop at Perfect Gear Company.

Machine name: Welding, plasma and shears		Activity description	Value adding	Non-value adding
MACHINE				
Number of operators per shift per machine	1			
Total employees other than operators	10	Total productive hours used in adding value	4095	
Total shifts	2	5S and PM		26
Total shift hours	8	Downtime due to		2925
5S and PM hours per shift	0.5	TOTAL	4095	2951
Available time	15	Total time used in value adding and non-value adding	7046	
Average downtime		Total time available per month	7488	
On each machine per day in hours	1.50	Total free available hours per month		442
Due to scrap per day on each machine	0.75	Value adding capacity percentage		55%
Due to rework per day on each machine	1.00	Non-value adding capacity percentage		39%
Due to wait for materials, inspections, etc. per day on each machine	1.50	Free capacity available		6%
Cycle time (hours/ton)	2.25			
MANPOWER				
Changeover time (hours):	0.50	Make for demand	4095	
Number of change over per day on each machine	3	5S and CLIT – 36 × 15 min × 26		234
Number of machines	18	Move material – 36 × 60 min × 26		936
Machine performance	65%	Tier 1 meeting and visual updates (36 employees × 26 times × 15 min)		234
Total machine available time (hours/day)	270	Hourly monitoring, inventory monitoring and report filling (36 × 30 min × 26)		468
Net machine available time (hours/day)	158	Manpower allocation (8 × 26 × 15 min)		52
Net flow rate (tons/day)	46	Tier 2 and 3 meetings (8 × 26 × 30 min)		104
Number of working days in the month	26	Abnormality management (8 × 26 × 30 min)		104
Average monthly production (in tons)	1183	Rework, wait for material, changeover		171
Running time during lunch and tea break of 30 minutes	0.5	TOTAL	4095	2303
		Total of value adding and non-value adding hours	6398	
		Total manpower time available hours per month	8970	
		Total free available hours per month	2572	
		Value adding capacity usage percentage	46%	
		Non-value adding capacity usage percentage	26%	
		Free capacity available	29%	

Table 8.6 Future State Map and Data Box for Fabrication Shop at Perfect Gear Company.

Machine name: *Welding, plasma and shears*	Activity description	Value adding	Non-value adding
	MACHINE		
1	Number of operators per shift per machine		
6	Total employees other than operators	Total productive hours used in adding value	5733	
2	Total shifts	5S and PM		26
8	Total shift hours	Downtime due to		1287
0.5	5S and PM hours per shift	TOTAL	5733	1313
15	Available time	Total time used in value adding and non-value adding		7046
	Average downtime:	Total time available per month		7488
0.75	*On each machine per day in hours*	Total free available hours per month		442
0.25	*Due to scrap per day on each machine*	Value adding capacity percentage		77%
0.50	*Due to rework per day on each machine*	Non-value adding capacity percentage		18%
0.50	*Due to wait for materials, inspections, etc. per day on each machine*	Free capacity available		6%
2.25	Cycle time (hours/ton)	**MANPOWER**		
0.25	Changeover time (hours):	Make for demand	5733	
3	Number of changeover per day on each machine	5S and CLIT – 36 operators × 15 min × 26		234
18	Number of machines	Move material – 36 × 30 min × 26		468
70%	Machine performance	Tier 1 meeting and visual updates (36 employees × 26 times × 15 min)		234
270	Total machine available time (hours/day)	Hourly monitoring, inventory monitoring and report filling (36 × 30 min × 26)		468
221	Net machine available time (hours/day)	Manpower allocation (8 × 26 × 15 min)		52
69	Net flow rate (tons/day)	Tier 2 and 3 meetings (8 × 26 × 30 min)		104
26	Number of working days in the month	Abnormality management (8 × 26 × 30 min)		104
1784	Average monthly production (in tons)	Rework, wait for material, changeover		72
0.5	Running time during lunch and tea break of 30 minutes	TOTAL	5733	1736
		Total of value adding and non-value adding hours		7469
		Total manpower time available hours per month		8190
		Total free available hours per month		721
		Value adding capacity usage percentage		70%
		Non-value adding capacity usage percentage		21%
		Free capacity available		9%

Table 8.7 Current State Map and Data Box for Stress Relieving Shop at Perfect Gear Company.

Machine name: Stress relieving furnace		Activity description	Value adding	Non-value adding
MACHINE				
Number of operators per shift per furnace	1			
Total employees other than operators	0	Total productive hours used in adding value	956	
Total shifts	3	5S and PM		39
Total shift hours	8	Downtime due to breakdown, scrap, rework, wait, changeover time		800
5S and PM hours per shift	0.5	TOTAL	956	839
Available time (hours per day)	23	Total time used in value adding and non-value adding usage	1794	
Average downtime		Total time available per month	1872	
On each furnace per day in hours	1.25	Total free available hours per month		78
Due to scrap per day on each furnace	0.50	Value adding capacity usage percentage		51%
Due to rework per day on each furnace	1.00	Non-value adding capacity usage percentage		45%
Due to wait for materials, inspections, etc. per day on each furnace	2.50	Free capacity available		4%
Cycle time (hours per ton)	0.60			
Changeover time (hours)	10.00	**MANPOWER** Make for demand	956	
Number of change over per day on each furnace	1	5S and CUT – 9 operators × 15 min × 26		59
Number of furnaces	3	Move material – 9 × 60 min × 26		234
Furnace performance	73%	Tier 1 meeting and visual updates 9 employees × 26 times × 15 min		59
Total furnace available time (hours per day)	68	Hourly monitoring, inventory monitoring and report filling – 9 × 30 min × 26	117	
Net furnace available time (hours per day)	37	Manpower allocation		0
Net flow rate (tons per day)	45	Tier 2 and 3 meetings		0
Number of working days in a month	26	Abnormality management		0
Average monthly production in tons	1163	Rework, wait for material, changeover		81
Running time during lunch and tea break of 30 minutes	1	TOTAL	956	549
		Total of value adding and non-value adding hours		1505
		Total manpower time available hours per month		1755
		Total free available hours per month		251
		Value adding capacity usage percentage		54%
		Non-value adding capacity usage percentage		31%
		Free capacity available		14%

Table 8.8 Future State Map and Data Box for Stress Relieving Shop at Perfect Gear Company.

Machine name: Stress relieving furnace		Activity description	Value adding	Non-value adding
Number of operators per shift per furnace	1	**MACHINE**		
Total employees other than operators	0	Total productive hours used in adding value	1209	
Total shifts	3	5S and PM		39
Total shift hours	8	Downtime due to breakdown, scrap, rework, wait, changeover time		546
5S and PM hours per shift	0.5	TOTAL	1209	585
Available time (hours per day)	23	Total time used in value adding and non-value adding usage		1794
Average downtime		Total time available per month		1872
On each furnace per day in hours	0.75	Total free available hours per month		78
Due to scrap per day on each furnace	0.25	Value adding capacity usage percentage		65%
Due to rework per day on each furnace	0.50	Non-value adding capacity usage percentage		31%
Due to wait for materials, inspections, etc. per day on each furnace	1.50	Free capacity available		4%
Cycle time (hours per ton)	0.60			
Changeover time (hours)	8.00	**MANPOWER**		
Number of change over per day on each furnace	1	Make for demand	1209	
Number of furnaces	3	5S and CLIT – 9 operators × 15 min × 26		59
Furnace performance	88%	Move material – 9 × 60 min × 26		234
Total furnace available time (hours per day)	68	Tier 1 meeting and visual updates 9 employees × 26 times × 15 min		59
Net furnace available time (hours per day)	47	Hourly monitoring, inventory monitoring and report filling – 3 × 30 min × 26		39
Net flow rate (tons per day)	68	Manpower allocation		0
Number of working days in a month	26	Tier 2 and 3 meetings		0
Average monthly production in tons	1773	Abnormality management		0
Running time during lunch and tea break of 30 minutes	1	Rework, wait for material, changeover		56
		TOTAL	1209	446
		Total of value adding and non-value adding hours		1655
		Total manpower time available hours per month		1755
		Total free available hours per month		100
		Value adding capacity usage percentage		69%
		Non-value adding capacity usage percentage		25%
		Free capacity available		6%

Table 8.9 Current State Map and Data Box for Machine Shop at Perfect Gear Company.

Machine name: Machine shop		Activity description	Value adding	Non-value adding
Number of operators per shift per machine	1	MACHINE		
Total employees other than operators	15	Total productive hours used in adding value	2925	
Total shifts	3	5S and PM		39
Total shift hours	8	Downtime due to breakdown, scrap, rework, wait, changeover time		5850
5S and PM hours per shift	0.5	TOTAL	2925	5889
Available time (hours per day)	22.5	Total time used in value adding and non-value adding usage		8814
Average downtime		Total time available per month		9360
On each machine per day in hours	3.00	Total free available hours per month		546
Due to scrap per day on each machine	0.50	Value adding capacity usage percentage		31%
Due to rework per day on each machine	1.00	Non-value adding capacity usage percentage		63%
Due to wait for materials, inspections, etc. per day	1.50	Free capacity available		6%
Cycle time (hours per ton)	1.75			
Changeover time (hours)	3.00	MANPOWER		
Number of changeover per day on each machine	3	Make for demand	2925	
Number of machines	15	5S and CLIT – 45 operators × 15 min × 26		293
Machine performance	70%	Move material – 45 × 60 min × 26		1170
Total machine available time (hours per day)	338	Tier 1 meeting and visual updates 45 employees × 26 times × 15 min		293
Net machine available time (hours per day)	113	Hourly monitoring, inventory monitoring and report filling – 45 × 30 min × 26		585
Net flow rate (tons per day)	45	Manpower allocation 10 × 26 × 15min		65
Number of working days in a month	26	Tier 2 and 3 meetings 15 × 26 × 30 min		195
Average monthly production in tons	1170	Abnormality management 15 × 26 × 30 min		195
Running time during lunch and tea break of 30 minutes	0.5	Rework, wait for material, changeover		540
		TOTAL	2925	3335
		Total of value adding and non-value adding hours		6260
		Total manpower time available hours per month		11700
		Total free available hours per month		5440
		Value adding capacity usage percentage		25%
		Non-value adding capacity usage percentage		29%
		Free capacity available		46%

Table 8.10 Future State Map and Data Box for Machine Shop at Perfect Gear Company.

Machine name: Machine shop		Activity description	Value adding	Non-value adding
Number of operators per shift per machine	1	MACHINE		
Total employees other than operators	15	Total productive hours used in adding value	4973	
Total shifts	3	5S and PM		39
Total shift hours	8	Downtime due to breakdown, scrap, rework, wait, changeover time		3803
5S and PM hours per shift	0.5	TOTAL	4973	3842
Available time (hours per day)	22.5	Total time used in value adding and non-value adding usage		8814
Average downtime		Total time available per month		9360
On each machine per day in hours	2.00	Total free available hours per month		546
Due to scrap per day on each machine	0.25	Value adding capacity usage percentage		53%
Due to rework per day on each machine	0.50	Non-value adding capacity usage percentage		41%
Due to wait for materials, inspections, etc. per day	1.00	Free capacity available		6%
Cycle time (hours per ton)	1.75			
Changeover time (hours)	2.00	MANPOWER		
Number of change over per day on each machine	3	Make for demand	4973	
Number of machines	15	5S and CLIT – 45 operators × 15 min × 26		293
Machine performance	75%	Move material – 45 × 60 min × 26		1170
Total machine available time (hours per day)	338	Tier 1 meeting and visual updates 45 employees × 26 times × 15 min		293
Net machine available time (hours per day)	191	Hourly monitoring, inventory monitoring and report filling – 45 × 30 min × 26		585
Net flow rate (tons per day)	82	Manpower allocation 10 × 26 × 15 min		65
Number of working days in a month	26	Tier 2 and 3 meetings 15 × 26 × 30 min		130
Average monthly production in tons	2131	Abnormality management 15 × 26 × 30 min		130
Running time during lunch and tea break of 30 minutes	0.5	Rework, wait for material, changeover		349
		TOTAL	4973	3014
		Total of value adding and non-value adding hours		7986
		Total manpower time available hours per month		11700
		Total free available hours per month		3714
		Value adding capacity usage percentage		43%
		Non-value adding capacity usage percentage		26%
		Free capacity available		32%

Table 8.11 Current State Map and Data Box for Gear Shop at Perfect Gear Company.

Machine name: Gear shop		Activity description	Value adding	Non-value adding
Number of operators per shift per machine	1	**MACHINE**		
Total employees other than operators	10	Total productive hours used in adding value	4680	
Total shifts	3	5S and PM		39
Total shift hours	8	Downtime due to breakdown, scrap, rework, wait, changeover time		4095
5S and PM hours per shift	0.5	TOTAL	4680	4134
Available time (hours per day)	22.5	Total time used in value adding and non-value adding usage	8814	
Average downtime		Total time available per month	9360	
On each machine per day in hours	3.00	Total free available hours per month	546	
Due to scrap per day on each machine	0.50	Value adding capacity usage percentage	50%	
Due to rework per day on each machine	1.00	Non-value adding capacity usage percentage		44%
Due to wait for materials, inspections, etc. per day on each machine	2.00	Free capacity available		6%
Cycle time (hours per ton)	3.75	**MANPOWER**		
Changeover time (hours)	1.00	Make for demand	4680	
Number of changeover per day on each machine	4	5S and CLIT – 45 operators × 15 min × 26		293
Number of machines	15	Move material – 45 × 60 min × 26		1170
Machine performance	80%	Tier 1 meeting and visual updates 45 employees × 26 times × 15 min		293
Total machine available time (hours per day)	338	Hourly monitoring, inventory monitoring and report filling – 45 × 30 min × 26		585
Net machine available time (hours per day)	180	Manpower allocation 10 × 26 × 15 min		65
Net flow rate (tons per day)	38	Tier 2 and 3 meetings 10 × 26 × 30 min		130
Number of working days in a month	26	Abnormality management 10 × 26 × 30 min		130
Average monthly production in tons	998	Rework, wait for material, changeover		338
Running time during lunch and tea break of 30 minutes	0.5	TOTAL	4680	3003
		Total of value adding and non-value adding hours		7683
		Total manpower time available hours per month		10725
		Total free available hours per month		3043
		Value adding capacity usage percentage		44%
		Non-value adding capacity usage percentage		28%
		Free capacity available		28%

Table 8.12 Future State Map and Data Box for Gear Shop at Perfect Gear Company.

Machine name: Gear shop		Activity description	Value adding	Non-value adding
		MACHINE		
Number of operators per shift per machine	1			
Total employees other than operators	7	Total productive hours used in adding value	6942	
Total shifts	3	5S and PM		39
Total shift hours	8	Downtime due to breakdown, scrap, rework, wait, changeover time		1833
5S and PM hours per shift	0.5	TOTAL	6942	1872
Available time (hours per day)	23	Total time used in value adding and non-value adding usage	8814	
Average downtime		Total time available per month	9360	
On each machine per day in hours	1.50	Total free available hours per month	546	
Due to scrap per day on each machine	0.25	Value adding capacity usage percentage	74%	
Due to rework per day on each machine	0.50	Non-value adding capacity usage percentage		20%
Due to wait for materials, inspections, etc. per day on each machine	0.45	Free capacity available		6%
Cycle time (hours per ton)	3.75	**MANPOWER**		
Changeover time (hours)	0.50	Make for demand	6942	
Number of changeover per day on each machine	4	5S and CLIT – 45 operators × 15 min × 26		293
Number of machines	15	Move material – 45 × 60 min × 26		1170
Machine performance	85%	Tier 1 meeting and visual updates 45 employees × 26 times × 15 min		293
Total machine available time (hours per day)	338	Hourly monitoring, inventory monitoring and report filling – 45 × 30 min × 26		585
Net machine available time (hours per day)	267	Manpower allocation 7 × 26 × 15 min		46
Net flow rate (tons per day)	61	Tier 2 and 3 meetings 7 × 26 × 30 min		91
Number of working days in a month	26	Abnormality management 7 × 26 × 30 min		91
Average monthly production in tons	1574	Rework, wait for material, changeover		144
Running time during lunch and tea break of 30 minutes	0.5	TOTAL	6942	2712
		Total of value adding and non-value adding hours	9654	
		Total manpower time available hours per month	10140	
		Total free available hours per month	487	
		Value adding capacity usage percentage	68%	
		Non-value adding capacity usage percentage		27%
		Free capacity available		5%

Table 8.13 Current State Map and Data Box for Heat Treatment Shop at Perfect Gear Company.

Machine name: Heat treatment shop		Activity description	Value adding	Non-value adding
Number of operators per shift per machine	1	**MACHINE**		
Total employees other than operators	5	Total productive hours used in adding value	2340	
Total shifts	3	5S and PM		39
Total shift hours	8	Downtime due to breakdown, scrap, rework, wait, changeover time		2340
5S and PM hours per shift	0.5	TOTAL	2340	2379
Available time (hours per day)	22.5	Total time used in value adding and non-value adding usage		4719
Average downtime		Total time available per month		4992
On each machine per day in hours	4.00	Total free available hours per month		273
Due to scrap per day on each machine	0.50	Value adding capacity usage percentage		47%
Due to rework per day on each machine	1.25	Non-value adding capacity usage percentage		48%
Due to wait for materials, inspections, etc. per day on each machine	4.00	Free capacity available		5%
Cycle time (hours per ton)	1.35	**MANPOWER**		
Changeover time (hours)	3.00	Make for demand	2340	
Number of changeover per day on each machine	0.5	5S and CLIT – 24 operators × 15 min × 26		156
Number of machines	8	Move material – 24 × 60 min × 26		624
Machine performance	65%	Tier 1 meeting and visual updates 24 employees × 26 times × 15 min		156
Total machine available time (hours per day)	180	Hourly monitoring, inventory monitoring and report filling – 24 × 30 min × 26		312
Net machine available time (hours per day)	90	Manpower allocation 5 × 26 × 15 min		33
Net flow rate (tons per day)	43	Tier 2 and 3 meetings 5 × 26 × 30 min		65
Number of working days in a month	26	Abnormality management 5 × 26 × 30 min		65
Average monthly production in tons	1127	Rework, wait for material, changeover		174
Running time during lunch and tea break of 30 minutes	0.5	TOTAL	2340	1585
		Total of value adding and non-value adding hours		3925
		Total manpower time available hours per month		5655
		Total free available hours per month		1731
		Value adding capacity usage percentage		41%
		Non-value adding capacity usage percentage		28%
		Free capacity available		31%

Table 8.14 Future State Map and Data Box for Heat Treatment Shop at Perfect Gear Company.

Machine name: Heat treatment shop		Activity description	Value adding	Non-value adding
		MACHINE		
Number of operators per shift per machine	1			
Total employees other than operators	3	Total productive hours used in adding value	3484	
Total shifts	3	5S and PM		39
Total shift hours	8	Downtime due to breakdown, scrap, rework, wait, changeover time		1196
5S and PM hours per shift	0.5	TOTAL	3484	1235
Available time (hours per day)	22.5	Total time used in value adding and non-value adding usage		4719
Average downtime		Total time available per month		4992
On each machine per day in hours	2.00	Total free available hours per month		273
Due to scrap per day on each machine	0.25	Value adding capacity usage percentage		70%
Due to rework per day on each machine	0.75	Non-value adding capacity usage percentage		25%
Due to wait for materials, inspections, etc. per day on each machine	1.75	Free capacity available		5%
Cycle time (hours per ton)	1.35	**MANPOWER**		
Changeover time (hours)	2.00	Make for demand	3484	
Number of change over per day on each machine	0.5	5S and CLIT – 24 operators × 15 min × 26		156
Number of machines	8	Move material – 24 × 60 min × 26		624
Machine performance	70%	Tier 1 meeting and visual updates 24 employees × 26 times × 15 min		156
Total machine available time (hours per day)	180	Hourly monitoring, inventory monitoring and report filling – 24 × 30 min × 26		312
Net machine available time (hours per day)	134	Manpower allocation 3 × 26 × 15 min		20
Net flow rate (tons per day)	69	Tier 2 and 3 meetings 3 × 26 × 30 min		39
Number of working days in a month	26	Abnormality management 3 × 26 × 30 min		39
Average monthly production in tons	1807	Rework, wait for material, changeover		90
Running time during lunch and tea break of 30 minutes	0.5	TOTAL	3484	1436
		Total of value adding and non-value adding hours		4920
		Total manpower time available hours per month		5265
		Total free available hours per month		346
		Value adding capacity usage percentage		66%
		Non-value adding capacity usage percentage		27%
		Free capacity available		7%

Table 8.15 Current State Map and Data Box for Gear Grinding Shop at Perfect Gear Company.

Machine name: Gear grinding shop		Activity description	Value adding	Non-value adding
Number of operators per shift per machine	1	**MACHINE**		
Total employees other than operators	5	Total productive hours used in adding value	1664	
Total shifts	3	5S and PM		39
Total shift hours	8	Downtime due to breakdown, scrap, rework, wait, changeover time		3016
5S and PM hours per shift	0.5	TOTAL	1664	3055
Available time (hours per day)	22.5	Total time used in value adding and non-value adding usage	4719	
Average downtime		Total time available per month	4992	
On each machine per day in hours	3.00	Total free available hours per month		273
Due to scrap per day on each machine	0.50	Value adding capacity usage percentage		33%
Due to rework per day on each machine	1.00	Non-value adding capacity usage percentage		61%
Due to wait for materials, inspections, etc. per day on each machine	4.00	Free capacity available		5%
Cycle time (hours per ton)	1.20	**MANPOWER**		
Changeover time (hours)	2.00	Make for demand	1664	
Number of changeover per day on each machine	3.0	5S and CLIT – 24 operators × 15 min × 26		156
Number of machines	8	Move material – 24 × 60 min × 26		624
Machine performance	82%	Tier 1 meeting and visual updates 24 employees × 26 times × 15 min		156
Total machine available time (hours per day)	180	Hourly monitoring, inventory monitoring and report filling – 24 × 30 min × 26		312
Net machine available time (hours per day)	64	Manpower allocation 5 × 26 × 15 min		33
Net flow rate (tons per day)	44	Tier 2 and 3 meetings 5 × 26 × 30 min		65
Number of working days in a month	26	Abnormality management 5 × 26 × 30 min		65
Average monthly production in tons	1137	Rework, wait for material, changeover		276
Running time during lunch and tea break of 30 minutes	0.5	TOTAL	1664	1687
		Total of value adding and non-value adding hours	3351	
		Total manpower time available hours per month		5655
		Total free available hours per month		2305
		Value adding capacity usage percentage		29%
		Non-value adding capacity usage percentage		30%
		Free capacity available		41%

Table 8.16 Future State Map and Data Box for Gear Grinding Shop at Perfect Gear Company.

Machine name: Gear grinding shop		Activity description	Value adding	Non-value adding
		MACHINE		
Number of operators per shift per machine	1			
Total employees other than operators	4	Total productive hours used in adding value	2756	
Total shifts	3	5S and PM		39
Total shift hours	8	Downtime due to breakdown, scrap, rework, wait, changeover time		1924
5S and PM hours per shift	0.5	TOTAL	2756	1963
Available time (hours per day)	22.5	Total time used in value adding and non-value adding usage	4719	
Average downtime		Total time available per month	4992	
On each machine per day in hours	2.00	Total free available hours per month	273	
Due to scrap per day on each machine	0.50	Value adding capacity usage percentage		55%
Due to rework per day on each machine	0.50	Non-value adding capacity usage percentage		39%
Due to wait for materials, inspections, etc. per day on each machine	2.50	Free capacity available		5%
Cycle time (hours per ton)	1.20	MANPOWER		
Changeover time (hours)	1.25	Make for demand	2756	
Number of changeover per day on each machine	3.0	5S and CLIT – 24 operators × 15 min × 26		156
Number of machines	8	Move material – 24 × 60 min × 26		624
Machine performance	85%	Tier 1 meeting and visual updates 24 employees × 26 times × 15 min		156
Total machine available time (hours per day)	180	Hourly monitoring, inventory monitoring and report filling – 24 × 30 min × 26		312
Net machine available time (hours per day)	106	Manpower allocation 4 × 26 × 15 min		26
Net flow rate (tons per day)	75	Tier 2 and 3 meetings 4 × 26 × 30 min		52
Number of working days in a month	26	Abnormality management 4 × 26 × 30 min		52
Average monthly production in tons	1952	Rework, wait for material, changeover		174
Running time during lunch and tea break of 30 minutes	0.5	TOTAL	2756	1552
		Total of value adding and non-value adding hours	4308	
		Total manpower time available hours per month	5460	
		Total free available hours per month	1152	
		Value adding capacity usage percentage	50%	
		Non-value adding capacity usage percentage		28%
		Free capacity available		21%

Table 8.17 Current State Map and Data Box for Assembly Shop at Perfect Gear Company.

Assembly		Activity description	Value adding	Non-value adding
Number of fitters per shift per station	4	MACHINE		
Total employees other than operators	5	Total productive hours used in adding value		
Total shifts	2	5S and PM		
Total shift hours	8	Downtime due to breakdown, scrap, rework, wait, changeover time		
PM hours per shift	0.5	Total		
Available time (hours per day)	15.0	Total time used in value adding and non-value adding usage		
Average downtime		Total time available per month		
On each workstation per day in hours	0.00	Total free available hours per month		
Due to scrap per day on each workstation	0.00	Value adding capacity usage percentage		
Due to rework per day on each workstation	0.50	Non-value adding capacity usage percentage		
Due to wait for materials, inspections, etc. per day on each workstation	2.00	Free capacity available		
Cycle time (hours per ton)	3.50	MANPOWER		
Changeover time (hours per changeover)	0.50	Make for demand	3055	
Number of change per days on each workstation	1.0	5S and CLIT – 40 operators × 15 min × 26		260
Number of assembly workstations	5	Move material – 40 × 60 min × 26		1040
Assembly performance	60%	Tier 1 meeting and visual updates 40 employees × 26 times × 15 min		260
Total manpower available time (hours per day)	375	Hourly monitoring, inventory monitoring and report filling – 10 × 30 min × 26		130
Net manpower available time (hours per day)	315	Manpower allocation 10 × 26 × 15 min		65
Net flow rate (tons per day)	54	Tier 2 and 3 meetings 10 × 26 × 30 min		130
Number of working days in a month	26	Abnormality management 10 × 26 × 30 min		130
Average monthly dispatch in tons	1404	Rework, wait for material, changeover		3120
		TOTAL	3055	5135
		Total of value adding and non-value adding hours		8190
		Total manpower time available hours per month		9750
		Total free available hours per month		1560
		Value adding capacity usage percentage		31%
		Non-value adding capacity usage percentage		53%
		Free capacity available		16%

Table 8.18 Future State Map and Data Box for Assembly Shop at Perfect Gear Company.

Assembly		Activity description	Value adding	Non-value adding
Number of fitters per shift per station	4	MACHINE		
Total employees other than operators	5	Total productive hours used in adding value		
Total shifts	2	5S and PM		
Total shift hours	8	Downtime due to breakdown, scrap, rework, wait, changeover time		
5S and PM hours per shift	0.5	TOTAL		
Available time (hours per day)	15.0	Total time used in value adding and non-value adding usage		
Average downtime		Total time available per month		
On each machine per day in hours	0.00	Total free available hours per month		
Due to scrap per day on each workstation	0.00	Value adding capacity usage percentage		
Due to rework per day on each workstation	0.25	Non-value adding capacity usage percentage		
Due to wait for materials, inspections, etc. per day on each workstation	1.00	Free capacity available		
Cycle time (hours per ton)	3.50	MANPOWER	6305	
Changeover time (hours per changeover)	0.25	Productive assembly hours		
Number of change per day on each workstation	1.0	5S and CLIT – 40 operators × 15 min × 26		260
Number of assembly stations	5	Move material – 40 × 30 min × 26		520
Assembly performance	85%	Tier 1 meeting and visual updates 40 operators × 26 times × 15 min		260
Total workstation available time (hours per day)	375	Hourly monitoring, inventory monitoring and report filling – 10 × 30 min × 26		130
Net workstation available time (hours per day)	360	Manpower allocation 10 × 26 × 15 min		65
Net flow rate (tons per day)	87	Tier 2 and 3 meetings 10 × 26 × 30 min		130
Number of working days in a month	26	Abnormality management 10 × 26 × 30 min		130
Average monthly dispatch in tons	2273	Rework, wait for material, changeover		1560
		TOTAL	6305	3055
		Total of value adding and non-value adding hours	9360	
		Total manpower time available hours per month	9750	
		Total free available hours per month	390	
		Value adding capacity usage percentage	65%	
		Non-value adding capacity usage percentage		31%
		Free capacity available		4%

Table 8.19   Current State Map and Data Box for Finished Good Supermarket and Logistics at Perfect Gear Company.

Finished good supermarket and logistics		Activity description	Value adding	Non-value adding
Number of dispatchers	6	MACHINE		
Total employees other than dispatchers	3	Total productive hours used in adding value		
Total shifts	1	5S and PM		
Total shift hours	8	Downtime due to breakdown, scrap, rework, wait, changeover time		
5S and PM hours per shift	0.5	TOTAL		
Available time (hours per day)	7.5	Total time used in value adding and non-value adding usage		
Average downtime		Total time available per month		
On each machine per day in hours	0.00	Total free available hours per month		
Due to scrap per day on each machine	0.00	Value adding capacity usage percentage		
Due to rework per day on each machine	0.00	Non-value adding capacity usage percentage		
Due to wait for materials, inspections, etc. per day on each machine	0.00	Free capacity available		
Cycle time (hours per ton)	1.00	MANPOWER		
Changeover time (hours)	1.00	Productive logistics hours	293	
Number of change per day on each machine	0.0	5S – 6 dispatchers × 15 min × 26		39
		Tier 1 meeting and visual updates 6 dispatchers × 26 times × 15 min		39
Logistics performance	70%	Hourly monitoring, inventory monitoring and report filling – 9 × 30 min × 26		78
Total logistics available time (hours per day)	67.5	Tier 2 and 3 meetings 3 × 26 × 30 min		39
Net logistics available time (hours per day)	47.3	Abnormality management 3 × 26 × 60 min		78
Net flow rate (tons per day)	47.3	Rework 3 × 26 × 1		78
Number of working days in a month	26	Wait for material 9 × 26 × 1.5 hours		351
Average monthly dispatch in tons	1229	Paperwork 3 clerks × 26 × 3 hours		234
		TOTAL	293	936
		Total of value adding and non-value adding hours		1229
		Total manpower time available hours per month		1755
		Total free available hours per month		527
		Value adding capacity usage percentage		17%
		Non-value adding capacity usage percentage		53%
		Free capacity available		30%

Table 8.20 Future State Map and Data Box for Finished Good Supermarket and Logistics at Perfect Gear Company.

Finished good supermarket and logistics		Activity description	Value adding	Non-value adding
Number of dispatchers	6	**MACHINE**		
Total employees other than dispatchers	3	Total productive hours used in adding value		
Total shifts	1	5S and PM		
Total shift hours	8	Downtime due to breakdown, scrap, rework, wait, changeover time		
5S and PM hours per shift	0.5	TOTAL		
Available time (hours per day)	7.5	Total time used in value adding and non-value adding usage		
Average downtime		Total time available per month		
On each machine per day in hours	0.00	Total free available hours per month		
Due to scrap per day on each machine	0.00	Value adding capacity usage percentage		
Due to rework per day on each machine	0.00	Non-value adding capacity usage percentage		
Due to wait for materials, inspections, etc. per day on each machine	0.00	Free capacity available		
Cycle time (hours per ton)	1.00			
Changeover time (hours)	1.00	**MANPOWER**	962	
Number of change per day on each machine	0.0	Productive logistics hours		
		5S – 6 dispatchers × 15 min × 26		39
		Tier 1 meeting and visual updates 6 dispatchers × 26 times × 15 min		39
Logistics performance	90%	Hourly monitoring, inventory monitoring and report filling – 9 × 15 min × 26		59
Total logistics available time (hours per day)	67.5	Tier 2 and 3 meetings 3 × 26 × 30 min		39
Net logistics available time (hours per day)	60.8	Abnormality management 3 × 26 × 30 min		33
Net flow rate (tons per day)	60.8	Rework 3 × 26 × 15 min		58.5
Number of working days in a month	26	Wait for material 9 × 26×× 1 hour		234
Average monthly dispatch in tons	1580	Paperwork 3 clerks × 26 × 1.5 hours		117
		TOTAL	962	618
		Total of value adding and non-value adding hours	1580	
		Total manpower time available hours per month	1755	
		Total free available hours per month	176	
		Value adding capacity usage percentage	55%	
		Non-value adding capacity usage percentage	35%	
		Free capacity available	10%	

Table 8.21   Current State and Future State Map for Maintenance Function at Perfect Gear Company.

Maintenance function	Current state map		Future state map	
Number of maintenance fitters	12		10	
Employees other than maintenance	7		5	
Number of shifts	3		3	
Hours per shift	8		8	
Rest hours per shift	0.5		0.5	
Available time (hours per day)	22.5	0.0	22.5	0.0
Number of working days in the month	26		26	
Activity description	Value adding time (in hours)	Non-value adding time (in hours)	Value adding time (in hours)	Non-value adding time (in hours)
Implementation of AM step 1, step 2 and step 3 on all the machines in all value streams. Assisting operators and operation department supervisors and executives in learning, implementing and sustenance of autonomous maintenance.		2340		1950
Implementation of PM step 1, step 2 and step 3 on all the machines in all value streams		3120		2730
Tier 1 meeting and visual updates 30 × 26 × 15 min		234		195
Tier 2 and 3 meetings 5 × 26 × 60 min		182		130
Monitor and control the energy bill of the company on monthly basis. Monitoring and reduction in the maintenance costs of all functions under value streams.		52		52
Monitor and control the OEE, MTBF and MTTR of all A-class machines in the company.		130		130
Prepare TBM and CBM sheets for all A-class machines in the company.		130		130
All work to be done under the jurisdiction of ERP system and to meet the changing requirements as lean production system is being implemented.		78		78
Implementation of PM step 4, spare parts management on all A-class machines.		208		208

Maintenance function	Current state map		Future state map	
Monitoring and follow up on all focused improvement projects under kobetsu kaizen pillars in all functions in the value streams.		260		260
Standardization work in the maintenance area, daily management, SOPs and checklists. SHE audit of the plant.		130		130
Maintenance executives and staff and fitters kaizen and technical training hours, implementation and sustenance of performance scorecard, skill matrix and training calendar 35 × 0.5 × 26	559		455	
Total	559	6864	455	5993
Total value adding and non-value adding hours	7423		6448	
Total usage time available hours per month	8385		6825	
Total free available hours per month	962		377	
Value adding capacity usage percentage	7%		7%	
Non-value adding capacity usage percentage	82%		88%	
Free capacity available	11%		6%	

Table 8.22   Current State and Future State Map for Quality Assurance Function at Perfect Gear Company.

Quality assurance	Current state map		Future state map	
Number of quality inspectors	10		7	
Employees other than quality inspectors	5		5	
Number of shifts	2		2	
Hours per shift	8		8	
Rest hours per shift	0.5		0.5	
Available time (hours per day)	15		15	
Number of working days in the month	26		26	
Activity description	Value adding time	Non-value adding time	Value adding time	Non-value adding time
Quality assurance coordination with customers (5 employees × 4 hours × 26 days)	520		650	

(Continued)

Table 8.22   (Continued)

Quality assurance	Current state map		Future state map	
Quality control reports for functions of value streams, at suppliers end and subcontracting (10 inspectors × 2 shifts × 5.5 hours × 26 days)		2600		1456
Tier 1 meeting and visual updates (20 inspectors × 15 min × 26 days)		130		91
Tier 2 and 3 meetings 5 operators, two shifts, 15 min, 26 days (divided by 60 to get the time in hours)		65		65
Keeping track of customer complaints in number and PPM, NCR, CAPA and cost of quality (5 employees × 1 hour × 26 days)		130		130
Quality control lab functions and tool room quality (2 shifts × 7.5 hours × 26 days)		390		390
SOPs, standard checklist preparation, welder qualifications, traceability (5 × 1 × 26, 20 × 1 × 26)		650		494
ISO9000, ISO14000, ISO18000 compliance – 2 × 2 × 26		104		104
Training for QA functions –5 × 1 × 26		130		130
Total	520	4199	650	2860
Total value adding and non-value adding hours		4719		3510
Total usage time available (hours per month)		4875		3705
Total free available hours per month		156		195
Value adding capacity usage percentage		11%		18%
Non-value adding capacity usage percentage		86%		77%
Free capacity available		3%		5%

Table 8.23   Current State and Future State Map for Purchase Function at Perfect Gear Company.

Purchase function	Current state map	Future state map
Number of purchasers	30	25
Purchase executives	5	4
Number of shifts	1	1
Hours per shift	8	8
Rest hours per shift	0.5	0.5
Available time (hours per day)	7.5	7.5
Number of working days in the month	26	26

Purchase function	Current state map		Future state map	
Activity description	Value adding time (in hours)	Non-value adding time (in hours)	Value adding time (in hours)	Non-value adding time (in hours)
Prepare POs as per the production schedule – 20 × 5 × 26		2600		2600
Chase suppliers for missed deliveries and expediting – 8 × 5 × 26		1040		1040
Tier 1 meeting and visual updates 35 × 26 × 15 min		228		189
Tier 2 and 3 meetings 5 × 26 × 60 min		130		104
Focus improvement projects on reduction in purchase price of large consuming raw materials, BOP and consumables and procurement directly from suppliers and not through traders – 5 × 2 × 26	260		208	
Focus improvement project on reducing/disposal of the non-moving and slow moving items – 5 × 1 × 26	130		104	
To analyze major causes of NCR for the purchase points and implementation of CAPA –5 × 2 × 26		260		208
Implementation of kanban system and regular repeat replenishment for RM, BOP, consumables and maintenance items. Creation of supermarkets in RM and stores – 5 × 4 × 26	520		520	
Executives and staff kaizen and technical training hours, implementation and sustenance of performance scorecard and training calendar – 20 × 0.5 × 26	260		260	
Total	1170	4258	1092	4141
Total value adding and non-value adding hours	5428		5233	
Total usage time available (hours per month)	6825		5655	
Total free available hours per month	1398		423	
Value adding capacity usage percentage	17%		19%	
Non-value adding capacity usage percentage	62%		73%	
Free capacity available	20%		7%	

Table 8.24 Current State and Future State Map for Finance Function at Perfect Gear Company.

Finance function	Current state map		Future state map	
Number of finance personnel	25		20	
Finance and accounting executives	6		5	
Number of shifts	1		1	
Hours per shift	8		8	
Rest hours per shift	0.5		0.5	
Available time (hours per day)	7.5		7.5	
Number of working days in the month	26		26	
Activity description	Value adding time (in hours)	Non-value adding time (in hours)	Value adding time (in hours)	Non-value adding time (in hours)
Invoice, voucher and payroll preparation		1560		1560
– Vetting of focused improvement projects across the plants and functions – Introduce incentives for the unit and functional heads and HODs to promote savings in the plants – Reduction in transactions for authorizations approvals and sign-off – Accounts payable – Explore possibility of eliminating need for matching receipts, POs and supplier invoices and authorization for payment on clearance of MRNs	260		390	
Tier 1 meeting and visual updates 31 × 26 × 15 min		202		163
Tier 2 and 3 meetings 6 × 26 × 60 min		156		130
Follow-up on accounts receivable and accounts payable		260		260
– Adherence of statutory responsibilities and balance sheet and P&L preparation		130		130

Finance function	Current state map		Future state map	
– Statutory compliance report for the plant – Release of quarterly report to the director for IT compliance				
Estimated contribution – percentage of the booked order (highlighting on monthly basis)		260		260
Monthly stock taking: – Raw material and store inventory reconciliation – MS plate, steel casting, job work items, store items – Introduction of perpetual inventory of runner – Repeater items		520		520
Supervision of ERP system and to meet the changing requirements as The lean production system is being implemented		260		260
To analyze major causes of NCR for the finance and accounts points and implementation of CAPA– 5 × 2 × 26		260		260
Resolve supplier and subcontractor problems		52		52
Executives and staff kaizen and technical training hours, implementation and sustenance of performance scorecard and training calendar 20 × 0.5 × 26	260		520	
Total	**520**	**3660**	**910**	**3595**
Total value adding and non-value adding hours	4180		4505	
Total usage time available (hours per month)	6435		4875	
Total free available hours per month	2256		371	
Value adding capacity usage percentage	8%		19%	
Non-value adding capacity usage percentage	57%		74%	
Free capacity available	35%		8%	

Table 8.25 Current State and Future State Map for Design Function at Perfect Gear Company.

Design function	Current state map		Future state map	
Number of marketing personnel	35		30	
Marketing executives	15		12	
Number of shifts	1		1	
Hours per shift	8		8	
Rest hours per shift	0.5		0.5	
Available time (hours per day)	7.5		7.5	
Number of working days in the month	26		26	
Activity description	Value adding time (in hours)	Non-value adding time (in hours)	Value adding time (in hours)	Non-value adding time (in hours)
– Preparation and modification of drawings and BOM based on proposal accepted by clients – Work order preparation for client order for internal use		4550		4550
– Set up development cell in the design department (R&D department) – Improvement in the current design by reducing weight and standardization, etc.	780		780	
Tier 1 meeting and visual updates 31 × 26 × 15 min		202		202
Tier 2 and 3 meetings 15 × 26 × 60 min		390		390
Duplicity of the item codes in drawings and BOMS to be removed		520		520
– Document control – Availability of standard drawings in plants – Availability of bought-out and quality standards – ERP update to allow issue of standard BOMs		130		130

Design function	Current state map		Future state map	
– Series standardization of equipment with the identification of key characteristics/parameter				
Estimated contribution – percentage of the booked order (highlighting on monthly basis)		260		260
Work in ERP system and meet changing requirements as the lean production system is implemented		260		260
To analyze major causes of NCR for the design department points and implementation of CAPA – 5 × 2 × 26		260		260
Allocation of slow moving and non-moving stocks to the new design to reduce their amounts in the company		217		182
– Executives and staff kaizen and technical training hours – Implementation and sustenance of performance scorecard and training calendar 30 × 0.5 × 26	390		390	
Total	**1170**	**6789**	**1170**	**6754**
Total value adding and non-value adding hours	7958		7924	
Total usage time available (hours per month)	8385		8190	
Total free available hours per month		427		267
Value adding capacity usage percentage		14%		14%
Non-value adding capacity usage percentage		81%		82%
Free capacity available		5%		3%

Table 8.26 Current State and Future State Map for Marketing Function at Perfect Gear Company.

Marketing function	Current state map		Future state map	
Number of marketing personnel	8		6	
Marketing executives	15		11	
Number of shifts	1		1	
Hours per shift	8		8	
Rest hours per shift	0.5		0.5	
Available time (hours per day)	7.5		7.5	
Number of working days in the month	26		26	
Activity description	Value adding time (in hours)	Non-value adding time (in hours)	Value adding time (in hours)	Non-value adding time (in hours)
– Offer preparation, customers visits, domestic and international strike rate to be achieved – Response time to customers and offer submission and clarifications – Repeat orders from old customers, set and achieve targets for both domestic and international – Monthly customer follow-up visit		1950		1248
– Contract manufacturing from small/mid-size companies in developed countries like Europe and Japan – These mid-sized companies could eventually become joint venture/technology partners for international market		52		52
Tier 1 meeting and visual updates 15 × 26 × 15 min		150		111
Tier 2 and 3 meetings 15 × 26 × 60 min		260		260
International spare orders booking, diversification into new products for current and new market		52		52
– To visit customers focusing on revamping jobs – Meaningful visits to old customers		130		130

Marketing function	Current state map		Future state map	
– What new equipment can be added? – New products that have been added – request them to visit us				
Estimating contribution of the new orders booked during the month		260		260
All work to be done under the jurisdiction of ERP system and to meet the changing requirements as the lean production system is being implemented		260		221
Customer complaint count, sales return value, customer satisfaction survey – format finalization and implementation	104		104	
– Approach independent consultants and stay in touch with them – To prepare a plan, act, have awareness seminars – To get an expert speaker from the industry for training		260		208
Selling of slow moving and non-moving finished good stocks		130		130
Executives and staff kaizen and technical training hours, implementation and sustenance of performance scorecard and training calendar 23 × 0.5 × 26	299		221	
Total	403	3504	325	2672
Total of value adding and non-value adding hours	3907		2997	
Total usage time available hours per month	3120		3315	
Total free available hours per month	−787		319	
Value adding capacity usage percentage	13%		10%	
Non-value adding capacity usage percentage	112%		81%	
Free capacity available	−25%		10%	

Table 8.27 Current State and Future State Map for HRD Function at Perfect Gear Company.

HRD function	Current state map		Future state map		Remarks
Number of HRD personnel	10		6		Four positions are to be relocated to other value streams.
HRD executives	5		4		One executive level position is to be relocated to other value streams.
Number of shifts	1		1		
Hours per shift	8		8		
Rest hours per shift	0.5		0.5		
Available time (hours per day)	7.5		7.5		
Number of working days in the month	26		26		
Activity description	**Value adding time (in hours)**	**Non-value adding time (in hours)**	**Value adding time (in hours)**	**Non-value adding time (in hours)**	
To ensure routine HRD function: – Attendance, recruitment, appraisal, monthly salary preparation and annual increment policy implementation – Induction program of staff and workmen – Handle labor disputes and disciplinary matters		1768		1092	
– Finalization of trainings based on workmen skill matrix and staff's performance scorecard – Executives and staff and workmen kaizen and technical training hours – Every month reminder mail to all functions regarding the hours put in		52		52	
Tier 1 meeting and visual updates 10 × 26 × 15 min		65		39	
Tier 2 and 3 meetings 5 × 26 × 60 min		130		104	
Safety PPE – helmet, shoes, gloves, goggles, welding screen, firefighting training – two monthly per plant or as per ISO14000 guidelines		52		52	

HRD function	Current state map	Future state map	Remarks
Workmen skill matrix finalization – Average score of workmen skill matrix – Department-wise reporting to all functions heads and HODs – Preparation of performance scorecard for all staff – Average score of performance scorecard for executives and staff – Department-wise reporting to all functions heads and HODs	130	130	
Corporate governance and risk management – Submission of all returns timely, legal compliance of policies and procedures regarding termination, dismissal, compensation, etc. – Liaison with statutory bodies under labor laws for registration, licenses, renewals, etc. – Workplace accident (man), fulfilling guidelines of ISO-18001–2007-OHSAS requirements. – Handle labor disputes and disciplinary matters	52	52	
All HRD work to be done in ERP system and implement changes as required by the lean production system	130	130	
Complete manning. Absenteeism control. Employee satisfaction (feedback through survey).	312	104	
Controlling attrition rate. Exit interview.	260	130	
Customer-centric workforce –creating product knowledge and end application awareness to workmen and staff through internal training.	130	78	
Keeping record of focused improvement projects for all functions. Quarterly payment of kaizen reward and recognition scheme.	195		130	
Total	195	3081	130	1963

(Continued)

Table 8.27   (Continued)

HRD function	Current state map	Future state map	Remarks
Total of value adding and non-value adding hours	2964	1989	
Total usage time available hours per month	3510	1950	
Total free available hours per month	546	−39	
Value adding capacity usage percentage	6%	7%	
Non-value adding capacity usage percentage	79%	95%	
Free capacity available	16%	−2%	

Table 8.28   Current State and Future State Map for Information Technology Function at Perfect Gear Company.

Information technology function	Current state map		Future state map	
Number of information technology supervisors	10		7	
Information technology executives	7		5	
Number of shifts	1		1	
Hours per shift (A)	8		8	
Rest hours per shift (B)	0.5		0.5	
Available time (hours/day) (A-B)	7.5		7.5	
Number of working days in the month	26		26	
Activity description	Value adding time (in hours)	Non-value adding time (in hours)	Value adding time (in hours)	Non-value adding time (in hours)
– Ensure uninterrupted working of ERP system – Complete capturing of data across all functions – Value stream from the user's terminal to the server – Maintenance of hardwares and close coordination with the ERP service provider – Implementation of cyber security		1768		1092

Information technology function	Current state map	Future state map
– Stock updation by month end – Complete cycle of all activity – Planning report and new packing list from ERP – Training on ERP	52	52
Tier 1 meeting and visual updates 17 × 26 × 15 min	111	78
Tier 2 and 3 meetings 7 × 26 × 60 min	182	130
Put in place an authority structure that can largely be automated and monitored through ERP	52	52
– Stock accuracy in all categories – RM, BOP, WIP and consumables accuracy – ERP data accuracy will be ensured all times with actuals	130	130
– Categorization as done in the item master must appear in all the BOMs while BOM preparation – New item coding is to be done by the PPC	52	52
All work to be done under the jurisdiction of ERP system and to meet the changing requirements as the lean production system is being implemented	130	130
Moving the material across ERP, store request by assembly, issue of all BOM materials by stores and depletion thru invoice	312	104
To bring the accurate material cost sheets preparation for all BOMs and all equipment dispatched for the month 'online' as the invoice is made	260	130
ERP system – to identify the areas where locks are to be put to follow the correct procedure. W.O Closure is to be done on ERP.	130	78

(Continued)

Table 8.28 (Continued)

Information technology function	Current state map		Future state map	
Programming training is to be given to ERP persons. Also ERP executives and staff kaizen and technical training hours, implementation and sustenance of performance scorecard and training calendar 17 × 0.5 × 26	221		156	
Total	221	3179	156	2028
Total of value adding and non-value adding hours	3088		2080	
Total usage time available hours per month	3510		2340	
Total free available hours per month	423		260	
Value adding capacity usage percentage	6%		7%	
Non-value adding capacity usage percentage	82%		82%	
Free capacity available	12%		11%"	

- Machine performance improved to 88% from 73%, which increased production by 293 tons

Improvements in the Machine Shop from Lean Implementation

- Average downtime on each furnace reduced by two hours and 15 minutes, which is a result of one hour reduction in downtime, 15 minutes scrap downtime, 30 minutes reduction rework and 30 minutes reduction in wait time for material and inspection
- Changeover time reduced from three to two hours
- Machine performance improved to 75% from 70%, which increased production by 481 tons

Improvements in the Gear Shop from Lean Implementation

- Average downtime on each furnace reduced by three hours and 30 minutes, which is a result of 90 minutes reduction in downtime, 15 minutes scrap downtime, 30 minutes reduction rework and 75 minutes reduction in wait time for material and inspection

- Changeover time reduced from 60 minutes to 30 minutes
- Machine performance improved to 85% from 80%, which increased production by 308 tons
- Three executive level positions relocated to other value streams

Improvements in the Heat Treatment Shop from Lean Implementation

- Average downtime on each furnace reduced by five hours, which is a result of two hours reduction in downtime, 15 minutes scrap downtime, 30 minutes reduction rework and two hours and 15 minutes reduction in wait time for material and inspection
- Changeover time reduced from three hours to two hours
- Machine performance improved to 70% from 65%, which increased production by 334 tons
- Two executive level positions relocated to other value streams

Improvements in the Gear Grinding Shop from Lean Implementation

- Average downtime on each furnace reduced by three hours, which is a result of one hour reduction in downtime, 30 minutes reduction rework and one hour and 30 minutes reduction in wait time for material and inspection
- Changeover time reduced from two hours to one hour and 15 minutes
- Machine performance improved to 85% from 82%, which increased production by 391 tons
- One executive level position relocated to other value streams

Improvements in the Assembly Shop from Lean Implementation

- Average downtime on each furnace reduced by one hour and 45 minutes, which is a result of 15 minutes reduction rework and one hour reduction in wait time for material and inspection and 30 minutes reduction in movement of materials
- Changeover time reduced from 30 minutes to 15 minutes
- Machine performance improved to 85% from 60%, which increased production by 681 tons

Improvements in a Year for the Finished Good Supermarket and Logistics from Lean Implementation

Performance improved to 90% from 70%, which increased production by 351 tons

Capacity Calculation for Machines – Summary

The capacity usage of machines by all functions is summarized in Table 8.29.

The total non-value adding hours, that is, hours lost on wasteful activities on the machines have decreased from 19,247 hours to 10,810 hours per month. This translates into a saving of 8437 hours in a month and a saving of 325 hours daily for the company. These hours, in addition to the free hours available, can now be used for additional production. These savings are a result of lean and kaizen improvement projects implemented consistently throughout the year. The company's non-value adding capacity usage has decreased from 50% to 28%, value adding usage has increased from 44% to 66% and the free capacity of 6% is still available on the machines.

Capacity Calculation for Manpower – Summary

The capacity of manpower utilized in each function is summarized in Table 8.30. The total non-value adding hours that are the spent on wasteful activities in the manpower activities have decreased from 53,442 hours to 44,263 hours per month. This translates into a saving of 9179 hours in a month and 353 hours (or 16 man-days) in a day for the company. These hours, in addition to the free hours available, can now be used for additional production. This non-value adding usage in the company has decreased from 53% to 49%, value adding usage has increased from 25% to 41% and free capacity of 10% is still available.

The production capacity in tons can also be calculated using the functional charts from current state to future state as on 31 March 2018 and 31 March 2019 from Table 8.5 to Table 8.28. In the example of Perfect Gear Company, the company's last 12 months were prolific. The capacity in tons increased due to reduction in non-value adding use of capacity and use of free capacity in both machines and manpower. Sales volume increased by 50%, from 1000 tons to 1500 tons. The top line grew by 65%, from USD 40 million to USD 66 million. Profits as a percentage of sales increased from 5% to 17.1%. This has happened due to increase awareness throughout the

Table 8.29 Company's Current State (2018) and Future State (2019) Capacity for Machines at Perfect Gear Company.

Data in hours	Current state March 2018					Future state March 2019				
Activities category	Value adding	Non-value adding	Free capacity available	Total hours consumed	Value adding	Non-value adding	Free capacity available	Total hours consumed
Fabrication shop	4095	2951	442	7488	5733	1313	442	7488
SR furnace	956	839	78	1873	1209	585	78	1872
Machine shop	2925	5889	546	9360	4973	3842	546	9361
Gear shop	4680	4134	546	9360	6942	1872	546	9360
Heat treatment shop	2340	2379	273	4992	3484	1235	273	4992
Gear grinding	1664	3055	273	4992	2756	1963	273	4992
Total per month	16660	19247	2158	38065	25097	10810	2158	38065
%	44%	50%	6%		66%	28%	6%	

Table 8.30 Company's Current State (2018) and Future State (2019) Capacity for Manpower at Perfect Gear Company.

Data in hours	Current state March 2018				Future state March 2019			
Activities category	Value adding	Non-value adding	Free capacity available	Total hours consumed	Value adding	Non-value adding	Free capacity available	Total hours consumed
Fabrication shop	4095	2303	2572	8970	5733	1736	721	8190
SR furnace	956	549	251	1756	1209	446	100	1755
Machine shop	2925	3335	5440	11700	4973	3014	3713	11700
Gear shop	4680	3003	3043	10726	6942	2712	487	10141
Heat treatment shop	2340	1585	1731	5656	3484	1436	346	5266
Gear grinding	1664	1687	2305	5656	2756	1552	1152	5460
Assembly	3055	5135	1560	9750	6435	2951	364	9750
Logistics	293	936	527	1756	962	618	176	1756
Quality assurance	520	4199	156	4875	650	2860	195	3705
Maintenance	559	6864	962	8385	455	5993	377	6825
Purchase	1170	4258	1398	6826	1092	4141	423	5656
Finance	520	3660	1866	6046	910	3595	371	4876
Design	1170	6788	427	8385	1170	6754	267	8191
Marketing	463	3504	-787	3180	325	2672	319	3316
HRD	195	2769	546	3510	130	1859	-39	1950
IT	221	2867	423	3511	156	1924	260	2340
Total per month	24826	53442	22420	100688	37382	44263	9232	90877
%	25%	53%	22%		41%	49%	10%	

Table 8.31 Production Capacity (in metric tons) per Month for All Functions at Perfect Gear Company.

Functions	Mar-18	Mar-19	Increased capability
Fabrication	1183	1784	601
Stress relieving shop	1163	1773	610
Machine shop and tool room	1170	2131	961
Gear cutting shop*	998	1574	576
Heat treatment shop	1127	1807	680
Gear grinding shop	1137	1952	815
Assembly and testing shop	1404	2273	869
Finished goods and logistics	1229	1580	351

*Gear cutting shop is the bottleneck function that limits the dispatches from the company

company about the capacity usage and reduction of non-value adding capacity usage. The increased awareness and regular monthly reviews contributed to key operational measures improvements as shown in Table 8.32.

Analysis of Capacity of Manpower

■ The *non-value adding use of capacity* by manpower decreased from 53% to 49%. This is due to reduction of wasteful hours in breakdowns, defects, scrap, waiting time for material, inspection and long changeover time. This extra capacity in manpower is now available in the company without any extra cost to the company.

■ The *value-adding use of capacity* increased from 25% to 41%. The company was able to use the free time available from the reduction of non-value adding capacity usage. The free manpower capacity is still available at 10%.

■ *Manpower deployment to other value streams – no layoff policy* Additionally, the company relocated 27 executives and 26 supervisors and workmen to other value streams successfully during this time without need for new hiring to meet additional demand. Table 8.33 summarizes these numbers. Perfect Gear Company assured its employees at the beginning of the lean and kaizen journey that no one will be laid off due to the improvements or automation in the operational parameters because this company is a proactive and farsighted company. Instead of laying off, it invested its efforts in planning for expansion in

Table 8.32   Improvement in Key Performance Measures at Perfect Gear Company.

Key parameters		UOM	Current state March 2018	Future state March 2019
Average dispatch per day		Tons	40	58
Average monthly dispatch		Tons	1000	1500
Average sales price		USD per kg	3.33	3.67
Monthly dispatch		USD (in Mn)	3.33	5.50
Annual turnover		USD (in Mn)	40	66
Capacity – Machines	Value adding capacity usage	%	44	66
	Non-value adding capacity usage	%	50	28
	Free capacity available	%	6	6
Capacity – Manpower	Value adding capacity usage	%	25	41
	Non-value adding capacity usage	%	53	49
	Free capacity available	%	22	10

the existing market and exploring diversification into new businesses so that these 53 personnel can be redeployed there.

Analysis of Capacity of Machines

■ The *non-value adding use of machine capacity* decreased from 50% to 28%. This is due to reduction in wasteful hours spent on breakdown, defects, scrap, waiting time for material, inspection and long change-over time. This extra capacity is available to the company without any investment.

■ The *value adding use of machine capacity* increased from 44% to 66%. The company was able to use the free time made available from reduction in non-value adding use of capacity to increase production by 50%, improve the revenue by 65% and surge profit by 12.1% in a span of one year of a lean and kaizen journey.

By the time the company reaches this stage, the managers have a thorough understanding of the capacity of the value stream, internal costs and the requirements of the customers. This enables them to revise the processes in order to improve customer service. Once the company identifies non-value

Table 8.33   Manpower Redeployment Plan at Perfect Gear Company.

Value stream cost centers	As of end of March 2019		
	Executives level	Supervisor/ workmen level	Total
Marketing	4	2	6
Design	3	5	8
Purchase, subcontracting and stores	1	5	6
Finance and accounts	1	5	6
Fabrication	4	0	4
Stress relieving shop	0	0	0
Machine shop and tool room	0	0	0
Gear cutting shop	3	0	3
Heat treatment shop	2	0	2
Gear grinding shop	1	0	1
Maintenance function – mechanical and electrical	2	2	4
Assembly and testing shop	0	0	0
Finished goods and logistics	0	0	0
Quality assurance	3	0	3
Information technology system	2	3	5
HRD	1	4	5
Total	27	26	53

adding activities in the value stream map, it should implement lean and kaizen tools aggressively to reduce time spent on these activities. The company must stretch its operations to the level of capacity utilization that fixed costs can support. The surplus capacity that will thus become available along with existing free capacity are excellent ingredients to look into expansion and diversification opportunities.

If the company diversifies and ventures into new product development or a new line of business, new products produced in the value stream will increase the revenue and bottom line without much impact on fixed costs. When the company increases production of existing products or commences production of new products, the average cost of production decreases since the company does not invest in new machinery or manpower. The only additional cost will be raw material cost along with marginal increase in variable cost of power, stores and consumables. Thus, capacity management results in increase in profits instead of capital investment.

Low average product cost empowers the company to reduce prices in the market and seize business from the competition. The company armed with information like free capacity available and scope of reduction in the non-value adding use of capacity makes better business and strategic decisions. Taking critical decisions like product pricing, outsourcing, purchase of capital equipment and new product development become easier with focus on lean company requirements.

Key Takeaways

1. Capacity data of a value stream is the missing link between lean operational improvements and visible financial improvements.
2. Higher production, higher manpower efficiency and better machine utilization than the standard reflect a good performance and profitability. Lower production, efficiency and utilization reflect poor performance and lower profits. *Lean accounting disapproves it*. Lean accounting expels the use of efficiency of manpower and utilization of machines in the company. Lean accounting focuses on customers with on time and full delivery of quality products or services to them.
3. Value adding capacity of the value stream is increased with release of capacity from non-value adding activities like breakdowns, minor or major stoppages, scrapping, reworking, waiting for material, decisions, changeover times, poor performance rate and so forth with the implementation of lean.
4. With the released capacity, the company can produce more products to generate additional revenue and profits. In doing so, revenue increases faster than the costs without investment in additional resources.
5. The company must stretch its operations to the level of capacity utilization that fixed costs can support. The surplus capacity that will thus become available along with existing free capacity are excellent ingredients to look into expansion and diversification opportunities.
6. Low average product cost empowers the company to reduce prices in the market and seize business from the competition.

Recommended List for Further Reading

1. Maskell.com. Blog- *"Capacity has value"*.
2. Maskell, B.H., Baggaley, B. and Grasso, L. (2012). *Practical lean accounting: A proven system for measuring and managing the lean enterprise*. Boca Raton, FL: CRC Press.
3. Stenzel, J. (2007). *Lean accounting: Best practices for sustainable integration*. Hoboken, NJ: John Wiley & Sons.

Chapter 9

Corporate Scorecard

When everything is a priority, nothing is a priority.

– Karen Martin

The companies embracing lean and kaizen tools initiatives observe improvement in throughput time, reduction in breakdowns and changeover time, improvement in quality, reduction in inventory and faster decision-making. The management evaluates the results to justify the budget of lean and kaizen initiatives.

The teams responsible for lean implementation calculate savings and present them to management to justify the future continuity of these improvement projects. In many companies this is a difficult hump to cross because on many occasions these initiatives cease at this stage or are relegated to a slow burner.

9.1 What Is a Corporate Scorecard (CSC)?

Lean Gurus James P. Womack and Daniel T. Jones[1] in their book *Lean Thinking: Banish Waste and Create Wealth in Your Corporation* underlined the importance of the implementation of the five principles of lean manufacturing for a company to become lean in a true aspect as discussed in Chapter 3. These five principles are as follows:

- *Identify Value* – Value must be defined from the standpoint of the final customer.

DOI: 10.4324/9781003221746-9

- *Map the Value Stream* – The entire set of activities needed to design and produce a product must be thoroughly understood and mapped out.
- *Flow* – The product must move along the value stream without interruption. It must flow.
- *Pull* – Organizations must be structured so that the customer can pull value from the producer.
- *Continuous Improvement* – The whole enterprise must pursue not its competitors, but rather perfection.

The outcome of implementation of these five principles can be captured in one sheet called a corporate scorecard that is a lean accounting tool that showcases monthly business performance to all stakeholders. It translates operational improvements into financial benefits and better utilization of capacity, a new concept many companies are unfamiliar with.

A corporate scorecard gives a three-dimensional view of operations, financials and capacity that enables managers to make better decisions for the value stream because it gives a multi-dimensional view of key business information. A corporate scorecard is a small table as shown in Table 9.1 and gives a 360-degree view of the company on a single sheet of paper.

Table 9.1   Sample Corporate Scorecard for Perfect Gear Company.

Aspect	Key performance indicator	UOM	Current state March 2018
Financial	**Sales revenue – monthly**	USD Mn	3.33
	Average product sales price	USD per kg	3.33
	Average product cost	USD per kg	2.84
	Value of inventory	USD Mn	6.27
	Profit before tax	USD Mn	0.17
	Profit before tax	%	5%
Operational	**Throughput time**	Days	113
	On time shipment	%	70%
	Total head count	Number	561
Capacity usage – manpower	**Value adding**	%	25%
	Non-value adding	%	53%
	Free capacity available	%	22%
Capacity usage – machine	**Value adding**	%	44%
	Non-value adding	%	50%
	Free capacity available	%	6%

It condenses operational and financial performance of the company along with capacity utilization of both manpower and machine. It summarizes the capacity used in value adding activities, non-value adding activities (i.e., for wasteful activities) and surplus capacity available. The capacity information is the missing link between operational and financial measures that is filled in by the corporate scorecard.

The financial aspect is an outcome of lean and kaizen initiatives and increase in value adding use of capacity, whereas the operational aspect of the corporate scorecard measures the performance of lean and kaizen initiatives. The capacity aspect of the corporate scorecard shows value adding use of capacity for which the customer pays the company, non-value adding wasteful activities that the company is forced to undertake and surplus capacity available. Capacity assessment encourages the company to evaluate how non-value adding usage will decrease month on month and get transferred either to value adding usage or surplus capacity. When non-value adding use of capacity decreases, the company experiences an increase in production, customer satisfaction and on-time performance and a reduction in inventory and throughput time.

Financial Aspect of a Corporate Scorecard

- *Monthly Sales Revenue and Production Value* – Invoice amount of shipment during the month. It is important to assess the monetary value of actual production during the month.
- *Average Product Sales Price* – Total revenue of the month/Number of units sold (either in numbers, tons, kg or liters, whatever is relevant for the company).
- *Average Material Cost Price* – Total material cost for the month/Number of units sold (either in numbers, tons, kg or liters, whatever is relevant for the company).
- *Inventory Value* – Value of all materials lying in the company (raw materials, stores materials, consumables, work in progress) and finished products yet to be dispatched, lying in the distribution centers or anywhere else in the supply chain along with slow moving and dead stock at the month end. The inventory is valued at current cost and cost of inventory lies in buying, storing, tracking, insurance, obsolescence and discount. This is also an opportunity to correct the books for actual material lying in various categories.
- In the lean journey, if the company is not able to see a decline in inventory, then it means the company is not practicing lean as per the

road map. The progress should be reviewed at this stage for corrective action. Inventory is the most important measure and must decrease at least 20% every year in initial years of lean implementation. This will be a sign of success of 'flow and pull'. The stock taking can be done in three days without hindering the operations. Finance and stores functions will coordinate with teams from each function for stock taking.

■ *Profit Before Tax (Value and %)* – It is the profitability of the company during the period, that is, the total earnings after deducting all expenses from the revenue. It includes sales value of all shipments from the value stream and all variables and fixed costs including cost of production labor, materials and support, operation support, facilities and maintenance and any other costs that are incurred for the value stream.

Operational Aspect of a Corporate Scorecard

■ *Throughput Time*
■ Throughput or lead time measures the flow of products from receipt of raw materials or customer orders to the shipment of finished goods. It shows the speed of conversion of raw materials or customer orders to finished product.
■ Throughput Time/Lead Time (in hours or days) = (Raw material + Store materials + Work in progress + Finished goods)/Products shipped in one hour or one day.
■ *On Time Shipment*
■ It measures the shipment of the right products in the right quantity as per the customer order. It shows the effectiveness of the production process in adhering to the schedule. It is updated monthly in the corporate scorecard to list the quantity shipped without any quality problems.
■ On time in full (OTIF) % = (Quantity shipped in full on time–customer return)/Scheduled quantity that was planned to be shipped.
■ *Total Headcount*
■ It is the total manpower in the company at the month end.

Capacity Aspect of a Corporate Scorecard

■ *Value Adding Use of Capacity*
■ Activities that convert the raw material into finished product constitute value adding use of capacity. This is calculated for both manpower and machine separately.

- *Non-Value Adding Use of Capacity*
- All activities that slow down or halt the processes like breakdowns, minor or major stoppages, scrapping, reworking, waiting for material, decisions and so forth, changeover times and poor performance rate are non-value adding use of capacity. Customers do not pay for it.
- The time spent in activities in functions like assembly, quality, logistics, purchase, design, marketing, finance and accounts, HRD, IT and maintenance are required to run the company and are partially value adding. What are the activities in these functions can be classified as 'value adding'? The relevant capacity calculations charts can be referred to in Chapter 8. This can vary from industry to industry.
- *Free Capacity Available*
- The available capacity or surplus capacity is the difference between total time available and the sum of both value adding capacity usage time and non-value adding capacity use of time. This is free time available for increasing production. The surplus capacity is further enhanced by reduction in the non-value adding use of capacity through lean and kaizen tools implementation.

9.2 How to Prepare a Corporate Scorecard

The CFO, his representatives or the value stream manager should take the responsibility of preparing the corporate scorecard on the first of every month. All major improvement initiatives must be included in the corporate scorecard. When the breakdowns, scrap, rework, wait time for materials and decision-making time reduces, it must be demonstrated by reduction in non-value adding use of capacity and creation of surplus capacity to produce more.

Table 9.2 shows the status of the company in the months of March 2018 and March 2019. The results can be compared to see how much the company has gained in one year due to improvements initiatives implemented in the company. Revenue increased by 50% and the bottom line by 10%. Throughput time has drastically decreased and the material flow is four times faster as the wasteful activities have reduced due to continuous improvement projects. Value adding use of manpower increased from 24% to 39% and of machine increased from 44% to 66%. Non-value adding use of capacity has declined in both manpower and machines.

Table 9.2 Corporate Scorecard for the Months of March 2018 and March 2019 for Perfect Gear Company.

Aspect	Key performance indicator	UOM	Current state March 2018	Future state March 2019
Financial	Sales revenue – monthly	USD Mn	3.33	5.50
	Average product sales price	USD per kg	3.33	3.67
	Average product cost	USD per kg	2.84	2.79
	Value of inventory	USD Mn	6.27	0.00
	Profit before tax	USD Mn	0.17	0.94
	Profit before tax	%	5%	17%
Operational	Throughput time	Days	113	31
	On time shipment	%	70%	80%
	Total head count	Number	561	508
Capacity usage – manpower	Value adding	%	25%	39%
	Non-value adding	%	53%	50%
	Free capacity available	%	22%	11%
Capacity usage – machine	Value adding	%	44%	66%
	Non-value adding	%	50%	28%
	Free capacity available	%	6%	6%

Corrective action can be taken promptly as the previous month's performance has been analyzed and next month can be planned realistically. The management should notice an increase in revenue faster than the costs. All functions must understand the financial outcomes of their lean operation measures and capacity usage. The companies move to weekly scorecards after successfully preparing and sustaining monthly a corporate scorecard. The swiftness in decision-making with up-to date information available on a weekly basis that is understood by functional managers will enhance business performance tremendously.

Advantages of a Corporate Scorecard

A corporate scorecard is a comprehensive report with financial and non-financial information and is useful in understanding the business performance. A corporate scorecard enables the company to analyze business operations month over month and reflect how operational performance improves the financial performance. The company can control the financial outcomes by controlling operational measures like operational processes, sales operation, design operation, purchase operations, production operations and administration operations.

Efficient processes ensure a healthy financial outcome. Operational performance improvement can be seen in the capacity box of manpower and machines. The non-value adding capacity use decreases as operations improve. A corporate scorecard is a crystal clear card where the company can see improvements every month. Therefore, the operations team does not need to explain savings every month to the top management for funding their lean and kaizen initiative projects.

A corporate scorecard gives a platform for taking accurate decisions and allows decision-making at the lower level. This is beneficial as people at the lower levels are aware of the workplace and the implications of the decision made on the company. This liberates the senior managers to devote time to strategy. The key advantage of a corporate scorecard is that it is understood by the non-finance managers because it eliminates complexity in presentation.

9.3 Corporate Scorecard and Decision-Making – A New Scientific Approach[2]

A corporate scorecard opens a new window for decision-making with a focus on lean company requirements. Unlike standard cost accounting practices, the company does not focus on an individual product. The company looks at the product portfolio and focuses on the profitability of the value stream. Due to better decision making, the company does not turn down orders due to lack of capacity or outsource if it is aware of cheaper in-house production. The company can assess operational parameters, capacity and financial health to make rational decisions. Lean accounting along with a corporate scorecard assists in logical and quick decision-making.

Product Part Pricing

Market determines the price of the product that further guides the price at which a company will be willing to sell a particular product. Traditional companies have a standard cost for each product. These traditional companies meticulously calculate material, production and overheads cost and then add a standard margin of profit set up by the management to derive the selling price that is used by marketing to prepare offers. Marketing assumes this price is the cost of the product and selling at a price lower than this will incur a loss. On the other hand, the company assumes that the standard cost of the product will remain the same and marketing can continuously use it for procuring or refusing orders. There is no affiliation with the actual costs and company's profitability. Suppose marketing receives a request from a customer that they want to buy an item X at a price of $95 per piece. The costing department has a standard cost for this product at $90 per piece. The management policy is to sell at 15% margin.

$$Selling\ price = 90 + 13.5 = \$103.5$$

The company would like to sell at $103.5 per piece, whereas the customer offers $95, that is, a 5.6% margin. The company might make a decision not to sell at this margin.

However, a lean company knows how much surplus capacity is currently available or is going to be available in the near future as the non-value adding use of capacity decreases. Therefore, a lean company does not refuse the order but negotiates best price before accepting the order and still make profit even after considering raw material and incremental conversion cost. There may be a situation where the customer offers the previous deal, but the company does not have internal capacity available. If the analysis reveals that overtime or partial machine outsourcing can earn a margin of 4% instead of the 5.6% margin as calculated earlier, the company can still accept the order because this 4% margin will be their incremental profit.

A corporate scorecard contains actual revenue, conversion cost, manpower cost and capacity. If the company has spare capacity available and continuously reduces non-value adding use of capacity, it will be in a better position to make a decision to sell at lower cost or deliver higher volumes to the customer instead of refusing the order and insisting on a higher price. This is the advantage with a corporate scorecard. Value stream production cost increases only if the level of resources changes, that is, the company buys additional resources or hires additional manpower. Without adding new facilities and using the spare capacity available the company can offer better prices in the market. This gives an insight into the importance of the costs. The key is to work in-house and reduce the internal costs to whatever extent possible. At this stage, the marketing function is expected to liaison with operations and value stream managers to make these decisions.

Outsourcing

If outsourcing gives the same product at a lower price than standard costs, a company might consider it to make a saving. But the company must first look at its capacity. If spare capacity is available, it will be cheaper to make it in-house as the company will expend only on material and incremental conversion costs. If spare capacity is not available, it should calculate the best option between outsourcing or running an extra shift and overtime for some operators.

If the company is using capacity for non-value adding activities, the manager should put in efforts to reduce non-value adding use of capacity. Also, the company must review currently outsourced activities and bring it in-house by fast pacing the lean initiatives. The company will be in a better position operationally and financially if it does so.

Capital Equipment Purchase

Traditional companies always analyze return on investment (ROI) through projected volumes from the new machine, payback period, impact on the present standard cost, future demand and so forth. But they do not check whether it is a bottleneck machine or not. The product price changes due to increase in cost of resources and standard costs are revised. The company continues to follow the same practice of standard costing system and decide to take orders based on the new standard costs.

However, a lean company will have a different perspective for this purchase. The capacities will be analyzed from the corporate scorecard, purchase will be evaluated from value stream's perspective and justified from capacity point of view. It will be checked if the new purchase addresses the bottleneck area where the cycle time is the highest. The company will calculate payback period and impact on value stream margins to evaluate this investment decision. For this, first impact on surplus capacity, current non-value adding use of capacity and status of the lean and kaizen initiatives in its reduction to release capacity for future use will be assessed. Then, change in future state of the value stream due to this investment will be computed highlighting projected increase in customer demand, capacity to produce, incremental revenue, increase in costs like depreciation, power, tooling and maintenance and new average cost of products in value stream. Also, impact on operational factors like reduction in throughput time, improvement in flow and reduction in delivery time to customers will be examined. Taking all these costs into account with new revenue figures based on the projected demand, the company can calculate new value stream margins and use it to calculate payback period.

Therefore, a corporate scorecard allows the company to make the decision to purchase a new machine from all three aspects – capacity, operations and finance.

Recruitment

Traditional companies hire people based on gaps arising during the monthly plan made in MRP and CRP. They view gaps based on projected demand as a call for fresh hiring and treat manpower cost as expense, like other resources.

Lean companies, on the other hand, calculate capacity for each function and know exactly how much manpower capacity is being utilized for value adding and non-value adding activities and how much free capacity is available in each function and across all the value streams in the company. They check whether the manpower demand is temporary or permanent and analyze opportunities to divert the surplus manpower available from one function to another, if feasible. Adding new manpower resources increases manufacturing costs and it is the last thing a lean company would want to do. For a lean company, additional hiring should be justified by increase in the revenue and margin in corporate scorecard for future state.

Budget for Continual Improvement Projects

The continual improvement teams require budget for expenditure on rectification and modification of machines and hardware resources, buying add-on features for existing machines, balancing small machineries in the main plant and hiring lean and kaizen agencies for guidance on implementation of initiatives. These expenses are borne by the existing value streams. The benefits achieved between current state and future state are explicitly mentioned in the capacity sheets of each function along with the monetary value of these initiatives. The initiatives should be successfully executed to justify the costs and benefits reaped should be higher than the costs incurred.

The improvement in the value streams and the company will result in surplus capacity due to continuous reduction in non-value adding use of capacity and awareness of the available capacity in the value stream. The focus of the lean company is to generate more capacity to meet customer demand and increase revenue. The released capacity must be used to acquire more orders for the existing products or new product development to increase the revenue and bottom line. The motto of continuous improvement initiatives is to bring higher growth in the bottom line than the top line. Reduction in machine and manpower resources brings overall cost reduction in the company, but this should be last resort for a lean company.

New Product Development

A lean company that is implementing continual improvement initiatives incessantly reduces wasteful use of capacity in its system and creates surplus capacity. This capacity is used to fulfill additional volume required by current customers or new customers. New product development is a key area for continuous attention in a lean company and until a product is developed and manufactured, it has to be supported by all value streams. All its expenses are underwritten by existing value streams till the product starts generating revenue.

A classic marketing approach should be used – can we sell more products to our existing customers? Can we acquire new customers to sell to our existing products to? Can we develop new products for existing customers? Can we develop new products for new customers?

The development of the new products should be brisk in meeting the current requirements of the customers and easy to manufacture so that it comes out swiftly into the market without compromise on quality. The faster the new product flows out of the company, the lesser will be the development cost.

Figure 9.1 shows responsibilities of the concerned functional managers for decisions based on the use of the corporate scorecard.

9.4 How Value Stream Managers and Functional Managers Use the Corporate Scorecard

Table 9.3 shows how top management, value stream managers and functional managers drive the key performance indicators (KPIs) in a value stream and in the company. A corporate scorecard provides a bird's-eye view of the value stream and the company. These improvements can be monitored on a weekly or monthly basis to assess revenue during this period, average sales price, average material cost and profit. Simultaneously,

Sl. No	Description	Refer chapter	CEO's	CFO's	Value stream managers**	Functional managers*	Concerned functional managers
1	Product part pricing		✓	✓✓	✓	✓	Marketing
2	Outsourcing		✓	✓✓	✓	✓	Purchase
3	Capital equipment purchase	Chapter-9	✓✓	✓✓	✓	✓	Purchase
4	Recruitment		✓✓	✓	✓	✓	HRD
5	Budget for the continual improvement projects		✓	✓✓	✓	✓	Concerned functional managers
6	New product development		✓✓	✓✓	✓	✓	Marketing, design, R&D, purchase

* Head of functions of fabrication, machining, gear cutting, heat treatment, gear grinding, assembly, logistics, quality, maintenance, purchase, finance, HRD, design and R&D.

** Only one value stream is referred to in detail in this book.

✓ = Direct responsibility to implement and sustain

✓ ✓ = Ultimate responsibility

Figure 9.1   Responsibilities for Decisions Based on the Use of Corporate Scorecard for Perfect Gear Company.

the inventory level, throughput time, delivery time, customer satisfaction and employee count can be reviewed. The most important thing to know is how much surplus capacity has increased and how much use of capacity in non-value adding activities decreased. If these parameters improve, it means continuous improvement initiatives are successful in the company.

The management and value stream managers can review these figures every month to check if they are on the right track. They can refine the corporate scorecard to make it relevant and meaningful for everyone. KPIs can be included or excluded and modified every six months if the requirement changes. The corporate scorecard is the starting point of preparing the balance scorecards for value stream managers, which are used in preparing performance scorecards for other executives and supervisors and in preparing skill matrix cards for the workmen on the plant floor. These will be discussed in detail in the next chapter.

The marketing function studies these charts from their perspective. They notice how on time delivery performance improved from 70% to 80% in a

Table 9.3   Corporate Scorecard for Gains and KPI Responsibility at Perfect Gear Company.

Aspect	Key performance indicator	UOM	Current state March 2018	Future state March2019- Change in 12 months	Explanation of gains		KPI responsibility
Financial	Sales revenue – monthly	USD Mn	3.33	5.50	2.17	Revenue increase of US$2.17 million in 12 months	Marketing and sales
	Average product sales price	USD per kg	3.33	3.67	0.33	Average product sales price per kg has increased by 0.33 US$	Marketing and sales
	Average product cost	USD per kg	2.84	2.79	−0.05	Average product cost per kg has dropped by 0.05 US$	All functions
	Value of inventory	USD Mn	6.27	0.00	−6.27	Inventory has gone down by 3.69 million US$	Operations, finance, SCM, R&D, marketing
	Profit before tax	USD Mn	0.17	0.94	0.77	Profit before tax per month has surged by 0.77 million US$	All functions
	Profit before tax	%	5%	17%	12%	Increase of profit before tax by 12%	All functions
Operational	Throughput time	Days	113	31	−82.00	Throughput has decreased by 82 days	All functions
	On time shipment	%	70%	80%	10%	On time shipment has increased by 10%	SCM, marketing, operations, all
	Total head count	Number	561	508	−53.00	Total 53 employees are to be redeployed to other value streams	All, HRD (coordinator)
Capacity usage – manpower	Value adding	%	25%	39%	14%	Value adding usage has increased by 14%	All functions
	Non-value adding	%	53%	50%	−3%	Non-value adding usage has decreased by 3%	All functions
	Free capacity available	%	22%	11%	−11%	11% free capacity is now available	All functions
Capacity usage – machine	Value adding	%	44%	66%	22%	Value adding usage has increased by 22%	All functions
	Non-value adding	%	50%	28%	−22%	Non-value adding usage has decreased by 22%	All functions
	Free capacity available	%	6%	6%	0%	No free capacity is now available	All functions

year. They see that since more capacity is available for the future, they have to book more orders and commit delivery dates to the customers. They also analyze the changes in the customer satisfaction level monthly. The production planning and control function prepares the schedule of operational activities for the next month based on the yearly budget and take corrective action required with respect to the previous month or previous quarter. The material and capacity resources will be based on this fundamental information.

The operational function uses the corporate scorecard to understand the outcome of the execution of the value stream improvement plans. The procurement function uses the corporate scorecard to monitor average product cost movement, inventories lying in the company and on time product shipment to customers. Value stream continuous improvement teams use the corporate scorecard for assessment of the outcomes of their projects, initiatives and course corrections. Continual improvement teams design their future improvement initiatives based on the corporate scorecard that will have highest impact on financial and operating results.

Skewing of the Production Toward the Last Week of the Month

Most of the companies have higher dispatches in the last week of the month. In some companies, 70% to 80% of the dispatches take place in the last two weeks of the month. This practice is eliminated when the corporate scorecard is prepared weekly. It is analyzed how the managers run the plants so efficiently in these last two weeks of the month. What is the true capacity of the plant? Is there some hidden capacity that managers use during this time? What are they producing? Are they producing the products to fulfill the finance requirement of machine and manpower utilization resulting in an increase in month end inventories? There is a need to know the true capacity of the plant. The plant should run on takt time (customer's requirements) on customer's pull throughout the month.

Key Takeaways

1. A corporate scorecard gives a three-dimensional view of operations, financials and capacity that enables managers to make better decisions for the value stream. A corporate scorecard is a crystal clear card where the company can see improvements every month.

2. The capacity information is the missing link between operational and financial measures that is filled in by the corporate scorecard.
3. Capacity assessment encourages the company to evaluate how non-value adding usage will decrease month on month and the company experiences increase in production, customer satisfaction, on time performance and reduction in inventory and throughput time. It means continuous improvement initiatives are successful in the company.
4. A corporate scorecard gives a platform for decision-making at the lower level.
5. Lean accounting along with a corporate scorecard assists in logical and quick decision-making.

Recommended List for Further Reading

1. Womack, J.P. and Jones, D.T. (2003). *Lean thinking: Banish waste and create wealth in your corporation.* New York: Free Press.
2. Maskell.com. Blog- *"Lean decision making: – 1. Making the leap. 2. A better lean way. 3. Every decision, all the time."*
   Maskell, B.H., Baggaley, B. and Grasso, L. (2012). *Practical lean accounting: A proven system for measuring and managing the lean enterprise.* Boca Raton, FL: CRC Press.
   Stenzel, J. (2007). *Lean accounting: Best practices for sustainable integration.* Hoboken, NJ: John Wiley & Sons.

Chapter 10

Lean Performance Measurement System

When performance is measured, performance improves. When performance is measured and reported, the rate of improvement accelerates.

– Thomas S. Monson

A company's strategy provides a 'line of sight' from strategic measures to operational activities. The strategy can be to increase sale revenues, cash flow, productivity, customer experience or employee satisfaction. Strategy may touch some of these goals or all of them. But how does a company assess if the strategy has been successful in accomplishment of the goals?

Each goal has success factors attached to it that are measurable and determine how successful the strategy has been. The right success factors are transformed into performance measures with targets for all functions and employees at all levels. Each employee in the company is involved in the continuous improvement initiatives to achieve the targets. The right strategy leads to increase in profits illustrated in Figure 10.1.

It is important that every employee in the company is well acquainted with their job responsibilities. However, usually only 5% of the workforce tends to understand the company's strategy because of the top-down approach. The company should have a system to ensure everyone in the company, from the senior managers to the workmen on the plant floor, knows what their key performing areas are. This brings clarity to the

DOI: 10.4324/9781003221746-10

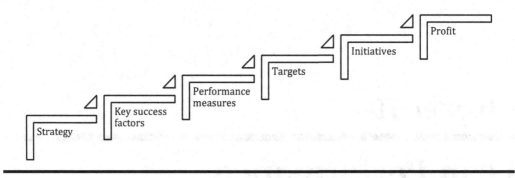

Figure 10.1 Strategy, Key Success Factors, Performance Measures and Profits Linkage.

individuals regarding their role in the company and helps the top management to monitor employee performance to link it to the reward and recognition scheme.

The need for the lean performance measurement system arises once the company implements lean tools like 5S, TPM, value streams, flow, supermarket, kanban and so forth and all workmen, staff and managers become part of some function in the value stream. They become mindful of customer needs and understand the significance of quality products and timely delivery. They fathom the next process is also their customer and commit not to produce defective materials, not to send the defective materials to the next process and not to accept defective materials from the previous process.

In a traditional company, the departmental approach for improvement is followed. The department teams focus on improvement of their departments only and are ignorant of customer needs. Consequently, neither the customers nor the company benefits, and everyone remains in firefighting mode. In a lean company that is a value stream-based company, flow and pull administer the processes. Everyone works on the lean approach, or a system approach, wherein everyone works to fulfill the needs of the customers and uplift the company as a whole.

The direction of the tiny arrows within the arrows in Figure 10.2 illustrates this point well. In the departmental approach, the directions are not clear and individual functions may work against each other. The system approach brings the functions together to focus on customer needs and overall company goals instead. The lean performance measurement system brings the goals of individual workmen, supervisors, managers, functional heads, value stream managers, the CFO and the CEO together so that everyone works toward the company goals, its vision and mission.

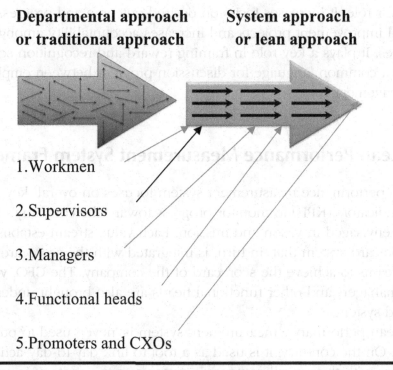

Departmental approach or traditional approach

System approach or lean approach

1. Workmen

2. Supervisors

3. Managers

4. Functional heads

5. Promoters and CXOs

Figure 10.2   Traditional Approach vs. Lean Approach.

10.1 Need for the Lean Performance Measurement System

The introduction, implementation and monitoring of the lean performance measurement system becomes a necessity once the lean production system is implemented. Performance measures are required because what is measured gets noticed, what is noticed gets acted upon and what is acted upon gets improved. The goal of the lean performance measurement system is *to manage the processes, not the results*. This change in perspective is essential because standard costing is result focused, whereas lean is process focused. It brings a change in employee behavior since focus on process improvement encourages employees to identify erroneous practices and reveal the defects without fearing impact on results.

The lean performance measurement system is a systematic way of measuring, reviewing and analyzing employee performance at each level in the company over a given period of time. This information is used for identification of training needs and skill up-gradation. Therefore, it acts as an appraisal system also. It aligns strategic objectives with customer needs and the company's expectations in order to bring clarity among the employees about their role. It increases focus on desired outcome and progress of continual improvement projects and increases accountability among the employees. It plays a key role in framing reward and recognition scheme and lays a common language for discussion progress between employees and management.

10.2 Lean Performance Measurement System Framework

The lean performance measurement system focuses on overall key performance indicators (KPIs) to monitor progress toward the company's strategic goals as envisaged in vision and mission. Each value stream establishes its own scorecard system that, in turn, is integrated with the scorecards of other value streams to achieve the scorecard of the company. The CFO, value stream managers and other functional heads are also brought under the scorecard system.

The lean performance measurement system is 'never' used to punish the staff. On the contrary, it is used as a tool to link day-to-day activities of employees with the overall company's strategy, so the strategy is engraved in everyone's daily activities. The monthly scores states current status and gives clarity on what needs to be done to improve the score. It brings transparency in the performance measurement and reward management system. For any company in a particular industry, the lean performance measurement system has to be designed on the basis of current status of the company and its vision and mission. A robust lean performance measurement system makes you perform better than your competition.

Why Selection of the Right Performance Measure Is Important

Before lean implementation, measures were based on the standard costing system, but the new measurement system must meet the requirements of the lean production system. Traditional measures focus on each department's efficiency and utilization of resources and serve internal individual interests, whereas in the lean management system, the focus is on value stream and customers. The strategic measures of the company should reflect in value stream measures, cell measures and functional process measures. This way the whole company is tied in one long rope speaking the same language and focusing on customers, who primarily pull this rope.

Consider the following scenario: a company implements flow and pull, establishes supermarket with kanban system, supplies products to customers to fulfill their demand. Whenever the products are dispatched, kanban triggers production and products are replenished in the supermarket. Processes are streamlined and customers are satisfied. Now, if in the month end review the CFO questions the operations team about lower machine or manpower utilization and unfavorable production volume variance, it will confuse and discourage the operations team. *How will they justify improvement in processes if old measures are used to review their performance? Hence, the earlier performance measures need to be scrapped and the new performance measures commensurate with the lean implementation should be used.*

Top management witnesses better results when people work in unison. Managing a company is hard work and needs the right set of measurements. Customers need quality material delivered in time as per the quantity required. Managers are responsible for the output and productivity of their teams and have a tough task of ensuring that employees produce results that are aligned with the customer requirements and organization goals. Also, employees have to realize the importance of concepts like first time right, waste elimination and consistency in processes.

The success from implementation of the lean production system, daily management system and lean accounting system in each function entails that the right questions are being asked by finance team and the right measures are being used to assess performance of the teams.

Financial results cannot be achieved in isolation. They are accomplished when operations improve, non-value adding use of capacity decreases and raw materials start flowing faster on the shop floor. This is why a CFO plays a pivotal role in the implementation of lean tools in a company. Operational improvements result in value addition in the company and reflect in both revenue and bottom line. The CFO should be fully committed to lean improvements projects and their execution in the company. Lean operational and financial measures should augment the value stream concept and should be practiced in every shift, every day and all the time. The performance measures should be simple and easy to calculate, and operators, supervisors and managers should be able to associate the measure with their job, that is, they should understand the repercussions of their activities on their function and value stream. They should understand how improvements in their measures convert into monetary value and reflect in value stream's P&L statement.

10.3 Implementation of the Lean Performance Measurement System

The lean performance measurement system is designed by the people for the people and is modified at regular intervals when the need of some new measure arises, or some measures become obsolete. The lean performance measurement system is not designed to be simply downloaded from the ERP system because lean ERP cannot think, so it has to be done manually but data, of course, are fetched from the ERP system.

A company needs different measurements for different levels in the company. Normally, a company will need at least three levels.

The lean performance measurement system is implemented in the companies using the following methodology:

- *Strategic Level* – This measures for the performance of the CEO, the CFO, value stream managers and functional HODs using corporate scorecard and VSM/functional scorecard.
- *Value Stream Level* – This measures for the performance of managers, first line of executives and supervisors using VSM/functional scorecard and performance scorecard.
- *Cell Level* – This measures for the performance of senior supervisors, supervisors and workmen using the performance scorecard and workmen skill matrix.

Corporate Scorecard

The corporate scorecard is covered in the previous chapter. The corporate scorecard condenses the company's financial and operational performance along with capacity utilization of both manpower and machine in a single chart as shown in Table 10.1.

VSM/Functional Managers Scorecards

Dr. Yoji Akao[1] of Tamagawa University was the primary architect of Policy Deployment (Hoshin Kanri) in the 1950s. In 1992, Robert S. Kaplan and David P. Norton at Harvard Business School Boston devised the balanced scorecard strategy[2].

Corporate scorecards/VSM scorecards/functional scorecards are created for the CEO, the CFO, value stream managers and functional managers to

Table 10.1 Sample Monthly Corporate Scorecard for Perfect Gear Company.

Aspect	Key performance indicator	UOM	Current state March 2018
Financial	**Sales revenue – monthly**	**USD Mn**	**3.33**
	Average product sales price	**USD per kg**	**3.33**
	Average product cost	**USD per kg**	**2.84**
	Value of inventory	**USD Mn**	**6.27**
	Profit before tax	**USD Mn**	**0.17**
	Profit before tax	**%**	**5%**
Operational	**Throughput time**	**Days**	**113**
	On time shipment	**%**	**70%**
	Total head count	**Number**	**561**
Capacity usage – manpower	**Value adding**	**%**	**25%**
	Non-value adding	**%**	**53%**
	Free capacity available	**%**	**22%**
Capacity usage – machine	**Value adding**	**%**	**44%**
	Non-value adding	**%**	**50%**
	Free capacity available	**%**	**6%**

measure their progress in achievement of company goals – operationally and financially. The scorecard should list the objectives of the company by measuring the parameters critical to accomplishment of the company's goals in line with its strategy. Scorecard methodology is based on the following five categories as illustrated in Figure 10.3.

- Financial measures
- Customer satisfaction measures
- Company processes measures
- Performance measurement system and training measures
- Safety health environment and quality measures

Financial Measures

It highlights the financial aspect of the company's strategy like revenue growth, profit margins and cash flow. Each function contributes to the financial results of the company because each process has monetary value.

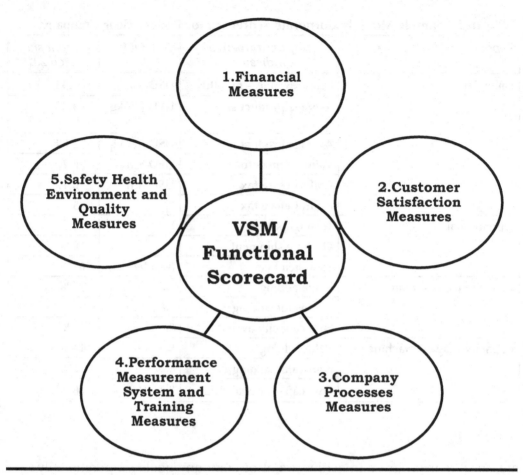

Figure 10.3   Five Categories of VSM/Functional Scorecard.

Key parameters like monthly dispatch and monthly value addition target are monitored under this measure.

Customer Satisfaction Measures

These key measures to monitor customer satisfaction could be OTIFEF and throughput time of the functions and customer complaints.

Company Processes Measures

Impeccable internal processes create products or services that placate customers and give competitive edge. These measures assess how the company will achieve financial measures and customer satisfaction measures and what developments can be brought in-house to achieve manufacturing excellence and improve the quality of product, processes, logistics and after sales services. Some of the most important initiatives (discussed in detail in previous chapters) that are focused upon are the following:

- Implementation of TPM – measurement of OEE, MTBF, MTTR of critical machines
- Changeover time reduction in critical machines
- Process standardization for repeated machined items and assembly
- Standardization of logistics process for incoming raw materials, inter-plant movement of goods, domestic as well as export sales
- Standardization of purchase procurement process
- Reduction in slow moving and non-moving stock
- Implementation of supermarket and kanban system
- Create vendor rating system for A-class items
- Standardize and implement quality control formats
- Freeze quality assurance checklists
- Technical certification of operators
- Participation in kaizen teams
- Material traceability and ISO compliance

Lean Performance Measurement System and Training Measures

In order to achieve key financial measures and customer satisfaction measures, the company monitors internal process measures. But who will administer these internal measures? Managers, executives, supervisors and workmen of the company can strive to achieve manufacturing excellence only if they are trained and skilled enough to handle it. That is why it is essential to have learning and growth measures.

Does Human Resources have enough skills, training and knowledge to enable the workforce to achieve their long-term targets of financial measures, customer satisfaction measures and internal measures using existing technologies and capabilities? The company has to upgrade its capabilities by training people and improving information systems. At Toyota, training plays a critical role. Initially the company starts with a ten hours per employee per year training hours target and gradually increases it to 40 hours per employee per year. Every employee must get 40 hours training per year. These trainings for workmen will comprise kaizen and technical training based on their skill matrix requirements, training for continual improvement projects and creating standards for quality controls. The training of supervisors and workmen will be conducted through the 'training within industry' (TWI)[3] tool. Job instruction (JI) cards will be used for the training. This powerful tool developed by the US Army in 1944 standardizes the training processes and helps the supervisors in training their operators effectively.

The training of managers, staff and supervisors will include seven basic quality control tools and knowledge of basic computer office software.

Safety Health Environment and Quality Measures

The safety of all employees and the business premise is critical. Audit and corrective and preventive actions based on these audits should not be ignored to maintain the continuity of operations:

Safety Health and Environment audit (SHE audit) is a system to protect health and environment in a company and make it a safe place to work. It is an organized effort by the company to identify the safety hazards and prevent accidents. It also includes training of personnel in accident prevention, accident response, emergency preparedness and use of personnel protective equipment. It encourages a friendly environment to prevent and reduce the risk of harm to personnel in the company. It is advisable to hire an expert who can conduct the SHE audits and help in identification and preventive and corrective action implementation on continual basis.

For 5S audit score the company is divided into zones and each zone is audited every month. The increased score indicates the people are following 5S practices. The zone that has the highest score should be rewarded with the gifts and a 5S trophy to be kept in that workplace for the month. Table 10.2 shows the methodology as how the gemba with the highest 5S score is identified and rewarded.

A quality control audit is done for all functions on the plant floor, and the function with the highest score is rewarded.

Table 10.3 shows the quality audit and evaluation score methodology where each plant is assessed on a monthly basis and how the score improves when the lean and kaizen tools are implemented and continual improvements are achieved.

Creation of Corporate/Functional Scorecards for CFO, Value Stream Manager and Managers[4]

The scorecards for Perfect Gear Company will be taken as samples to showcase the methodology. The scorecards are prepared for the marketing,

Table 10.2   5S Score for Different Zones at Perfect Gear Company.

Function	Area	Team leader name	Oct-18	Nov-18	Dec-18	Jan-19	Feb-19	Mar-19
Machine shop	Conventional machine area		75	70	70	72	70	72
Machine shop	CNC machine area 1		70	70	70	72	70	72
Machine shop	CNC machine area 2		75	70	70	72	70	72
Machine shop	Lathe machine area		70	70	70	72	70	72
Gear cutting and gear grinding shop	Gear cutting and gear grinding shop		77 Best gemba in the plant	70	75 Best gemba	79 Best gemba	76 Best gemba in the plant	75 Best gemba
Assembly shop	Area 1		75	75	75 Best gemba	77	70	72
Assembly shop	Area 2		70	70	70	72	70	72
Assembly shop	Area 3		70	75	70	72	70	72
Fabrication shop	Fabrication shop		70	70	70	72	65	70
Store			75	77 Best gemba	70	72	70	72
Component store	Component store						45	60
Maintenance room	Maintenance room						45	60
Yard	Front yard		65	70	70	72	65	70
			73%	71%	71%	73%	66%	70%

Table 10.3 Quality Audit and Evaluation Score on 1 April 2019 at Perfect Gear Company.

Sl no.	Description	Total score	Month							
			Oct-18	Nov	Dec	Jan-19	Feb	Mar
1	Resource management							
1.1	Provide operational and quality training – NDT (UT, PT, MT)	5	2	2	2	3	3	3.5
1.2	Welder qualification by external agency	4	2	2	2.5	3	3	3.5
1.3	Internal auditor, kaizen and QC tools training	5	3	3	5	5	5	5
1.4	Proper recording and record keeping of different projects	5	3	3.5	4.5	5	5	5
2	Metrology, inspection and recording							
2.1	Identification and update calibration with record of inspection equipment	5	2.5	2.5	3.5	4	4.5	5
2.2	Record of update calibration with agency traceability with source	5	2.5	3	3.5	4	4.5	5
3	In process control and recording							
3.1	Ensure the quality of incoming material before issue for further processing	5	3	3.5	4.5	5	5	5
3.2	SOP developed and being used in manufacturing process in shop and at supplier end	5	4	4	4	4	4	4.5
3.3	Inspection and test performed at right stage and recorded in assembly process	5	4	4	4.5	5	5	5
3.4	Assembly inspection as per STD checklists developed to ensure completeness and quality	5	4	4	4.5	5	5	5

4	At supplier end							
4.1	Control the first time right percentage	3	2	2.5	2.5	2	2	3
4.2	Vendor rating based on quality and resources	3	2	2.5	2.5	3	3	3
4.3	Identification and traceability at suppliers end	3	1	2	2	2.5	2	2.5
5	Identify NCR with CAPA							
5.1	Identify the NCR in case of abnormality observed	5	4	4	5	5	5	5
5.2	Corrective and preventive action on NCR within two weeks	5	2	2	3	4	4	4
5.3	Reduction in NCR percentage	4	2	2	3	3.5	3.5	4
5.4	Effectiveness of CAPA	4	3	3	3	3.5	3.5	4
6	Audit in process and at supplier end							
6.1	In process audit	3	2	2	2.5	3	2.5	3
6.2	Supplier audit	3	2	2	3	3	3	3
6.3	Dispatch audit	3	2	2.5	3	3	3	3
7	Customer relationships							
7.1	Reduction in customer complaints	5	3	4	4	4	4	4
7.2	To attend to the complaint within the minimum possible time	5	3	3	3	3	4	4
8	Certification by external agency							
8.1	Annual audit by external agency TUV and certification for ISO 9001:2008	5	5	5	5	5	5	5
Total		100	63	68	80	87.5	88.5	94
			63%	68%	80%	87.5%	88.5%	94%

finance, operations, design, fabrication, assembly, quality, maintenance, HRD and projects. These functional scorecards can be modified based as per relevance to the individual industry.

Eleven scorecards are displayed here as Table 10.4 to Table 10.14 based on the Perfect Gear Company for the following people:

- Vice President (Marketing and Business Development)
- Chief Financial Officer
- GM (Design and R&D)
- Vice President (Purchase)
- Plant General Manager
- DGM (Fabrication)
- Senior Manager (Assembly)
- General Manager (Quality)
- DGM (Maintenance)
- General Manager (HRD)
- GM (Projects)

Please note that these scorecards are for a capital machinery manufacturer. These will give a good insight into what should be measured for every function. One can prepare the scorecard for their industry based on the ideas used here. Some of these scorecards also have the actual score data that has been achieved for that particular month.

Design should work with customer inputs as well as being discussed internally. The design should not create inefficiencies in manufacturing like more time, poor yield, costly materials and so forth and not achieve desired profit levels.

Summary[5]

Improvement in scores due to the Perfect Gear Company's lean journey from October2018 to March 2019 after implementation of the lean production system, daily management system and lean accounting is summarized in Table 10.15. The increase in the score signifies that the operational parameters are improving. The improvement in financial parameters will reflect in the P&L statement.

Table 10.4 Functional Scorecard for Vice President (Marketing and Business Development) at Perfect Gear Company.

				Month	Mar-19
	A) Financial Measures (83%)				
	Objectives	Target figure	Score weightage	Responsibility	Score achieved
1	Develop new international customers – both direct and distribution (OEM)				
1a.	International sales target		90		
	Achieving sales – International – Europe-Russia-CIS				
	Achieving sales – International – South America-North America-Mexico				
	Achieving sales – International – Africa and Middle East				
	Achieving sales – International – Egypt				
	Achieving sales – International – Iran				
	Achieving sales – International – SAARC-Bangladesh, Nepal, Sri Lanka, Pakistan				
	Achieving sales – International – developed countries including Japan				
2	Contract manufacturing from ten small/mid-size companies in developed countries like Spain, Germany and Japan. These mid-sized companies could eventually become joint venture/technology partners.	Full implementation	60		
3	To develop joint venture/technology partners in Europe	Full implementation	60		
4	International spare orders booking to be treated as priority	Full implementation	30		
5	International business in the tube industry	Full implementation	30		
6	To visit customers focusing on revamping jobs	Full implementation	30		
7	To approach all independent consultants. Stay in touch with them. To prepare a plan and act.	Full implementation	10		
8	To have awareness seminars. To get one expert speaker from the industry. Should be done every two months.	Full implementation	10		
9	Why don't we look at defense and railway? 'A' supplies equipment to railways. 'B' is railway equipment suppliers – expanding in a big way.	Full implementation	10		
10	Estimated contribution (sales value–material costs) – in percentage of the booked orders for the month	Aim for 55% to 60% contribution	20		
11	Preparing marketing expenses budget	To calculate	5		
12	Strike rate – international	5% — target	10		

(Continued)

Table 10.4 (Continued)

	Objectives	Target figure	Score weightage	Month Responsibility	Mar-19 Score achieved
	A) Financial Measures (83%)				
13	Domestic sales target (order booking should be Rs.100 crores)		90		
	Achieving sales – Domestic – North				
	Achieving sales – Domestic – East/Central				
	Achieving sales – Domestic – East				
	Achieving sales – Domestic – South				
14	Domestic spare orders booking to be treated as priority		30		
15	New product development – crane business		10		
16	To visit customers focusing on revamping jobs	Full implementation	10		
17	To approach all domestic independent consultants. Stay in touch with them. To prepare a plan and act.	Full implementation	10		
18	To have seminars in five big industrial towns. To get one expert speaker from the industry. Should be done every two months.	Full implementation	10		
19	Meaningful visits to old customers. What new equipment can be added – new products that have been added – request them to visit us.	Full implementation	10		
20	Customer follow-up – ten-day visit every month to the customers	Full implementation	10		
21	Finished good inventory lying in the plants		10		
22	Fixed cost monthly marketing department – (salary)		5		
	Total		550		
	B) Customer Satisfaction Measures (5%)				
1	Important customer visits to company	Full implementation	10		
2	Response time to customers – offers submission and clarifications	Full implementation	5		
3	Repeat customer (share of order booking from old customers)	List (%)	5		
4	Customer complaints in numbers	0	5		
5	Customer return in value	0	5		
6	Customer satisfaction survey – format finalization and implementation	Full implementation	5		
	Total		35		

C) Company Processes Measures (8%)					
1	Freeze organization chart and roles and responsibilities of all staff. Recruitment as per the proposed organization chart.	Full implementation	5		
2	Recruitment for new business – design/marketing cum execution	Full implementation	5		
3	To prepare promotional material for business	Full implementation	5		
4	Work order closing in the ERP after dispatch	Full implementation	5		
5	Work order should capture the sequence of delivery of equipment and it should be visible in the work order	Full implementation	5		
6	Finalize SOPs for marketing department	Full implementation	4		
7	To develop the marketing/sales CRM	Full implementation	10		
8	Strike rate – domestic	5% – target	6		
9	Marketing strategy monthly MD review	Full implementation	10		
		Total	55		
D) Performance Measurement System and Training Measures (%)–					
1	Executives and staff kaizen and technical training hours	10 hours per man per year	10		
2	Average score of performance scorecard for executives and staff	85%	10		
3	Implementation of training calendar	Full implementation	5		
		Total	25		
		Grand total	665		
		%	100		70%

Table 10.5 Functional Scorecard for Chief Financial Officer at Perfect Gear Company.

SI no.	Objectives	Target score	Month Score weightage	Mar-19 Responsibility	Achieved score
A) Financial Measures (55%)					
1	Reduction in inventories in RM, BOP, slow moving – non-moving items. Plant-wise list available. Non-moving is – and slow moving is –. Total –. Cross-functional team to be set up with purchase, design, stores	Reduction from present from – to – **8030**			
2	**Vetting of focused improvement projects across the plants and functions. Introduce incentives for the unit heads, functional heads and HODs to promote savings in the plants.**		50		10
3	**Estimated contribution – percentage of the booked orders highlighting on a monthly basis.**		25		10
4	**Introduce incentives for the marketing department to promote achieving stretched targets in orders bookings and new business launch.**		10		10
5	How to reduce the costs with interaction with functional heads when the order book is low for the month.		20		20
		Total	185		80
B) Company Processes Measures (34%)					
1	Freeze organization structure and roles and responsibilities (KPIs/MBO) of all individuals in finance department.		5		5
2	Reduction in transactions in authorizations – approvals and sign-off.		20		15
3	Accounts payable – look at possibility to eliminate need for matching receipts, POs and supplier invoices and authorization for payment on clearance of MRNs.		10		5
4	Introduction of standard work and checklist for all up to supervisory level.		10		2

5	Initiation of focused improvement projects in finance.	20	2
6	Statutory compliance report for the plant and release of quarterly report to the directors for IT compliance.	5	5
7	Enhancing the credit rating. BB+ is target, current BB.	10	5
8	Help evolve a capital structure that will help improve the debt-equity ratios.	5	
9	Put in place and monitor key controls particularly those relating to financial commitments before they are entered into.	5	5
10	Stock accuracy in all categories – RM, BOP, WIP, and consumables accuracy. ERP data accuracy will be ensured.	25	15
	Packing list through ERP. Packing list modification to enable multi-selection.	5	5
	To bring the accuracy material cost sheets preparation – regular analysis for not picking up complete information – correction through user/ERP only. To incorporate the job work value in the material cost sheet.	25	15
	Implementation of reserving option in ERP – planning sheet is to be created showing stocks at all stages and the unallocated ones.	10	5
	If PO has been issued for any RM/BOP item and if design dept is revising this item in the drawing/BOM, ERP will prevent and block this revision. It can be done only after discussion among design, purchase and PPC and ERP person.	5	5
	ERP system – to identify the areas where locks are to be put to follow the correct procedure.	10	5
	ERP should prompt the balance work. When the main equipment has gone the system should be able to tell us what is the balance work.	5	2
	Work order closure is to be done on ERP.	5	2
	Programming training is to be given to ERP persons.	5	5

(Continued)

Table 10.5 (Continued)

Sl no.	Objectives	Target score	Month Score weightage	Mar-19 Responsibility	Mar-19 Achieved score
11	Monthly stock taking – All raw material and store inventory and reconciliation – MS plate, steel casting, job work items, store items. Introduction of perpetual inventory of runner, repeater items.		10		5
12	Implementation of cyber security.		10		
		Total	205		108
C) Performance Measurement System and Training Measures (11%)					
1	Kaizen and functional training to staff and executives Total hours to be logged in per month.	Ten hours per person per year	20		10
2	Finalization of performance scorecard for finance staff.	85%	20		8
3	Knowledge of computer basics (Excel, PowerPoint, Word).		10		8
4	Training calendar implementation.		10		5
		Total	60		31
		Grand total	450		219
			100%		64%

Table 10.6 Functional Scorecard for GM (Design and R&D) at Perfect Gear Company.

Sl no.	Objectives	Target	Target score	Responsi-bility	Achieved score
				Month	Mar-19
A) Customer Satisfaction Measures (57%)					
	Order under execution – -drawing and BOM issue on time				
1	Customer A		30		
2	Customer B		30		
3	Customer C		30		
4	Customer D		30		
5	Customer E		30		
6	Customer F		30		
7	Customer G		30		
8	Customer H		30		
		Total	240		
B) Company Processes Measures (37%)					
1	Finalization of the organizing chart with responsibilities	Full implementation	5		
2	Set up development cell in the design department (R&D department) – improvement in critical areas	Full implementation	5		
3	Duplicity of the item codes – to be removed	Full implementation	15		
4	Design daily review meeting	Full implementation	3		
5	Work order preparation as per new format – incorporation of BOM number/Item code number – equipment name and sub-assembly-wise	Full implementation	3		
6	Implementation of sequence of issue of drawings	Full implementation	3		
7	SOP implemented so far	Full implementation	15		
8	Concept of putting 'hold' on drawings and BOM for the bought-out items for which the certified drgs are not recd	Full implementation	5		

(Continued)

Table 10.6 (Continued)

Sl no.	Objectives	Target	Target score	Month — Responsibility	Mar-19 — Achieved score
9	Document control; availability of standard drawings in plants; availability of bought-out and quality standards; ERP update to allow issue of standard BOMs. Standardization for all equipment along with the identification of key characteristics/parameters.	Full implementation	20		
10	In all BOMs, all items' weight should be put. Currently many weights are missing.	Full implementation	15		
11	BOM/drawing description for casting/forging/other items should be sufficient for the procurement and quality point of view for putting in the PO.	Full implementation	15		
12	Standardization of putting specifications for BOP items	Full implementation	5		
13	Finalization of fasteners specifications and release of SOP	Full implementation	2		
14	Finalization of foundation bolts specifications and release of SOP	Full implementation	2		
15	POE items – appoint a person to work on the correction of POE drgs/BOM. With help from assembly starting with all gearboxes, shears and housing less. Special focus to be on implementing pipeline drawings and fabrication BOM for gearboxes, shears and housing less mills.	Full implementation	10		
16	To ensure no duplication of item codes in BOM	Full implementation	2		
17	Allocation of slow moving and non-moving stocks to the tune of USD will result in the interest saving of USD of interest per month	Full implementation	20		
18	FIP – Review the design of the intermediate shaft of the gearbox		10		
		Total	155		
C) Performance Measurement System and Training Measures (6%)					
1	New software, kaizen and technical (material, heat treatment) training	10 hours per employee per year	10		
2	Staff performance scorecard	80%	10		
3	Implementation of training calendar	Full implementation	5		
		Total	25		
		Grand total	420	%	72

Table 10.7 Functional Scorecard for Vice President (Purchase) at Perfect Gear Company.

Sl no.	Objectives	Target	Target score	Month Responsibility	Mar-19 Achieved score
A) Financial Measures (53%)					
1	Focus improvement project on purchasing from OEMs instead of traders and reduction in the purchase price	Annual 10% reduction	45		
2	FIP on reduction in purchase price of large consuming BOP and consumables	Annual 5% reduction	45		
3	FIP on reducing/disposal of the non-moving and slow moving items		45		
4	FIP on reducing the price of specific large category of purchase items A	Full implementation	10		
5	FIP on reducing the price of specific large category of purchase items B	Full implementation	10		
6	FIP on reducing the price of specific large category of purchase items C	Full implementation	10		
		Total	165		
B) Customer Satisfaction Measures (10%)					
1	FIP on reducing the throughput time of the equipment – FIP on throughput time of product A to be reduced	Full implementation	10		
2	FIP on reducing the throughput time of product B	Full implementation	10		
3	FIP on reducing the throughput time of product C	Full implementation	10		
		Total	30		
C) Company Processes Measures (39%)					
1	Organizing chart – keep it updated	Full implementation	2		
2	Introduction of daily management	Full implementation	10		
3	Weekly analysis of gap between PR raising and PO issued	Full implementation	10		
4	Focused improvement projects – standardization of BOM/drawing description should be sufficient for the procurement and quality point of view for putting in the PO	Full implementation	5		
5	(a) To analyze major causes of NCR for the purchase points	Full implementation	5		
	(b) To develop action plan to reduce and eliminate NCRs for the purchase points	Full implementation	5		

(Continued)

Table 10.7 (Continued)

Sl no.	Objectives	Target	Target score	Month Responsibility	Mar-19 Achieved score
6	SOP implemented so far. (Total no. of SOP – 11 mos.)	Full implementation	5		
7	Audit system for review of the implementation of kanban system and regular repeat replenishment of kanban items	Full implementation	10		
8	Implementation of kanban system and regular repeat replenishment for – RM	Full implementation	5		
9	Implementation of kanban system and regular repeat replenishment for BOP - -project items	Full implementation	5		
10	Implementation of kanban system and regular repeat replenishment for BOP --fasteners and keys	Full implementation	5		
11	Implementation of kanban system and regular repeat replenishment for consumables and toolings	Full implementation	5		
12	100+ job vendors should be reduced to around 50. Suitable action plan with target is to be decided. Vendor rating system is to be introduced.	Full implementation	5		
13	Vendor job rates are to be scrutinized by scientific calculations	Full implementation	5		
14	FIP on removing duplicity of item codes. These duplicates should be eliminated ASAP.	Full implementation	5		
15	Focused improvement projects to start with cross-functional team – first time right is to be improved for purchase items, which is around 70%. A deterrent is to be built in for the suppliers for whom the first time right rating is poor.	Full implementation	5		
		Total	92		
D) Performance Measurement System and Training Measures (28%)					
1	Executives and staff kaizen and technical training hours – 220 hours of training per year – 18 hours training per month	10 hours per man per year	10		
2	Average score of performance scorecard for executives and staff	85%	10		
3	Training calendar implementation	Full implementation	5		
		Total	25		
		Grand total	312		74%

Table 10.8 Functional Scorecard for Plant General Manager at Perfect Gear Company.

					Month	Mar-19
Sl no.	Objectives	Target figure	Target score	Respon-sibility		Achieved score
A) Financial Measures (52%)						
1	Achieving minimum monthly dispatch in value		90			
2	Achieving minimum monthly value addition targets		90			
3	Fixed costs – staff, workmen – salary and wages including overtime		10			
4	Offloading cost		10			
5	First time right (internal)	100%	5			
6	Oils and lubricants per month		5			
7	Carbide inserts and accessories per month		5			
8	Electricity and diesel expenses for power generation		5			
9	Paint		5			
10	Gas		5			
11	Fabrication rate	4 tons/man/month	5			
		Total	235			
B) Customer Satisfaction Measures (5%)						
1	Throughput time of product A	140 man days	5			
2	Throughput time of product B	112 man days	5			
3	Throughput time of product C	112 man days	5			
4	OTIFEF of plant (manufacturing only)	85%	5			
5	Completeness of dispatch as per BOM of all orders	100%	5			
		Total	25			

(Continued)

Table 10.8 (Continued)

Sl no.	Objectives	Target figure	Target score	Month Respon-sibility	Mar-19 Achieved score
C) Company Processes Measures (35%)					
1	Grinding wheel and grinding disc –fabrication shop		5		
2	Cost of internal power generation –Rs/unit		5		
3	OEE of machine A	90%	5		
4	OEE of machine B	90%	5		
5	OEE of machine C	90%	5		
6	5S score	90%	5		
7	Implementation of AM step 1 on 28 machines	100%	5		
8	Implementation of AM step 2 on 10 machines	100%	5		
9	Implementation of AM step 3 on 6 machines	100%	5		
10	Implementation of PM step 2 on 28 machines	100%	5		
11	Implementation of PM step 3 on 28 machines	100%	5		
12	Implementation of PM step 4 on 28 machines. Spare parts management.	100%	5		
13	Implementation of SMED on ten machines	100%	10		
14	Introduction of standard work and checklist for all up to supervisory level	100%	10		
15	Focused improvement project A – average savings per month $	100%	5		
16	Focused improvement project B – average savings per month $	100%	10		
17	Focused improvement project C – average savings per month $	100%	10		
18	(a) Compiling standard hours for job A through introduction of job route card	100%	5		
	(b) Standard hours for machining of critical component-setting target and monitor reduction through job route card	100% 100%	5		
19	(a) Compiling standard hours for assembly of critical component through introduction of job route card	100%	5		
	(b) Standard hours for assembly of critical component-setting target and monitor	100%	5		

20	Visual management	100%	3				
21	Packing list through ERP	100%	3				
22	a) Utilization of excess inventory slow moving – non-moving of stores item plus inventory reduction category-wise as per the stock taking for the other items	100%	10				
23	Stock taking – purchase versus issue of consumables	100%	2				
24	Reconciliation of vendors pending updated	100%	2				
25	(a) To analyze major causes of NCR in plant (machine shop, fabrication and assembly)	100%	5				
	(b) To be developed action plan to reduce NCRs (machine shop, fabrication and assembly)	100%	5				
		Total	155				
D) Performance Measurement System and Training Measures (6%)							
1	Executives and staff kaizen and technical training hours	10 hours per man per year	5				
2	Workmen kaizen and technical training hours	10 hours per man per year	5				
3	Average score of performance scorecard for executives and staff	85%	5				
4	Average score of workmen skill matrix	85%	5				
5	Knowledge of computer basics (Excel, PowerPoint, Word, Outlook, ERP)	100%	5				
		Total	25				
E) Safety Health Environment and Quality Measures (2%)							
1	SHE audit score	100%	5				
2	Quality audit score	85%	5				
		Total	10				
		Grand total	450				
		%	%				78%

Table 10.9 Functional Scorecard for DGM (Fabrication) at Perfect Gear Company.

Sl no.	Objectives	Target figure	Target score	Month Responsibility	Mar-19 Achieved score
A) Financial Measures (58%)					
1	Achieving minimum monthly dispatch	$ – minimum or as per budget for the month	90		55
2	Achieving minimum monthly value addition targets	$ – minimum or as per budget for the month	90		70
3	Fixed costs – staff, casual, temporary – salaries and overtime	$--	10		10
4	Grinding wheels (fabrication)	$--	10		10
5	Diesel for furnace SR operation	$--	10		10
6	Fabrication rate	4 Tons/man/month	15		11
7	Gas	$--	5		7
8	Focused improvement project A	Savings/month-$--	30		5
9	Focused improvement project B	Savings/month-$--	25		3
10	Focused improvement project C	Savings/month-$--	10		7
		Total	295		188
B) Company Processes Measures (26%)					
1	Diesel for furnace stress relieving operation	$	20		20
2	Introduction of AM step 1 on CNC cutting machine	%	10		5
3	5S score – fabrication shop	%	10		7
4	Cutting list preparation by the planning and fabrication and material issue list by planning and fabrication	audit	20		20
5	All consumable items issue request from fab shop and subsequent stores issuing these	audit	20		20

6	(a) To analyze major causes of NCR in plant (fabrication)	%	25	20
	(b) To be developed action plan to reduce NCRs (fabrication)	%	25	10
		Total	130	102
C) Performance Measurement System and Training Measures (13%)				
1	Number of SOP made and implemented	10 numbers in year	20	10
2	Training and kaizen hours for workmen	11 hours/man/year	10	10
3	Training and kaizen hours for staff	10 hours/man/year	10	10
4	Average score of workmen skill matrix	85%	10	8
5	Average score of performance scorecard	85%	10	10
6	Knowledge of computer basics (Excel, PowerPoint, Word, Outlook, ERP)	Full implementation	5	5
		Total	65	53
D) Safety Health Environment and Quality Measures (3%)				
1	SHE audit score and attending the NCRs in fabrication shop	Full implementation	15	10
		Total	15	10
		Grand total	505	353
			%	70

Table 10.10 Functional Scorecard for Senior Manager (Assembly) at Perfect Gear Company.

				Month	Mar-19
Sl no.	Objectives	Target figure	Target score	Responsibility	Achieved score
A) Financial Measures (54%)					
1	Achieving minimum monthly dispatch	$ – minimum or as per budget for the month	90		55
2	Achieving minimum monthly value addition targets	$ – minimum or as per budget for the month	90		64
3	Fixed costs – staff, workmen, casuals, temporary – salary, wages, overtime	$	10		10
4	Grinding wheels and grinding disc	%	5		5
5	Electricity and diesel expenses for power generation	$	10		
6	Paint	$ per month	5		5
7	Focused improvement project A	Full implementation	20		5
8	Focused improvement project B	Full implementation	20		5
9	Focused improvement project C	Full implementation	20		5
		Total	270		154
B) Customer Satisfaction Measures (11%)					
1	Throughput time of assembly of product A	4 days	10		10
2	Throughput time of assembly of product B	8 days	10		10
3	Throughput time of assembly of product C	20 days	5		3
4	Throughput time of assembly of product D	10 days	10		10
5	Throughput time of assembly of product E	15 days	10		10
6	Completeness of dispatch as per BOM of all orders		10		10
		Total	55		53
C) Company Processes Measures (18%)					
1	5S score (assembly shop)		10		7
2	Customer complaint		10		10
3	Focus improvement project – eliminate rust		20		20

No.	Measure	Target		
4	(a) Compiling standard hours for assembly of critical component through introduction of job route card		20	20
5	(b) Standard hours for assembly of critical component-setting target and monitor reduction through job route card		20	0
6	(a) To analyze major causes of NCR in plant (assembly)		5	5
	(b) To be developed action plan to reduce NCRs (assembly)		5	5
		Total	90	67
D) Performance Measurement System and Training Measures (14%)				
1	Number of SOP made and implemented	10	30	10
2	Training and kaizen hours for workmen	11 hours/man/year	10	10
3	Training and kaizen hours for staff	10 hours/man/year	5	10
4	Average score of workmen skill matrix	85%	10	7
5	Average score of performance scorecard	85%	10	6
6	Knowledge of computer basics (Excel, PowerPoint, Word, Outlook, ERP)	Full implementation	5	3
		Total	70	46
E) Safety Health Environment and Quality Measures (3%)				
1	SHE audit score and attending the NCRs in assembly shop	Full implementation	15	10
		Total	15	10
		Grand total	500	330
		%		66

Table 10.11 Functional Scorecard for General Manager (Quality) at Perfect Gear Company.

Sl no.	Objectives	Targets	Target score	Month Responsi-bility	Mar-19 Achieved score
A) Customer Satisfaction Measures					
1	Total number of customer complaints in the month and YTD	Zero	10		5
2	Customer complaints in PPM and YTD	5S, 233 PPM, non-acceptance – 0.02%	10		5
3	Cost of poor quality/cost of quality – NCR to be closed in writing before dispatch, unit head to sign before dispatch, QA head is to be aware of all the deviations/NCRs. NCRs are to be closed before the balance scorecard meeting.	To establish the current cost and as a % of sales and then benchmark for improvement	50		30
4	Corrective action related to process deviations/customer complaints – NCRs closing	Zero NC	30		20
5	Holding monthly meeting with director and quarterly MD review. For CAPA of customer complaint.	For CAPA from HOD units to achieve the zero complaint	20		8
6	Completeness of dispatch as per BOM of all orders	100% in quality and quantity	20		10
7	Control of fixed costs	$	5		5
	Total		145		83
B) Company Processes Measures					
1	Setting up responsibility of QA department – in all plants	Full implementation	5		5
2	Introduction of standard work and checklist for all up to supervisory level	Full implementation	10		7
3	Focused improvement projects – development of critical part A a) activity sheet from supplier b) QAP + update PO with technical specification, c) pattern checking, d) identification of integral test piece + inspection	Full implementation	20		15

#	Measure	Target		
5	Focused improvement project – measurement system analysis – assess MSA trust level	9% or less	15	10
6	Focused improvement project –traceability of all components	From suppliers to customers	30	25
7	Focused improvement projects with cross-functional team – customer complaint regarding product part failure at site	To bring it down to zero	15	12
8	Focused improvement projects with cross-functional team – customer complaint	To bring it down to zero	15	12
9	Ensuring geometrical tolerances at the supplier's end	Full implementation	5	5
10	Use of standard checklist of all products quality check before dispatch	Full implementation	15	11
11	ISO 14000 compliance – monitoring of progress and final certificate	Full implementation	15	12
12	ISO 18001–2007 – preparation of quality manual	Full implementation	15	6
	Total		170	124
C) Performance Measurement System and Training Measures				
1	Repairing, identification and calibration updation of all measuring and monitoring instruments, gauges and granite surface plates	100% as per schedule before due date, calibration certificate	10	7
2	Welder qualification by TUV	W Qualification Certificate by Agency	10	8
3	Training of internal auditor for IS14001–2004 and IS18001:2007		5	2
4	Training of NDT level II testing (UT, MPT, LPT)		5	5
5	Executives and staff kaizen and technical training hours	10 hours per man per year = (10 × 18) 180 hours	20	20
6	Average score of performance scorecard for executives and staff	0.85	20	15

(Continued)

Table 10.11 (Continued)

Sl no.	Objectives	Targets	Target score	Month Responsi-bility	Mar-19 Achieved score
7	Measuring instrument training in all plants to production persons through QC department	1 training/month/unit over 10 person total 3 training/month	10		6
	Total		80		63
D) Safety Health Environment and Quality Measures					
1	QC audit score	Full implementation	15		13
	Total		15		13
	Grand total		410		283
			%		69

Sl no.	Objectives	Target	Target score	Month Responsi-bility	Mar-19 Achieved score
A) Financial Measures (54%)					
1	**Achieving minimum monthly dispatch + value addition targets to meet the break-even point**	**$ – minimum or as per the monthly budget**	90		55
2	**Achieving minimum monthly value addition targets to meet the break-even point**	**$ – minimum or as per the monthly budget**	90		70
3	**Fixed costs – staff, workmen, temporary – salaries, wages, overtime**	**$--**	10		10
4	**Oils and lubricants in $ per month**	**$--**	5		4
5	**Electricity and diesel expenses for power generation**	**$--**	5		4
6	**Cutting oils**	**$--**	5		4
		Total	205		147
B) Company Processes Measures (39%)					
1	**Cost of internal power generation – $ per unit**		5		4
2	**OEE of critical machine A**	90%	5		3
3	**OEE of critical machine B**	90%	5		3
4	**OEE of critical machine C**	90%	5		3
5	**OEE of critical machine D**	90%	5		3
6	**5S score – maintenance**	90%	5		3
7	**Implementation of AM step 1 on 22 machines**	100%	5		4
8	**Implementation of AM step 2 on 22 machines**	100%	5		3
9	**Implementation of AM step 3 on 22 machines**	100%	5		4
10	**Implementation of PM step 2 on 22 machine**	100%	5		4
11	**Implementation of PM step 3 on 22 machines**	100%	5		3
12	**Implementation of PM step 4 spare parts management on 22 machines**	100%	5		5

(Continued)

Table 10.12 (Continued)

SI no.	Objectives	Target	Target score	Month Responsibility	Mar-19 Achieved score
13	**Implementation of SMED on 10 machines**	**Full implementation**	50		15
14	**Introduction of standard work and checklist for all up to supervisory level**	**Full implementation**	20		8
15	**Focused improvement project A – average savings per month $--**	**Full implementation**	5		5
16	**Focused improvement project B – average savings per month $--**	**Full implementation**	5		1
17	**Focused improvement project C – average savings per month $--**	**Full implementation**	5		2
18	**Visual management**	**Full implementation**	3		3
		Total	148		76
C) Performance Measurement System and Training Measures (6%)					
1	Executives and staff kaizen and technical training tours	10 hours per man per year = 600 hours	5		5
2	Workmen kaizen and technical training hours	11 hours per man per year = 660 hours	5		4
3	Average score of performance scorecard for executives and staff	85%	5		4
4	Average score of workmen skill matrix	85%	5		2
5	Knowledge of computer basics (Excel, PowerPoint, Word, Outlook, ERP)	Full implementation	5		5
		Total	25		20
D) Safety Health Environment and Quality Measures (1%)					
1	SHE audit score	100%	5		4
		Total	5		4
		Grand total	383		247
		%			64

Table 10.13 Functional Scorecard for General Manager (HRD) at Perfect Gear Company.

Sl no.	Objectives	Target	Target score	Month Responsi-bility	Achieved score
A) Financial Measures (25%)					
1	Achieving minimum monthly manufacture targets to meet the budget	$ – for plant	90		55
2	Fixed costs – staff, temporary – salary, wages, overtime	Cost reduction in the year as planned 15% OPY	80		40
Total			170		95
B) Customer Satisfaction Measures (2%)					
1	Customer-centric workforce – creating product knowledge and end application awareness to workmen	6 trainings/quarter	10		0
Total			10		0
C) Company Processes Measures (10%)					
1	Complete manning of critical machines	Full implementation	5		5
2	Complete manning of balance machines	Full implementation	5		5
3	Reduce manpower turnover/exit interview	<2%	5		5
4	Absenteeism control	<4%	10		8
5	Employee satisfaction (feedback through survey)	80%	10		7
6	Safety PPE – helmet, shoes, gloves, goggles, welding screen	Full implementation	15		12
7	Tobacco, spitting control, no mobile use near the machine	zero	15		12
Total			65		54
D) Performance Measurement System and Training Measures (48%)					
1	Finalization of training topics based on workmen skill matrix and staff's performance scorecard	Topics to increase the training quality index	30		24

(Continued)

Table 10.13 (Continued)

Sl no.	Objectives	Target	Target score	Month Responsi-bility	Achieved score
2	Monitoring of the introduction of standard work and checklist for all up to supervisory level	Full implementation	30		0
3	Executives and staff kaizen and technical training hours, every month reminder mail to all functions regarding the hours put in	10 hours per man per year – hours	30		20
4	Workmen kaizen and technical training hours, every month reminder mail to all functions regarding the hours put in	10 hours per man per year – hours	30		18
5	Measuring instrument training in all plants to production persons through QC department	3 training in a month	10		7
6	Induction program of new entrant (staff)	Full implementation	10		8
7	Induction training of new entrant (associates)	Full implementation	10		6
8	Knowledge of computer basics (Excel, PowerPoint, Word)	Full implementation	10		7
9	Workmen skill matrix finalization	Full implementation	20		12
10	Average score of workmen skill matrix – department-wise reporting to all functional heads and HODs	85%	30		10
11	Preparation of performance scorecard for all staff	100%	20		15
12	Average score of performance scorecard for executives and staff. Department-wise reporting to all functional heads and HODs.	85%	30		0
13	Record keeping of focused improvement projects for all functions	Full implementation	20		15
14	Quarterly payment of kaizen reward and recognition scheme	100%	30		20
Total			310		162

E) Safety Health Environment and Quality Measures (15%)			
1	Timely submission of all returns	Full implementation	15	15
2	Ensure legal compliance of policies and procedures, termination, dismissal, compensation, etc.	Full implementation	15	15
3	Liaison with statutory bodies under labor laws for registration, licenses, renewals, etc.	Full implementation	15	5
4	Workplace accident	Zero	5	0
5	Firefighting training – 2 monthly per plant or as per ISO14000 guidelines	Full implementation	10	10
6	Fulfilling all guidelines of ISO-18001–2007 – OHSAS requirements	Full implementation	25	25
7	Take care of labor disputes and disciplinary matters	Full implementation	10	10
		Total	95	80
		Grand total	650	391
			%	60

Table 10.14 Functional Scorecard for GM (Projects) at Perfect Gear Company.

Sl no.	Objectives	Target figure	Target score	Month Respon-sibility	Mar-19 Achieved score
A) Financial Measures (20%)					
1	Capturing of erection site costs – order-wise expenses	Annual reduction of 15%	20		
2	Capturing of rectification costs at the site – all sites	Annual reduction of 15%	20		
3	Fixed costs – staff, workmen – salary, wages, overtime	Current figure – 10% reduction	10		
		Total	50		
B) Customer Satisfaction Measures (34%)					
1	Throughput time of erection and commissioning of customer site A	Reduction of 30%	10		
2	Throughput time of erection and commissioning of customer site B	Reduction of 30%	10		
3	Throughput time of erection and commissioning of customer site C	Reduction of 30%	10		
4	Through put time of erection and commissioning of customer site D	Reduction of 30%	10		
5	Through put time of erection and commissioning of customer site E	Reduction of 30%	10		
6	Completeness of dispatch as per BOMs	100%	5		
7	Customer complaints – numbers	Zero	10		
8	Customer complaints – value in US$	Zero	10		
9	Customer supplied equipment – coordination with customer for timely arrival at site for timely completion of the erection	100%	10		
		Total	85		
C) Company Processes Measures (34%)					
1	Finalize the organization chart with allocation of work – lamination and display	Full implementation	5		
2	Dispatch as per sequence of erection at the site – non-compliance – orders	Full implementation	5		
3	Feedback to plant and design for the problems encountered at site and due diligence closing of all points with suitable corrective action to be taken	Full implementation	5		

#	Description	Criteria	Points	
4	Sales support to marketing dept – to attend to the technical meetings wherever needed	Full implementation	5	
5	Authenticate the weight of the equipment for the marketing department wherever needed	Full implementation	5	
6	Preparation of standard format for capturing daily schedule of erection people at site	Full implementation	5	
7	Preparation of erection manuals for all critical equipment – 5 SOPs	Full implementation	10	
9	Preparation of commissioning procedure for all machines – 15 numbers	Full implementation	10	
10	Preparation of standard format for customer complaint	Full implementation	5	
11	Preparation of testing procedure for all machines preparation in the plant before dispatch	Full implementation	10	
12	Commissioning trouble shooting checklist for critical equipment	Full implementation	10	
13	SOP for communication procedure from site to HO	Full implementation	5	
14	Coordination between project, marketing and PPC for communicating customer status to the PPC	Full implementation	5	
		Total	85	
D) Performance Measurement System and Training Measures (8%)				
1	Training calendar implementation	100%	5	
2	Kaizen and technical training	10 man hours per employee per year	5	
3	Preparation of the performance scorecards for all staff members	Full implementation	5	
4	Knowledge of computer basics (Excel, PowerPoint, Word, Outlook, ERP)	Full implementation	5	
		Total	20	
E) Safety Health Environment and Quality Measures (4%)				
1	Safety at site	Zero accidents	10	
		Total	10	
		Grand total	250	
		Percentage	%	59%

Table 10.15 Status of the Functional Scorecards – Score Rating for Six Months at Perfect Gear Company.

Sl no.	Name	Design-ation	Function	Oct-18	Nov-18	Dec-18	Jan-19	Feb-19	Mar-19
1		VP	Marketing	41	48	55	61	66	70
2		CFO	Finance	45	47	49	55	60	64
3		GM	Design, R&D	50	55	58	62	69	72
4		GM	Purchase	54	54	62	70	72	74
5		GM	Operations	55	57	64	69	72	78
6		DGM	Fabrication	46	56	59	59	69	70
7		DGM	Assembly	33	46	50	52	55	64
8		GM	Quality	43	48	58	59	68	72
9		DGM	Maintenance	45	47	55	58	59	64
10		GM	HRD	33	45	48	52	55	60
11		GM	Projects	41	44	51	55	56	59

Performance Scorecard

A performance scorecard is created for the middle level staff up to supervisors and first line of engineers or managers. They have financial and operational parameters that link them to their functional heads and enable them to monitor and control their workplace through standardized work. Supervisors are more successful when scorecards focus on the rights tasks.

Please note that the performance scorecards in Table 10.16 through Table 10.18 are for a capital machinery manufacturer. These will give a good insight into what should be measured for every function. One can prepare the performance scorecard for their industry based on the ideas used here. Some of these performance scorecards have the actual score data also which has been achieved for that particular month.

Workmen Skill Matrix

Traditional companies carry a notion that the older the workmen are, the better experience they have. They understand the job well and the company can trust them to manufacture quality products. This is true to some extent, but a lean company will not judge its workmen's skill on the basis of

Table 10.16 Performance Scorecard for Machine Shop Supervisor at Perfect Gear Company.

Name: Function: Machine Shop   Designation: Supervisor

For the year of 2018–2019

Sl no.	Activity	Target and point award criteria	Maximum Points	Points achieved in the month						Total Points	Date / Remarks %
				Oct-18	Nov-18	Dec-18	Jan-19	Feb-19	Mar-19		
A) Finance Measures											
1	First time right (internal) %	<<85%=0,,85%=3,,86 to 90%=6,,91 to 95%=8,,96 to 100%=10	10	6	6	6	7	7	7	39	65%
2	Carbide inserts and shims for machine shop-$per month	15% reduction	5	2	2	3	3	3	3	16	53%
3	Oils and lubricants in $ per month.	15% reduction	10	6	6	6	6	6	6	36	60%
B) Company Processes Measures											
1	OEE of HB-01-skoda,,CNC2,CNC3,CNC4	80%	5	3	3	4	4	4	4	22	73%
2	5S Score - 39 Plant (machine shop)	Minimum 85%	5	2	2	2	2	3	3	14	47%
3	Implementation of AM Step 1, step2, step3 on 22 machines	100%	10	4	4	5	5	6	5	29	48%
4	Compiling standard hours for machining of critical component	30% process time reduction	10	5	5	4	6	6	7	33	55%
5	Standard hours for machining of critical components - setting target and monitor reduction	30% process time reduction	10	4	4	4	5	4	5	26	43%

(Continued)

Table 10.16 (Continued)

SI no.	Activity	Target and point award criteria	Maximum Points	Oct-18	Nov-18	Dec-18	Jan-19	Feb-19	Mar-19	Total Points	%	Date	Remarks
	Name:								**Designation: Supervisor**				
	For the year of 2018–2019												
				Points achieved in the month									
6	To analyse major causes of NCR in plant (machine shop)	25% reduction	10	5	5	5	5	6	6	32	53%		
7	To develop action plan to reduce NCR's in machine shop	25% reduction	10	4	4	4	5	4	5	26	43%		
C) Performance Measurement System and Training													
1	Kaizen basics, 3M's, 7 M's	100%	5	4	4	4	4	4	4	24	80%		
2	5 'S concept	100%	5	3	3	3	3	4	4	20	67%		
3	AM step 1 to 3, OEE,MTTR,MTBF	100%	5	4	4	4	3	3	3	21	70%		
4	Lean flow-throughput time	100%	5	3	3	3	3	3	3	18	60%		
5	Participation in focused improvement projects	2 in a year	5	2	3	3	3	4	4	19	63%		
6	No.of leave without information (self & workmen)	Zero	5	3	3	3	4	4	4	21	70%		
7	Training taken/given per month	As per schedule	10	9	9	7	7	7	7	46	77%		
8	Skill matrix preparation & display	100%	10	6	6	6	6	7	6	37	62%		
9	7 basics of QC tools	100%	10	6	6	6	7	7	7	39	65%		
D) Safety Health Environment and Quality													
1	Safety NCR's	Zero	15	10	10	11	11	11	11	64	71%		
	Total		160	91	92	93	99	103	104	582			
	Performance of machine shop supervisor			57%	58%	58%	62%	64%	65%		61%		

Function: Machine Shop

Table 10.17 Performance Scorecard for Assembly Supervisor at Perfect Gear Company.

Sl no.	Activity	Target	Max points	Oct-18	Nov-18	Dec-18	Jan-19	Feb-19	Mar-19	Total Points	%	Remarks
						Points achieved in the month						
A) Company Processes Measures												
1	**Number of completed assembly Vs planned in month**	100%	20	10	10	11	13	11	15	70	58%	
2	**Reduction in through put time of assembly**	15%	10	4	3	4	2	3	2	18	30%	
3	**All project BOM issue list by assembly department through ERP**	100%	10	5	5	6	6	7	7	36	60%	
4	**All consumable items issue request from assembly Shop and subsequent store through ERP**	100%	10	6	5	5	7	7	7	37	62%	
5	**Compiling standard hours for assembly of critical component on job card**	100%	10	4	4	5	5	6	5	29	48%	
6	**Standard hours for assembly of critical component setting target and monitor reduction through job route card**	100%	10	5	5	4	6	6	7	33	55%	
7(a)	**No. of NCR raised in assembly for assembly fault fabrication & assembly**	Zero	10	6	6	5	5	6	6	34	57%	
(b)	**To be developed action plan to reduce NCR's (machine shop, gear shop, fabrication & assembly)**	25% reduction	10	4	4	3	5	2	5	23	38%	

Name: *Function: Assembly*   *Designation: Supervisor*

For the year of 2018–2019

(Continued)

Table 10.17 (Continued)

Name:			Function: Assembly								Designation: Supervisor		
For the year of 2018–2019					Points achieved in the month								Remarks
Sl no.	Activity	Target	Max points	Oct-18	Nov-18	Dec-18	Jan-19	Feb-19	Mar-19	Total Points	%	
B) Performance Measurement System and Training Measures												
1	Kaizen basics, 3M's, 7 M's	100%	5	4	4	4	4	4	4	24	80%	
2	5'S concept	100%	5	3	3	3	3	4	4	20	67%	
3	LEAN flow-throughput time	100%	5	4	4	4	3	3	3	21	70%	
4	Visual management	100%	5	3	3	3	3	3	3	18	60%	
5	Knowledge of basics computer (excel,power point & word)	85%	5	2	3	3	3	4	4	19	63%	
6	Participation in focused improvement projects	2 in a year	10	3	3	3	4	4	4	21	35%	
7	No.of leave without information (self & workmen)	Zero	10	9	9	10	9	9	10	56	93%	
8	Training taken/given per month	As per schedule	10	6	6	6	6	7	6	37	62%	
9	Skill matrix preparation & display	100%	10	7	7	7	7	7	7	42	70%	
10	7 basics of QC tools	100%	10	4	5	5	5	5	5	29	48%	
C) Safety Health and Environment Measures												
1	Safety NCR's	Zero	15	10	10	11	11	11	11	64	71%	
Total			180	99	99	102	107	109	115	631		
				55%	55%	57%	59%	61%	64%			
Performance of assembly supervisor											58%	

Table 10.18 Performance Scorecard for PPC Supervisor at Perfect Gear Company.

Name: For the year of 2018–2019				Function: Planning					Designation: Supervisor		Date Remarks
				Points achieved in the month							%
										Total Points	
Sl no.	Activity	Target	Max Points	Oct-18	Nov-18	Dec-18	Jan-19	Feb-19	Mar-19		
A) Finance Measures											
1	Offloading costs. 15% on $ per year/$ per month	$ per month	15	11	10	11	10	10	11	63	70%
2	Increase the usage of slow moving, non moving stocked items & End pieces	05 items	15	8	8	8	8	9	9	50	56%
B) Customer Satisfaction Measures											
1	Reduce throughput time of an order by better co-ordination and proper planning	15% reduction	15	7	7	7	8	8	9	46	51%
2	Completeness of dispatch as per BOM's for all orders	100%	15	12	12	2	13	13	3	55	61%
C) Company Processes Measures											
1	Ensure correct cutting list through ERP	100%	10	6	6	7	8	8	8	43	72%
2	Proper correct packing list through ERP	100%	10	4	2	4	4	5	6	25	42%
3	Stock taking WIP,FG	100%	10	6	6	6	7	7	7	39	65%
D) Performance Measurement System and Training											
1	Kaizen basics, 3M's, 7M's	100%	5	4	4	4	4	4	4	24	80%
2	5'S concept	85%	5	2	2	3	3	4	4	18	60%

(Continued)

Table 10.18 (Continued)

Sl no.	Activity		Function: Planning							Designation: Supervisor			Date	Remarks
Name:														
For the year of 2018–2019		Target	Max Points	Points achieved in the month						Total Points	%			
	Activity			Oct-18	Nov-18	Dec-18	Jan-19	Feb-19	Mar-19					
3	Visual management	85%	10	2	2	4	3	3	3	17	28%			
4	Knowledge of basics computer (Excel, power point & word)	100%	10	3	2	2	3	3	3	16	27%			
5	Participation in focused improvement projects	2 in a year	10	2	3	2	3	4	4	18	30%			
6	No.of leave without information (self)	Zero	10	6	6	6	8	7	8	41	68%			
7	Training taken/given per month	As per schedule	10	6	6	7	7	7	7	40	67%			
8	7 Basics of QC tools	100%	10	4	4	4	5	5	6	28	47%			
Total			160	83	80	77	94	97	92	523	54%			
Performance of planning supervisor				52%	50%	48%	59%	61%	58%		54%			

number of years of experience. Toyota was first to question this wisdom and found that workmen need the proficiency in each skill required to do their job well and have to be trained regularly to improve specific skills or learn new skills.

Workmen Skill Matrix is used to assess skill up-gradation and training requirements for workmen. It is created for all the workmen (operators and fitters) and is in continuity to performance scorecards of their supervisors and first line manager of the function. Workmen performance is linked with their skill requirements and how well they perform their daily work to achieve timely production, product quality and meeting cycle times. The aim is to identify skill gaps and equip them with upgraded skills, better attitude and good attendance. They must have skills, knowledge and capabilities to do their job well. The link between their skill matrix and performance scorecard and the value stream manager's function scorecard should be explained to them.

Individual workmen shall also be judged for their attitude, that is, the commitment of the workmen toward their job. A positive attitude is 'it can be done, it will be tried and it will be done' and a negative attitude is 'it is not possible' or 'why change the present practices?' When there is a positive attitude in a workplace, there is always a positive feeling that anything can be accomplished. Good attitude also brings in punctuality.

Please note that these skill matrix charts in Table 10.19 through Table 10.23 are for a capital machinery manufacturer. These will give a good insight into every function. One can prepare the skill matrix charts for their industry based on the ideas used here. Some of these skill matrix charts have the actual score data that has been achieved for that particular month.

These skill matrices will lead to the methodology to freeze the training needs and continual skill improvements. Based on the evaluation of the skill matrices the priority will be set which skills are to be inculcated first. Accordingly, job instruction (JI) cards will be created for training and a training plan will be made. This repeated training will increase the skill levels of the workmen and will enable the organization to get the optimum and consistent production rate per hour.

Table 10.19   Assembly Workmen Skill Matrix for Perfect Gear Company.

Department-Assembly   Month: March 2019   Function-HR

Category	Skill	1	2	3	4	5	6	7	8	9	10	11	12	Total	%
	Sl no	1	2	3	4	5	6	7	8	9	10	11	12		
	Card number														
	Name														
	Photo														
	Designation	Fitter	Fitter	Fitter	Fitter	Fitter	Fitter	Fitter	Fitter	Fitter	Fitter	Helper	Helper		
Subject Knowledge	Hand grinding	2	2	2	3	2	4	2	2	2	4	4	2	31	65%
	Measuring & marking	2	2	2	3	1	4	1	0	1	0	0	0	16	33%
	Hacksaw cutting	2	2	2	2	2	2	2	2	4	4	4	2	30	63%
	Gear fitting	2	2	2	1	2	2	3	1	3	2	2	0	22	46%
	Bearing fitting	2	2	2	1	2	2	3	1	3	2	2	1	23	48%
	Pipeline fitting	1	0	3	1	3	3	1	0	2	1	0	0	15	31%
	Understanding drawings	1	1	1	3	0	2	0	0	1	1	1	0	11	23%
	Checking backlash and tooth contact	2	3	2	0	2	3	0	0	0	0	0	0	12	25%
	Fastener's skill	3	3	3	3	2	3	2	1	2	3	2	2	29	60%
	Couplings fittings	3	3	3	0	3	2	2	1	2	2	2	1	24	50%
	Crane operating skills	1	1	1	1	2	2	2	0	2	1	2	0	15	31%
	General assembly	2	2	2	2	2	2	1	0	2	2	2	0	19	40%
General	Attitude and late coming	2	2	3	4	2	2	3	0	3	2	2	2	27	56%
	Unauthorized absentism	2	2	3	3	2	3	1	0	3	2	3	2	26	54%
	Tool handling	4	4	3	3	3	3	2	0	3	2	2	2	31	65%
	5S and safety.	2	2	3	3	2	3	2	0	2	2	2	1	24	50%
Function-HR	Marks achieved	33	33	37	33	32	42	27	8	35	30	30	15	355	
	in %	52%	52%	58%	52%	50%	66%	42%	13%	55%	47%	47%	23%		46%

There are total four levels of skills. 1 – I know, but can not do. 2 – I can do, under guidence. 3 – I can do independently. 4 – I can do independently & can train others. The marks are to be given accordingly from 1 to 4.

Table 10.20 Machine Shop Workmen Skill Matrix for Perfect Gear Company.

Department: Machine shop 1 Month: March 2019

Sl no.	Designation	Subject Knowledge												General				Function-HR	
		Tool selection and fixing in conv. Turning	Adjustment of speed, feed and depth of cut in conv. shaping	Understanding CAD drawing	Adjustment of speed, feed and depth of cut in machine	Measurement with Slide Calliper	Measurement with bore gauge	Measurement with Inside/Outside micrometre	Measurement with slip gauge	Adjustment of speed, feed and depth of cut in drilling	Drill and tap selection in conv. drilling	Band saw operation	Crane operator-ating	Attitude and late coming	Unauthorized absentism	Tool handling	5s and safety	Marks	Marks in %
1	shaper m/c operator	1	2	2	4	2	2	4	4	1	1	1	0	1	1	2	2	30	47%
2	shaper m/c operator	2	2	1	2	2	1	2	2	2	0	1	1	1	1	2	4	26	41%
3	Drill m/c operator	2	2	2	4	2	0	0	0	4	4	1	0	2	4	2	1	30	47%
4	Lathe m/c operator	4	1	2	4	4	4	4	1	2	4	1	0	0	1	1	0	33	52%
5	Lathe m/c operator	4	1	2	4	4	4	4	0	2	4	0	0	0	1	1	0	31	48%
6	Lathe m/c operator	2	1	2	4	2	2	2	0	2	2	0	0	0	1	1	0	21	33%
7	Lathe m/c operator	1	1	1	1	1	1	2	0	2	2	0	0	0	1	1	0	14	22%
8	milling m/c operator	0	1	1	1	4	4	4	4	2	0	0	0	0	0	1	0	22	34%
9	milling m/c operator	1	1	2	2	2	1	4	4	1	0	0	0	2	4	2	1	27	42%
10	milling m/c operator	1	2	2	2	2	2	2	4	2	1	0	1	4	4	2	1	32	50%
11	Hacksaw m/c operator	1	0	0	0	0	0	0	0	0	0	4	0	1	2	2	2	12	19%
12	Hacksaw m/c operator	1	1	0	0	0	0	0	0	0		2	0	1	2	1	1	9	14%
		20	15	17	28	25	21	28	19	20	18	10	2	12	22	18	12	287	37%
		42%	31%	35%	58%	52%	44%	58%	40%	42%	38%	21%	4%	25%	46%	38%	25%		

There are total four levels of skills. 1 - I know, but can not do. 2 - I can do, under guidence. 3 - I can do independently. 4 - I Can do independently & can train others. The marks are to be given accordingly from 1 to 4.

Table 10.21 Fabrication Shop Workmen Skill Matrix for Perfect Gear Company.

Function: Fabrication
Month: March 2019

Sl no.	Card number	Name	Photo	Subject Knowledge									General			Points	Total points	% age
				CNC machine	Welding	Hand grinding	EOT crane operator	Fitter	Shot blasting	Hydra operator	Bevel generator	Gas cutting	Punctuality	5S and safety	Attitude			
1				2	4	2	2	1	2	2	1	2	4	3	3	28	48	58%
2				4	4	1	2	4	1	2	2	3	2	2	2	29	48	60%
3				4	4	3	2	2	1	1	2	2	2	3	3	27	48	56%
4				3	4	2	2	2	1	1	2	3	4	3	2	29	48	60%
5				2	2	2	2	4	2	1	3	3	4	3	3	31	48	65%
6				0	0	2	2	0	3	1	2	0	2	2	2	16	48	33%
7				0	0	2	1	0	3	2	2	0	4	3	4	21	48	44%
8				0	0	2	1	0	1	2	1	0	4	4	4	19	19	40%
9				2	2	2	1	4	1	3	1	3	2	2	2	25	48	52%
10				0	0	2	3	0	1	4	1	0	4	3	3	21	48	44%
11				0	0	2	3	0	2	2	1	0	2	2	4	18	48	38%
12				0	0	2	3	0	1	1	3	0	2	2	2	16	48	33%
Total				15	20	24	24	17	19	22	21	16	36	32	34	280	576	49%
				31%	42%	50%	50%	35%	40%	46%	44%	33%	75%	67%	71%			

There are total four levels of skills. 1 - I know, but can not do. 2 - I can do, but under guidence. 3 - I can do independently. 4 - I Can do independently & can train others. The marks are to be given accordingly from 1 to 4.

Table 10.22 Main Stores Workmen Skill Matrix for Perfect Gear Company.

Function: Store Month: March 2019

Sl no.	Card Number	Name	Photo	Documentation	Physical verification	Material loading, unloading	Material identification	5 S and safet	Computer knowledge	FIFO	Fork operating	Crane operating	Supermarket, kanban	Material, safety knowledge	Punctuality	Attitude	Points	Total points	% age
																General			
								Subject Knowledge											
1				4	4	1	2	2	0	2	0	1	2	2	4	2	26	52	50%
2				2	4	4	2	2	2	2	2	4	1	2	2	1	30	52	58%
3				4	4	1	4	2	4	2	0	1	2	2	1	4	31	52	60%
4				1	2	4	2	2	0	2	0	1	2	2	4	4	26	52	50%
5				0	2	4	2	2	0	1	0	2	0	2	4	4	23	52	44%
6				1	2	4	2	2	0	1	0	1	0	1	4	4	22	52	42%
7				0	1	4	2	2	0	1	0	1	0	1	2	2	16	52	31%
8				1	2	4	2	2	0	1	0	4	2	2	4	2	26	52	50%
Total				13	21	26	18	16	6	12	2	15	9	14	25	23	200	416	
				41%	66%	81%	56%	50%	19%	38%	6%	47%	28%	44%	78%	72%			48%

There are total four levels of skills. 1 – I know, but can not do. 2 – I can do. 3 – I can do independently. 4 – I can do independently & can train others. The marks are to be given accordingly from 1 to 4.

Table 10.23 Electrical Maintenance Workmen Skill Matrix for Perfect Gear Company.

SI no.	Photo	Name	Card no	Electrical contactor	Panel wiring	Electrical fitting	Pneumatic line repair/FRL	Bearing fitting	5S and safety	Attitude	Punctuality	Points	Total points	% age
Department: Electrical maintenance				**Month: March 2019**										
				Activity										
1				0	0	0	4	4	3	4	4	19	32	59
2				0	0	0	2	4	3	3	4	16	32	50
3				2	0	4	0	0	2	3	4	15	32	47
4				4	2	4	0	0	3	4	4	21	32	66
5				2	0	4	0	0	1	3	2	12	32	38
6				2	0	2	0	0	1	2	2	9	32	28
Total				10	2	14	6	8	13	19	20	92	192	48
				42%	8%	58%	25%	33%	54%	79%	83%			48%

There are total four levels of skills. 1 – I know, but can not do. 2 – I can do, under guidance. 3 – I can do independently. 4 – I can do independently and can train others. The marks are to be given accordingly.

10.4 How Should Employees at Every Level Utilize Their Time in a Lean Company?

In a lean company, it is important that employees at every level understand how to divide their time during the day, week and month.

- The CEO and the CFO must not spend, on an average, more than 20% of their time in the current operational activities. They should spend at least 40% of their time in improvement initiatives and industry watch and balance time in formulating strategic initiatives.
- Employees at manager level must spend more than 50% of their time in current activities, 40% of their time in improvement of the current operations to identify challenges and root cause of the problems and 10% of their time in innovation advancements in competition and industry.

- Supervisors should use 70% of their time on standardized processes and balance 30% of their time for kaizen activities and improvements of their current operation.
- Workmen must use 95% of their time on executing processes as per standardized operational procedures.

Value stream managers will have to ensure that individual as well as company goals are being met while preparing the functional scorecard, performance scorecard and workmen skill matrix for their staff, supervisors and workmen. The measures should be SMART – *Specific, Measurable, Achievable* stretched but *Realistic*. The *Timeline* for accomplishment of goals should be set up upfront and should be achievable. The functional managers, if required, should not hesitate to hold hands, spoon feed, coach and motivate so that the supervisors and workmen are able to achieve these goals.

Supervisors and workmen are to be accoladed with reward and recognition when they achieve some good results, however small. The rewards should be in the form of household utilities so that they can share it with their families and feel proud in front of them. Cash rewards should be avoided. The performance scorecard and skill matrix must be displayed at the workplace so that continuous feedback can be given. Functional managers must ensure that supervisors and workmen will accept the measurement system positively without any fear of results when scorecards and the workmen skill matrix are displayed.

What Is the Target Score?

There is no minimum score to pass. Audit current score and implement lean accordingly to improve the scorecards. Every month end audit the score based on scorecards and link it to factual information. Increasing trend and improving processes is more important than achieving a target score.

Who Is Going to Monitor It Every Month?

There should be a self-assessment before a value stream manager or kaizen coordinator or an authorized person audits the scorecards. Finance should also be a part of the team. Figure 10.4 highlights the responsibility for implementation of the lean performance measurement system.

Sl. No	Description	Refer chapter	CEOs	CFOs	Lean sensei	Kaizen promotion champion	Value stream managers**	Functional managers*	Concerned functional managers
1	Corporate scorecard	Chapter 9	✓✓	✓✓	✓	✓	✓	✓	Finance
2	Functional scorecard	Chapter 10	✓✓	✓✓	✓	✓	✓	✓	All
3	Performance scorecard		✓✓	✓	✓	✓	✓	✓	All with HRD help
4	Workmen skill matrix		✓✓	✓	✓	✓	✓	✓	All with HRD help

* Head of functions of fabrication, machining, gear cutting, heat treatment, gear grinding, assembly, logistics, quality, maintenance, purchase, finance, HRD, design and R&D.

** Only one value stream is referred to in detail in this book.

✓ = Direct responsibility to implement and sustain

✓ ✓= Ultimate responsibility

Figure 10.4 Responsibility for Implementation of the Lean Performance Measurement System at Perfect Gear Company.

The Need for a Lean Expert

A lean and kaizen expert has expertise in implementation of the functional scorecard to measure the performance of the managers, achieve the corporate strategies and reward and recognize the performers. This ensures sustenance of the lean performance measurement system. These experts, along with kaizen promotion office, work with functional teams and top management to ensure that scorecards are finalized and implemented and reviewed monthly. A lean and kaizen expert provides guidance in implementation of functional scorecard, performance scorecards and workmen skill matrix. These scorecard measures result in growth of the company's revenue and profits and ensure gains are sustained. In few months, these scorecards become the habit and culture of the organization.

Key Takeaways

1. The lean performance measurement system brings the goals of individual workmen, supervisors, managers, functional heads, value stream managers and the CFO and the CEO together so that everyone works toward the company goals, its vision and mission. This way the whole company is tied in one long rope speaking the same language and focusing on customers, who primarily pull this rope.
2. The goal of lean performance measurement system is to manage the processes, not the results.
3. It increases focus on desired outcome and progress of continual improvement projects and increases accountability among the employees.
4. The lean performance measurement system is 'never' used to punish the staff.
5. The lean performance measurement system is designed by the people for the people and is modified at regular intervals when the need of some new measure arises, or some measures become obsolete.
6. Traditional companies carry a notion that the older the workmen are, the better experience they have. Toyota was first to question this wisdom and found that workmen need the proficiency in each skill required to do their job well and have to be trained regularly to improve specific skills or learn new skills.
7. Supervisors and workmen are to be accoladed with reward and recognition when they achieve some good results, however small.
8. A robust lean performance measurement system makes you perform better than your competition.

Recommended List for Further Reading

1. Akao, Yoji and Mazur, G.H. (1991). *Hoshin Kanri[1] – Policy deployment for successful TQM*. Cambridge, MA: Productivity Press.
2. Kaplan, Robert S. and Norton, David P. (1992). Working Paper 10-074. *Using the balanced scorecard[2] as a strategic management system and conceptual foundations of the balanced scorecard*. Boston, USA: Harvard Business School, Harvard University.
3. 'Training within Industry' (TWI)[3] tool. The Training Within Industry (TWI) program developed by the United States in 1944, has been used by Toyota for decades!

4. Fayad, V. and Rubrich, L. (2009). *Policy deployment & lean implementation planning: 10 step roadmap to successful policy deployment using lean as a system: Development workbook*. Fort Wayne, IN: WCM Associates.
5. Maskell.com. Blog- *"Performance measurements."*
Liker, KJ. and Convis, G.L. (2012). *The Toyota way to lean leadership'*. New Delhi, India: Tata McGraw-Hill.

Chapter 11

Finance for Non-Finance

The single most powerful asset we all have is our mind. If it is trained well, it can create enormous wealth in what seems to be an instant.

– Robert T. Kiyosaki

11.1 How Much Do Your Managers Know About the Finance of the Company?

It is assumed that managers in a company understand financial jargon like contribution, variable costs, fixed costs and corporate overheads or they are equipped to answer questions like how much inventory (in days) the company is carrying, should it be more or less, what is the difference between accounts payable and accounts receivable and so forth. If a company examines the financial skills of its managers, the average score percentage will not exceed 30. Business is tough. *There is no easy way to make money. Employees must understand this basic concept. They should develop the capabilities to convert daily activities around them into money so that they can understand from where the profits are being generated in the company.*[1] If your managers shy away from financial numbers, the company will surely get into trouble.

The majority of the traditional companies confine operations teams to production, maintenance teams to machines, the marketing team to procurement of customer orders and only the finance and accounts team to financial reporting and profitability discussion. This is how traditional companies

DOI: 10.4324/9781003221746-11

promote individual interests. But in a lean company, the value stream manager is expected to know cost incurred and profit made during the month as well as the needs of the customers.

In dynamic competitive markets, companies have to deliver higher revenue and sustainable profits to remain relevant in the market. Managers must understand the concept of 'making money'. Are the company's profits growing, declining or flat?

The purpose of this book is to make finance comprehensible to the managers so that they can understand the financial performance of the business, evaluate the outcome of their monthly activities and contribute to improving the business performance and financial health of the company.

11.2 Bonding with the Profit and Loss Statement

Table 11.1 shows the profit and loss statement based on value stream costing. The detail preparation and importance of each

constituent is discussed in detail in Chapter 7. It is very important to understand how a P&L statement is made under lean accounting so that value stream managers and functional managers can see the financial outcome of their operational efforts in the value streams. This is the core of lean accounting. Functional managers must understand the link between operational parameters and contribution and profit outcome for the month. Managers should be able to appreciate the monetary value of their efforts in order to drive performance of the value stream by linking their chores to the P&L statement, specifically to the bottom line. If the bottom line does not show a double-digit percentage growth, then focus is required on changing the course of action toward improving value stream processes. Simple arithmetic, calculator, computer and knowledge of Excel spreadsheet is sufficient to start understanding financial performance.

11.3 Key Performance Responsibilities of Functional Managers

Table 11.2 shows the key performance responsibilities of functional managers for financial and operational parameters and use of capacity of manpower and machine.

Table 11.1 Profit and Loss Statement as per Lean Accounting for Perfect Gear Company in USD'000.

Key parameters	Current state March 2018			Future state March 2019		
	Annual P&L	Monthly average	% of sales	Annual P&L	Monthly average	% of sales
Monthly quantity dispatched	1000 tons			1500 tons		
Sales price	$3.33 per kg			$3.67 per kg		
Sales revenue	40000	3333		66000	5500	
Material cost	17280	1440	43.2%	31200	2600	47.3%
Contribution 1 (A)	22720	1893	56.8%	34800	2900	52.7%
Total variable expenses (B)	6778	565	16.9%	9794	816	14.8%
Consumables and stores	1093	91		1640	137	
Oil and lubricants	208	17		312	26	
Inserts	160	13		240	20	
Accessories	80	7		64	5	
Grinding wheels	88	7		144	12	
Cutting oil	120	10		208	17	
Tool cutter	101	8		144	12	
Gas	53	4		80	7	
Paints	82	7		122	10	
Grease	27	2		56	5	
Others	480	40		800	67	
Power and fuels	2019	168		3040	253	
Job works	1547	129		2384	199	
Other plant misc. expenses	720	60		560	47	
Contribution 2 (C) = (A-B)	15942	1329	39.9%	25006	2084	37.9%
Total fixed expenses (D)	9971	831	24.9%	9213	768	14.0%
Wages – workers	1893	158		2240	187	
Wages – fabrication	373	31		312	26	
Overtime	773	64		736	61	
Salary – executives	3600	300		2885	240	
Other corporate overheads	3333	278		3040	253	
Net profits-EBITDA (E) = (C-D)	5971	498	14.9%	15794	1316	23.9%
Depreciation and amortization	2107	176		2400	200	
EBIT	3864	322	9.7%	13394	1116	20.3%
Bank interest	933	78		960	80	
Interest on term loans	907	76		1120	93	
Net earnings before tax (EBT)	2024	169	5.1%	11314	943	17.1%

Table 11.2 Key Performance Responsibilities of Functional Managers at Perfect Gear Company.

Monthly corporate scorecard						
Aspect	Key performance indicator (KPI)	UOM	Current state March 2018	Future state March 2019	Change in 12 months	KPI responsibility
Financial	Sales revenue – monthly	USD Mn	3.33	5.50	2.17	Marketing and sales
	Average product sales price	USD per kg	3.33	3.67	0.33	Marketing and sales
	Average product cost	USD per kg	2.84	2.79	−0.05	All functions
	Value of inventory	USD Mn	6.27	0.00	−6.27	Operations, finance, SCM, R&D, marketing
	Profit before tax	USD Mn	0.17	0.94	0.77	All functions
	Profit before tax	%	5%	17%	12%	All functions
Operational	Throughput time	Days	113	31	−82.00	All functions
	On time shipment	%	70%	80%	10%	SCM, marketing, operations, all
	Total head count	Number	561	508	−53.00	All, HRD (coordinator)
Capacity usage – manpower	Value adding	%	25%	39%	14%	All functions
	Non-value adding	%	53%	50%	−3%	All functions
	Free capacity available	%	22%	11%	−11%	All functions
Capacity usage – machine	Value adding	%	44%	66%	22%	All functions
	Non-value adding	%	50%	28%	−22%	All functions
	Free capacity available	%	6%	6%	0%	All functions

Contribution Is Important, Not Revenue

Contribution is sales price of a product minus costs of raw material and bought-out products that are required to manufacture final product. In simple words, this is what left out of sales revenue when you have paid for the material and bought-out items that you have procured from outside to build the product. Further, contribution minus the variable costs, fixed costs, corporate expenses is the net profit (EBITDA). Higher contribution increases probabilities of higher profits.

Marketing brings in customer orders. Marketing and finance monitor the sales revenue and profits in traditional companies. But a lean company monitors the contribution instead of revenue when a customer order is received. This is to evaluate how much contribution or value addition the company will earn for this product. This is why marketing is encouraged to learn about drivers of contribution to augment profitability because if a company has to shell out substantial funds to buy raw materials and is left with little funds to cover variable and fixed expenses, then the essence of revenue earned would be diminutive.

For a lean company, revenue of each product is important but more important is how much contribution it brings in. Therefore, it is important to know the expenditure on raw materials to manufacture a product while booking the order because profits will be derived only when each product or basket of products purchased by the customer makes significant value addition (contribution). In simple words, the value addition or contribution of a product is what is left out of revenue after the company pays for raw materials. From this balance amount that is called contribution, the company pays for variable cost and fixed cost incurred in manufacturing of the product and support function required to run the company smoothly. The residual value is net profit (EBIDTA) for the product. Therefore, monitoring only revenue will not ensure that the sale price of the product will fund the activities that are required to manufacture and deliver it to the customer.

How Much Attention Should the Value Stream Manager and Functional Managers Pay to Each Expense Item in the P&L Statement?

A question that is always raised is how much attention the company should pay to each expense incurred during the month. The answer is simple and logical. It has to be proportional to the expenses in the P&L statement. The higher the amount, the higher should be the attention. Companies should understand this concept.

Most managers spend an enormous amount of time on frivolous things. When the company is burgeoning, all expenses seem logical and necessary, but when the company starts deteriorating, the managers start micromanaging each expense.

Table 11.3 elaborates on the expenses as a percentage of sales in the P&L statement. The percentages will differ from company to company for

Table 11.3 Profit and Loss Statement Showing Expenses as a Percentage of Sales for Perfect Gear Company in USD'000.

Key parameters	Current state map March 2018				Future state map 2019			Priority to be given to for improve-men
	Annual P&L	Monthly average	% of sales		Annual P&L	Monthly average	% of sales	
Monthly quantity dispatched	1000 tons				1500 tons			
Sales price	$3.33 per kg				$3.67 per kg			
Sales revenue	40000	3333			66000	5500		
Material cost	17280	1440	43.2%	First	31200	2600	47.3%	First
Contribution 1 (A)	22720	1893	56.8%		34800	2900	52.7%	
Total variable expenses (B)	6778	565	16.9%		9794	816	14.8%	
Consumables and stores	1093	91	2.7%		1640	137	2.5%	Fifth
Oil and lubricants	208	17	0.5%		312	26	0.5%	
Inserts	160	13	0.4%		240	20	0.4%	
Accessories	80	7	0.2%		64	5	0.1%	
Grinding wheels	88	7	0.2%		144	12	0.2%	
Cutting oil	120	10	0.3%		208	17	0.3%	
Tool cutter	101	8	0.3%		144	12	0.2%	
Gas	53	4	0.1%		80	7	0.1%	
Paints	82	7	0.2%		122	10	0.2%	
Grease	27	2	0.1%		56	5	0.1%	
Others	480	40	1.2%		800	67	1.2%	
Power and fuels	2019	168	5.0%		3040	253	4.6%	Third
Job works	1547	129	3.9%		2384	199	3.6%	Fourth
Other plant misc. expenses	720	60	1.8%		560	47	0.8%	
Contribution 2 (C) = (A-B)	15942	1329	39.9%		25006	2084	37.9%	
Total fixed expenses (D)	9971	831	24.9%		9213	768	14.0%	Second
Wages – workers	1893	158	4.7%		2240	187	3.4%	
Wages – fabrication	373	31	0.9%		312	26	0.5%	
Overtime	773	64	1.9%		736	61	1.1%	
Salary – executives	3600	300	9.0%		2885	240	4.4%	
Other corporate overheads	3333	278	8.3%		3040	253	4.6%	
Net Profits-EBITDA (E) = (C-D)	5971	498	14.9%		15794	1316	23.9%	
Depreciation and amortization	2107	176			2400	200		
EBIT	3864	322	9.7%		13394	1116	20.3%	
Bank interest	933	78			960	80		
Interest on term loans	907	76			1120	93		
Net earnings before tax (EBT)	2024	169	5.1%		11314	943	17.1%	

different industries. The following example is for a capital machine build-ing company. But the concept will remain the same, that is, *focus on 'expenses' that are higher as a 'percentage of sale'.* Use the Pareto principle for selection.

In Table 11.3, for the year ending 31 March 2018, the largest expenses in descending order are material costs – 43.2%, total fixed costs – 24.9%, power and fuel – 5% and job work – 3.9%. These four categories are accountable for 77% of the total costs incurred. Hence, maximum attention needs to be given to the reduction of material costs and fixed costs to reduce the over-all cost of production. Of course, these are big-ticket expenditures and are to be further broken down into smaller categories before the project teams start working on it for reduction.

Daily Operational Activities and Their Link with the Profit and Loss Statement

Figure 11.1 shows how operational activities are linked to each row of the P&L statement to enable a non-finance person to link the P&L statement with his daily activities. For a value stream manager, it is important to deliver the ordered products on time in full without any quality problem along with meeting or exceeding the sales revenue and net profit targets with his value stream team for the company.

A company with several families of products is advisable to run on the concept of value streams. They are mini companies within the company and each one should be profitable. Each mini company should have its own P&L statement so that a company can assess which product family is subsidizing other product families.

For a company to continuously make profits it must have a mechanism to capture the true cost of each product as soon as it comes out of the finish-ing line for dispatch. No product should subsidize another product. When this practice is implemented in the company, it will be stupefied to discover that the high revenue customers could be giving negative return. The cost structure of these products should be analyzed to take corrective action by reviewing the internal processes that it goes through and the product specifications to take necessary corrective action. If internal processes and product specification are unblemished, then price correction should be negotiated with the customers.

Sl. No	Daily operational issues faced	Benefits achieved after implementation of kaizen and lean improvements	Impact on profit and loss statement
1	Regular breakdowns	Hours saved will result in increased production	Sales revenue will increase
2	Long changeovers times	Hours saved will result in increased production	Sales revenue will increase
3	Quality issues like defects, rework and scrap generation	Higher yield, increased productivity, reduced variations	Material costs will decrease, sales revenue will increase
4	Waiting for material and inspection	Hours saved will result in increased production	Sales revenue will increase
5	High inventory levels	Reduction in inventories in raw materials, WIP and FG, slow moving and non-moving materials, stores material will result in lead time/throughput time reduction	Interest on working capital will decrease. Sales revenue will increase, cash flow will increase.
6	Logistic losses due to excess transportation and poor layout	Increase in productivity of man and machine	Fuel bill, maintenance costs will decrease. Net profit will increase.
7	Oil and lubricants, electrical, diesel, paints, gas, consumable items expenses	Savings coming out of these expenses will result in reduction of total variable costs	Net profits will increase
8	Large consuming raw materials, bought-out items and consumables	Reduction of purchase prices of these categories will result in big savings in the cost of production	Total material costs will decrease. This is the largest expense on the profit and loss statement. Net profit will increase.
9	Procurement time reduction and just-in-time arrival of raw material, bought-out items and consumables	The throughput time/lead time to customer will decrease	Interest on working capital will decrease. Sales revenue will increase, cash flow will increase.
10	Higher fixed costs	Enhanced focus on fixed costs and all major expenses. Standardization, balancing of workstations and functions will be done.	Fixed costs will decrease. Net profit will increase.

Figure 11.1   Daily Operational Activities and Their Link with P&L Statementat Perfect Gear Company.

Sl. No	Daily operational issues faced	Benefits achieved after implementation of kaizen and lean improvements	Impact on profit and loss statement
11	Issue time of specifications, drawings and BOM and standardization of drawings and BOM from the design function	The throughput time/lead time to customer will decrease	Sales revenue will increase
12	Marketing department increasing focus on higher contribution products while taking orders	Higher contribution will mean high value addition	Net profit will increase
13	Accounts receivable	Marketing will keep focus on accounts receivable	Net profit will increase, cash flow will increase
14	Too many transactions across the functions in the company	Reduction in transactions will give managers free time to give more attention to kaizen and lean improvements projects	Both revenue and profit will increase
15	Low sustenance of improvements brought in	Daily management will help hourly production achievement, increase in productivity of man and machine	Sales revenue and net profit will increase

Figure 11.1 (Continued)

How Much Inventory Should the Company Keep?

The primary goal of kaizen and lean implementation is to reduce the throughput time, which means inventory should be reduced in the company. This large drop in inventory will release funds tied up in handling and storage of inventory, which will improve cash flow in the company and eliminate the need for short-term bank loans to fund working capital, resulting in saving in interest cost and increase in net earnings before tax (EBT). The company will further save on space used, obsolescence or selling raw materials and products at discount.

The company generates substantial savings by reduction in inventory through implementation of supermarket with kanban system where the company stores calculated stock of each item that is replenished as soon as it is consumed.

Some companies believe that with a higher level of inventory they will be able to serve their customer better. They procure raw material at discount and purchase in bulk, but this is not a right approach for a company that is not in the trading business. Too much inventory of some items will almost always result in short supply of some other items and the company is unable to complete manufacturing and dispatch the products. In a lean company, there is focus on uninterrupted flow of raw material driven by pull system through designed supermarket principles for replenishment.

Monster Cost Center

Often when a company embarks on lean journey, there are large machines or facilities that need to be shared by a number of value streams in the company or within the group. The group or the company should be careful in allocating such costs to the value streams. Allocate the costs with logic. Dig deeper. A large boring machine, large gear grinding machine, a large boiler supplying steam, a large bank of cooling towers, a large gas plant or a large oxygen plant are some of the examples of large facilities that serve a number of value streams.

Depreciation – Less or More – Which One Is Better?

When a machine is purchased, it is treated as an asset for the company and shown in the balance sheet. Every month, the company accounts for the obsolescence of the machine as depreciation that is shown as an expense in P&L statement. Lower depreciation signifies the company is not investing in new technologies. If the company has higher depreciation and it is making healthy profit, then this company is doing well financially. It also means company has a modern plant with top-of-the-line machinery.

Accounts Receivable (Debtors)

The company earns revenue when it dispatches a product and raises the invoice but unless the entire amount receivable against each product is not received in the bank, the company will not have tangible or liquid funds to sponsor other activities in the organization. Revenue is the preliminary element of finance activity and is essential to fund other activities (cost centers). Increase in accounts receivable indicates that the funds are tied, not yet received and cash flow is low. The receivables that are disputed and not paid at all by the customers will result in direct write-off of profits earned from that sale. A designated collections team in a company should monitor 'debtor outstanding days' that reveals after how many 'days of sale' does a customer take to pay the money to the company.

Accounts Payables (Creditors)

As important collection from accounts receivable is to the company, it is equally important to pay the suppliers in time also. Lean companies consider suppliers or vendor as part of family. Toyota's vendor management function implements relevant lean tools at the plants of their vendors so that they are also lean and are able to supply the material on time and at low cost. Lean companies pay their vendors on time to ensure receipt of material or service on time. But the company monitors creditors' outstanding days to maintain a healthy cash flow to ensure availability of funds for routine business activities.

In conclusion, in just few months of following the P&L statement, non-finance managers can comprehend it and understand the correlation between business processes and their impact on the P&L statement. It is very important for the non-finance managers to collaborate with finance managers in the lean and kaizen journey in order to achieve the maximum gains in operational parameters, which will eventually translate into financials gains.

Key Takeaways

1. Revenue is the preliminary element of finance activity and is essential to fund other activities (cost centers).
2. Revenue of each product is important but more important is how much contribution it brings in. Higher contribution increases probabilities of higher profits.
3. There is no easy way to make money. Managers must understand the concept of 'making money'. They should develop the capabilities to convert their daily activities into money so that they can understand from where the profits are being generated in the company. They should as well understand the needs of the customers.
4. How much attention should a manager pay to each category of expense incurred during the month? The answer is simple and logical. It has to be proportional to the expenses in the P&L statement. The higher the amount, the higher should be the attention. Companies should understand this concept.

5. No product should subsidize another product.
6. Too much inventory of some items will almost always result in short supply of some other items resulting in delayed deliveries to customers.
7. Lower depreciation signifies the company is not investing enough in new technologies.

Recommended List for Further Reading

1. **Finance for Non Finance**
   Cunningham, J.E. (2017). *Real numbers: Management accounting in a lean organization*. Evanston, IL: JCC Press.

Chapter 12

New Role of Finance Team

Conformity is the jailor of freedom and enemy of growth.

– John F. Kennedy

Accountants in the finance team in the traditional companies are 'book-keepers'. Their job is to prepare and present a true picture of the financial health of the company. The role of an accountant in a traditional company can be summarized as follows:

- Maintenance of books of accounts
- Preparation of financial statements
- Budgeting and forecasting
- Working capital and cash flow management
- Bank and payroll
- Taxation
- Management advisory services
- Audit, statutory and regulatory compliances
- ERP and IT responsibility
- Finance confidentiality

When the company embarks on a lean journey, it starts scrutinizing the processes for waste in the company. 'Waste' is broadly defined as the activities for which the customer does not pay. An accountant's role, as defined earlier, consists primarily of non-value adding activities because the customer does not pay for these activities, he pays only for the product. But in the process

DOI: 10.4324/9781003221746-12

of manufacturing a product, the company has to perform certain non-value adding activities that are essential and contribute to successful outcome of the value adding activities. Lean accounting does not minimize or eliminate the role of accountants. Rather, accountants play the most critical role in lean implementation.[1] Lean also takes into consideration the requirements of GAAP, statutory and legal compliances that a business must comply with.

12.1 Why Is It Difficult to Onboard the Finance Team on a Lean Accounting Journey?

Lean accounting challenges the long-followed practices of standard cost accounting. Finance personnel find it difficult to accept. They are apprehensive to come on board. They assume lean accounting does not comply with principles of generally accepted accounting practices (GAAP) and its focus on reduction in inventory will not reflect well in balance sheet where inventory is shown as an asset. Also, since banks grant short-term loans for working capital funds against inventory stock, the company will struggle with availability of funds due to reduction in inventory. They want to continue reviewing business performance using variance analysis for deviation from budget instead of adopting new measures that focus on operational performance.

Lean brings the traditional methods of standard costing under fire. As the industry advances in technology, a company's performance cannot be based on numbers generated in the traditional system. The true arena of value addition is the plant floor and profits are steered by efforts of operations team. The numbers generated in the back office are only an outcome of the activities on plant floor. A traditional accountant cannot be ignorant of the company's processes and operations or oblivious to the products, market and customers.

The finance team lacks knowledge about technicalities of a company's product because they rarely utilize an opportunity to understand the intricacies of the manufacturing process or spend time in the finishing area of the company to understand the product lines.

They do not understand the function or uniqueness of the products. Hence, the finance team cannot divide activities, based on value addition, in isolation or identify major a cost center on the plant floor. The finance team interacts primarily with management team and external stakeholders like banks, rating agencies, government departments like excise and taxation, auditors, SEC or investors.

Breaking Stereotypes

The role of finance is no longer limited to generation of financial reports. The scope of their activities in progress of a company extends beyond historical practices being followed in the company. The CFO's role should transform into that of a business partner, strategic thinker and technology driver, and his team should be well trained and equipped to help him execute this role in the company. The finance team has to step out of their confined offices into the workplace where the actual value addition takes place. The myths associated with traditional companies should be busted to give them freedom to operate in the new environment. Some of these myths are discussed next.

Profits Are Generated in the Finance Function

Profit is an outcome of activities conducted on the company's plant floor where value addition takes place. It stems from operational excellence on the plant floor or operating function in a service industry. The role of the finance team is to translate the outcome of operational activities into meaningful information and highlight best practices and opportunities for improvement to the people running the processes in the company. This is how operational performance drives the goal of financial excellence.

Finance Personnel Are Watchdogs for the Company

Accountants should not scrutinize the operations team like quality inspectors scrutinize products on the plant floor. Accountants are not business policemen who patrol to find fault in the work of the operations team. Functional managers are competent in their work and aware of their responsibilities and accountabilities. The finance team should partner with different function project teams to contribute to operational improvement by spending time on plant floor, observing operational activities. They can help operations managers/executives calculate the financial gains being accrued due to operational improvements happening on the workshop floor. They can take charge of financial measures as outlined in Chapter 6 on a monthly or weekly basis as the need be. This will help functional managers to improve their processes.

Only the Finance Team Should Understand the Financial Numbers

Operations managers are experts in their operational area but do not know how to comprehend the complexity of financial statements. The finance team should simplify and communicate the business performance to functions after understanding their need through scorecards. They should establish a correlation between non-finance business drivers and financial outcomes to help the operations team understand how they contribute to the financial health of the company. Financial reports should not be restricted to top management. The top management views outcome of operational activities that are carried out on the plant floor in financial statements. Unless the financial performance is not communicated to the operations managers, they will be unable to link profit to the manufacturing process. Accountants should play a key role in making finance easier for non-finance executives in the business. The complexity of the balance sheet, P&L statement and cash flow statements should be simplified to enable managers to use them for improving business processes.

Budget Is Sacrosanct and Variances Analysis Is the Best Tool for Business Performance Evaluation

Budgets lay the vision for financial and operational goals for the year but the budget prepared at the beginning of the year using forecasting models and planning done using MRP and CRP is bound to give variances. The actual demand at the start of the month is different and this is bound to give variances. However, variances are not measured in a lean company. The meetings arising to discuss variances are considered a waste of time for managers. While accountants should analyze and report deviations in the financial statement, they should also understand that rectifications can be made at the plant floor only. The financial measures should not work against the lean production system and the company should work on flow and pull basis with supermarkets to reduce the variances.

12.2 How the Role of the Finance and Accounts Team Transforms in Lean Accounting[2]

Lean gives finance personnel an opportunity to learn lean accounting to proliferate their role in the company. When lean tools are implemented in the company, the existing workload of finance teams decreases by 20% to 50% due to reduction in transaction volume generated as a result of data collection and analysis under standard cost accounting. Like 'finance for non-finance' is recommended for other functions, finance teams need orientation in production, quality and procurement processes. They need to collaborate with other functions and participate in manufacturing and continuous improvement teams. Lean companies run exclusive courses to induct finance professional into the operational areas.

Lean accounting is useful for all the functional managers in the value stream. Radical changes in the company redefine the role of operation, maintenance, design, procurement and quality teams along with the finance team. Finance and accounting are also company processes. When manufacturing and services improve, the financial processes also evolve as per changing business requirements. But the finance team should become a team player and not a barrier. Although their primary responsibility is to track where the money is being spent and whether it is justified, they should still collaborate with the operations teams on the plant floor to remove wastes in the workplace.

Traditionally, the finance function gets involved in the journey a few months down the line when the lean improvement project teams calculate the savings from lean initiatives to present it to the top management and solicit funds for their projects. In the lean production system and lean accounting implementation, the idea is to free the finance personnel from their routine book-keeping and chasing transactions and instead train them to apportion their time between book-keeping, financial statement preparation and analysis and becoming data analyst and valued business partners. Accounting and book-keeping activities like recording transactions and handling accounts payable and accounts receivable should be made simple and automated. Functional activities should be analyzed and, where possible, the processes should be automated.

The implementation of the lean production system calls for elimination of wasteful transactions across the company. Accountants should partner with the operations engineers, designers, quality, maintenance and other support functions for reduction or elimination of these transactions. Some of the most wasteful transactions have an origin in the finance function like book-keeping, ledger transaction recording, daily tracking of material, labor and inventory, three-way matching of accounts payable, accounts receivable, month end closing, variance reporting, corporate overheads allocations and so forth.

Finance team is thus asked to come on board in the lean production system and lean accounting implementation journey from the very beginning. Rather, the lean production system and lean accounting implementation must be initiated by the finance function but rarely do companies start the lean journey from the finance function. Ninety-nine percent of the companies embarking on the lean journey start their lean implementation from the plant floor, or functional areas in the service industry.

Wasteful Processes in the Finance Function

The new role of the finance team will be to implement and monitor lean continuous improvement projects in the finance function and identify wasteful practices. Following are wasteful processes in the finance function that bring in heavy transactions and consume time:

- Book-keeping
- Material tracking
- Manpower tracking
- Inventory tracking for raw material, WIP and finished goods and main stores
- Budgeting and forecasting
- Variance reporting
- Overheads allocation
- Accounts payable and accounts receivable

All these transaction-heavy topics are discussed in detail in Chapter 16.

12.3 How Is Lean Accounting Implemented in the Finance Function?

Step 1 – Cross-Functional Training of the Finance Team to Gain Operational Knowledge

Finance teams are introduced to the concept of gemba walks to commence their learnings of operational processes. Representatives from each non-finance function should explain how the processes in their function flow, which process or function is from their suppliers and customers, what value do they create and what do they use to create that value. If the finance team is educated about cross-functional processes in this way, budget approval will become logical and easier and implementation of new techniques will accelerate. Hence, the finance team should move out of their cubicles and spend half a day, daily for five days, in the finance and the other half in other functions of the value stream. They should observe where the parts are getting manufactured and assembled, how they are designed and how they are procured. Business partnering should be an important goal of the finance team. They should obtain operational training to thoroughly understand the product of the company, its industry and customer market in order to share meaningful insights in financial statements. They should also be educated on kaizen tools and change management.

For example, in Perfect Gear Company, accountants spent a half day in each function – fabrication and stress relieving, machine shop, gear shop, heat treatment shops, gear grinding shop, maintenance, assembly and logistics. In the next round, they started with marketing, design and R&D, purchase and projects. The aim was to understand the functioning and bottlenecks, identify areas that need improvement and continuous improvements projects that are under implementation in those functions.

Step 2 – 5S Implementation

5S is to be implemented in the finance department and hardware, software and server areas of IT department. 5S organizes the workplace so that work can be done efficiently, effectively and safely because a messy and unorganized workplace will lead to oversight of opportunities for improvements that lie in the workplace. Unnecessary and obsolete files, unfiled paperwork lying on desks, unorganized data, redundant IT application and so forth should be reviewed under 5S (see Chapter 2).

Step 3 – Identify Value, Map the Processes of the Finance Function and Identify Non-Value Adding Activities

The first step is to identify the customers of the finance team. External customers of the finance department include, but are not limited to, auditors, investors, banks, lenders and regulatory agencies while internal customers include the management team and cross-functional managers. The next step is to study the processes used to generate relevant reports for these customers. For example, preparation of the P&L account as per GAAP[3] for regulatory compliances, tax filings, management reporting, monthly review decks, bank reconciliations and so forth. The next step is to map the processes and identify non-value adding activities like duplicate reports, redundant internal reports, over-analysis, last minute adjustment entries and so forth that need to be eliminated or reduced. A decision should be made about precision and accuracy of data. How much time can a company spend in correcting the data to the third decimal place (see Chapter 16)?

Step 4 – Prepare a Road Map

A road map for the finance function for adapting to lean accounting, implementation of measures and preparation of the P&L as per lean accounting, business partnering and continual improvement in reduction of transactions and transaction time should be prepared. Since implementation of lean tools commences from finance, it is important that the paradigm shift evolves from finance (see Chapter 16).

Step 5 – Select Leaders

As discussed in Chapter 4, there will always be some employees enthusiastic to embrace lean and implement it in their work. The company should select leaders from this group of employees to implement lean and drive continuous improvement projects by forming small groups within the function as well as some cross-functional teams.

Step 6 – Audit the Results Monthly

The lean assessment audit will become a new norm to track progress of the teams in implementation of lean tools and the improvements generated from them and to see where the company stands on its path to become a world-class company (use Assessment Audit sheets in Chapter 17).

The New Role of Finance and Accounts Team in the Company

The finance function transforms into a collaborative team who continuously partners with other functions for success in the implementation of the lean production system, daily management system and lean accounting.

- *Operations* – Accountants will become the finance business partner for continuous operational improvement projects and support through calculation of savings and review of operational improvement plans from a finance perspective.

- *Procurement* – The finance team will provide support through reduction in suppliers, vendor rating, outsourcing decisions, simplifying accounts payable, stock taking and cycle stock take.
- *Sales and Marketing* – Accountants will move away from calculating product cost using allocations, which is misleading and prone to wrong decision-making, and start using value stream-based product costing and simplify accounts receivable.
- *Human Resources* – Accountants will drive the implementation of a reward and recognition scheme in collaboration with HRD.
- *Corporate, Functional, Performance Scorecard and Skill Matrix Implementation* – The finance team will replace old measures with new measures that add value to the lean implementation journey. They will frame and implement the lean performance measurement system for all functions and coordinate the scorecard readiness for presentation in the monthly review meeting to provide meaningful and timely information.
- *Financials* – The finance team will replace standard cost accounting with value stream-based costing for better cost management and implementation of lean accounting across the company.
- *Prepare Annual Budget* – The finance team will prepare month-wise and function-wise budgets for the current year for easy understanding by the functional managers and projected budget for next three years. Since finance personnel now understand the operational aspect of manufacturing, they can provide proactive suggestions for reduction in waste and cost of manufacturing. They can eliminate complexity from the financial statements and prepare the P&L statement as per lean accounting, which would be useful for all functional managers.
- *One-Day Closing* – We live in a world of instant gratification. If we can obtain real-time information about the weather, current news, stock market, banking and so forth, the company can also aim for one-day closing (i.e., preparing the P&L on the first day of the following month).

  The importance of one-day closing can be determined by how much time, effort and cost goes into month end closing activity. The cost of preparing the P&L can be computed by identifying how many accountants work on preparing the P&L, how many days they take and how much are their salaries. This would be a significant amount but is it worth it if the month end reports are prepared after a week of previous month? It is too late to be of any value because costs have been incurred and plans have been made for the new month. The operations function has moved ahead and is busy tackling new challenges of the current month without any improvement on obstacles of previous month. The problem persists, the costs are still high and the sales are still low.

In order to initiate one-day closing, start by closing every day of the month. The variable costs add up every day. Post the approved bills on the same day and ensure no bills are pending. Keep corporate costs, payrolls, warranty and depreciation updated. Fixed costs do not change much month to month and can be updated in advance. Leave as few items for the closing window as possible like sales revenue, material costs and closing inventory, the first two entries in the P&L statement for the last day. Month-wise financial performance should highlight what improvements have been achieved and the focus should be on partnering with the function teams to make them understand the monetary value of their activities.

■ *Capacity Calculations* – The finance team should lead the capacity calculation to highlight opportunities for increase in production or business expansion. It should also lead the preparation and updation of the corporate scorecard for each function every month along with the functional teams and value stream managers.

■ *Transaction Elimination* – Identification and elimination of transactions across the company along with the functional teams and value stream managers will be one of the key objectives of the finance team in the new lean environment.

■ *Lean Assessment and Audit* – Accountants have to lead with operations teams in conducting a 'lean production system, daily management system and lean accounting system' assessment audit along with the functional teams and value stream managers.

■ *Lean ERP* – Accountants have to lead with operations teams in implementing lean ERP changes along with the functional teams and value stream managers.

■ *Conduct Monthly Budget Review Meeting* – The finance team will help to conduct this meeting to discuss performance of the previous month, orders for the financial year, reasons for shortfall of manufacturing and dispatch value, if any, inventory status, status of scorecards for all functions, financial review for the month and course correction for the next month and quarter.

The role of 'finance and cost accountants' are totally transformed from the earlier 'book-keeper' status to active members of the continual improvement projects teams.

Key Takeaways

1. A traditional accountant cannot be ignorant of the company's processes and operations or oblivious to the products, market and customers. Rather, an accountant plays the most critical role in lean implementation.
2. Accountants are not only 'book-keepers'. Also accountants are not business policemen who patrol to find fault in the work of operations team. Rather, the lean implementation must be initiated/supported by the finance function and companies must start their lean journey from finance function.
3. The complexity of the balance sheet, P&L statement and cash flow statements should be simplified for non-finance executives by accountants to enable them to use these for improving their business processes.
4. We live in a world of instant gratification. If we can obtain real-time information about the weather, current news, stock market, banking and so forth, the company can also aim for one-day closing (i.e., preparing the P&L on the first day of the following month). *It is possible.*

Recommended List for Further Reading

1. Brewer, P.C. and Kennedy, F.A. (feb2013 cover story). *Putting accountants on a "lean" diet* (Vol. 94, Issue 8). Strategic Finance: Institute of Management Accountants. *Article preview available online at Gale Academic Onefile.*
2. Maskell, B.H. (2009). *Making the numbers count: The accountant as change agent on the world class team.* Boca Raton, FL: CRC Press.
3. **Lean Accounting and GAAP**
   Maskell.com. Blog- *"Lean accounting and GAAP, part 1,2 and 3."*
   Maskell.com. Blog- *"Lean accounting and generally accepted accounting principles."*

Chapter 13

Budgeting

A budget is telling your money where to go instead of wondering where it went.

– Dave Ramsey

The annual budget process is a major business exercise. A budget group is formed in the company among the functional managers that is steered by the finance team. Each function formulates a budget for the funds required during the year for operational and capital expenditure. The finance function plays an important part in the approval process. It is a crafted exercise to be executed diligently and the success lies in the absence of deviations throughout the year. The finance team consolidates and presents the budget to top management and showcases the funds required for operational and capital investment in the current year and expected return on money invested in the company.

The teams should have stretched targets to exceed profit target. Internally, the company has to ensure that broad thrust areas are opportunities that can be converted into strengths by leveraging manpower and sound managerial systems and processes. Involving frontline people, backed by immaculate management processes, will ensure that the company's capabilities are sustainable.

The company needs to be fortified to achieve the targets irrespective of changes in the business environment. That is precisely why we need competent managers in the company who understand and perform in the interest of stakeholders like investors, customers, promoters, management and

DOI: 10.4324/9781003221746-13

employees of the company because stakeholders expect the company to deliver value irrespective of whether the environment is kind to the company or not. Higher productivity from existing assets and rationalization of excess capacity should be the preliminary objective for overall cost management. Focus on asset productivity ensures that capital investments are made efficiently, and the organizations grow with low risk. The company needs to reduce its working capital substantially and release the funds for investment in better technology and productive assets.

13.1 What Is a Business Budget Plan?

A business budget plan is a formal written document containing business goals, the methods on how these goals can be attained and the time frame within which these goals need to be achieved. It also describes the company's financial projections and the strategies it intends to implement to achieve the stated targets. This document serves as a road map that provides direction to the business.[1]

A business budget plan is both internally and externally focused. Internally, the business plan focuses on internal goals to be achieved to accomplish financials goals because financial performance is driven by operational performance. The budget also covers development of new products, refurbishing of infrastructure, any new service, new IT system and so forth. A business or budget plan is often developed in conjunction with a list of critical success factors and scorecards targets.

A business budget plan thus becomes the beacon for the CEO, the CFO, value stream managers and all managers. This is a dynamic plan. One cannot foresee the market situations that will roll out during the year, so a revised forecast is required every month and every quarter to make a rolling plan that gives an outlook of the financial year. In this book, the preparation of budgets will focus on key aspects of cost that should be considered or analyzed while making the budget.

13.2 How to Make a Budget for a Lean Company

The preparation of budget or a business plan for a company is a critical, formal and structured exercise. Everything needs to 'fit' and make sense. All aspects of the plan should invigorate and support one another. In lean accounting, it involves preparation of the budget for the current year and projections for the next three years based on the performance of the past three years of the company (3 + 1 + 3). The budget team assimilates operational, financial and infrastructure data from respective functions to develop a raw picture of the proposed budget that is analyzed and stipulated before finalizing the current year budget and future years' projections. The budget details expenses – fixed, variable and capital, internal process improvement plans and HR and IT related plans to generate a budgeted balance sheet, P&L statement, cash flow statement, financial ratios, EVA and so forth.

The real purpose of the budget preparation exercise is to lay out an expenditure and profitability road map aligned with the strategy, mission, targets and goals of the company. Budgeting accounts for anticipated business challenges like increase in direct or indirect material cost, raw material shortage, government or regulatory changes, intense competitive pressure, stagnant demand, employee turnover and foreign exchange and stock market fluctuations as well as seasonality of customer demand.

The *Business Plan Preparation* is an eight-step exercise. It commences assimilation of data and first cut numbers that are then brainstormed upon to freeze the current and future year projections. Figure 13.1 shows the eight steps involved in the preparation of the budget for the company.

Review of the Market and Industry Environment

The appraisal of the industry environment is pivotal to the formulation of an infallible business plan. It is essential to study the forces that have shaped the current state of the industry in order to identify future growth opportunities in the industry. These forces can be political, economic, social, technological or environmental and may have a favorable or unfavorable impact on the business plan. For example, changes in GDP, inflation rates, government subsidies, technology advancement or environmental laws may come as a boon or a bane for the company. Also, it is important to understand the value chain in the industry since it comprises the company's suppliers and customers who determine the prices of raw material and final products respectively.

The budget team should brainstorm and discuss with the top management what are the political, economic, social, technological, legal and environment elements that can change the dynamics of the industry. What impact would it have on the company and how to factor this in the business plan? This will give them an idea of obstacles that could hinder the

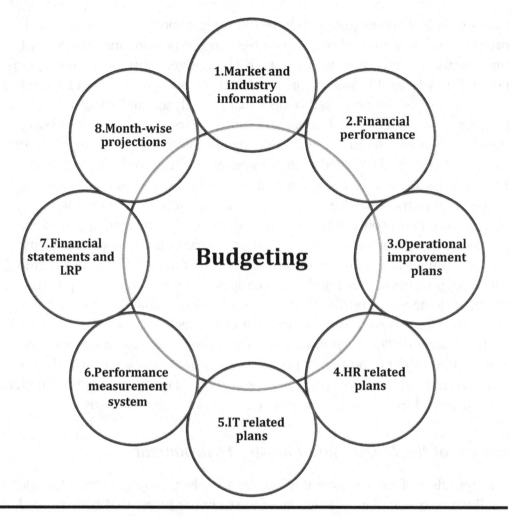

Figure 13.1 Process of Budget Preparation.

achievement of desired goals. There are certain questions that one needs to have answers to like the political situation of the country, and how it can affect the industry. Is there any current legislation that is likely to have an impact on the industry? A rise in the inflation rate of any economy would affect the way a company prices its products and services. Also, the purchasing power of consumers will decide the sales volumes. Other factors to be considered are inflation rate, interest rates, foreign exchange rates, economic growth rate, cultural trends, demographics, population analytics, automation, R&D, consumer laws, safety standards, labor laws, geographical location, global changes in climate, environmental offsets and so forth.

To review the industry environment, management should analyze the annual growth trends, profitability and competitors in the industry.

Distinguish your company from others. Identify features that will make customers buy your products over your competition. This helps to estimate how much organic and inorganic growth is possible for the company. Organic growth is driven by growth in population and price inflation (selling same volume of goods at higher prices). Inorganic growth comes from new product development, entering a new market or capturing market from competition.

For example, if a company manufactures electronic bulbs, it will study how the electronic goods industry is expected to grow, how much profit does the industry make and how are the competitors in the industry performing in terms of sales and profitability. It also needs to know about the latest technology in the industry to meet the needs of customers. The company should then make a stretched but achievable target on being a low-cost, high-quality, profitable manufacturer. The company needs to be agile in making necessary adjustments swiftly to successfully respond to the rapid and ever-changing business imperatives. The company should believe this to be an organizational capability that it needs to acquire and practice. Also, it should analyze its product portfolio to add products equipped with latest technology (like LED and halogen bulbs) and remove obsolete products (incandescent bulbs).

With the previous analysis, the company can formulate a strategy to bring the 15%–20%–25%–30% growth for the current year with respect to the previous year depending upon its comfort level. This analysis will allow the budget team to derive the expected revenue for the current year and the next three years from key products and identify opportunities or need for market segmentation, capital investment, business from competitors and plans to counter the competitors.

Review of the International Market

In the era of globalization, the sky is the limit for companies. With advancement in technology and supply chain, there are limited barriers on companies to be ambitious enough to launch their products in the international market. The international market offers better prices and wider growth prospects than the domestic market. However, the international market can be tough and demanding in terms of quality and delivery requirements.

Further, with transportation becoming faster and cheaper, companies can explore the option of procurement of cheaper raw material from international markets. But this decision should be taken only after all the possibilities of in-house production or low-cost domestic procurement have been exhausted. This will help the company in fulfilling its objective of becoming a low-cost manufacturer.

But exchange rates play a crucial role in making the previous decisions as they determine whether the import of raw material or export of final product will be beneficial for the company. With growing volatility in exchange rates, the company needs to hedge itself against losses arising due to unfavorable rates. Export benefits, subsidies, competition and supply chain for the international market – these are other important factors that are not to be ignored. Depending on the industry the company is in, these factors may become important factors that are to be kept in mind when making decisions.

SWOT Analysis

SWOT analysis is a strategic planning technique used to help a company identify its strengths and weaknesses and discover opportunities and threats from competition or external environment.

This technique is designed for use in the preliminary stages of the decision-making process and can be used as a tool for evaluation of the strategic position of company. It intends to specify the objectives of the business venture and identify the internal and external factors that are favorable and unfavorable to achieving those objectives. Users of a SWOT analysis often ask and answer questions to generate meaningful information for each category and make the tool useful for ascertaining their competitive advantage. SWOT analysis assumes that strengths and weaknesses are frequently internally related, while opportunities and threats are more commonly external. The name is an acronym for the four parameters the technique examines:

- *Strengths* – Characteristics and capabilities of the business that give it an advantage over others.
- *Weaknesses* – Characteristics, lack of capabilities or flaws in processes that place the business at a disadvantage relative to others.
- *Opportunities* – Elements in the environment that the business could exploit to its advantage.
- *Threats* – Elements in the environment that could cause trouble for the business or project.

The degree to which the internal environment of the company aligns with the external environment is expressed by the concept of strategic fit.[2] SWOT analysis is an important tool for a realistic assessment of attainability of objectives that the company wants to pursue during the year. The following is an example of SWOT analysis of the Indian automobile industry.

STRENGTHS	WEAKNESSES
■ Expertise in production of small cars ■ Large pool of engineers ■ Availability of capacity to cater to rise in demand	■ Low labor productivity ■ Low investment in R&D area ■ Lack of skilled labor
OPPORTUNITIES	THREATS
■ Growing population ■ Improved road conditions ■ Rise in standard of living ■ Increase in income level of middle class ■ Increase in demand in rural areas	■ Increase in demand for European cars ■ High interest rate ■ Demand for low-cost vehicles ■ Increase in the input tariff ■ Increase in congestion in urban areas

Let us now take the example of Perfect Gear Company. The company does SWOT analysis twice a year because it wants to radically grow its profits and get ahead of the completion in delivering customer satisfaction. The management of the Perfect Gear Company proactively prepares itself to address these concerns.

STRENGTHS	WEAKNESSES
■ Advanced technological machine setup ■ Technical collaboration with three reputed technology suppliers in Japan, Germany and Sweden ■ Appointment of sales XE "**sales**" agents overseas in Europe, United States and Latin America ■ Updated in-house design facilities and modern state-of-the-art facilities ■ Extensive training trips for skill up-gradation of managers and executives to the plants of foreign collaborators	■ Poor HR XE "HR:HR-related plans" policies ■ Increase in turnover of high-performing employees ■ Highest sales XE "**sales**" price in the market ■ Unable to acquire customers in new markets ■ Unskilled workmen on plant floor ■ Lack of coordination within the departments ■ Poor logistics framework ■ Inefficient customer service
OPPORTUNITIES	THREATS
■ High industrial growth in India ■ Government subsidy for infrastructural growth ■ New geographical market like South Africa, South America ■ Rise in standard of living ■ Revamping or reconditioning of the existing infrastructure	■ Entry of foreign players in capital machinery industry in India ■ Volatile foreign exchange rates

Review of the Financials for the Previous Year

Once the industry and market environment have been analyzed, the next step is to review the past performance of the company. Table 13.1 shows the corporate scorecard for the year 2018–2019 – March 2018 and as of March 2019. It shows the company parameters after one year of a lean and kaizen journey and what improvements have been achieved. The financial and operational results achieved are commendable.

The yearly dispatch volumes have increased by 50% over the last year with a 65% increase in revenue growth. The average product mix selling price increase of 10% also helped this. The profits have jumped from 5% to 17%. The inventory has dropped from US$6.27 million to

Table 13.1 Corporate Scorecard for the Months of March 2018 and March 2019 for Perfect Gear Company.

Aspect	Key performance indicator	UOM	Current state March 2018	Future state March 2019	Change in 12 months
Financial	Sales revenue – monthly	USD Mn	3.33	5.50	2.17
	Average product sales price	USD per kg	3.33	3.67	0.33
	Average product cost	USD per kg	2.84	2.79	−0.05
	Value of inventory	USD Mn	6.27	0.00	−6.27
	Profit before tax	USD Mn	0.17	0.94	0.77
	Profit before tax	%	5%	17%	12%
Operational	Throughput time	Days	113	31	−82.00
	On time shipment	%	70%	80%	10%
	Total head count	Number	561	508	−53.00
Capacity usage – manpower	Value adding	%	25%	39%	14%
	Non-value adding	%	53%	50%	−3%
	Free capacity available	%	22%	11%	−11%
Capacity usage – machine	Value adding	%	44%	66%	22%
	Non-value adding	%	50%	28%	−22%
	Free capacity available	%	6%	6%	0%

US$2.58 million – a drop of 60%. The throughput time has decreased from 113 days to 31 days. There was a massive war on the inventory that made it possible. The customer on time delivery has increased to 80% as timely and complaint-free material is reaching the customers. The operational excellence initiatives on reduction of downtime, changeover times, waiting time for material and manpower and drop in defects, rework, scrap have resulted in reduction of non-value adding capacity usage for machine from 50% to 28%. This in turn resulted in increased value adding capacity usage. Marketing was prompt in getting more orders and in one year the revenues increased by 65%. The change in product mix also helped in increase. The drop in variable expenses as a percentage of sales by 2% also helped here. The raw material cost increased by 4%. There was no layoff. There was a manpower rationalization and redeployment of manpower to other businesses of the group. This resulted in a drop of 7% in fixed charges in absolute value over the year but as a percentage of sales it dropped by 11%.

When the finance team prepares the budget, it uses the trends established in past years to understand the growth pattern of volume, customers and revenue; seasonality of business; and outcome of previous cost saving initiatives and have a record of each and every revenue and cost activity in the company that impacted the P&L in last three years.

A company's life cycle starts from launch of the company followed by growth, maturity and decline. This means the company will not grow at the same rate each year. Past performance review helps to establish at which stage of the life cycle the company currently is on. This exercise also lays down the basis for month-on-month budgeted P&L statement because there will be months in which demand is higher than other months. For example, demand for air conditioners is higher in summers compared with winter months or a specific cost has to be incurred only in one month, for example, the quarterly bonus of the sales team. This is important to make the cash flow statement and ensure availability of funds for respective activities. Also, when the finance team discusses the budget inputs shared by each function, they will need logical reasons for the increase in fixed cost from the respective function compared with previous years.

Table 13.2 outlines improvements in operational and financial parameters in the 12-month lean journey from March 2018 to March 2019. Figure 13.2 shows the lean and kaizen tools that were implemented in Perfect Gear Company in the last 12-month period to improve the operational parameters that resulted in the improvements in the financial parameters. Table 13.3

shows the profit and loss statement for the months of March 2018 and March 2019 and for full year ending March 2018 and March 2019.

Let's discuss the key points for the past year to be reviewed in detail:

Table 13.2 Improvements in Operational and Financial Parameters in the 12-Month Lean Journey from March 2018 to March 2019.

Key parameters	UOM	Current state March 2018	Future state March 2019	Improvements in one year
Average material costs	USD per kg	1.44	1.73	Please Note: 20% increase in raw material costs has taken place as of March 2019
Average manpower costs	USD per kg	0.55	0.34	40% drop in manpower costs
Average conversion costs	USD per kg	0.84	0.71	16% drop in conversion costs
Average total costs	USD per kg	2.84	2.79	2% drop in average costs despite 20% increase in raw material costs
Average sales price	USD per kg	3.33	3.67	10% increase in sales price
Average dispatch per day	Tons	40	58	1.5 times
Average monthly dispatch	Tons	1000	1500	1.5 times
Annual turnover	USD (in Mn)	40	66	65% increase
Annual net profit	%	5.10%	17.10%	3.35 times

Review of Contribution and Raw Material Cost[3]

The Perfect Gear Company is embarking on a path of revenue growth along with profit growth. *The company's ambition is to be the lowest cost producer of quality products.* This will keep it financially secure even during a downturn. Contribution as a percentage to sales revenue is sacrosanct and non-negotiable. If the company is further investing in improving operations, it must reflect in improvement of contribution percentage. To improve contribution without investing in projects and new equipment, the company has to be transparent and

SI. No.	Hours wasted in manpower and machine due to the following losses	Kaizen and lean tools available for improvements. (Refer to chapter 2 and chapter 6)	Benefits achieved
	Main losses resulting in generation of non-productive hours and kaizen and lean tools available to reduce/eliminate these losses		
1	Breakdowns	TPM (AM, PM)	Hours saved for increased production
2	Long changeovers	SMED	Hours saved for increased production
3	Quality issues like defects, rework and scrap generation	TQM, COPQ, MSA, Six Sigma, poka yoke, jidoka, standard work, root cause analysis	Higher yield, increased productivity, reduced variations
4	Waiting for material inspection	Workload balance, flow layout, problem-solving methodology, PDCA, SDCA, data stratification, root cause analysis	Hours saved for increased production
5	High inventory levels	Inventory management, pull system, supermarket, kanban system	Reduced lead time/ throughput time, reduced inventory, increased cash flows
6	Logistic losses due to excess transportation and poor layout	Workload balancing, flow layout and cellular manufacturing, mizusumashi	Hourly production achievement, increase in productivity of man and machine
7	Low sustenance of improvements brought in	Standard work, SOPs, daily management tools like leader standard work, leader checklists, accountability and attendance boards	Hourly production achievement, increase in productivity of man and machine
8	Change paradigm to accept the changes being brought in. Cluttered workplace.	Kaizen mindset, kaizen principles and mudas understanding, 6S tool	Understand wastages in the company, build kaizen thinking. Clutter-free and well-kept workplace.

Figure 13.2   Lean and Kaizen Tools that Were Implemented in the 12-Month Period to Improve Operational Parameters.

Table 13.3 Profit and Loss Statement for Perfect Gear Company in USD'000.

Key parameters	Current state map 2018			Future state map 2019		
	Annual P&L	Monthly average	% of sales	Annual P&L	Monthly average	% of sales
Monthly quantity dispatched	1000 tons			1500 tons		
Sales price	$3.33 per kg			$3.67 per kg		
Sales revenue	40000	3333		66000	5500	
Material cost	17280	1440	43.2%	31200	2600	47.3%
Contribution 1 (A)	22720	1893	56.8%	34800	2900	52.7%
Total variable expenses (B)	6778	565	16.9%	9794	816	14.8%
Consumables and stores	1093	91		1640	137	
Oil and lubricants	208	17		312	26	
Inserts	160	13		240	20	
Accessories	80	7		64	5	
Grinding wheels	88	7		144	12	
Cutting oil	120	10		208	17	
Tool cutter	101	8		144	12	
Gas	53	4		80	7	
Paints	82	7		122	10	
Grease	27	2		56	5	
Others	480	40		800	67	
Power and fuels	2019	168		3040	253	
Job works	1547	129		2384	199	
Other plant misc. expenses	720	60		560	47	
Contribution 2 (C) = (A-B)	15942	1329	39.9%	25006	2084	37.9%
Total fixed expenses (D)	9971	831	24.9%	9213	768	14.0%
Wages – workers	1893	158		2240	187	
Wages – fabrication	373	31		312	26	
Overtime	773	64		736	61	
Salary – executives	3600	300		2885	240	
Other corporate overheads	3333	278		3040	253	
Net profits-EBITDA (E) = (C-D)	5971	498	14.9%	15794	1316	23.9%
Depreciation and amortization	2107	176		2400	200	
EBIT	3864	322	9.7%	13394	1116	20.3%
Bank interest	933	78		960	80	
Interest on term loans	907	76		1120	93	
Net earnings before tax (EBT)	2024	169	5.1%	11314	943	17.1%

The necessary price increase has to be obtained to compensate for increases in variable costs like raw material, power and fuel, utilities and supplies. This will be applicable for items that account for 90% of variable costs. Yield improvement initiatives need to be thought through with aggressive execution plans.

For long-term survival, it is important that the company targets a minimum 10% reduction in variable costs for the first year in its business plan. If hard negotiations are required, it must be listed in the functional scorecard for the CEO and the value stream manager. Managing contribution levels is the true reflection of strength of the business. To do this, the company must remember to compete on costs. There are external costs like price of power or raw material over which the company has limited control so the company should focus on controllable costs like administration and overheads to offset the setback arising from uncontrollable elements.

Also, the company can increase rate of productivity of assets, their yield or recovery; optimize consumption of utility; streamline logistics; and increase productivity of manpower in general, and of management in particular, because there is always a gap between the theoretical best and what the company is achieving at present. There is a need to narrow this gap that will ensure that assets sweat better, thereby improving profits and returns. Once better scores like highest daily production, lowest cost or best yields are achieved, the company should be able to sustain these gains and not allow concept of average to pull these down.

The company should have a low break-even level that mandates improvement in contribution and reduction in fixed costs. This is essential for survival in a highly competitive business environment. Contribution should be the governing factor at the time of finalization of orders. Historical data available with the company should be analyzed to identify product families with poor contribution and a target cost should be set for these products.

Review of Variable Costs

The business should get back to basics on theoretical variable costs and make the business robust even in a downturn. Price cycles are bound to repeat; therefore, the company has a small window to fine-tune itself. For aggressively improving the variable and fixed costs, the company needs to be aggressive in terms of better shop floor practices, maintenance and investing in technologies that make manufacturing efficient and manpower productive through automation.

As part of the business planning exercise, the company must identify steps that reduce variable costs by at least 10% annually. This can be done by identifying negative or low contributing segments or segments with low EBIT to sales ratio. Reconstruction of the cost structure for these segments should be planned to witness impact on overall and fixed cost to contribution ratio.

The largest scope of cost savings lies in the cost of raw materials. The company has to move away from traders to original equipment manufacturers (OEMs). Traders, or middlemen, should be avoided. Reduction in the purchase price of large categories of raw materials and bought-out projects should be planned with minimizing off-loading costs. Focused improvements projects like material yield improvements, setup time (changeover time) and reduction through SMED (single-minute exchange of dies) should be accelerated. Energy cost reduction, compressor power usage reduction, defects reduction, waiting time reduction, and more such projects should be started. The budget should contain targets for improvement projects so that the company does not lose focus on them.

Review of Fixed Costs

Fixed cost refers to the cost that the company will incur irrespective of any production or usual business activity like salaries, rent of corporate office and interest on loans. The company must target a 20% reduction in fixed cost when it attempts a zero-based buildup of fixed costs. This should be explicitly built in the business plan along with initiatives to be taken in this direction. A cardinal principle of a good business model is fixed costs as a percentage of sales should be less than 50% of the contribution as a percentage of sales. Reducing fixed does not mean laying off manpower but instead redeployment of personnel to new value streams, expansion and diversification, that is, the focus should be on the denominator.

Review of Working Capital

Working capital is a wasteful deployment of critical financial resources. When a company plans high-growth, high-investment projects, it needs internal funds for investment before soliciting external debt. Traditional companies retain a certain percentage of sales as a budget for working capital. However, a company can operate with half of this percentage if the overall inventory level declines, which happens in a lean company in its maiden journey.

In most companies, the working capital is not rigidly controlled. Optimal use of working capital can release locked-in funds for investment in better technology and productive assets. Asset deterioration, obsolescence and their carrying cost result in absolute losses. Bad debts also lead to losses. Funds released from such assets could be put to better use by reinvesting in productive fixed assets through technology up-gradation or capacity enhancement. Figure 13.3 links reduction in fixed costs, variable costs and inventory with the P&L statement to explain how the released funds from working capital, upgraded technology and increased productivity result in increase in profit or revenue.

Sl no	Daily operational issues faced	Benefits achieved after implementation of kaizen and lean improvements	Impact on profit and loss statement
1	Regular breakdowns	Hours saved will result in increased production	Sales revenue will increase
2	Long changeovers times	Hours saved will result in increased production	Sales revenue will increase
3	Quality issues like defects, rework and scrap generation	Higher yield, increased productivity, reduced variations	Material costs will reduce, sales revenue will increase
4	Waiting for material and inspection	Hours saved will result in increased production	Sales revenue will increase
5	High inventory levels	Reduction in inventories in raw materials, WIP and FG, slow moving and non-moving materials, stores material will result in lead time/throughput time reduction	Interest on working capital will decrease. Sales revenue will increase, cash flow will increase.
6	Logistic losses due to excess transportation and poor layout	Increase in productivity of man and machine	Fuel bill, maintenance costs will decrease. Net profit will increase.
7	Oil and lubricants, electrical, diesel, paints, gas, consumable items expenses	Savings coming out of these expenses will result in reduction of total variable costs	Net profits will increase

Figure 13.3   Link of Reduction in Fixed Costs, Variable Costs and Inventories with the Profit and Loss Statement.

Sl no	Daily operational issues faced	Benefits achieved after implementation of kaizen and lean improvements	Impact on profit and loss statement
8	Large consuming raw materials, bought-out items and consumables	Reduction of purchase prices of these categories will result in big savings in the cost of production	Total material costs will decrease. This is the largest expense on the profit and loss statement. Net profit will increase.
9	Procurement time reduction and just-in-time arrival of raw material, bought-out items and consumables	The throughput time/lead time to customer will decrease	Interest on working capital will decrease. Sales revenue will increase, cash flow will increase.
10	Higher fixed costs	Enhanced focus on fixed costs and all major expenses. Standardization, balancing of workstations and functions will be done.	Fixed costs will decrease. Net profit will increase.
11	Issue time of specifications, drawings and BOM and standardization of drawings and BOM from the design function	The throughput time/lead time to customer will decrease	Sales revenue will increase
12	Marketing department increasing focus on higher contribution products while taking orders	Higher contribution will mean high value addition	Net profit will increase
13	Accounts receivable	Marketing will keep focus on accounts receivable	Net profit will increase, cash flow will increase
14	Too many transactions across the functions in the company	Reduction in transactions will give managers free time to give more attention to kaizen and lean improvements projects	Both revenue and profit will increase
15	Low sustenance of improvements brought in	Daily management will help hourly production achievement, increase in productivity of man and machine	Sales revenue and net profit will increase

Figure 13.3 (Continued)

The company must work on operational profit and not stock profit *(profit from increase in market value of unsold inventory)*. Often, the stock profit made by storing inventory is thrown away when price increase is not taken at the right time. When the price of raw material increases, the company should immediately pass on this increase to its customers in order to secure profits. Manufacturing companies should not resort to holding excessive inventories, as a drop in market value will smear the profits. Manufacturing and trading should not be mixed because these are two different businesses. It is a double-edged sword that can hurt the business whenever prices of raw material are rolled back. The company should also aim for to maintain inventory at less than 30 days to avoid capitalization of inventory in the balance sheet and deviate from the actual P&L statement.

As accounts receivable age, the quandary of collection may result in total loss of sale value and waste time and efforts of management in follow-up and review. As inventory ages, it becomes vulnerable to obsolescence, which may result in write-offs. Therefore, a target to reduce the working capital to half of the current level must be built into the budget. Working capital as a percentage of sales must decrease with decrease in inventory and receivables. Slow moving and non-moving items should be disposed of with the help of the design and purchase functions. A plan for disposal of non-performing assets and the use of funds derived from this disposal should also be outlined in the budget plan.

Review of Economic Value Added (EVA)

EVA is an estimate of a company's economic profit, or the value created in excess of the required return by the company's shareholders.

EVA = Net operating profit after tax − (Weighted average cost of capital × capital invested)

The idea is that value is created when the return on the company's capital employed exceeds the cost of that capital. In simple language, EVA is the amount the company earns over and above what the shareholders would have earned if they invested their money in a bank and earned interest from it. The company's profit should be significantly higher than the bank interest for the shareholders so that the decision to invest in the company turns out to be a prudent one.

The company should have a positive EVA in order to confidently bid for bigger orders. The business makes tremendous effort to improve the performance and over-achieve their planned targets for the year. Though the increase in raw material prices may affect the profitability of the business, it should be offset through higher volumes and lower operational costs resulting in better profitability.

The company needs to 'lock in gains' wherever it achieves the best. Hence, each value stream manager should strive to make their unit EVA positive, which will also boost the shareholders' confidence. Division must focus on reducing debtors aging and hold back supplies to erring customers so that real sales with positive effect on the profits are achieved.

Operational Improvement Plans

The operational excellence initiatives for reduction in downtime, change-over time, waiting time for material and manpower and decrease in defects, rework and scrap have resulted in reduction of non-value adding capacity usage for machine from 50% to 28%, a reduction of 22% (see Table 13.2).

There is a scope to reduce non-value adding and wasteful activities through kaizen and lean improvement initiatives. There is a 60% drop in the inventory in the last year. (see Table 13.2).

These initiatives are to be continued.

Once the financial aspect of the past three years has been reviewed, the next step is to outline initiatives for improvement in operations that would help in meeting cost reduction, revenue growth and operational excellence targets. For the purpose of operational improvement, the following areas or initiatives can be focused upon:

- *Training, Training and Training* – Toyota has a target of training their employees for 40 hours per employee per year even after 60 years of kaizen and lean implementation because it believes that successful sustenance is an outcome of continual training efforts. A new lean company can take a target of ten hours per employee per year in its first few years. Gradually it can increase the target. For Perfect Gear Company this translates to approximately annual 6000 hours. The company must put in 500 hours per month of training.
- *Standardization* – Each team should thoroughly understand its processes and draft standard operating procedures (SOPs) to bring standardization in processes. SOPs also contain the methods and techniques

selected by the company for carrying out an activity to bring consistency in outcomes. Tools like PDCA and SDCA ensure continuous improvement so that standardization does not bring stagnation in advancement.

- *Business Development and Fulfillment* – Marketing must develop key customer contacts, gathering market and business intelligence, and develop new product portfolios in order to increase business volume while functional managers must focus on improving OTIFEF to improve customer experience.

- *Quality Improvement* – The management team should thoroughly analyze the reasons for customer rejections and continuous customer complaints and survey customer satisfaction to identify scope for improvement in quality because it is a key driver to gain a competitive edge in the market and improve market share.

- *New Product Development* – A prophetic company ensures a certain percentage of sales turnover in a year is contributed from new product development. The higher the percentage, the better are the odds of the company's survival in the long term. This gives an advantage over competitors and an opportunity to diversify into new market segments or products. Therefore, marketing needs to understand the stated as well as unstated needs of the customer and be ahead of the competition in fulfillment of those needs. The lead time for new product development needs to be abridged. In a free market scenario, competitive advantage can be gained by innovation in products and services at a low cost. The company should implement measures to evaluate the lead time for new product development and the success rate of new products.

- *Productivity and Yield Improvement* – Higher productivity can be achieved only if there are fewer unscheduled stoppages, which implies maintenance of equipment should be robust resulting in higher mean time between failure (MTBF). When costs reduction drive is commenced, it is a general tendency to reduce maintenance expenses by delaying maintenance activities, but this is a shortsighted approach that leads to higher costs and unwanted breakdowns at critical moments. Productivity improvement should predominantly focus on three core areas – throughput time, quality and utilization. It is imperative that we constantly measure throughput levels, quality of products produced and working capital asset turnover ratios to diagnose the root cause of problems and launch corrective actions. Reduction in defects, rework and rejections in the process can improve yield of the processes and be one of the largest potential saving opportunity in some companies.

- *Power Consumption* – Parameters like power units per ton, fuel consumption for power generation and cost of internal power generation per unit should be monitored and tracked for improvement. Solar power and energy efficient appliances should be used to optimize use of power in the company.

- *Consumables Stores* – Operations, purchase and stores personnel should focus on reduction in expenditure on consumables and stores. A budget should be prepared for all work centers and accordingly included in the functional scorecard and performance scorecards for control.

- *Subcontracting* – As discussed in detail earlier, a cost benefit analysis should drive the decision for in-house production or outsourcing.

- *Revision of Product Portfolio* – The product portfolio should be analyzed to pinpoint product with low or negative contribution. The raw material cost and product mix should be revised in order to improve overall contribution in the P&L statement. Marketing, operations, PPC and purchase, design and R&D department should collaborate on devising a precise improvement plan in this direction.

- *Asset Utilization, Capacity and Capital Expenditures* – There is a lot of scope to improve asset utilization while simultaneously making an investment toward improving technical capabilities and in new technology, failing which the company will lose out on quality and productivity in the long run. In times of growth, it is always a good practice to have a little extra capacity or to invest to create this capacity. However, the company should be cautious against significant increase in capacity without maximizing existing asset utilization during a boom period.

In many companies, most of the manufacturing assets operate below their true theoretical operational capabilities. Poor asset performance could be due to higher capacity creation, poor shop floor practices or poor planning, resulting in higher cost of capital and lower returns to shareholders.

Inefficient work practices consume excess capacity, result in poor productivity and necessitate higher manpower related cost in payroll, welfare and administration. Over a period of time, this production level becomes a norm and rise in demand is concomitant with additional investment in capacity and higher cash outflow. Companies need to achieve higher productivity from existing assets and rationalize excess capacity to improve overall cost management. Focus on asset productivity ensures that capital investment is an industrious decision and not driven by persistence of inefficiencies in the organization. However, the company needs to practice this consistently. This is the reason why theoretical capacity of critical equipment is important because it helps in understanding performance gaps, pinpoint bottlenecks and identify root cause for problems.

Asset productivity signifies that we not only generate higher output per hour or per shift but also produce quality and first time right products. The aim is to generate maximum marketable products at lowest cost and in time from any given equipment. This is a vivid example of investing in the right technology to improve our competitiveness in a product segment that otherwise was in the stronghold of either cheap imports or other competitors. Capital expenditure identification and execution skills are key to achieving the cost structures a company aspires for.

Calculate the return on capital employed (ROCE) of each investment, payback period, cost-benefit analysis and review whether it delivers the benefits envisaged. Use the value stream approach while decision-making.

Human Resources Related Plans

The benefit of a strong and skilled workforce in a company will be appreciated by now. Therefore, the following factors should be built in the functional scorecards for all functions:

- Improvement in employee engagement
- Skill up-gradation
- Nurturing and retention of key employees
- Creating a customer-centric workforce with product knowledge and end application awareness
- Reducing recruitment lead time
- Statutory compliances like EPF
- Training hours
- Productivity and value added per employee
- Manpower count, manpower cost, manpower cost per ton dispatch and average manpower cost per employee and so forth

Information Technology Related Plans

Information technology (IT) is a critical function in a company because it handles all the communication and technologies in the company. The company should review the IT related plans for investment and maintenance of hardware, license fees and up-gradation of software, integration support, ERP implementation, data security and communication systems within the organization.

Lean Performance Measurement System

Once the financial and operational excellence targets have been decided and budgeted for, the next step is to update the functional scorecards, performance scorecards and skill matrix with the new target based on the company's strategy for the year. The initiatives for operational excellence, cost reduction and reduction in non-value adding use of capacity should be explicitly mentioned in the scorecards along with required training and skill up-gradation plan to achieve the above in skill matrix. This is important to track the progress each element of the company during the year.

Financial Statements and Long-Run Planning

All the previous steps lay the foundation for projection of revenue, volume and profitability for the current year and next three years. Sales revenue is estimated based on the past trends and order position in hand. It also depends on new products, new customers, industry and market growth because past year trends usually give growth projection for business as usual. Material consumption is estimated based on the consumption in previous year and yield and inflation impact should be built into the estimation. Material consumption is sales driven while dispatch is target driven. Wages and other operational overhead are calculated based on average increase over the previous years. Wages are also governed by compensation scheme of government (minimal wage rate) and industry rate. Administrative expenses are estimated based on past trends and new control measures.

The company has to be aggressive in vying for the business. The increase in cost of raw material due to inflation should be factored in the sales price and meticulous planning of material should be done to offset the impact of inflation. The company has to focus on improving its design facilities and capabilities to enhance quality. It has to reduce costly material procurement, negotiate aggressively and explore alternate source.

The P&L statement, cash flow statement and balance sheet derived from the previous activities will be used as a target for performance measurement and act as a guide for the decision-making process.

Inventory Control

The company must plan for major reduction in piled inventory. High inventory has significant repercussions on working capital and gradually becomes fixed capital. It increases the cost of the products, results in obsolescence and symbolizes poor planning.

System controlled planning of inventory with proper checks and balances for ordering of material can help initiate inventory control. Sourcing of material should be linked with customer delivery schedule, which means material should be bought in when it is required for use in production and not earlier than required. Better coordination with sales, design, production planning and control and purchase functions helps to bring control at the time of raising request for new material. The design and planning team should take care of liquidation of non-moving material at the earliest as this material adds to carrying cost. The company must put all consumables and bought-out standard materials in one store and their sourcing should also be centralized.

Month-Wise Projected Finance Statements and Scorecards

The target of the current year should be broken down into monthly sales targets. The adjustment for seasonal fluctuations, as discussed in step 1, should be made as per business need. These monthly targets for the next 12 months will become the budget for the year. Any shortfall in a month should be covered in the upcoming month or quarter so that when the year ends the company reaches or exceeds the yearly target for revenue. The company performance improves considerably when the company switches to rigorous control through monthly review meetings and quicker decision-making because monthly results are made available on the first day of next month. The results were understandable and linked to the processes.

13.3 Responsibility for Preparation of the Business Plan

A business plan can be great on paper, but it requires kosher execution. Figure 13.4 shows direct as well as ultimate responsibility of functional heads, value stream managers, the CFO and the CEO in preparation and execution of the business plan. The ultimate role of the CEO and the CFO is to ensure that a business plan is implemented, reviewed and sustained on a monthly basis.

Sl. No	Description	Refer chapter	Responsibility					Concerned functional managers
			CEO's	CEO's	Kaizen promotion champion	Value stream managers**	Functional managers*	
1	Review of the financial figures for the last financial year		✓	✓✓	✓	✓	✓	Finance
2	Review of the marketing, industry environment		✓✓	✓✓	✓	✓	✓	Marketing
3	Review of operational improvement plans		✓✓	✓	✓	✓	✓	All
4	HR related plans		✓✓	✓	✓	✓	✓	HRD
5	IT related plans		✓	✓✓	✓	✓	✓	Finance
6	Review of corporate, functional scorecards of value stream managers and HOD – functions, performance scorecards for the staff and skill matrix for the workmen	Chapter 13	✓✓	✓✓	✓	✓	✓	All, main – finance, HRD
7	Development of the financials data for the current and the next three years		✓✓	✓✓	✓	✓	✓	Finance, marketing
8	Development of projected finance results month-wise for easy understanding by the functional managers		✓✓	✓✓	✓	✓	✓	Finance
9	Implementation and monthly review		✓✓	✓✓	✓	✓	✓	All, finance

* Head of functions of fabrication, machining, gear cutting, heat treatment, gear grinding, assembly, logistics, quality, maintenance, purchase, finance, HRD, design and R&D.

** Only one value stream is referred to in detail in this book.

✓ = Direct responsibility to implement and sustain

✓✓ = Ultimate responsibility

Figure 13.4 Responsibility for Preparation of the Business Plan of Perfect Gear Company.

The company's CEO and CFO work with value stream managers and functional teams to ensure that a logical and achievable plan is finalized and implemented for the current year and the next two years. Then the CEO chairs monthly review meetings to ensure conversion of lean benefits into sustainable top-line and bottom-line growth and inculcate lean in the culture of the organization. The finalized plan is communicated down the line so that everyone works together in the right direction. The company keeps its objectives clear and simple and addresses the areas for improvement identified as a part of the business plan. The business plan is prepared extensively for the current year, but projections for the next three years will be outlined based on the company's vision and mission.

The marketplace determines our future, and as a group and as individuals we need to spend quality time there. The customer always must take precedence over everyone else. The business has to gain the knowledge and experience to counter these challenges, and going ahead, this learning will be key for all. The key requirement is perfect execution of the outrageous growth plans. The company has to keep the growth curve going; however, the holes will need to be plugged quickly to help ensure that the growth rates remain aggressive, profitable and sustainable.

The current year plans should be stretched but achievable. The customers tell what more they expect and how big the opportunity really is. And when the CEO and the CFO talk to their managers, they should get the confidence in achieving these targets. The company can and must aim for a little more stretch over the plan, in both top and bottom line. The company must plan to do better, not just incrementally but radically. How can a business not just grow, but grow exponentially? And a failure to grow can be a catastrophe.

Key Takeaways

1. The marketplace determines our future, and as a group and as individuals we need to spend quality time there. The customer always must take precedence over everyone else.
2. The key requirement is perfect execution of the outrageous growth plans. The company has to keep the growth curve going; the growth rates remain aggressive, profitable and sustainable.
3. The teams should have stretched but achievable targets to exceed profit target to keep the company a low-cost, high-quality, profitable manufacturer.
4. The company needs to be fortified to achieve the targets irrespective of changes in business environment.

5. The company must plan for major reduction in piled inventory. High inventory has significant repercussions on working capital and gradually becomes fixed capital.
6. Contribution as a percentage to sales revenue is sacrosanct and non-negotiable. Contribution should be the governing factor at the time of finalization of orders. Managing contribution levels is the true reflection of strength of the business.
7. Working capital is a wasteful deployment of critical financial resources. Therefore, a target to reduce the working capital to half of the current level must be built into the budget.
8. The company should have a low break-even level that mandates improvement in contribution and reduction in fixed costs. This is essential for survival in a highly competitive business environment.
9. A prophetic company ensures a certain percentage of sales revenue in a year is contributed from new product development. The Higher the percentage, the better are the odds of company's survival in the long term.

Recommended List for Further Reading

1. Abrams, R. and Vallone, J. (2006). *Business plan in a day- get it done right, get it done fast*. New Delhi: Prentice Hall of India.
2. Ananthanarayanan, R. (2000). *The totally aligned organisation- a foundation of TQM culture'*. Chennai, India: Productivity & Quality Publishing Private Ltd.
3. Pandey, I.M. (2003). *Financial management*. New Delhi: Vikas Publishing House Pvt. Ltd.

Chapter 14

Business Plan Review

Mistakes should be examined, learned from, and discarded; not dwelled upon and stored.

– Tim Fargo

The process and responsibility of preparation and implementation of a business plan is detailed in the previous chapter. The next step is to review the performance of the company monthly with respect to the business plan so that timely action can be initiated to accomplish the targets laid out in the business plan.

The team reviews financial as well as non-financial drivers to analyze the performance of business in a particular month. The meeting acts as a platform for discussion of challenges being faced and scope for improvement with focus on processes, not the person. This one-hour meeting offers tremendous benefit to the company under lean implementation. Value stream managers and functional managers become familiar with their function's data when the company implements the lean production system, daily management system and lean accounting system. They participate in the preparation of the business plan to some extent as well. Functional scorecards and performance scorecards accustom them to the importance of their responsibilities, key result areas and targets.

DOI: 10.4324/9781003221746-14

14.1 What Is the Agenda of Business Plan Review?

Let's discuss the agenda or the process of the monthly performance review meeting using the example of Perfect Gear Company. The following agenda is designed for a capital machine building company and acts as a guidance for companies to design the meeting agenda and documentation suitable to them.

Perfect Gear Company started working on pull from customers. Therefore, production of only those products that were likely to be dispatched or sold by the end of the month was planned. No order is planned for production that is unlikely to be dispatched and would land in the warehouse forever. The performance of the company for the financial year 2018–2019 will be discussed in the meeting that will be held on 2 April 2019 after all the documentation is updated till 31 March 2019 and financial statements are prepared according to one-day closing.

The CEO, CFO, value stream and functional managers will be present in the meeting and other managers can be asked to join if they are needed to give any particular information. The performance update is circulated to the respective stakeholders a day in advance so that everyone comes prepared and avoids discussion on data discrepancies. *The meeting duration is restricted to one hour and is to be strictly adhered to, but the entire agenda is to be addressed in the meeting. This means each agenda item has a set time. These 60 minutes are 'power time' and only the corrective action strategy, if any required, will be discussed.* Managers must sort out the data discrepancies among themselves before coming to the meeting. This is one area where the precious meeting time is wasted. If initially the meeting exceeds one hour, it is acceptable, but target to bring it down to one hour within six to nine months. The targets suggested during the meeting for continuous improvement teams will be difficult to implement initially as they demand a substantial change, but this should not discourage the teams from pursuing these initiatives.

The CEO chairs the meeting, but the CFO is the central coordinator, and his team will prepare the minutes for circulation after the meeting. The monthly review process is divided into five broad areas:

Financial Review

The financial performance in the month of March 2019 and performance in the financial year 2018–2019 are reviewed on 2 April 2019.

The P&L statement presented in Table 14.1 gives a detailed outlook of volume dispatched, revenue earned and cost incurred on production of items dispatched including fixed overheads. Each line item is thoroughly analyzed and discussion on deviation from the targets in the budget remains the prime agenda of the review. Reasons for shortfall in dispatches, if any, value of finished goods lying after month end, material cost and inventory status are discussed. The review should focus on profitability for the month, deviation from targets in the business plan, reason for lower sales value and contribution percentage. Following would be the key points to discuss:

The production budgeted for the month in the annual budget, revised target finalized at the beginning of the month for production after factoring customer demand and operational challenges, actual production and actual dispatch numbers for the month and cumulative for the financial year (year-to-date) are presented in the meeting. In Table 14.2, the company achieved budgeted target for dispatch volume for the year and the finished goods inventory was 263 tons at closing of the year.

In case of shortfall in the previous month, a proactive plan to make up for shortfall in dispatch is formulated. The targets for next month and next quarter are finalized and areas in which support of management is required are discussed.

The financial performance for the month and year-to-date (YTD) is discussed using the corporate scorecard found in Table 14.3. Reduction in non-value adding use of capacity and free capacity available are analyzed to contemplate where to deploy them in upcoming months. This is an important aspect to deliberate after discussion on dispatch in order to make productive use of resources in the next month.

After the financial performance for the current month is reviewed, discussion on current orders (see Table 14.4), status of their fulfillment and potential orders or new business development opportunities are brainstormed upon to forecast the production required in the next month or during the financial year.

This discussion is done each month and the reasons for failure to dispatch the orders planned for the month are reviewed using the format attached in Table 14.5 to discern which function delayed it and what the challenges were. The most common reasons for missing the targets are a shortage in bought-out items because they did not reach the plant in time that delayed assembly and the product could not be finished for dispatch. Also, last minute rejections of manufactured items, inability of sub-vendors to supply machine, breakdown in heat treatment furnace, unavailability of

Table 14.1 Profit and Loss Statement for the Month of March 2019 and Financial Year 2018–2019 for Perfect Gear Company in USD'000.

Key parameters	Current state map March 2018			Future state map March 2019		
	Annual P&L	Monthly average	% of sales	Annual P&L	Monthly average	% of sales
Monthly quantity dispatched	1000 tons			1500 tons		
Sales price	$3.33 per kg			$3.67 per kg		
Sales revenue	40000	3333		66000	5500	
Material cost	17280	1440	43.2%	31200	2600	47.3%
Contribution 1 (A)	22720	1893	56.8%	34800	2900	52.7%
Total variable expenses (B)	6778	565	16.9%	9794	816	14.8%
Consumables and stores	1093	91		1640	137	
Oil and lubricants	208	17		312	26	
Inserts	160	13		240	20	
Accessories	80	7		64	5	
Grinding wheels	88	7		144	12	
Cutting oil	120	10		208	17	
Tool cutter	101	8		144	12	
Gas	53	4		80	7	
Paints	82	7		122	10	
Grease	27	2		56	5	
Others	480	40		800	67	
Power and fuels	2019	168		3040	253	
Job works	1547	129		2384	199	
Other plant misc. expenses	720	60		560	47	
Contribution 2 (C) = (A-B)	15942	1329	39.9%	25006	2084	37.9%
Total fixed expenses (D)	9971	831	24.9%	9213	768	14.0%
Wages – workers	1893	158		2240	187	
Wages – fabrication	373	31		312	26	
Overtime	773	64		736	61	
Salary – executives	3600	300		2885	240	
Other corporate overheads	3333	278		3040	253	
Net profits-EBITDA (E) = (C-D)	5971	498	14.9%	15794	1316	23.9%
Depreciation and amortization	2107	176		2400	200	
EBIT	3864	322	9.7%	13394	1116	20.3%
Bank interest	933	78		960	80	
Interest on term loans	907	76		1120	93	
Net earnings before tax (EBT)	2024	169	5.1%	11314	943	17.1%

Table 14.2 Performance Chart for Perfect Gear Company.

Financial year 2018–2019			March 2019		
All values in USD'000	Budget	Actual plan budget at the start of the month	Month closing finished goods stock	Actual manufacturing	Actual dispatched
	Budget cumulative	Actual plan budget cumulative		Actual manufacturing cumulative	Actual dispatched cumulative
Monthly	5500	6600	263	6263	6000
Cumulative	66000	67000		66263	66000

Table 14.3 Monthly Corporate Scorecard for March 2019 for Perfect Gear Company.

Aspect	Key performance indicator	UOM	Current state March 2018
Financial	Sales revenue – monthly	USD Mn	3.33
	Average product sales price	USD per kg	3.33
	Average product cost	USD per kg	2.84
	Value of inventory	USD Mn	6.27
	Profit before tax	USD Mn	0.17
	Profit before tax	%	5%
Operational	Throughput time	Days	113
	On time shipment	%	70%
	Total head count	Number	561
Capacity usage – manpower	Value adding	%	25%
	Non-value adding	%	53%
	Free capacity available	%	22%
Capacity usage – machine	Value adding	%	44%
	Non-value adding	%	50%
	Free capacity available%	6%	

tooling, mistakes in drawings found during assembly, delay due to rework and delay in customer payment (Perfect Gear Company has a policy of not dispatching the products if full payment is not received from the customers) are some prominent reasons due to which dispatch targets are not met. Based on these reasons, a proactive action plan is devised during the month using the Pareto principle to identify the three major reasons for failure to deliver on time. Also, impending decisions are reviewed during the month.

Table 14.4 Customer Orders in Hand as on 1 April 2019 for Perfect Gear Company.

Sl no	Work order no.	Date	Customer name	Order in hand in USD'000	Remarks
Domestic customers				**Basic value**	
1	WO-9874385231	06/08/18	A	2304	
2	WO-9874385321	19/09/18	B	810	
3	WO-9874385369	23/09/18	C	1570	
4	WO-9874385370	14/10/18	D	7435	
5	WO-987438768	02/01/19	E	1923	
6	WO-9874385851	03/02/19	F	1500	
Indirect export customers					
1	WO-	19/09/18	X	2905	
2	WO-	03/11/19	Y	6335	
3	WO-	03/03/19	Z	3380	
Export					
1	WO-	07/07/18	G	2070	
2	WO-	08/08/18	H	4294	
3	WO-	19/09/18	I	810	
4	WO-	29/10/18	J	1371	
5	WO-	11/11/18	K	3000	
6	WO-	12/01/19	L	9490	
			Grand total	38500	7 months

Table 14.5 Reasons for Shortfall in March 2019 for Perfect Gear Company.

Functions due to which the products could not be dispatched in this month	Value of shortfall for March 2019	Value of shortfall till date – cumulative	Write product/ BOM number that are delayed and reasons why	What countermeasures are in place so that it doesn't recur
Shortfall due to fabrication shop				
Shortfall due to machine shop				
Shortfall due to design and R&D				
Shortfall due to purchase + outsourcing				
Shortfall due to gear cutting function				
Shortfall due to gear grinding function				
Shortfall due to heat treatment function				
Shortfall due to assembly function				
Shortfall due to logistics				
Shortfall due to any other reason				
Total				

However, when the dispatches are higher than the target, the teams should be complimented, and best practices that helped in achieving that result should be identified and practiced every month.

Next the marketing functional head should present the costing of the dispatched material and the product mix for the month. The value stream manager and functional managers should have an idea of the costing pattern and profitability of each product so that they can monitor the contribution of the value stream by prioritizing high profitable products on the plant floor. Material costs as a percentage of the sales value and current rate per unit are important indicators to monitor contribution level in the company. Also being in the capital machine building industry, Perfect Gear Company should monitor the weight of the dispatched equipment compared with the weight as per design in BOM as illustrated in Table 14.6.

Table 14.6   Material Cost Status for March 2019 for Perfect Gear Company.

Product-wise material costs and BOM weight vs. shipping weight for the month								
BOM – 685745 – Customer name							*Month*	*Mar-19*
Sl no	*Name of product*	*Material value – US$*	*Sale value – US$*	*Material cost % as a % of sales value*	*BOM Weight*	*Shipping weight*	*Shipping weight/ BOM weight*	*Rate US$ per kg*
1	Product A	7012	16520	42%	2765	2500	0.9	6.61
2	Product B	282502	663295	43%	91268	92210	1.0	7.19
3	Product C	28613	58986	49%	12250	11000	0.9	5.36
4	Product D	75653	208139	36%	34580	32500	0.9	6.40
5	Product E	621680	1533333	41%	246500	245000	1.0	6.26
6	Product F	54454	125828	43%	36580	37500	1.0	3.36
7	Product G	100979	279760	36%	89533	88000	1.0	3.18
	Grand total	1170893	2885861	41%	513476	508710	1.9	5.67

Inventory management is a persisting nuisance that the company cannot escape unless it brings the level of inventory under control because inventory halts flow and creates wastes. The inventory level should be equivalent to the designed level as per flow and pull (Table 14.7). In each review meeting, inventory aging and list of slow moving (Table 14.8) and non-moving (Table 14.9) items should be reviewed by management to assess the funds blocked in inventory and take action.

plan for disposal of slow moving and non-moving items from the procurement functional head for that value stream. Also, the management should take note of the finished goods inventory (Table 14.10) after the month is over. The sales and marketing team should plan how to sell these finished goods before they land in the slow moving bucket of inventory.

Customer Satisfaction Review

To review the level of customer satisfaction, status of customer complaints, first time right data, non-conformities reports (NCRs) for all functions and their current status will be discussed using the following formats.

Customer Complaints

A database of customer complaints should be maintained, the top five frequent complaints should be reviewed and an action plan must be given in

Table 14.7   Inventory Status in March 2019 for Perfect Gear Company.

Particulars	Current state March 2018			Future state March 2019		
Average dispatch per day in tons	40			58		
Average monthly dispatch in tons	1000			1500		
Average sales price (USD/Kg)	3.33			3.67		
Monthly dispatch (USD Mn)	3.33			5.50		
Annual turnover (USD Mn)	40			66		
Category	Current state			Future state		
	RM cost USD/kg	Weight (in tons)	Value (USD'000)	RM cost USD/kg (5% increase)	Weight (in tons)	Value (USD'000)
Raw materials	0.67	2210	1473	0.70	750	525
Job work with suppliers	1.60	95	152	1.68	100	168
Stores	4.00	466	1864	4.20	200	840
WIP – fabrication	0.67	510	340	0.70	200	140
WIP – machine shop	1.60	147	235	1.68	100	168
WIP – gear shop	1.60	84	134	1.68	50	84
WIP – gear-grinding shop	1.60	100	160	1.68	50	84
Assembly shop	1.47	409	600	1.54	200	308
Finished goods	3.33	392	1307	3.50	75	263
Total inventory		4413	6265		1725	2580

the meeting by the quality head and the customer service head. Separate meetings must take place during the month between quality functions and others functions before the monthly meeting so that only critical issues are discussed in this meeting. Table 14.11 shows the format for status of customer complaints and corrective action register as used by Perfect Gear Company.

Non-Conformities Reports and First Time Right Data

Whenever the process is not carried out at first time right, an NCR is raised for counter action. This is an internal quality control measure. 'First time right' (FTR)

Table 14.8 List of Slow-Moving Items in Perfect Gear Company in US$ as of the End of March 2019.

Sl no.	Item description	Item code	Quantity				Rate per unit	Total amount	Sub group
			Opening	Inward	Outward	Closing			
1	Bearing 6201 2RSR		23	20	8	35	2	70	Bearing and accessories
2	Deep groove ball bearing 6205 /2Z		21	40	8	53	3	159	Bearing and accessories
3	Plain spherical bearing GE 40 ES		6	20	5	21	4	84	Bearing and accessories
4	V-belt 5V pitch length-150" matched pair		14	7	6	15	15	225	belts
5	Roller chain duplex 1"P 102 link and connecting links		86	0	10	76	56	4256	chains
6	Panel light 11 W		45	0	3	42	7	294	control desk and panels
7	Control desk		3	2	1	4	3500	14000	control desk and panels
8	Motorised globe valve 200 NB		5	2	2	5	1800	9000	Control valves
9	Fit bolt for gear couplings 107		156	40	9	187	2	374	couplings
10	Tyre couplings T-8 B		55	1	6	50	43	2150	couplings
11	Pneumatic cylinder 250 Bore x 350 Stroke		23	0	1	22	785	17270	cylinders
12	Door limit switch		77	0	2	75	144	10828	electricals
13	Disc spring A90		98	0	8	90	6	540	fasteners
14	Bevel helical gear motor 5.5 KW 47 RPM 400V 60HZ		24	2	2	24	600	14400	geared motors
15	Hydraulic power pack		10	1	1	10	1987	19870	hydraulic power pack
16	Pyrometer - model AST-250		12	9	10	11	1900	20900	instruments and sensors
17	Pressure transmitter (0-25 bar)		24	7	7	24	169	4056	instruments and sensors
18	Key 14 x 2 9 x 300		28	12	5	35	1	35	key
19	Air pressure regulator with gauge 1/2" BSP		65	5	7	63	19	1197	lubrication unit
20	Grease nipple B-PT 1/8		77	0	5	72	1	72	lubrication unit
21	A.C. Motor 7.5 kw 1000 rpm 50 hz foot type		18	0	5	13	750	9750	motors
22	Welding helmets		45	0	3	42	53	2226	operating tools
23	Ratchet handle -20 sq (female)		19	0	2	17	35	595	operating tools
24	Ball valve 3/4"		42	12	11	43	4	172	pipe fittings

Table 14.9 List of Non-Moving Items in Perfect Gear Company in US$ as of the End of March 2019.

SI no.	Item description	Item code	Quantity				rate per unit	Total amount	Sub group
			Opening	Inward	Outward	Closing			
1	Adapter sleeve H2320		21	0	0	21	8	168	Bearing and accessories
2	Adapter sleeve H2322		1	2	0	7	40	280	Bearing and accessories
3	V - belt SPC 2000 long		23	0	0	23	9	207	Belts
4	V Belt A 34		34	0	0	34	2	68	Belts
5	Duplex chain - 3/4" pitch 232 link + connecting link		54	0	0	54	54	2916	Chain
6	Duplex chain - 3/4" pitch 97 link + connecting link		45	0	0	45	27	1215	Chain
7	Coupling gfa 56		5	2	0	7	45	315	Coupling
8	Fit bolt for gear coupling 104		118	16	0	134	1	134	Coupling
9	Breaker block 1602 - 06/09R2		4	0	0	4	13	52	Cylinder
10	Crown wheel 1602 - 06/06R2		16	0	0	16	98	1568	Cylinder
13	Worm gear box 8" 5:1 type - B		5	5	0	10	985	9850	Gear Boxes
14	Worm gear box -7.5 kw 960 RPM 7.5:1 6" handling b type MAKE-ALLROYD		8	1	0	9	1200	10800	Gear Boxes
15	Bevel geared motor - 5.5 kw 21 RPM 400V 60HZ S5 IP55 INS CL-F VVVF B3 with inbuilt brake		9	4	0	13	654	8502	Geared motors
16	Geared motor 1.5 KW 105 RPM		23	0	0	23	265	6095	Geared motors
17	Gun metal rod		67	3.5	0	70	16	1128	Hydraulic power pack
18	Hyd power pack 60 LPM		32	0	0	32	3657	117024	Hydraulic power pack
19	Display unit		4	0	0	4	46	184	Instruments and sensors
20	orifice plate 200NB		89	0	0	89	12	1068	Instruments and sensors
21	key 70 x 36 x 614 long		45	0	0	45	37	1665	key
22	Parallel key 56 x 32 x 290 long		23	0	0	23	12	276	key
23	Banjo fitting WH8PSRKD		67	0	0	67	5	335	Lubrication units
24	AC Motor - 37.5 kw 1450 rpm		7	1	0	8	2579	20632	Motors
	Total Value in US$							1,84,482	

Table 14.10 Finished Goods Inventory Status for Perfect Gear Company for 2 April 2019.

Sl no.	Customer	Description of product	Quantity	Value in USD'000	Action plan	Timeline	Responsibility
1	A	Gearbox 334141	1	20	Payment expected in 6 days	April 19 dispatch	Marketing
2	B	Gearbox 331651	1	9	Customer canceled order. To get order from new customer.	May-19	Marketing
3	C	Gearbox 337871	1	12.2	Gearbox to be modified for another customer	Jun-19	Design and Marketing
4	D	Gearbox 331721	6	14	Payment expected in 15 days	April 19 dispatch	Marketing
5	E	Gearbox 313418	2	0.6	Customer canceled order. New customer to be identified.	June dispatch	Marketing
36	F	Gearbox 343419	1	1.5	Customer needs modification	May dispatch	Design to issue new drawings
37	G	Gearbox 384201	1	4	Payment expected by next month	May 19 dispatch	Marketing
38	H	Gearbox 354221	1	3	Customer needs modification	May dispatch	Design to issue new drawings
39	I	Gearbox 394252	2	10.8	Payment expected in 6 days	April 19 dispatch	Marketing
40	J	Gearbox 348746	8	1	Customer needs modification	May dispatch	Design to issue new drawings
Total				263			

data and the status of NCRs should be captured for all functions and a summary chart should be presented briefly by the functional head with measures for improvement. Table 14.12 and Table 14.13 show the formats used by Perfect Gear Company.

Table 14.11   Status of Customer Complaints and Corrective Action Register for Perfect Gear Company.

Perfect Gear Company									*Format no*		
									Rev. date		
Customer complaints/corrective action register for the financial year 2018–2019											
SI no.	*Date*	*Source*	*Name of customer*	*Plant location*	*Item's name*	*Details of complaints and root cause.*	*Corrective and preventive action.*	*Responsible person*	*Target date*	*Effective date*	*Authorized signatory*

Table 14.12   Status of First Time Right Data for In-House Functions at Perfect Gear Company for March 2019.

First time accepted of purchase function	78.1%
First time accepted of subcontracting function	84.3%
First time accepted of in-house machine shop	97.5%
First time accepted of in-house fabrication	97.7%
First time accepted of in-house gear shop	98.9%
First time accepted of company	62.0%

Status of Major NCRs

The list shown in Table 14.14 should be continuously updated and regular meetings on corrective and preventive action should be held and the quality head should brief during the review meeting accordingly.

Internal Business Process Review

Internal business process review focuses on status of kanban implementation, 5S, TPM-AM-PM score and training schedule and topics.

Table 14.13 Status of NCRs for Perfect Gear Company from October 2018 to March 2019.

Sl no.	Function	Total NCR raised	Closed NCR	Balance NCRs
1	Design	45	32	13
2	Subcontracting	15	6	9
3	Machine shop	154	113	41
4	Purchase	14	4	10
5	Fabrication	7	2	5
6	Quality control	2	2	0
7	Assembly	7	6	1
8	PPC	8	6	2
9	Gear section	1	0	1
10	Others	4	1	3
	Total	257	172	85

Kanban Implementation

Kanban is implanted in the finished goods stores, raw material stores, consumable stores and in the manufacturing plants between all the production centers to control inventory and maintain flow and pull. This avoids sales loss along with control on inventories and is the responsibility of procurement function. Table 14.15 shows the format for kanban implementation process.

5S

The kaizen promotion manager presents the 5S audit report as per Table 14.16 and the best workplace team is given gifts and allowed to keep the 5S trophy for the month.

TPM-AM-PM Score

TPM-AM-PM scoreboard as per Table 14.17 is presented in the meeting by the maintenance functional head. The best workplace team is rewarded and allowed to keep the TPM trophy for the month. The format is attached as used by Perfect Gear Company.

Table 14.14 Status of Major NCRs for Perfect Gear Company in April 2019.

Sl no.	Date	Part details	NC no	Details of non-conformance	Deviation	Dept	Final decision	Status after CAPA
1	08.01.2019	Screw down shaft	171	Thread 70 x 4P, direction req. R.H & Obs. L.H.	Thread hand changed	Process	Closed	Used after rework
6	27.01.2019	Input pinion	181	Helix angle variation	Helix angle change	Process	Closed	Rejected
7	29.01.2019	Input pinion shaft	183	MOT undersized by 0.08 mm	MOT undersized	Process	Closed	Used after rework
8	29.01.2019	1st pinion shaft	184	MOT undersized by 0.39 mm	MOT undersized	Process	Closed	Used after rework
9	05.02.2019	Hollow shafts	188	Keyway length oversize by 18.0 mm	Keyway size variations	Process	Closed	Used after rework
10	06.02.2019	Bearing housings	189	Machining allowance 7 mm not given on bottom face	NO machining allowance	Process	Closed	Used after rework
11	18.02.2019	Housing for gearbox	193	Bore oversized by 0.04 mm	Bore oversized	Process	Closed	Used after rework
58	17.03.2019	Gear and input pinion	275	Chamfer required 3 x 45 deg but observed 7 x 45	Chamfer/radius	Process	In process	No action taken
59	22.03.2019	Gear and input pinion	276	No grinding allowance left in ID	Grinding allowance	Process	In process	No action taken
60	23.03.2019	Housing for gearbox	278	Bore oversized by 0.04 mm	Bore oversized	Process	In process	No action taken

Table 14.15 Status of Kanban Implementation Process for Perfect Gear Company on 1 April 2019.

	1	2	3	4	5	6	7	8	9	10	11	12	13	14	15
1st replenishment made			✓	✓	✓	✓	✓	✓	✓	✓					✓
Putting Maximum and average stock level in ERP by ERP dept			✓	✓	✓	✓	✓	✓	✓	✓			✓	✓	✓
MOU signing with the suppliers	Price settled with 2 suppliers		✓	✓	✓	✓	✓	✓	✓	✓	✓		✓	✓	✓
Initial stock brought to Maximum level	✓	✓	✓	✓	✓	✓	✓	✓	✓	✓	✓	✓	✓	✓	✓
material will be recd by	✓	✓	✓	✓	✓	✓	✓	✓	✓	✓	✓	✓	✓	✓	✓
Order placed	✓	✓	✓	✓	✓	✓	✓	✓	✓	✓	✓	✓	✓	✓	✓
Procurement status prepared	✓	✓	✓	✓	✓	✓	✓	✓	✓	✓	✓	✓	✓	✓	✓
Laminated kanban made	✓	✓	✓	✓	✓	✓	✓	✓	✓	✓	✓	✓	✓	✓	✓
Kanban laminated sheet made	✓	✓	✓	✓	✓	✓	✓	✓	✓	✓	✓	✓	✓	✓	✓
Calculation done	✓	✓	✓	✓	✓	✓	✓	✓	✓	✓	✓	✓	✓	✓	✓
Description of stock item	EN-9 forged material	EN-9 rolled and MS round	Structure	Fasteners	Piping on equipment	Key	Bought out products	Consumables plus tooling	Steel plate	18cr material	Pipes	TMT	Housing less	Twin chennal	Blade holders for shear
Average inventory level in $ millions															
Average inventory level in tons.															
Maximum inventory level in $ millions															
Maximum inventory level in tons.															
Responsible person															
Sl no.	1	2	3	4	5	6	7	8	9	10	11	12	13	14	15

Table 14.16   5S Score Status for Perfect Gear Company as of the End of March 2019.

Function	Area	Team leader name	Oct-18	Nov-18	Dec-18	Jan-19	Feb-19	Mar-19
Machine shop	Conventional machine area		75	70	70	72	70	72
Machine shop	CNC machine area 1		70	70	70	72	70	72
Machine shop	CNC machine area 2		75	70	70	72	70	72
Machine shop	Lathe machine area		70	70	70	72	70	72
Gear cutting and gear grinding shop	Gear cutting and gear grinding shop		77 Best gemba in the plant	70	75 Best gemba	79 Best gemba	76 Best gemba in the plant	75 Best gemba
Assembly shop	Area 1		75	75	75 Best gemba	77	70	72
Assembly shop	Area 2		70	70	70	72	70	72
Assembly shop	Area 3		70	75	70	72	70	72
Fabrication shop	Fabrication shop		70	70	70	72	65	70
Store			75	77 Best gemba	70	72	70	72
Component store	Component store						45	60
Maintenance room	Maintenance room						45	60
Yard	Front yard		65	70	70	72	65	70
			73%	71%	71%	73%	66%	70%

Training Topics and Training Schedule Monitoring

Training is the only way to measure and upgrade the skills of the personnel. The HRD functional head anchors the training pillar and presents the status in each review meeting. Function-wise training calendar is prepared as per format in Table 14.18 and Table 14.19 with a list of the training topics

Table 14.17   Status of TPM-AM-PM for Perfect Gear Company as of March 2019.

	AM	PM	AM	PM	AM	PM	Scoring criterion
	Gear shop	Gear shop	Machine shop	Machine shop	Utilities	Utilities	For both AM and PM: step 1, the score is 10; step 2, the score is 20; step 3, the score is 30. Machines will get final scores based on status of both AM and PM and display on the gemba.
Total number of machines	22	22	28	28	6	6	
Machines in step 1	7	16	6	2	0	0	
Machines in step 2	7	0	15	0	0	0	
Machines in step 3	8	6	7	26	6	6	
Display on the gemba	80%	80%	80%	80%	80%	80%	
Score	450	340	570	800	180	180	
Avg %	74%	66%	74%	88%	90%	90%	
Score for September 2018	46%						
Score for October 2018	55%						
Score for November 2018	66%						
Score for December 2018	77%	66%	74%	88%	76%	80%	
	76.8%						
Score for January 2019	72%	66%	80%	85%	88%	88%	
	80%						
Score for February 2019	69%	61%	69%	83%	85%	85%	
	75%						
Score for March 2019	74%	66%	74%	88%	90%	90%	
	80%						

and personnel by HRD. The training topics should be synchronized with SOPs, OPLs, workmen skill matrix, performance scorecards and functional scorecards.

Lean Performance Measurement System Review

Status of functional scorecards, performance scorecards and workmen skill matrix implementation is discussed.

Table 14.18 Example of Training Topics for the Finance Function.

Key	SOP No.	What	Trainer	Trainees
	SOP/FD/001	Accounts payable posting		
	SOP/FD/002	Accounts payable reports		
	SOP/FD/009	Creditors aged analysis		
	SOP/FD/036	Management accounts reports		
	SOP/FD/037	SOP for rollover		
	SOP/FD/024	Costing for imports		
	SOP/FD/025	Costing for finished goods		
	SOP/FD/027	SQL transaction processing		
	SOP/FD/030	DCT reports on Excel		
	SOP/FD/031	DST reports on Excel		
	SOP/FD/033	Updating DCT report from Syspro		
	SOP/FD/034	Updating DPT report from Syspro		
	SOP/FD/007	General ledger posting		
	SOP/FD/008	General ledger reports		
	SOP/FD/012	VAT returns		
	SOP/FD/018	Stock take		
	SOP/FD/019	Stock movement		
	SOP/FD/020	Stock reconciliation		
	SOP/FD/021	Stock valuation analysis		
	SOP/FD/026	Control work in progress		
	SOP/FD/032	DPT reports		
	SOP/FD/035	Posting journals		

Functional Scorecard

The current functional scorecard summary is presented in the review meeting. If the score is increasing month on month, it means lean production system and lean accounting implementation is bearing results and the company is in the right direction. Otherwise, remedial action can be taken, if needed. Table 14.20 shows the trend of functional scorecards for 11 senior managers of the Perfect Gear Company. There is an upward trend that is commendable. It means the teams are working sincerely and vigorously on the continuous improvement projects.

Table 14.19 Example of a Training Schedule for the Finance Function.

SOPs Training Schedule – Score 1 & 2 – Finance						
Training time					*Weekdays: 2.00 pm–4.00 pm*	
Sunday	*Monday*	*Tuesday*	*Wednesday*	*Thursday*	*Friday*	*Saturday*
		1	2	3	4	5
6	7	8	9	10	11	12
13	14	15	16	17	18	19
			SOP/FD/001	SOP/FD/036	SOP/FD/025	
			SOP/FD/002	SOP/FD/037	SOP/FD/027	
			SOP/FD/009	SOP/FD/024	SOP/FD/030	
20	21	22	23	24	25	26
	SOP/FD/031		SOP/FD/019	SOP/FD/021	SOP/FD/032	
	SOP/FD/033		SOP/FD/020	SOP/FD/026	SOP/FD/035	
	SOP/FD/034					
27	SOP/FD/007	29	30	31		
	SOP/FD/008					
	SOP/FD/012					
	SOP/FD/018					

Table 14.20 Functional Scorecard Rating

Sl no.	Name	Desig-nation	Function	Oct-18	Nov-18	Dec-18	Jan-19	Feb-19	Mar-19
1		VP	Marketing	41	48	55	61	66	70
2		CFO	Finance	45	47	49	55	60	64
3		GM	Design, R&D	50	55	58	62	69	72
4		GM	Purchase	54	54	62	70	72	74
5		GM	Operations	55	57	64	69	72	78
6		DGM	Fabrication	46	56	59	59	69	70
7		DGM	Assembly	33	46	50	52	55	64
8		GM	Quality	43	48	58	59	68	72
9		DGM	Maintenance	45	47	55	58	59	64
10		GM	HRD	33	45	48	52	55	60
11		GM	Projects	41	44	51	55	56	59

Performance Scorecard Implementation

The HRD team will present the status of implementation of performance scorecards for first line executives and supervisors.

Workmen Skill Matrix Implementation

The implementation of the workmen skill matrix will bring sustenance to the company's operations. This summary is presented in the review meeting by the HRD functional head as per the format in Table 14.21.

Table 14.21   Status of Workmen Skill Matrix Implementation Progress at Perfect Gear Company.

SI no.	Skill matrix	Progress of completion					
		Oct-18	Nov-18	Dec-18	Jan-19	Feb-19	Mar-19
1	Functions identification	✓	✓	✓	✓	✓	✓
	Skill identification	✓	✓	✓	✓	✓	✓
	Person identification	✓	✓	✓	✓	✓	✓
	Format made	✓	✓	✓	✓	✓	✓
2	Test preparation						
	Assembly (13 skills)	✓					
	Maintenance (8 skills)		✓				
	MC shop (9 skills)			✓			
	Fabrication (6 skills)				✓		
	Gear grinding (8 skills)					✓	
	Store (8 skills)						✓
3	Test of all employees						
	Assembly (13 skills)	✓					
	Display		✓				
	Maintenance (8 skills)		✓				
	Display			✓			
	MC shop (9 skills)			✓			
	Display				✓		
	Fabrication (6 skills)				✓		
	Display					✓	
	Gear grinding (8 skills)					✓	
	Display						✓
	Store (8 skills)					✓	
	Display						✓

Safety Health and Environment Review

Safety Health and Environment (SHE) audit scores and status of quality audit and evaluation score for all functions are discussed here.

Status of Quality Audit and Evaluation Score

Quality function anchors this and the quality audit is done for all functions. The summary is presented in the meeting. A sample as per Table 14.22 is attached here. Audit scores must have an upward trend.

SHE Audit

The HRD functional head will present the safety health and environment status and SHE audit score. Normally an outside expert agency is used for this audit and monitoring the implementation of corrective and preventive action and is directly under the control of the CEO.

Figure 14.1 outlines the accountability for preparation and conduct of monthly review meeting among functions. It shows who has the direct responsibility to implement and sustain monthly review meetings. It is only a guideline that companies can use to draft their own responsibility matrix.

The monthly budget review is a structured process that stimulates quicker decisions, better cooperation and communication among functional managers. Value stream functional managers become more empowered and passionate to exceed month end results beyond the annual budget. The other outcomes of these meetings are that functional managers understand how their roles contribute to the overall company's objectives, how it benefits when the consensus on some issue is reached and how it gradually reduces daily firefighting.

14.2 Aim to Become a World-Class Company

To become a world-class company, the policies and processes of the company should surpass excellence, stand the test of time and prove that the company is headed in the right direction to fulfill its mission. Such a company has well-defined strategic objectives and continuously strives to achieve an edge over its competitors. Mutual vision, goals and objectives are framed for both company and employees with a focus on innovation

Table 14.22 Status of Quality Audit and Evaluation Score for Perfect Gear Company on 1 April 2019.

Sl no.	Description	Total score	Month					
			Oct-18	Nov	Dec	Jan-19	Feb	Mar
1	Resource management							
1.1	Provide operational and quality training – NDT (UT, PT, MT)	5	2	2	2	3	3	3.5
1.2	Welder qualification by external agency	4	2	2	2.5	3	3	3.5
1.3	Internal auditor, kaizen and QC tools training	5	3	3	5	5	5	5
1.4	Proper recording and record keeping of different projects	5	3	3.5	4.5	5	5	5
2	Metrology, inspection and recording							
2.1	Identification and update calibration with record of inspection equipment	5	2.5	2.5	3.5	4	4.5	5
2.2	Record of update calibration with agency traceability with source	5	2.5	3	3.5	4	4.5	5
3	In process control and recording							
3.1	Ensure the quality of incoming material before issue for further processing	5	3	3.5	4.5	5	5	5
3.2	SOP developed and being used in manufacturing process in shop and at supplier end	5	4	4	4	4	4	4.5
3.3	Inspection and test performed at right stage and recorded in assembly process	5	4	4	4.5	5	5	5
3.4	Assembly inspection as per STD checklists developed to ensure the completeness and quality	5	4	4	4.5	5	5	5
4	At supplier end							
4.1	Control the first time right percentage	3	2	2.5	2.5	2	2	3
4.2	Vendor rating based on quality and resources	3	2	2.5	2.5	3	3	3
4.3	Identification and traceability at suppliers end	3	1	2	2	2.5	2	2.5

(Continued)

Table 14.22 (Continued)

Sl no.	Description	Total score	Month					
5	Identify NCR with CAPA							
5.1	Identify the NCR in case of abnormality observed	5	4	4	5	5	5	5
5.2	Corrective and preventive action on NCR within two weeks	5	2	2	3	4	4	4
5.3	Reduction in NCR percentage	4	2	2	3	3.5	3.5	4
5.4	Effectiveness of CAPA	4	3	3	3	3.5	3.5	4
6	Audit in process and at supplier end							
6.1	In process audit	3	2	2	2.5	3	2.5	3
6.2	Supplier audit	3	2	2	3	3	3	3
6.3	Dispatch audit	3	2	2.5	3	3	3	3
7	Customer relationships							
7.1	Reduction in customer complaints	5	3	4	4	4	4	4
7.2	To attend to the complaint within the minimum possible time	5	3	3	3	4	4	4
8	Certification by external agency							
8.1	Annual audit by external agency for ISO 9001:2008	5	5	5	5	5	5	5
	Total	100	63	68	80	87.5	88.5	94
			63%	68%	80%	87.5%	88.5%	94%

Sl no.	Description	Refer chapter	CEO's	CFO's	Kaizen promotion champion	Value stream managers**	Functional managers*	Concerned functional managers
1	Performance of the month	Chapter 14	✓✓	✓✓	✓	✓	✓	All, finance
2	Performance of the month and current financial year budget and corrective action plan		✓✓	✓✓	✓	✓	✓	All, marketing
3	Orders for the financial year (target – $ millions)		✓✓	✓	✓	✓	✓	Marketing
4	Reasons for shortfall of production and dispatch		✓✓	✓	✓	✓	✓	All
5	Material cost figures of the current month dispatch		✓	✓✓	✓	✓	✓	Finance
6	Inventory status – raw materials, work in progress, finished goods and stores material		✓✓	✓✓	✓	✓	✓	All, main – finance, purchase, marketing, operations
7	Financial review – based on dispatch and actual production		✓✓	✓✓	✓	✓	✓	Finance
8	Value of finished goods lying after month end – $ millions		✓✓	✓✓	✓	✓	✓	Marketing
9	Kanban implementation status		✓✓	✓	✓	✓	✓	Purchase
10	Status of functional scorecards, performance scorecards and workman skill matrix for all functions		✓✓	✓	✓	✓	✓	Kaizen champion
11	HRD – status		✓✓	✓	✓	✓	✓	HRD

* Head of functions of fabrication, machining, gear cutting, heat treatment, gear grinding, assembly, logistics, quality, maintenance, purchase, finance, HRD, design and R&D.

** Only one value stream is referred to in detail in this book.

✓ = Direct responsibility to implement and sustain

✓ ✓ = Ultimate responsibility

Figure 14.1   Responsibilities for Conducting Monthly Budget Review Meeting at Perfect Gear Company.

and transformation to cope with changing dynamics of business environment. Customer satisfaction and exceptional quality are idiosyncrasies that drip from each process in the company. Such a company is a forerunner in use of latest technology with unswerving business ethics and professional standards. It has a profound understanding of its value chain and maintains excellent and respectful relations with its vendors and other elements of supply chain.

Changes in the macro-environment are inevitable – inflation will increase price of raw materials, new competitors will enter the market, substitute products or technological advancements will make existing products obsolete and so forth but the company should be equipped to combat the challenges arising in such a dynamic environment. While the company should capitalize on favorable economic factors, it should also be a significant contributor to the economic prosperity of its stakeholders, and a company's credibility with stakeholders is dependent on achievement of its targets or going beyond them. Therefore, a company should accelerate the process of optimizing cost structures and working capital, which may continue to be unsustainable and unhealthy for a long time if they are not focused upon.

Increase in productivity of the value streams and exceeding customer expectations are the most important goals. Going forward, a lean company should keep its objectives clear and simple and address the areas for improvement identified in functional scorecards, performance scorecards and workmen skill matrix. Once the managers have control over their function's cost structure (materials, consumables, energy and common facilities, fixed costs and other expenses), the company will be intellectually adept to proactively respond to changing needs of the customers. Also, a parsimonious culture among the functional managers will help to reduce time expended on analysis and post event firefighting for funds.

A company should consistently lock the gains – once a high score like best monthly dispatch volume, best machining hours, best yield and so forth are achieved, the company should hold onto the best practices that helped to achieve these scores instead of using averaging concept to pull it down. OTIFEF should be measured for everything the company does. The company must use stretched targets not only in manufacturing but also in all the functions. It should upgrade current technologies to improve process efficiencies and manpower productivity, and a provision for this should be regularly made in the yearly budget.

These previous arguments should be the focus areas of the company for its journey toward becoming a world-class company.

Key Takeaways

1. The business plan review meeting duration is restricted to one hour and is to be strictly adhered to. These 60 minutes are 'power time' and only the corrective action strategy is to be reviewed.
2. The managers must sort out the data discrepancies before coming to the meeting. This is one area where the precious meeting time is wasted.
3. The review should focus on profitability for the month, deviation from targets in the business plan, reason for lower sales value and contribution percentage and the corrective and preventive action.
4. The value stream manager and functional managers should have an idea of the costing pattern and profitability of each product so that they can monitor the contribution of the value stream by prioritizing high profitable products on the plant floor.
5. The value stream functional managers become more empowered and passionate to exceed month end results beyond the budget.

Chapter 15

Lean ERP for Lean Accounting

A company can employ the most sophisticated software in the world, but unless the information is managed, timely, accurate and complete, the system serves little purpose.

– Wayne L. Staley

15.1 What Is Lean ERP?

Enterprise resource planning (ERP) is the management of all the information and resources involved in a company's operations by means of an integrated computer system. Lean enterprise resource planning is a planning tool that consolidates and presents the data generated by all the functions as meaningful information to help the company in better decision-making. If the company is already using ERP, it can refine its current ERP with the help of the service provider to make it suitable for kaizen and lean. The ERP system from all well-known service providers have inbuilt lean production system tools that can be activated and modified. Lean production system, daily management system and lean accounting system are to be implemented with the help of lean ERP. All the base data will have to be captured through the lean ERP system. The following tools shall be successfully deployed through lean ERP.[1]

- Value Stream Mapping – Value Adding Ratio and Throughput Time
- Capacity – Value Adding, Non-Value Adding and Surplus Available
- Quality at Source

- Workplace Reorganization – 5S
- TPM-AM, PM – OEE, MTTR, MTBF
- TQM
- Visual Management
- Setup Time Reduction
- Batch Size Reduction
- Cellular Manufacturing
- Standardized Work
- Work Balance
- Production Leveling
- Point-of-Use Systems
- Supermarket
- E-Kanban system
- Daily Management
- Lean Accounting

Lean and kaizen tools eliminate waste and create value in the organization to deliver quality products and exceptional services. The daily management system helps in sustenance. Lean accounting tools help in observing the results in the financial parameters ongoing basis. Lean ERP helps track the progress of implementation, increase control, collect data in real time and make quicker decisions.

Every industry is unique in its own way, but lean and kaizen tools are universal. It is the skill of the lean expert and lean implementation teams that determines how successfully these tools can be implemented in the company. Value stream integrates all the functions like marketing, design, production planning and control, purchase, maintenance, assembly, logistics, quality, finance and IT into one large team that is responsible for timely delivery of products from the product family to its customers. Lean ERP helps in integration of functional data in the value stream for swift analysis and decision-making.

Figure 15.1 shows how the lean ERP system metamorphoses data collection, cross-functional synchronization and decision-making for capital machine building company that is implementing the lean production system, daily management system and lean accounting system. Each function determines how they require the report from the data collected in lean ERP and the finance team establishes the logic for fabrication of these reports with the help of the lean ERP service provider. The objective is that all workings, transactions and approvals should be executed through lean ERP only.[2]

		Perfect Gear Company
		How lean ERP system makes a difference for all functions from current ERP system?
Sl no.	Functions	How ERP helps in lean production system, daily management and lean accounting implementation
1	Marketing	Product costing available soon after dispatch. Costing available customer-wise and product-wise. Profit/loss can be seen in real time at the time of dispatch.
2	Design	Standardization becomes easy. Time required to issue specifications, BOM and drawings are reduced. Throughput time decreases. Results in timely delivery to customers.
3	Planning	Real status of any product becomes possible. True stock position is available in all categories of inventories. Easier to monitor the weekly and monthly rolling plan in real time.
4	Procurement	Real-time purchase master, easier PR-PO-MRN-invoice linkage for efficient working. Inventory management and purchase through e-kanban and maintaining ROL and MOQ. Easier monthly stock taking.
5	Operations	Machine-wise collection of data for breakdowns, changeovers, rework, scrap, waiting time for material, manpower and decision and consumable costs becomes possible for easier control over expenses for critical machines, capacity of machines and free capacity available for quick and logical decision-making. Real-time throughput time is available for all products. Daily work schedule and typical checklist data available online.
6	Maintenance	Online equipment control ledger is maintained for critical machines. OEE, MTBF, MTTR, TBM and CBM data for critical machines are available in real time.
7	Quality control	Internal rejection data, non-conformity reports – function-wise, product code-wise, customer order-wise available in real time. Monthly cost of quality can be generated in real time.
8	Finance and accounts	Profit and loss statement on first of every month, product pricing on dispatch, product pricing decisions, vendor management, inventory management, preparation of functional scorecards, corporate scorecard generation weekly or monthly. Financial transactions reduction becomes easier.

Figure 15.1　Lean ERP to Track Progress of Lean Implementation.

Marketing is able to see the manufacturing status and warehouse inventories, or design and manufacturing is able to see customer data through ERP. This means if the design team prepares a bill of material (BOM) containing items with a description and an item code number, these data should appear in the inquiries that the purchase function makes from vendors. The vendor's invoice matches this code number, and the company can validate these three sources before making payment. The same material can be issued with this item code from the stores for in-house use and will continue the manufacturing cycle till it is ready for dispatch. When an invoice and a packing list is made for this item as part of the product now ready for dispatch to customer this particular material is flushed out from the inventory by the ERP. The key is exact and uniform information available to everyone in the company.

The raw material and standard bought-out items received from the suppliers move through the stores and manufacturing processes and are assembled into a finished product that is then invoiced and shipped and amount due for it is collected. The intention is to carry out all these activities on the lean ERP platform. Examples of reports or formats that can be produced from lean ERP (for understanding purpose) are categorization of BOM, purchase request creation by stores for C-class items, BOM status through ERP, job work PR – cutting list, plan BOM, PPC menu for stocks in all plants, raw material PR, job work PR, new PO format, purchase master through ERP, packing list, highlighting slow moving and non-moving items in the stores, rolling plan weekly meeting list through ERP, daily breakdown and machine loading report, challans pending at job work end (more than 20 days), equipment control ledger for all machines, TBM and CBM sheets for all critical machines, machine-wise consumables issue through ERP and machine-wise spare parts issue through ERP.

Lean ERP processes the data and shares useful information in real time. Without a robust lean ERP, a company will not be able to sustain the process improvements achieved through lean initiatives.[3]

Lean ERP Institutionalizes Lean Accounting in the Company

The lean production system defines the parameters that are to be adhered to to eliminate waste and create value. Lean accounting helps in tracking these parameters to facilitate the teams in deciding a future course of action. And this is where lean ERP plays a pivotal role to provide logical, accurate and timely data.[4]

Lean accounting helps in tracking lean parameters to take timely corrective action and achieve the desired results. Lean ERP believes in small data. Small data are relevant to the particular work center of the function. Small data in simple form are understandable to supervisors and team leaders. Big data for the whole function in a big Excel sheet are immaterial for supervisors, team leaders and workmen. The big data ERP is modified in a lean company because it does not need big data during the lean journey. If the company is able to run the operation and track data product-wise, value stream-wise, plant-wise and group-wise, then the company can have their profit and loss statement on first of every month for the previous month. It will give managers enough time for corrective and preventive action to be taken.[5]

15.2 Use of Lean ERP in All Functions

Each manager and supervisor has to be trained and equipped to use lean ERP in their function on the computer terminals provided to them. Managers should be able to implement tools of the lean production system, daily management system and lean accounting system through the lean ERP.

Sales and Marketing

The marketing team can track monthly item-wise, product-wise and value stream-wise costs in real time for better decision-making and assessment of product profitability at the time of dispatch. When marketing receives a customer's order, it captures all the customer requirements in a work order that is shared with the design and R&D team. The design team incorporates customer's requirements in the design and a bill of materials (BOM) is created. Lean ERP updates the work order with inputs from BOM information. This rolling plan and packaging list in ERP are also updated accordingly. This eliminates chaos and confusion in the workplace and improves coordination within different functions. When the marketing function receives a customer's orders, it allots the same code number that was used when the item was manufactured. This ensures historical cost structure is available for guidance in future. The design and R&D function use historical codes to review designs before generating any new codes. If an item was previously ordered, lean ERP prevents its design revision. Marketing also can check the contribution level of potential orders through the lean ERP system before taking orders.

For the sales team, sales order management, sales analysis and sales forecasting are done through lean ERP.

Design and R&D

How are item codes defined? What are the various categories of material? It can be defined and coded in the lean ERP like bought-out series, C-class items like fasteners, oil seals and circlips and manufacturing item series with a code for each item, each product, each value stream. As discussed earlier, historical coding is used if the items are used again without any modification to avoid duplication. New coding provision is there for new items but numbers for new series should be generated with the authorization of group leaders in design and R&D only. Lean ERP helps in standardization, that is, preparation of standard description for items. Duplicate items are easily detected in lean ERP and clubbed, and wrong series items are corrected. Design can ensure use of standard products from certified sources by building it in ERP.

Production Planning and Control

Lean ERP helps in production planning through capacity planning since all the data of the value stream are available on ERP. Value adding capacity usage, non-value adding capacity usage and free capacity can be tracked through lean ERP for all functions for both manpower and machines. Routing of the BOM received as per the work order is outlined in ERP and PR raised for procurement of kanban and non-kanban items after validating existing stock though the ERP system will automatically prevent ordering of slow moving and non-moving items using codes to track and match new requirement against existing inventory.

Standardization is done across the plant so that all value streams are tied together and no excess stock is generated. A company can freeze the quantities of the consumables through lean ERP so that their consumption does not exceed budget and each item being used within the value stream can be tracked in the ERP.

Procurement

Material planning, raising purchase requisition (PR) and purchase order (PO), receipt of goods in stores, stock taking and stock movement, inventory management, slow moving and non-moving items in the stores and procurement of capital goods can be done through lean ERP. Approvals, if any, are also routed through ERP. Procurement can track PR to PO timing and raise alarm for the delay. Similarly, PO to material receipt delay can be monitored. Also, the system can stop the receipt of materials before its due date and credit period arrangements with accounts payable can be automated to free the accountant's time. E-kanban can be issued and monitored through lean ERP.

Production and Assembly

The production and assembly section controls the shop floor, production schedule, daily breakdown and machine loading report through the lean ERP. Throughput time of products can be captured through lean ERP. Daily management Tier 3 meeting can be made online by lean ERP terminal. Rework and scrap generation can be reported through lean ERP.

Maintenance

The maintenance function will use the lean ERP to maintain real-time stock of the plant maintenance spares, machine maintenance – electrical, machine maintenance – mechanical, non-stock items, machine-wise consumables/ spare parts issue through lean ERP. The capturing of changeover timings, downtime timings, OEE, MTBF, MTTR, calculation of 16 losses, time-based maintenance sheets and condition-based maintenance sheets of critical machines can be tracked through lean ERP.

Quality Assurance and Quality Control

Quality assurance and quality control can function through lean ERP for customer coordination, inspection and approval because value stream products are shipped subject to their clearance. The quality function can track customer complaints, internal rejections and non-conformity reports through lean ERP. Cost of quality calculations can also be automated through lean ERP.

Logistics and Dispatch

The logistics and dispatch department prepares packing slips and erases the stock from inventory in the ERP through invoicing, warehouse management and transport management.

Finance

The finance function updates general ledger, accounts receivable, accounts payable, assets management, treasury management, vendor management and vendor rating on quality and delivery. Finance can generate the corporate scorecards and monthly or weekly profit and loss statement through lean ERP.

Since each component of the product is tracked on lean ERP, real-time product costing becomes feasible. If the company is able to track cost in real time, then the actual cost of the product can be easily determined at the time of dispatch that will help in prompt assessment of the product's profitability. Therefore, there will be no need for standard costs.

Lean ERP also streamlines stock taking because the physical stock in the warehouse should incessantly reconcile with the ERP stock. Additionally, this reconciliation also ratifies accuracy of transactions in lean ERP and augments accountability in the organization.

Human Resources

The HR function can prepare a performance scorecard for all supervisors and skill matrix for team leaders and workmen and monitor kaizen reward and recognition system through the lean ERP system.

All functions can also use the lean ERP to generate the update balance scorecards, performance scorecards and skill matrix for their function.

Reduction in Transactions

All functions can use the lean ERP to track the unnecessary transactions that are happening in their functions that are not value adding and can be avoided and the unnecessary transactions identified can be dropped after due deliberations.

However, recurrent training and persistent support to employees is indispensable to extract the best out of lean ERP because lean initiatives will eventually collapse if considerable attention to specific lean ERP aspects is not given. Lean addresses how processes should work, and lean ERP ensures the processes consistently work in that manner. The ERP team, with help from the ERP service providers, has the potential to be the game changer in implementation of lean in the company.

15.3 Benefits of Lean ERP

Lean ERP is an integrated system that brings uniformity and discipline by setting a code of conduct and inviolable source of data.[6]

Lean ERP becomes a single source of authentic information that is used by each function resulting in reduction in issues related to data disparity. Access is given to all employees according to their level and if someone feeds incorrect data, it is easier to track it since lean ERP increases accountability and brings in efficiency and prompt attention to issues.

Lean ERP reduces errors in operations including billing, wrong delivery and so forth and eradicates duplication of data. Managers can track actuals costs as per lean accounting and calculate savings due to lean and kaizen improvement initiatives effortlessly. Management information reports can be generated from the lean ERP system in agreed formats. Lean ERP helps in implementation of lean accounting by updating capacity data for manpower and machines, functional scorecards, performance scorecards and skill matrix. It makes preparation of the corporate scorecard and monthly profit and loss statement faster and easier so that it is ready on the first day of the following month.

Lean ERP eliminates unnecessary transactions in the company that makes managers more productive. But the IT function has to modify existing ERP in line with requirements of lean and lean accounting implementation efficiently so that ERP issues do not become a challenge in lean implementation.

Lean manufacturing operates in real time and lean ERP also share information in real time that enables the entire company to operate in real time. The real-time collection of data is significant. Since all the data for the value stream are captured in the ERP, each activity, such as submission of offers to customers, order receipt, design, planning, procurement, plant operations, dispatch and logistics and collection of payment from the customers, is captured in ERP. The base data, such as customer purchase orders, specifications and bill of materials, are entered once in the ERP by the authorized person and go to the relevant users. This becomes a prominent reason for healthy inter-department relationships since accountability and conflict resolution become easier due to transparency brought by the lean ERP system.

Key Takeaways

1. Lean manufacturing operates in real time and lean ERP also share information in real time that enables the entire company to operate in real time and make quicker decisions.
2. The lean production system, daily management and lean accounting is to be implemented with the help of lean ERP. The intention is to carry out all activities on the lean ERP platform.
3. Without a robust lean ERP, a company will not be able to sustain the process improvements achieved through lean initiatives.
4. The big data ERP is modified in a lean company because it does not need big data during the lean journey.
5. The capturing of changeover timings, downtime timings, OEE, MTBF, MTTR, calculation of 16 losses, time-based maintenance sheets and condition-based maintenance sheets of critical machines, cost of quality and product costs can be automated in real time through lean ERP.
6. Corporate Scorecards and a monthly profit and loss statement can be made available on the first of every month through lean ERP.

Recommended List for Further Reading

1. Balogh, S. (2019). *How ERP improves lean manufacturing* [online]. Available at: https://www.encompass-inc.com/7-ways-erp-improves-lean-manufacturing/
2. Doug, B. (2012). *Can lean and ERP work together?* [online]. Available at: www.industryweek.com/technology-and-iiot/systems-integration/article/21957403/can-lean-and-erp-work-together
3. Richard, C. (2014). *ERP Implementation: Lessons from Toyota on achieving ROI* [online]. Available at: www.erpvar.com/blog/bid/109048/ERP
4. Saraswati, S. (2018). *Hybrid ERP lean system implementation framework for small and medium manufacturing enterprises*. Thesis for the Degree of Master of Science in Engineering Management., Department of Mechanical engineering, University of Alberta.
5. Maskell.com. Blog- "*Data gathering-how lean companies create control*".
6. Jean, Thilmany. *For the lean manufacturer, ERP plays a vital role., How running ERP in a lean manufacturing environment can improve the bottom line., When using ERP to go lean, experts advise starting small., Avoiding the pitfalls of configuring your ERP system for a lean environment.* SearchManufacturingERP.com Contributor.com., www.iqms.com

Chapter 16

Reduction in Transactions

So we need to eliminate the transactions that are no longer needed without losing control of the business – perform 'konmari' on your company's transactions.

A transaction is any kind of action involved in conducting business, or an interaction between people. When someone goes to the bank to fill out a form and deposit a paycheck, then that person has made a *transaction*. Transactions in business mean what a company does to conduct its business. These transactions can be making purchase indents; preparing purchase orders; preparing material receipt reports; receiving invoices from the vendors; detail tracking of material and manpower on the plant floor; detail tracking of all inventories including consumable stores from receipt to issue to the processes, its movement in the plant to assembly and dispatch; physical inventory and cycle counting; issuing machinery spare parts; tooling; preparing shipping documents and customer invoices at the time of dispatch; corporate overheads; and accounts payable process and accounts receivable process.

Most of these transactions are wasteful activities that the customers are not paying for and have to be eliminated. These transactions consume the time of supervisors, executives and managers. These non-essential transactions are to be minimized. The time consumed in conducting each of these transactions is also to be looked into and to be minimized.[1]

Transaction elimination is the focus of the lean accounting system similar to inventory that was targeted to reduce during the lean production system implementation.

DOI: 10.4324/9781003221746-16

16.1 Standard Cost Accounting Is Transaction Heavy

Traditional standard cost accounting supports mass production. It promotes manufacturing of large batches to lower per unit cost. It utilizes manpower and machine at full capacity to absorb overheads and build inventory without analyzing the demand of the customers.

Standard cost accounting system requires thousands and thousands of transactions each month as stated earlier. People and computers are used to collect large information.[2]

The aforementioned exercise leads to preparation of long reports. The focus is to determine the actual situation in the company with respect to the budget figures, and the variances are plotted for man, material and machine utilization. The operations people are made to explain these variances. It results in long meetings and reconciliation exercises. This imposes avoidable heavy demand on the people's time in explaining variances. People feel they will lose their job if they are free.

Traditional companies operate with a paradigm that all processes are mostly out of control and to bring semblance of discipline, the finance function should bring in transactions that have a sign-off and approval from the heads of the operations and finance functions. The finance function has the operating control over the company.[3]

The ERP system calculates labor and overheads cost by assigning labor and overhead rates to work centers and by creating routings how it will travel from one work center to next till the end. With cycle time data you will get the cost at each station. This has to be done for all products. The company will put in manpower resources to collect this information. This will involve cost and efforts. The company will undertake these activities because your MRP-based ERP will demand it every day. This will give the cost incurred at each workstation and it can be all added up and you will get the product cost. The cycle time will vary for each individual. There will be minimum value, maximum value and an average value. Which value will you take? Some operators will run the machine faster. Some operators will run it slower. In an assembly line some can assemble faster, some slower. Just imagine how big data are being generated with a huge number of transactions that is leading you to confusion and bringing in approximation to come to some end. Is this the right way? No. It is not the right way to cost calculations. Lean accounting will show you the right way.

16.2 Why the Finance Function Has More Say in a Traditional Company

A traditional company is run through the finance function as most of the financial controls are in the hand of promoters and top management. These companies have an approval matrix (An approval matrix ensures that the correct individuals are involved in decision-making at the appropriate time. Sometimes also referred to as a 'schedule of authority'.). Proposals like documents, invoices, monthly budgets, purchase orders, capital expenditure budget, marketing initiatives or any other spending approval run through the hierarchy and reaches the finance department who coordinate with the promoters and top management in approving or rejecting.

Promoters/top management perceives the finance function as the most suited to do the business control of the company as only they understand the value of money.

The finance department is unaware of the implications of most of the operational financial decisions as how it will facilitate the customers in getting the better services from the company like getting supplies and service on time.

Promoters/top management believes first, that operations people have no financial knowledge, and second, the processes on the plant floor also are not under control so operations people can't be trusted with giving this additional responsibility of approvals.

Promoters/top management feels the finance function does its job well with cross-checking every detail and their reports can be trusted.

The areas where most of the transactions are mostly carried out are operational areas, material procurement, manpower tracking, inventory tracking in raw material, WIP and finished goods and main stores inventories counting, material issue from stores, consumables stores, machinery spare parts, corporate overheads, accounts payable, accounts receivable. This leads to millions of transactions in a large company annually. These have been performed for decades, so the practice continues. It will give a very amazing picture if they are documented and analyzed. How much of a manager's time goes into signing these transactions on a daily basis? Managers in traditional companies rather enjoy this power but these do not add any value to the company. Most of these transactions are non-value adding and do not bring control with them.

Detailed tracking is required to be done in a traditional company as the lead times are running into weeks and months.

16.3 Transactions in a Lean Company

This is set to change in a lean company.

In the lean production system, lead times have decreased to days and inventories have reduced with formation of supermarkets. Throughput time has decreased. Material is flowing smoothly in the processes. There is no appreciable variation in the processes. The processes are standardized.

Decision-making is gradually encouraged in the operational areas where the value addition is taking place and people at the lower commands are trained to make their own decisions. With time the authority is given to value stream managers and functional managers for faster decision-making to help reduce the throughput time and timely supplies to customers with no quality problems. When this shift of decision-making from finance to operations is happening there is no loss of control on the system. The value stream manager assumes the responsibility and authority of his value stream and is authorized to make financial decisions. Later, functional managers are given some financial authority where they can approve purchase orders of vendors and payments can be made to vendors by their approval. The control will shift to where it will help in providing the best service to the customer. These ideas have worked well in many companies where they have eliminated the waste of time and energy that goes in chasing the needless transactions.

16.4 Lean Production System Practices that Help in the Reduction of Transactions and Transaction Time

The following are lean production system practices that help in the reduction of transactions and transaction time – a close watch over throughput time to bring it to minimum, TPM tools to reduce the downtime of the machines, TQM to enhance the quality and reduce variability, kanban system to implement flow and pull, standard work and daily management to bring control down to the plant floor, visual display system, supplier/vendor certification, workplace quality right first time right, implementation of the lean performance measurement system.

16.5 Lean Accounting Takes Your Focus Away from Data Collection

Data are plain statistics collected during the operations of a business. Data can be used to measure/record a wide range of business activities and are crucial for the business. Data are measured, collected, reported, analyzed and converted to required information with which decisions can be made. In a lean company many categories of data can be done away with. This will lead to a reduction of a lot of information/formats in use now.

To start with, in a lean company, there is no need of the internal work orders to capture the costs. Customer order number and BOM number is sufficient, for example, in a capital machine builder like Perfect Gear Company.

New lean methods are implemented to reduce and eliminate the data tracking without loss of control. Controls are slowly transferred to operations on the plant floor and unnecessary entries are eliminated. There will be a reduction in entry of many categories of data in the ERP system. The target is now to identify and eliminate the non-value adding data collection.

The spotlight in lean accounting will be issuing open POs, using actual costs, dropping allocations, using the kanban system, self-certification, authorizing suppliers to dispatch and voucher on receipt there by eliminating three-way matching of price of MRN-PO-supplier's invoice. This will considerably reduce the wasteful transactions.

16.6 Lean Accounting Focuses the Company on Live Data Analysis

It provides live information allowing for any proactive action. Control is with the value stream manager as weekly or monthly performance is tracked through the corporate scorecard and the monthly P&L statement is prepared and the company is running live. Value stream managers have finance and accounts and sales and marketing personnel reporting to them. Value stream managers are directly in touch with the customers. Corrective action is taken quickly now. Lean manufacturing with daily/hourly dispatch to customer's assembly line does not increase transactions. The kanban system is there to control it.

Live data are captured at the workplace by terminals provided nearby and also through mobiles of key personnel identified in this regard.

16.7 How to Identify and Reduce/Eliminate Wasteful Transactions in the Company

The following are the areas where heavy transactions take place that leads to wastages of the manager's, executive's and supervisor's time and efforts. These transactions are making purchase indents; preparing purchase orders; preparing material receipt reports; receiving invoices from the vendors; detail tracking of material and manpower on the plant floor; detail tracking of all inventories including consumable stores from receipt to issue to the processes, its movement in the plant to assembly and dispatch; physical inventory and cycle counting; issuing machinery spare parts; tooling; preparing shipping documents and customer invoices at the time of dispatch; corporate overheads; and accounts payable process and accounts receivable process.

To initiate the transactions identification and elimination process, the functional managers have to prepare the process chart for their function based on the day-to-day working to record each transaction of their function that can be further discussed within the function, across functions and with the lean experts. The lean production system and lean accounting methodology will guide the new way of doing the tasks, which will be bringing down the number of transactions and time involved in doing the transactions.

The processes across the functions are analyzed, opportunities are identified and subsequently elimination of transactions without losing control on the system is taken up and a new lean system is developed for the company.

The following are details of the company operations where major transactions are carried out.

Operational Movements

The lean implementation in the company generates a lot of transactions initially if we continue to follow traditional practices in operational areas.

These transactions can be preparation and approvals for purchase indents, design issues, preparing material receipt reports, detail work order-wise tracking of material, manpower and machines on the plant floor during their movement in the plant from raw materials stockyard to assembly and dispatch, issuing components, consumables, machinery spare parts, tooling, maintenance data, quality control data, daily management system data, preparing shipping documents and customer invoices at the time of dispatch.

Any mistake, deviation, rework, non-conforming reports or quality rejections will bring in the non-value adding transactions for preventive and corrective action.

There will be a surge in the transactions initially when the lean production system is implemented. The large batch size is replaced with single piece flow or the small batch flow. As the tracking is done batch-wise the number of transactions will multiply till the lean methodology is implemented. In the lean production system the individual batch tracking is not done but backflushing is introduced. This itself will bring a huge reduction in transactions.

Further, if processes are under control, the need for transactions is reduced. No more measures like manpower or machine utilization are used. This eliminates long debate in monthly meetings. This way the transactions and transaction time are reduced. Excess capacity to the extent of 20% in the machines and manpower is welcome.

Material Procurement

These transactions can be making purchase indents, preparing purchase orders, preparing material receipt reports, receiving invoices from the vendors, detail tracking of all inventories including consumable stores from receipt to issue to the processes, physical inventory and cycle counting.

The process of procurement is simplified in the lean production system with introduction of just-in-time/flow and pull through kanban and supermarket concept. This reduces the transactions and transactions time considerably.

For all major, critical and repetitive raw material and standard bought-out components, the prices and terms and conditions can be negotiated and open purchase orders with maximum time validity can be released. Release actual requirement through e-kanban whenever the free kanban comes to purchase for procurement. These kanban can then be relayed to the suppliers. There can be more than one supplier for each item. Even the company shares their forecasting figures with the vendors so that they can also implement lean production in their companies in order to serve better. They can keep the material ready when it is needed.

Start a vendor certification scheme with the help of the quality control department and continue this exercise to bring maximum vendors under this scheme. Decide at what frequency these audits are to be done.

Gradually introduce vendor-managed inventories at the company. The vendor will not hesitate but will welcome this. Who does not want assured customers? The vendor material is received in the plant and material receipt note is made. This material receipt note will become the document for releasing the payment. The date on the material receipt note is the day one for the accounts payable process.

Take the pull backward from finished good supermarket back to the previous processes all the way through the plant to the suppliers. Use kanban for triggering the action.

Further in the lean production system and lean accounting system the materials costs are directly credited to the work orders/bill of materials on ERP as soon as the materials enter the company gate.

The material movement inside the plant from one process to another is regulated by use of internal kanban and the use of earlier move cards or job cards is discontinued. If the company does not do this, then it is causing confusion and it is doing this only to satisfy the accounting people but not the company.

Common material is posted when it is issued from stores for the work orders/bill of materials.

All these practices will considerably reduce your transactions.

Manpower Tracking

In traditional companies the manpower costs are tracked at every step every day on the plant floor and in departments for every work order or job card and credited to work orders/bill of materials on ERP. This involves filling up data manually or in ERP at the end of shift. At the end of the month the variance is calculated, and functions have to explain this variance if it on the negative side.

In lean these practices are totally stopped. All personnel are allocated to the value streams and functions and the manpower expenses are accounted accordingly. At the month end these costs are added up and credited to P&L accounts for the value streams or company.

The company eliminates shift detail tracking. This results in considerable reduction of transactions. If the company wants to calculate the costing of the individual product it can use these total manpower costs proportionally to the sales value of each product for its P&L calculations. There are no direct and indirect costs in lean accounting. All costs are direct. All contract workmen are counted as equivalent of own workmen.

Inventory Tracking

In traditional standard accounting, detailed tracking is done for all material movement from raw material to finished goods on the plant floor and allocated to the work orders on a continuous basis daily. It involves the number of transactions happening daily.

Physical inventory for all stock keeping units is done diligently for all the materials inside the company by stopping the company's operations for a couple of days.

Inventory tracking is done in a different way in lean accounting with few transactions. The raw materials are credited to the work order as soon as its material receipt note is made at entry. With one transaction the material shifts in ERP to the value stream and to its work order/bill of material.

The common material is received in the stores and is credited to a work order/bill of material as it is issued from main stores. The standard bought-out and smaller item that are purchased in bulk are issued at a time of assembly or final process in the process industry as part of a kit and at that moment it is credited to its work order/bill of material on the ERP.

Under lean the inventory is considered as evil as explained earlier and continuous strides are made to reduce it. The slow moving and non-moving stocks are also under attack. With reduction in inventory, the job of monthly stock counting becomes easy. With kanban system, visual displays and proper storage practices, the inventories are even easier to track.

To make the monthly stock taking work more easily, the regular cycle counting of each category is taken up on a daily basis. There is no need to stop the plant for stock taking, which is an annual elaborate feature in traditional companies with three to four days of plant closure. This annual practice is discontinued in a lean company.

Material Issue from Stores

All materials are issued from the stores through a request on the ERP system. When this item is issued the cost shifts to work order/bill of material number in the ERP. This is common material that could not be credited to any work order/bill of material when it was received in the company.

All functions are to send their material issue requests on ERP by the evening of the day before and material is delivered to point of use by stores. Except for emergency and urgent needs no one is encouraged to come to the stores.

Consumables Stores

Cost of consumables issued to the functions should be allotted to that particular function. This brings better control. These expenses are compared with the budgets in the balance scorecard for functional heads to control.

Machinery Spare Parts

Each machine in the lean company has a user code. The spare parts for specific machines are credited to the maintenance function on issue from the stores. The common items are issued through ERP to the maintenance function at stores. The tooling that goes out and comes back to stores after use is regarded as capital purchase.

Corporate Overheads

This is part of the fixed cost. Corporate overheads are allocated to each individual value stream or products as part of the pricing exercise in proportion to their sales value.

Accounts Payable

Lean companies consider their suppliers or vendors as part of the company. Toyota's vendor management department implements relevant lean tools at their vendor's workplace or plant to make them lean and procure material on time and at low cost.

Payable process is a non-value adding activity. This process is to be not only standardized but also simplified so that the transaction cost per voucher is minimum. Transaction cost is the average cost of each transaction happening in the company. The company should know what this cost is. The second step is to continuously reduce this cost by eliminating the non-value adding transactions.

How many vouchers are prepared in a month and how many accountants are engaged in this activity and what are their salaries and perks? The company can calculate the average transaction cost per voucher. It should be brought down to minimum.

In a traditional company a three-way matching is done between purchase order, the material receipt note (the receiving documents) and the supplier invoice before payment. A slight discrepancy can disrupt the whole process.

The mistakes can be in incorrect specifications or work order number. This leads to the finance team spending a considerable amount of time in rectifying or seeking clarifications for correction. There may be less than 5% of the total invoices with discrepancies that does not justify the time spent on the present system of three-way reconciliation.[4]

Lean accounting recommends introduction of auto voucher receipt and triggering the auto payment at the time of receipt of material for vendors with a high rating. This triggering will begin the period of time of payment negotiated with the vendor. This will considerably reduce the transactions.

The three-way matching can be eliminated for routine materials and components by use of e-kanban and long-term purchase orders. This will also create good relations with vendors. In a lean company this process is simplified with continual improvement projects. All duplicate, repetitive and incorrect data are erased from the ERP. Product names and specifications are standardized in the ERP by the relevant function like design or R&D. Any specific data in the ERP are entered only once. ERP prompts item names and code numbers and their specifications that are entered by the design. This eliminates reconciliation activities and transaction time. In many established companies it is a common practice to release a new product code instead of searching for the code in the system.

Accounts Receivable

The company must work with their customers for auto payment on dispatch or at the time of receipt of materials at their end similar to the company procedure of making payments to their vendors as per accounts payable. Old customers can be convinced. This practice can be discussed with new customers at the negotiations stage.

This practice will increase the cash flow for the company if successful. This will not be easy, but a start can be made.

16.8 Benefits of Reduction of Transactions and Transaction Time

Managers can focus more on value adding activities and lean project implementation with reduction in transactions. The time spent in reconciliation meetings can be utilized for strategic thinking about the next phase of lean or process improvement. Managers feel empowered and productive.[5] They start working on ERP efficiently through their terminals in their work area or through their mobiles and use less paper.

16.9 Elimination of Transactions Without Losing Control[6]

We eliminate a transaction when we create a system that does not require that transaction. The lean production system, daily management system and lean accounting system make such a system feasible. Transactions are abolished when the top management, specifically the CFO, attains confidence in the capability of the new system to create the right level of control. Functional managers can identify the transactions and discuss with cross-functional teams, finalize and take the CFO's approval and eliminate those transactions.

Key Takeaways

1. Most of a company's transactions are wasteful activities that customers are not paying for and that have to be minimized/eliminated.
2. Transaction elimination is the focus of lean accounting system similar to inventory that was targeted to reduce during the lean production system implementation.
3. Traditional standard cost accounting supports mass production. The standard cost accounting system requires thousands and thousands of transactions each month.
4. Traditional companies operate with a paradigm that all processes are mostly out of control and to bring semblance of discipline, the finance function should have operating control over the company as they only understand the value of money.
5. In lean companies, value stream managers assume the responsibility and authority of their value streams and are authorized to make financial decisions. The control will shift to where it will help in providing the best service to the customer.
6. We eliminate a transaction when we create a system that does not require that transaction and the top management, specifically the CFO, attains confidence in the capability of the new system to create the right level of control.

Recommended List for Further Reading

1. Cunningham, J.E. (2017). *Real numbers: management accounting in a lean organization*. Evanston, IL: JCC Press.
2. Maskell.com. Blog- *"Why do we need work orders? We don't"*.
3. Maskell.com. Blog- *"Data gathering- Why are our processes out of control"*.
4. Maskell.com. Blog- *"Getting to the root of the AP 3-way match"*.
5. Maskell, B.H. (2009). *Making the numbers count: The accountant as change agent on the world class team*. Boca Raton, FL: CRC Press.
6. Maskell, B.H., Baggaley, B. and Grasso, L. (2012). *Practical lean accounting: A proven system for measuring and managing the lean enterprise*. Boca Raton, FL: CRC Press.

Chapter 17

System Assessment/Audit

I have always believed that if you put in the work, the results will come.

– Michael Jordan

The workmen skill matrix, performance and functional scorecards focus on performance of individuals at various levels and the corporate scorecard is an outcome of efforts of the company as a whole. An assessment of these scorecards articulates if the company making progress or if amelioration is required. The assessment scorecard is beneficial for monitoring the monthly company score and set targets for the future months. A lean assessment is not merely an audit of the current operations while implementing the lean production system, daily management and lean accounting but also a directive to take the company to the next level of operations. *Lean assessment steers the focus of the decision-makers in the right direction and acts as the true North Star for the company by laying down the road map for the future.*

17.1 Lean Assessment Score Card

A lean assessment scorecard is designed for this purpose. Every company in each industry is unique in its own way, and before any company starts benchmarking against the industry's best players, it can use this assessment tool to assess what is the current status of the company and analyze the progress achieved every quarter.

Table 17.1 through Table 17.18 show the assessment audit score methodology. It has 18 yardsticks to judge the company's implementation journey of the lean production system, daily management system and lean accounting

DOI: 10.4324/9781003221746-17

system. The assessment is initiated after evaluating the progress of implementation of the following benchmark areas:

- 5S Audit Score of the Company
- TPM – OEE, MTTR, MTBF, TBM, CBM
- TQM
- Flow and Pull of Kanban System
- Progress of Continual Improvement Projects in Hand across Functions
- Flow and Pull – Supermarket Kanban System Implementation as a Percentage of Total Products Applicable
- Daily and Visual Management
- Value Stream Implementation
- Performance Measures on the Work Center and Value Streams
- Performance Measurement System
- Production Capacity Measurement
- Corporate Scorecard
- Product Costing Based on Lean Accounting
- Value Stream Budgeting and Planning
- Continual Improvement Projects across Functions
- Financial Benefits Due to Implementation of Lean Production System and Daily Management.
- Transactions Elimination and Transaction Time Reduction
- Change in Role of Finance People Due to Lean Implementation

If the assessment scorecard has an increasing trend, then the lean production system, daily management system and lean accounting system implementation will be giving positive results. A negative trend of the lean assessment score will mean the implementation process needs to be reviewed. Increasing trend in the assessment scorecard will motivate managers, staff and workmen to work harder to achieve the target score in the future.

Perfect Gear Company lean assessment was done as per the above methodology every month from 31st March 2018. Only two lean assessment scorecards for the months of March 2018 and March 2019 are exhibited here in detail to showcase the methodology.

17.2 Lean Assessment Score Card of Perfect Gear Company as on March 2018

Table 17.1 through Table 17.9 show the lean and lean assessment format filled up as on 31 March 2018 to assess the lean production system, daily

Table 17.1 Format for Assessment of 6S Audit, TPM, TQM and Continual Improvement Projects at Perfect Gear Company as on 31 March 2018.

Category			1. 6S	2. TPM OEE, MTTR, MTBF, TBM, CBM implementation						3. TQM	4. Continual improvement projects in hand
Ref chapter			2	2						2	2
	Sub-category		6S audit score	AM step1	AM step2	AM step3	PM step1	PM step2	PM step3		
Score	Audit score	Maximum score	Achieved score	Achieved score	Achieved score	Achieved score	Achieved score	Achieved score	Achieved score	Achieved score	Achieved score
Level 1	10%	1									
	20%	2									
Level 2	30%	3						2	2		
	40%	4	4		4	3	3			3	3
Level 3	50%	5		5							
	60%	6									
Level 4	70%	7									
	80%	8									
Level 5	90%	9									
	100%	10									
Level 6											
Score as on date			4	5	4	3	3	2	2	3	3
Total score			4	3.5						3	3

Table 17.2 **Format for Assessment of Flow and Pull – Supermarket, Kanban System, Daily Management and Visual Management at Perfect Gear Company as on 31 March 2018.**

Category		5. Flow and pull – supermarket kanban system		6. Flow and pull – supermarket kanban system		7. Daily management and visual management	
Reference chapter		2		2		3	
Sub-category		Kanban system		% of total products applicable		Daily management and visual management	
Score	Maximum score	Stage	Achieved score	Stage	Achieved score	Stage	Achieved score
Level 1	1	Dispatch to warehouse		Dispatch to warehouse		Daily work schedule for managers and supervisors and function-wise display is initiated	
	2						
Level 2	3	Warehouse to plant FG store	3	Warehouse to plant FG store	3	Daily work schedule for managers and supervisors in advance stage	3
	4						
Level 3	5	FG store to last production cell		FG store to last production cell		Typical checklists are being prepared	
	6						
Level 4	7	Within the production cells and stores		Within the production cells and stores		Daily performance board, action plan board of the operations implemented	
	8						
Level 5	9	Stores to purchase function		Stores to purchase function		Obeya room implemented. Daily meeting module on the plant floor implemented.	
	10						
Level 6	11	Purchase function to suppliers		Purchase function to suppliers		All the previous four daily management activities in full implementation	
	12						
Score as on date			3		3		3
Total score			3		3		3

Table 17.3 Format for Assessment of Value Stream Implementation and Performance Measures at Perfect Gear Company as on 31 March 2018.

Category		8. Value stream implementation		9. Performance measures basis	
Reference chapter		2		6	
Sub-category		*Define value streams, functions clarity as who is in which value stream and function*		*Follow lean measures*	
Score	Maximum score	Stages	Achieved score	Stages	Achieved score
Level 1	1	No value stream culture. Everyone is department oriented.		Standard costing still in use, using variance analysis to judge department efficiencies	
Level 1	2		2		
Level 2	3	Value stream is introduced on shop floor		Company still structured department-wise. Lean implementation started. Cycle time, throughput time, first time quality, inventory turns concepts introduced, still P&L is made with standard costing – variance analysis method	
Level 2	4				4
Level 3	5	Also includes shipping		Value streams defined and implemented 25% and new measures like hourly production at cells, first time through, throughput time, on time delivery, average cost, OEE of critical machines, monthly basis, partially done by accounts department	
Level 3	6				
Level 4	7	Also includes quality		Value streams defined and implemented 50% and new measures like hourly production at cells, first time through, throughput time, on time delivery, average cost, OEE of critical machines on monthly basis, partial done by accounts department	
Level 4	8				
Level 5	9	Also includes purchase and finance		Value streams defined and implemented 75% and new measures like hourly production at cells, first time through, throughput time, on time delivery, average cost, OEE of critical machines, AR days, AP days, being done by value stream accountant reporting to value stream manager, done on weekly basis	
Level 5	10				
Level 6	11	Also includes sales and marketing		Value streams defined and implemented 100% and new measures like hourly production at cells, first time through, throughput time, on time delivery, average cost, OEE of critical machines, AR days, AP days, being done by value stream accountant reporting to value stream manager, done on weekly basis	
Level 6	12				
Score as on date			2		4
Total score			2		4

Table 17.4 Format for Assessment of Performance Measurement System and Production Capacity at Perfect Gear Company as on 31 March 2018.

Topic		10. Performance measurement system					11. Production capacity of the company	
Reference chapter		10					8	
Sub-topic		Workmen skill score measurement		Executive performance scorecard		Managers functional scorecard	Awareness of how much capacity is productive, non-productive, surplus available	
Score	Max score	Stage	Achieved score	Stage	Achieved score	Stage	Achieved score	Stage	Achieved score
Level 1	1	Not aware of the concept		Not aware of the concept		Not aware of the concept		Not aware of the concept	
Level 1	2								
Level 2	3	Process initiated		Process initiated		Process initiated		Capacity of only manpower is calculated	3
Level 2	4		4		4		4		
Level 3	5	Score >20%		Score >20%		Score >20%		Capacity of machines also is calculated monthly	
Level 3	6								
Level 4	7	Score >40%		Score >40%		Score >40%		Capacity of manpower and machines also is calculated weekly	
Level 4	8								
Level 5	9	Score >60%		Score >60%		Score >60%		Capacity information is used for decision-making – taking additional orders, outsourcing, NPD, capital purchase. Standards costs are never used for these kinds of decisions.	
Level 5	10								
Level 6	11	Score >80%		Score >80%		Score >80%		The capacity concept is well understood and diligently followed	
Level 6	12								
Score as on date			4		4		4		3
Total score		4							3

Table 17.5 Format for Assessment of Corporate Scorecard and Product Costing at Perfect Gear Company as on 31 March 2018.

Topic		12. Corporate scorecard		13. Product costing	
Reference chapter		9		7, 12	
Sub-topic		*Monthly and then weekly corporate scorecard is used*		*Earlier costing based on internal cost plus profits to summary direct costs*	
Score	*Max score*	*Stages*	*Achieved score*	*Stages*	*Achieved score*
Level 1	1	Concept not understood		Product cost is calculated on material plus labor and overhead plus margin and any deviation in the department is questioned	
	2				
Level 2	3	Training given, concept explained	3	Product cost is calculated on material plus labor and overhead plus margin and any deviation in the department is questioned. Concurrently, training is being given to finance and value streams about lean accounting	4
	4				
Level 3	5	Filling of operation data initiated		Product costing is initiated, company is divided into value streams and average product cost in the value stream costing is calculated on monthly basis	
	6				
Level 4	7	Filling of finance data also initiated		Value stream costing (summary direct costing of the value stream) is widely used. When the costs of individual products are required we use features and characteristics costing	
	8				
Level 5	9	Filling of capacity data also initiated		Value stream direct costing is being used for individual product costing. Monthly reporting is promptly done.	
	10				
Level 6	11	Concept understood and weekly filling started		Value stream direct costing is being used for target costing for the existing and new product development	
	12				
Score as on date			3		4
Total score			3		4

Table 17.6 **Format for Assessment of Budgeting, Planning and Continual Improvement at Perfect Gear Company as on 31 March 2018.**

Category		14. Budgeting and planning		15. Continual improvement	
Reference chapter		13		2, 3, 4, 5	
Sub-category		Shift from managing by departmental budgets to managing by value stream, driven by the sales and operations planning process		From a department-based organization to a company embracing lean production system and lean accounting	
Score	Maximum score	Stage	Achieved score	Stage	Achieved score
Level 1	1	We have extensive and detailed budgeting for every department and cost center and for every account and sub-account. This way we can plan and control our expenditures. We have a formal annual budget development process in which each department manager develops his own budget for approval. Budget vs. actual reports are prepared monthly by department and reviewed in meetings.	2	The financial reports are made quarterly and department managers are unable to link it with plant floor performance. All departments are busy improving their own efficiencies. Customer is very far from them.	2
Level 1	2				
Level 2	3	We have greatly simplified the annual budgeting process by eliminating most cost centers and accounting codes from the items that need to be budgeted. We have begun to implement a formal sales operations and financial planning process each month and we plan by value stream.		We have established value stream continuous improvement teams. The lean tools are being understood by all functions and improvement initiatives are in progress. Training for value streams and changes are being brought in to work on the philosophy of value stream management.	
Level 2	4				
Level 3	5	We have eliminated department budgets. We create monthly (periodic) rolling budgets for each value stream from our sales, operations and financial planning process. Our budgeted values include both financial and non-financial performance. We regularly include value stream targets for elimination of waste and for increasing available capacity through the application of lean initiatives.		Continuous improvement is now routine within the value stream. The capacities of functions are being calculated and thrust toward minimization of non-value adding capacity usage is on. Corporate scorecards on monthly basis are prepared and understood by all functions.	
Level 3	6				
Level 4	7	The company is managed by value streams both operationally and financially. The monthly rolling budgets are key to the ongoing continuous improvements of the value streams and the overall business.		Almost everybody is actively involved in week-by-week continuous improvement projects, performance improvement and cost impacts, freed up capacity.	
Level 4	8				
Level5	9				
Level5	10				
Level 6	11				
Level 6	12				
Score as on date			2		2
Total score			2		2

Table 17.7 Format for Assessment of Financial Benefits of Lean at Perfect Gear Company as on 31 March 2018.

Category		16. Financial benefits of lean changes	
Reference chapter		5, 6, 7, 8, 9, 14, 17	
Sub-category		Focus to shift from calculating financial benefits from lean initiatives to understanding the total concept of capacity usage	
Score	Maximum score	Stage	Achieved score
Level 1 — 1	1	The financial benefits of lean project initiatives implementation are being calculated but the effect of these benefits is difficult to link with the topline and the bottom line.	
Level 1	2		2
Level 2	3	We monitor financial benefits from the lean initiatives and understand how these improvements are linked with the non-value adding capacity usage reduction. Understanding how much free capacity is available and how it can be used for taking more orders. Also started making outsourced products/items in-house.	
Level 2	4		
Level 3	5	We have established monthly financial gains calculations from all lean initiatives and teams are understanding this and are able to correlate with freeing up the capacity.	
Level 3	6		
Level 4	7	All functions are in the teams for lean initiatives, resulting in huge gains to bottom line. The teams are motivated looking at the financial results they are achieving.	
Level 4	8		
Level 5	9		
Level 5	10		
Level 6	11		
Level 6	12		
Score as on date			2
Total score			2

Table 17.8 Format for Assessment of Transactions Elimination and Role of Finance Team at Perfect Gear Company as on 31 March 2018.

Category	17. Transactions elimination		18. Role of finance people	
Reference chapter	16		12	
Sub-category	Material cost, labor costs, inventory tracking, accounts payable, accounts receivable, month end closing. Focus to shift from tracking individual costs to direct expense of the materials, labor. Reduction of inventory helps in switching to cycle counting.		Shift in the role of finance from detached evaluators of the lean results to integral members of the value stream teams.	
Score / Maximum score	Stages	Achieved score	Stages	Achieved score
Level 1 — 1, 2	Conventional system of material tracking, daily tracking of labor, inventory tracking in the process, yearly full inventory counting, three-way matching to arrive at accounts payable, mailing invoices to customers and monthly closing reports are made well into end of next month.	2	The finance people are attuned to old practices of book-keeping and gathering data from ERP and maintaining records and trying the utmost correct status of the finance of the company. They understand only the numbers but have no clue as to how these numbers are linked with the working on the plant floor.	2
Level 2 — 3, 4	The backflushing of labor and overhead costs and material cost allocation to work order as it enters the company, cycle counting of inventory, authority to approve is being lowered down the hierarchy and open POs to suppliers, e-kanban system, requested customers to give open POs and dispatch invoice to work as payment request – all these are in the work in progress.		The finance people have moved out of their offices and are part of teams of lean initiatives and are beginning to understand the operations and better understanding of the finances also. They are getting lean production system and lean accounting training. Started making capacity calculations and finalizing corporate scorecards.	
Level 3 — 5, 6	The process is established. Further value stream costing is also established, accounts payable to suppliers when they deliver materials to assembly line get paid based on kanban, similarly customers have started paying based on kanban. Authorization has come to value stream manager and below and only high value items prior approval is required. Quarterly book closing and monthly P&L is prepared on 2nd of next month.		All finance activities are now done on value stream basis and performance measures are used, which are commensurate with the lean methodology. They are sitting with the operations teams reporting to value stream managers. Corporate scorecard is well entrenched and positive movements have been achieved in the results.	
Level 4 — 7, 8	The transactions are eliminated to great extent as these practices are well trenched in the company now. The corporate scorecard is now made weekly. The managers are now free to spend more times on value added activities.		P&L comes out on 1st of every month. All managers understand the plusses or minuses of financial figures and finance is part of the integral team.	

Category		17. Transactions elimination			18. Role of finance people		
Level 5	9						
	10						
Level 6	11						
	12						
Score as on date				2			2
Total score				2			2

Table 17.9   Format for Consolidated Assessment at Perfect Gear Company as on 31 March 2018.

Sl no.	Category	Maximum score	Achieved score
1	6S audit score	10	4
2	TPM-OEE, MTTR, MTBF, TBM, CBM	10	3.5
3	TQM	10	3
4	Continual improvement projects in hand	10	3
5	Flow and pull – supermarket kanban system	12	3
6	Flow and pull – supermarket kanban system	12	3
7	Daily management and visual management	10	3
8	Value stream implementation	12	2
9	Performance measures basis	12	4
10	Performance measurement system	12	4
11	Production capacity of the company	12	3
12	Corporate scorecard	12	3
13	Product costing	12	4
14	Budgeting and planning	8	2
15	Continual improvement	8	2
16	Financial benefits of lean changes	8	2
17	Transactions elimination	8	2
18	Role of finance people	8	2
	Total score	186	53
	Total score in %		28%

Table 17.10 Format for Assessment of 6S Audit, TPM, TQM and Continual Improvement Projects in Hand at Perfect Gear Company as on 31 March 2019.

Category			1.6S	2. TPM-OEE, MTTR, MTBF, TBM, CBM implementation						3. TQM.	4. Continual improvement projects in hand
Reference chapter			2	2						2	2
Sub-category			6S audit score	AM step1	AM step2	AM step3	PM step1	PM step2	PM step3		
Score	Audit score	Maximum score	Achieved score	Achieved score	Achieved score	Achieved score	Achieved score	Achieved score	Achieved score	Achieved score	Achieved score
Level 1	10%	1									
Level 1	20%	2									
Level 2	30%	3									
Level 2	40%	4									
Level 3	50%	5									
Level 3	60%	6								6	6
Level 4	70%	7	7				7	7	7		
Level 4	80%	8		8	8	8					
Level 5	90%	9									
Level 5	100%	10									
Level 6											
Score as on date			7	8	8	8	7	7	7	6	6
Total score			7	7.5						6	6

Table 17.11 Format for Assessment of Flow and Pull – Supermarket, Kanban System, Daily Management and Visual Management at Perfect Gear Company as on 31 March 2019.

Category		5. Flow and pull – supermarket kanban system		6. Flow and pull – supermarket kanban system		7. Daily management and visual management	
Reference chapter		2		2		3	
Sub-category		Kanban system		% of total products applicable		Daily management and visual management	
Score	Maximum score	Stage	Achieved score	Stage	Achieved score	Stage	Achieved score
Level 1	1	Dispatch to warehouse		Dispatch to warehouse		Daily work schedule for managers and supervisors and function-wise display is initiated	
Level 1	2						
Level 2	3	Warehouse to plant FG store		Warehouse to plant FG store		Daily work schedule for managers and supervisors in advance stage	
Level 2	4						
Level 3	5	FG store to last production cell	6	FG store to last production cell	6	Typical checklists are being prepared	
Level 3	6						
Level 4	7	Within the production cells and stores		Within the production cells and stores		Daily performance board, action plan board of the operations implemented	7
Level 4	8						
Level 5	9	Stores to purchase function		Stores to purchase function		Obeya room implemented. Daily meeting module on the plant floor implemented.	
Level 5	10						
Level 6	11	Purchase function to suppliers		Purchase function to suppliers		All the previous four daily management activities in full implementation	
Level 6	12						
Score as on date			6		6		7
Total score			6		6		7

Table 17.12 Format for Assessment of Value Stream Implementation and Performance Measures Basis at Perfect Gear Company as on 31 March 2019.

Category	8. Value stream implementation			9. Performance measures basis	
Reference chapter	2			6	
Sub-category	Define value streams, functions clarity as to who is in which value stream and function			Follow lean measures	
Score	Maximum score	Stages	Achieved score	Stages	Achieved score
Level 1	1	No value stream culture. Everyone is department oriented.		Standard costing still in use, using variance analysis to judge department efficiencies	
	2				
Level 2	3	Value stream is introduced on shop floor		Company still structured department-wise. Lean implementation started. Cycle time, throughput time, first time quality, inventory turns concepts introduced, still P&L is made with standard costing – variance analysis method.	
	4				
Level 3	5	Also includes shipping		Value streams defined and implemented 25% and new measures like hourly production at cells, first time through, throughput time, on time delivery, average cost, OEE of critical machines, monthly basis, partially done by accounts department.	
	6				
Level 4	7	Also includes quality		Value streams defined and implemented 50% and new measures like hourly production at cells, first time through, throughput time, on time delivery, average cost, OEE of critical machines on monthly basis, partially done by accounts department.	
	8				
Level5	9	Also includes purchase and finance		Value streams defined and implemented 75% and new measures like hourly production at cells, first time through, throughput time, on time average cost, OEE of critical machines, AR days, AP days, being done by value stream accountant reporting to value stream manager, done on weekly basis.	
	10				
Level 6	11	Also includes sales and marketing	11	Value streams defined and implemented 100% and new measures like hourly production at cells, first time through, throughput time, on time delivery, average cost, OEE of critical machines, AR days, AP days, being done by value stream accountant reporting to value stream manager, done on weekly basis.	11
	12				
Score as on date			11		11
Total score			11		11

Table 17.13 Format for Assessment of Performance Measurement System and Production Capacity at Perfect Gear Company as on 31 March 2019.

		Perfect Gear Company							
		Lean and lean accounting assessment march 2019							
Topic		10. Performance measurement system						11. Production capacity of the company	
Reference chapter		10						8	
Sub-topic		Workmen skill score measurement		Executive performance score card		Managers functional scorecard		Awareness of how much capacity is productive, non-productive, surplus available	
Score	Max score	Stage	Achieved score	Stage	Achieved score	Stage	Achieved score	Stage	Achieved score
Level 1	1	Not aware of the concept		Not aware of the concept		Not aware of the concept		Not aware of the concept	
Level 1	2								
Level 2	3	Process initiated		Process initiated		Process initiated		Capacity of only manpower is calculated	
Level 2	4								
Level 3	5	Score >20%		Score >20%		Score >20%		Capacity of machines also is calculated monthly	
Level 3	6								
Level 4	7	Score >40%		Score >40%		Score >40%		Capacity of manpower and machines also is calculated weekly	8
Level 4	8								
Level 5	9	Score >60%		Score >60%		Score >60%		Capacity information is used for decision-making – taking additional orders, outsourcing, NPD, capital purchase. Standards costs are never used for these kinds of decisions.	
Level 5	10		10						
Level 6	11	Score >80%		Score >80%		Score >80%		The capacity concept is well understood and diligently followed	
Level 6	12								
Score as on date			10		10		10		8
Total score		10						8	8

Table 17.14 Format for Assessment of Corporate Scorecard and Product Costing at Perfect Gear Company as on 31 March 2019.

Topic		12. Corporate scorecard		13. Product costing	
Reference chapter		9		7,12	
Sub-topic		Monthly and then weekly corporate scorecard is used		Earlier costing based on internal cost plus profits to summary direct costs	
Score	Max score	Stages	Achieved score	Stages	Achieved score
Level 1	1	Concept not understood		Product cost is calculated on material plus labor and overhead plus margin and any deviation in the department is questioned.	
	2				
Level 2	3	Training given, concept explained		Product cost is calculated on material plus labor and overhead plus margin and any deviation in the department is questioned. Concurrently, the training is being given to finance and value streams about lean accounting.	
	4				
Level 3	5	Filling up of operational data initiated		Product costing is initiated, company is divided into value streams and average product costs in the value stream costing is calculated on monthly basis	6
	6				
Level 4	7	Filling up of finance data initiated		Value stream costing (summary direct costing of the value stream) is widely used. When the costs of individual products are required, we use features and characteristics costing.	
	8				
Level 5	9	Filling up of capacity data initiated	9	Value stream direct costing is being used for individual product costing. Monthly reporting is promptly done.	
	10				
Level 6	11	Concept understood and weekly filling started		Value stream direct costing is being used for target costing for	
	12			the existing and new product development	
Score as on date			9		6
Total score			9		6

Table 17.15   Format for Assessment of Budgeting, Planning, Continual Improvement at Perfect Gear Company as on 31 March 2019.

Category		14. Budgeting and planning			15. Continual improvement	
Reference chapter		13			2, 3, 4, 5	
Sub-category		Shift from managing by departmental budgets to managing by value stream, driven by the sales and operations planning process			From a department-based organization to a company embracing lean production system and lean accounting	
Score	Maximum score	Stage	Achieved score		Stage	Achieved score
Level 1	1	We have extensive and detailed budgeting for every department and cost center and for every account and sub-account. This way we can plan and control our expenditure. We have a formal annual budget development process in which each department manager develops his own budget for approval. Budget vs. actual reports are prepared monthly by department and reviewed in meetings.			The financial reports are made quarterly and department managers are unable to link it with plant floor performance. All departments are busy improving their own efficiencies. There is no interaction with the customers.	
Level 1	2					
Level 2	3	We have greatly simplified the annual budgeting process by eliminating most cost centers and accounting codes from the items that need to be budgeted. We have begun to implement a formal sales operations and financial planning process each month and we plan by value stream.			We have established value stream continuous improvement teams. The lean tools are being understood by all functions and improvement initiatives are in progress. Training for value streams and changes are being brought in to work on the philosophy of value stream management.	
Level 2	4					
Level 3	5	We have eliminated department budgets. We create monthly (periodic) rolling budgets for each value stream from our sales, operations and financial planning process. Our budgeted values include both financial and non-financial performance. We regularly include value stream targets for elimination of waste and for increasing available capacity through the application of lean initiatives.	6		Continuous improvement is now routine within the value stream. The capacities of functions are being calculated and thrust toward minimization of non-value adding capacity usage is on. Corporate scorecards are prepared on monthly basis and understood by all functions.	6
Level 3	6					
Level 4	7	The company is managed by value streams both operationally and financially. The monthly rolling budgets are key to the ongoing continuous improvements of the value streams and the overall business.			Almost everybody is actively involved in week-by-week continuous improvement projects, performance improvement and cost impacts, freed up capacity.	
Level 4	8					
Level 5	9					
Level 5	10					
Level 6	11					
Level 6	12					
Score as on date			6			6
Total score			6			6

Table 17.16   Format for Assessment of Financial Benefits of Lean at Perfect Gear Company as on 31 March 2019.

Category		16. Financial benefits of lean changes	
Reference chapter		5, 6, 7, 8, 9, 14, 17	
Sub-category		*Focus to shift from calculating financial benefits from lean initiatives to understanding the total concept of capacity usage*	
Score	Maximum score	Stage	Achieved score
Level 1	1	The financial benefits of lean project initiatives implementation are being calculated but the effect of these benefits is difficult to link with the topline and the bottom line.	
	2		
Level 2	3	We monitor financial benefits from the lean initiatives and understand how these improvements are linked with the non-value adding capacity usage reduction. Understand how much free capacity is available and how it can be used for taking more orders. Also started making outsourced products items in-house.	
	4		
Level 3	5	We have established monthly financial gains calculations from all lean initiatives and teams are understanding this and are able to correlate with the freeing up the capacity.	5
	6		
Level 4	7	All functions are in the teams for lean initiatives, resulting in huge gains to bottom line. The teams are motivated looking at the financial results they are achieving.	
	8		
Level 5	9		
	10		
Level 6	11		
	12		
Score as on date			5
Total score			5

Table 17.17 Format for Assessment of Transactions Elimination and Role of Finance at Perfect Gear Company as on March 2019.

Category		17. Transactions elimination		18. Role of finance people	
Reference chapter		16		12	
Sub-category		*Material cost, labor costs, inventory tracking, accounts payable, accounts receivable, month end closing. Focus to shift from tracking individual costs to directly expense the materials, labor to the value streams. Reduction of inventory helps in switching to cycle counting.*		*Shift the role of finance from detached evaluators of the lean results to integral members of the value stream teams*	
Score	*Maximum score*	*Stages*	*Achieved score*	*Stages*	*Achieved score*
Level 1	1	Conventional system of material tracking, daily tracking of labor, inventory tracking in the process, yearly full inventory counting, three-way matching to arrive at accounts payable, mailing invoices to customers and monthly closing reports are made well into end of next month		The finance people are attuned to old practices of book-keeping and gathering data from ERP and maintaining records and trying the utmost correct status of the finance of the company. They understand only the numbers but have no clue as to how these numbers are linked with the working on the plant floor.	
Level 1	2				
Level 2	3	The backflushing of labor and overhead costs and material cost allocation to work order as it enters the company, cycle counting of inventory, authority to approve is being lowered down the hierarchy and open POs to suppliers, e-kanban system, requested customers to give open POs and dispatch invoice to work as payment request – all these are in the work in progress		The finance people have moved out of their offices and are part of teams of lean initiatives and are beginning to understand the operations and better understanding of the finances also. They are getting lean production system and lean accounting training. Started making capacity calculations and finalizing corporate scorecards.	4
Level 2	4				
Level 3	5	The process is established. Further value stream costing is also established, accounts payable to suppliers when they deliver materials to assembly line get paid based on kanban, similarly customers have started paying based on kanban. Authorization has come to value stream manager and below and only high value items prior approval is required. Quarterly book closing and monthly P&L is prepared on 2nd of next month.	5	All finance activities is now done on value stream basis and performance measures are used which are commensurate with the lean methodology. They are sitting with the operations teams reporting to value stream managers. Corporate scorecard is well entrenched and positive movements have been achieved in the results.	
Level 3	6				
Level 4	7	The transactions are eliminated to great extent as these practices are well trenched in the company now. The corporate scorecard is now made weekly. The managers are now free to spend more times on value added activities.		P&L comes out on 1st of every month. All managers understand the plusses or minuses of financial figures and finance is part of the integral team.	
Level 4	8				
Level 5	9				
Level 5	10				
Level 6	11				
Level 6	12				
Score as on date			5		4
Total score			5		4

Table 17.18 Format for Consolidated Assessment at Perfect Gear Company as on 31 March 2018 and 31 March 2019.

Perfect Gear Company				
Lean and lean accounting assessment- consolidated		*Date*	*31 March 2018*	*31 March 2019*
Sl no.	*Category*	*Maximum score*	*Achieved score*	*Achieved score*
1	6S audit score	10	4	7
2	TPM-OEE, MTTR, MTBF, TBM, CBM	10	3.5	7.5
3	TQM	10	3	6
4	Continual improvement projects in hand	10	3	6
5	Flow and pull – supermarket kanban system	12	3	6
6	Flow and pull – supermarket kanban system	12	3	6
7	Daily management and visual management	12	3	7
8	Value stream implementation	12	2	11
9	Performance measures basis	12	4	11
10	Performance measurement system	12	4	10
11	Production capacity of the company	12	3	8
12	Corporate scorecard	12	3	9
13	Product costing	12	4	6
14	Budgeting and planning	8	2	6
15	Continual improvement	8	2	6
16	Financial benefits of lean changes	8	2	5
17	Transactions elimination	8	2	5
18	Role of finance people	8	2	4
	Total score	188	53	127
	Total score in %		28%	67%

management system and lean accounting system implementation journey. There are nine audit sheets. The first eight audit sheets show the achieved score against each benchmark. The ninth audit in Table 17.9 is the consolidated chart that gives the score as on 31 March 2018.

Table 17.9 shows the lean and lean accounting assessment for March 2018 consolidated. The score in March 2018 is 28%.

17.3 Lean Assessment Score Card of Perfect Gear Company as on March 2019

Table 17.10 through Table 17.17 show the lean and lean assessment format filled up as on 31 March 2019 to assess the status of the lean production system and lean accounting implementation journey after one year.

17.4 Consolidated Monthly Assessment Audit Score

A consolidated statement of the Assessment Audit is prepared as on 31st march 2018 and as on 31st march 2019 as per the Table 17.18.

The lean and lean accounting score increased from 28% to 67%, as shown in Figure 17.1.

Figure 17.1 shows the assessment audit score from March 2018 to March 2019 and the audit score was continually rising. This reaffirmed the Perfect Gear Company was on the right path and the corresponding operational, capacity enhancement and financial gains were taking place. The next chapter will aptly describe the two years kaizen and lean

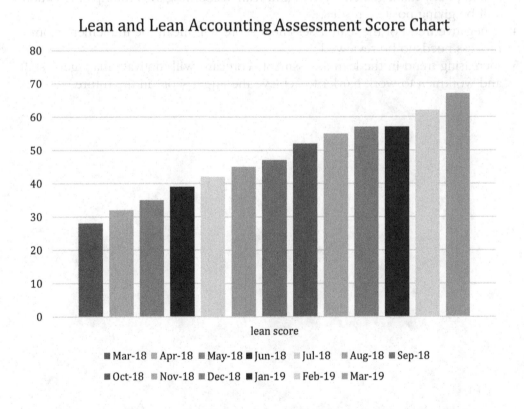

Figure 17.1   Consolidated Monthly Assessment Audit Score from March 2018 to March 2019.

journey at Perfect Gear Company, the process adopted and the resulting outcome.

Key Takeaways

1. A lean assessment is not merely an audit of the current level of operations while implementing the lean production system, daily management system and lean accounting system but also a directive to take the company to the next level of operations. It steers the focus of the decision-makers in the right direction and acts as the true North Star for the company by laying down the road map for future. The lean assessment scorecard is designed for this purpose.
2. Every company in each industry is unique in its own way and before any company starts benchmarking against the industry's best players, it can use this lean assessment tool to assess what is the current status of the company and analyze the progress achieved every quarter.
3. If the lean assessment scorecard has increasing trend, then the lean production system, daily management system and lean accounting system implementation will be giving positive results.
4. A negative trend of the lean assessment score will mean the implementation process needs to be reviewed.
5. Increasing trend in the lean assessment scorecard will motivate managers, staff and workmen to work harder to achieve the target score in the future.

Chapter 18

Lean Transformation Journey of Perfect Gear Company

There are four purposes of improvement: easier, better, faster and cheaper. These four goals appear in the order of priority.

– Shigeo Shingo

Shigeo Shingo appropriately summarized the lean and kaizen journey in the previous quote. There are four elements in the quote. The first element is 'easier'. If the workplace improvements are not 'reducing efforts' in operations, the workforce will not accept the changes. The second element is 'better'. The customers must get the 'quality' products in full quantities. The third element is 'faster'. The customer must get their products or services within the 'agreed time'. The fourth element is 'cheaper'. The company must achieve the first three elements and then, to achieve more profits, it should continuously 'reduce cost of production' by implementing lean and kaizen. This will be the 'win-win' situation for all stakeholders involved.

Perfect Gear Company is a capital machine builder group with three divisions for capital machinery – hot rolling mills, cold rolling mills and gearbox division. The company had many teething problems and was unable to serve its clientele. The clients were unhappy with the repetitive quality issues. The products were not delivered on time and in full quantities. Internally, there were manufacturing issues in the bottleneck operations. The breakdowns in the machines were hampering smooth operations. The changeover times on the critical machines were high. The layout of the

DOI: 10.4324/9781003221746-18

plant was poor and excessive internal transportation was adding delays and increased costs of production. The first time right quality was poor, leading to rework and rejections. Poor skills of the workmen and supervisors were a matter of concern. There was a high level of inventory in the raw material, WIP and finished goods. Customers were cancelling the orders at the last moment due to delay in supply and quality issues. The market for their product was growing at a decent pace and more export opportunities were opening up on the other hand.

Perfect Gear Company took the decision to implement the lean production system, daily management system and lean accounting system simultaneously to come out of the sticky situation.

Perfect Gear Company availed the services of three members of an external sensei team who were experts in the field of lean production system, daily management system and lean accounting system. The outsourced sensei team decided to take four actions. The process was initiated first with the assessment, second was to identify the gaps and set the improvement targets, third was to estimate the summary of financial benefits and fourth was to create the road map.

A session with top management was conducted to apprise them of the assessment and the road map for improvement and share potential benefits and goals. The obvious next step was to train internal change agents and then start implementation/actions as per the road map.

The following lean and kaizen tools methodology was formulated for Perfect Gear Company. The focus was broadly kept on the implementation of the following tools:

- 6S
- Total Productive Maintenance – Concepts of OEE, MTTR, MTBF, TBM, CBM
- Total Quality Maintenance
- Kobetsu Kaizen (Focus Improvement) Projects across Functions
- Flow and Pull – Supermarket Kanban System Implementation
- Daily Management
- Value Stream Implementation
- Selection of 'Lean Measures' at the Work Centers and Value Streams
- Value Stream Costing
- Plant Capacity Measurement
- Corporate Scorecard
- Performance Measurement System

- Lean ERP Implementation
- Product Costing Based on Lean Accounting
- Value Stream Budgeting and Planning and Review Mechanism
- Continual Improvement Projects across Functions
- Financial Benefits Due to Implementation of Lean Production System, Daily Management System and Lean Accounting System
- Transactions Elimination and Transaction Time Reduction
- Change in Role of Finance People Due to Lean Implementation

The following tentative road maps were finalized in three phases with 24 workshops. Each phase had eight workshops and was executed in eight months. The road maps focused on the previous 18 yardsticks to guide the company's journey of lean production system, daily management system and lean accounting system.

The first phase road map as per Figure 18.1 focused on training of basic tools to change the paradigm of the staff and workers to accept the changes being brought in and implementation of the basic tools starting with 5S, TPM, SMED, flow and pull and initiating the TQM and lean accounting by selecting the quality projects and selection and implementation of performance measures. After a month down the line the sustenance tools were also brought in and a kaizen and lean steering committee was formed.

The second phase road map as per Figure 18.2 was focused more on lean and pull, performance measurement system, capacity calculations, incorporation of corporate scorecard and product costing based on lean accounting. A profit and loss statement based on production was initiated along with the dispatch-based profit and loss statement.

The third phase road map as per Figure 18.3 was focused on implementation of budgeting and planning, monthly budget review and making the managers comfortable with the corporate scorecard and full understanding of product costs, transactions reduction and linkages of daily activities with the costs incurred and profit and loss statement on the first of every month and product costing at the touch of computer keyboard as soon as it is dispatched.

The kaizen approach is well suited for application in gemba (where the value addition is done). Here the emphasis is not only to identify the gap between target versus actual on various operating parameters on the basis of past performance but also on actual implementation of ideas generated by the cross-functional teams. The manager model machines were selected for improvement. These machines were normally the weakest machines in the

Tentative lean and kaizen implementation road map   Date

Phase I

Objectives	Means	Activities planned – projects in the workshops	Workshop								
			0	1	2	3	4	5	6	7	8
Kaizen awareness for management team, and participants of phase I including finance and accounts team	Training	One week of pre-implementation 'kaizen awareness' training; three sessions of two days each	▓								
		TPM – education and training pillar				▓	▓	▓	▓	▓	▓
Implement 5S, visual management methods in model areas including finance and accounts department	5S	5S and visual management on the shop floor			▓						
		Kaizen office level 1					▓				
		Kaizen office level 2, 3, 4					▓		▓		▓
Implement TPM with 4 pillars for selected model equipment	TPM	Planned maintenance step 1 and 2				▓					
		Planned maintenance step 3						▓			
		Kobetsu kaizen projects originating from PM					▓		▓		▓
		AM step 1 on model machine 1				▓					
		AM step 2 on model machine 1					▓				
		AM step 3 on model machine 1						▓			
		AM step 1 on model machine 2						▓			
		AM step 2 on model machine 2							▓		
		AM step 3 on model machine 2								▓	
Implement SMED for selected model equipment	SMED	SMED on model machine 1					▓				
		SMED on model machine 2							▓		
		SMED on model machine 3									▓
Inventory management for FG and distribution management	Pull flow	Finished goods									
		Distribution management									▓

Inventory management – ENGG spares	Pull	5S and materials management for selected ENGG spares
Quality	TQM	Select and work on quality improvement projects
Performance measures selection and implementation	Lean accounting	Top management, value stream, work floor level key measures
Sustenance	TCM, SDCA, daily management	Creating visual standards, audit procedures for sustenance, daily work schedule, typical checklists, action plan board and attendance board
	Steering committee	Kaizen promotion/communication; standardization, audits; recognition and rewards, multiskilling, obeya room

Figure 18.1 Tentative Lean and Kaizen Road Map for Phase I.

Tentative lean and kaizen implementation road map

Phase II

Objectives	Means	Activity planned – projects in the workshops	T	9	10	11	12	13	14	15	16	Date
						Workshop						
Training of finance to non-finance leaders, training of operational aspects to finance people	Training	Three weeks – ten sessions of two days each	▪	▪							▪	
		TPM, TQM, LPS – education and training pillar, lean accounting, PMS		▪	▪	▪	▪	▪	▪	▪	▪	
Implement TPM with 4 pillars for selected model equipment	TPM	Planned maintenance step 3/kobetsu kaizen projects originating from PM				▪						
		Planned maintenance step 4						▪				
		AM step 3			▪							
		AM step 4 planning and preparation					▪			▪		
Implement SMED for selected model equipment	SMED	SMED on model machine 3										
		SMED on model machine 4							▪			
		SMED on model machine 5						▪		▪		
Heijunka (leveled planning) for FG and distribution management	Pull and flow	Kanban implementation		▪								
		Design and implementation of heijunka in-house				▪						
		Logistics design (scheduled delivery routes and timetables)			▪							
		Distribution management – model channel partners									▪	
		Horizontal deployment – cross docks										
Inventory management	Pull	Kanban for packing material		▪								
		Kanban for ENGG spares			▪			▪		▪		
Quality	TQM	Select and work on quality improvement projects		▪		▪	▪	▪	▪	▪		
Implementation of performance measurement system	PMS	Workmen skill matrix		▪			▪		▪			
		Executive performance scorecard										
		Managers functional scorecard	▪									

Implementation of production capacity	Capacity	Capacity for manpower									
		Capacity for machines									
Implementation of corporate scorecard	Corporate scorecard	Incorporation of operational data									
		Incorporation of financial data									
		Incorporation of capacity data									
Introduction of product costing based on lean accounting	Lean accounting	Concept of average value stream costing									
		Cost of individual product costs on dispatch									
Profit and loss statement to be made as per lean accounting (on production basis additionally)		Profit and loss statement on 1st of every month									
Kaizen qualification for kaizen promotion office executives	Lean black belt	Yellow belt, green belt, black belt, master black belt certification									
Promotion and sustenance	TCM, SDCA, daily management	Creating visual standards, audit procedures for sustenance, daily work schedule, typical checklists, action plan board and attendance board									
	Kaizen promotion office/ steering committee	Creating visual standards, audit procedures for sustenance									
		Kaizen promotion/communication; standardization, audits; recognition and rewards, multiskilling, obeya room									

Figure 18.2 Tentative Lean and Kaizen Road Map for Phase II.

Tentative lean and kaizen implementation road map

Phase III   Date

Objectives	Means	Activity planned – projects in the workshops		Workshop							
			T	17	18	19	20	21	22	23	24
Training of finance to non-finance leaders, training of operational aspects to finance people	Training	Three weeks – ten sessions of two days each									
		TPM, TQM, LPS – education and training pillar, lean accounting, PMS									
Kaizen office – transaction elimination and Transaction time reduction	Lean accounting	Kaizen Office Level 2 (Standards for effective teamwork)									
		Kaizen Office Level 3 (Process Mapping and Improvement)									
		Easier operational movements									
		Backflushing of accounts									
		Material procurement simplifications, cycle counting of stores, e-kanban and open POs, three-way matching simplifications									
		Simplified accounts payable									
Value stream budgeting and planning	Budgeting and planning	Development of annual budgeting process value stream-wise									
		Monthly budget review meetings									
Calculations of the financial benefits of lean changes	Lean accounting	Linkages of reduction of non-value adding capacity usage with the financial benefits									
		Usage of free capacity available									
		Operations and financial team to calculate the monthly value stream profits									

			New role of finance managers
			Profit and loss statement to be made as per lean accounting.
		TCM, SDCA, daily management	Creating visual standards, audit procedures for sustenance, daily work schedule, typical checklists, action plan board and attendance board
Promotion and sustenance		Kaizen promotion office/steering committee	Creating visual standards, audit procedures for sustenance
			Kaizen promotion/communication; standardization, audits; recognition and rewards, multiskilling, obeya room

Figure 18.3   Tentative Lean and Kaizen Road Map for Phase III.

system. These machines were then given special attention by maintenance/operations and all attention was focused here so that there was a noticeable improvement in productivity, quality and yield on these machines. There was a widening gap in productivity figures between the manager model machines and the other machines. A whiff of change was than observed in the company.

The sensei team worked for five days in a week every month with the company's teams to achieve the targets. At the end of each kaizen intervention week, each team leader gave a formal presentation of improvements done and targets achieved to the top management. A three-week gap was kept between each workshop for the teams to finish their homework and for horizontal deployment. This methodology empowered the local teams to absorb the new practices being implemented.

A half-day virtual review session was conducted in between the two workshops. Based on the review, areas for further improvement were identified in consultation with the value stream managers and teams. Tangible gains were visible by the end of each workshop. Attitudinal and cultural changes were inevitable outcome with this approach.

Lots of visual displays were carried out so as to involve the shop floor workforce as well as various support services.

The continual improvement teams worked relentlessly to reduce the internal waste like downtime due to breakdown, minor stoppages, long changeover times and machines running at lower speeds, low quality levels and non-standard working. The teams diligently worked and implemented daily work scheduling, typical checklists, daily performance board, daily meetings schedule, action plan board and they also focused on skill level and training, performance measurement system and capacity measurement system. The financial team came out to the workplace and worked actively with the functional team in implementing lean accounting. The CEO and the CFO regularly monitored the progress and provided necessary resources and support when required.

The following major improvements were achieved during these three phases over a period of 24 months of kaizen and lean journey.

18.1 Lean Audit Score

The assessment was conducted initially in the last week of March 2018 when the first phase of eight months was over and the achieved score was

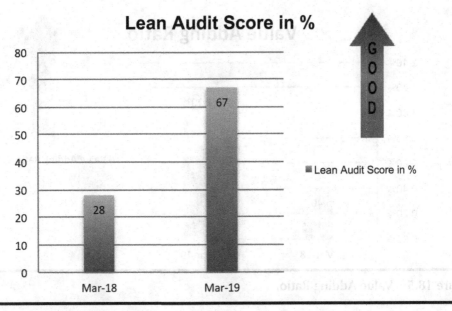

Figure 18.4   Lean Audit Score.

28%. The assessment was done again for evaluating the progress of implementation after one year in the last week of March 2019 when the second phase was over and the company was four months into the third phase. The achieved score was 67%. This happened due to continuous improvement projects in place. This was commendable. See Figure 18.4.

18.2 Value Adding Ratio

The value adding ratio went up by more than three times but a lot of scope was still there for improvements. See Figure 18.5.

18.3 Value of Inventory in US$ Millions

The inventory in raw material, work in progress and finished goods and consumables was very large at the start of the first phase. The implementation of flow and pull through kanban system and inventory management resulted in a large drop of inventory from 4413 tons to 1725 tons. The value of the total inventory came down from US$6.27 million to US$2.6 million. This is despite the fact that the cost of the raw material went up by 20%.

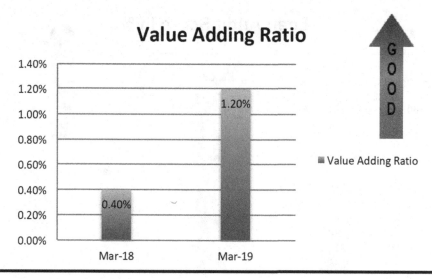

Figure 18.5   Value Adding Ratio.

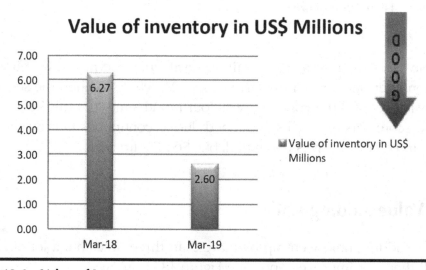

Figure 18.6   Value of Inventory.

This resulted in improved cash flows and profits as well as freed the workplace and stores. See Figure 18.6.

18.4 Throughput Time in Days

The company's ability to deliver the products had become four times faster. The throughput time, the time required for raw material to travel through the company's plant and become finished products, went down from 113 to 31 days. See Figure 18.7.

18.5 On Time Shipment in %

On time shipment with full ordered quantities went up from 70% to 80%. The clients appreciated it. See Figure 18.8.

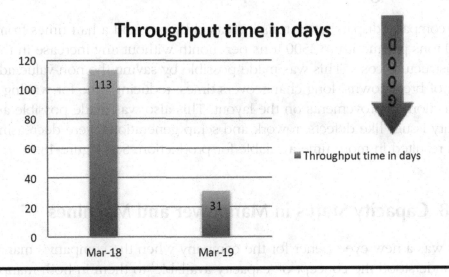

Figure 18.7 Throughput Time in Days.

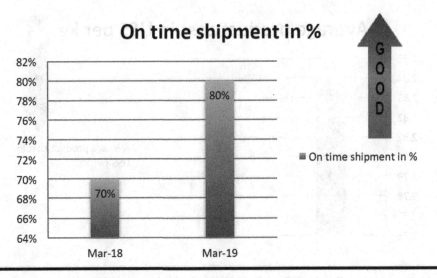

Figure 18.8 On Time Shipment in Percentage.

18.6 Average Products Costs in US$ per Kg

Due to the 40% reduction in the manpower costs and 16% drop in the conversion costs and despite the increase of raw material prices by 20% over one year the average product costs dropped by 2%. This was a creditable achievement. See Figure 18.9.

18.7 Average Monthly Dispatch in Tons

The company dispatches in tons increased by one and a half times from 1000 tons per month to 1500 tons per month without any increase in the infrastructure costs. This was made possible by saving the non-value adding time of breakdowns, long changeovers times, reducing time for waiting and inspection, improvements on the layout. This also was made possible as the quality issues like defects, rework and scrap generations were decreasing. This resulted in more time available for production. See Figure 18.10.

18.8 Capacity Status in Manpower and Machines

This was a new eye opener for the company when the company's managers understood the concept of 'capacity available' to them in both manpower

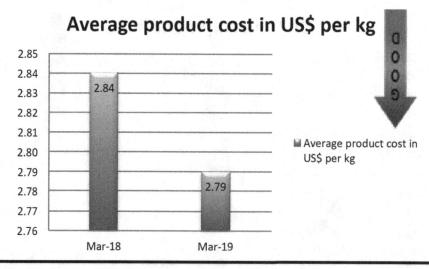

Figure 18.9   Average Product Cost in US$ per Kg.

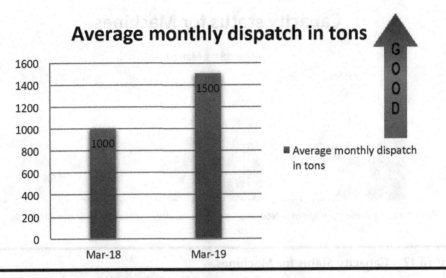

Figure 18.10 Average Monthly Dispatch in Tons.

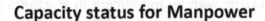

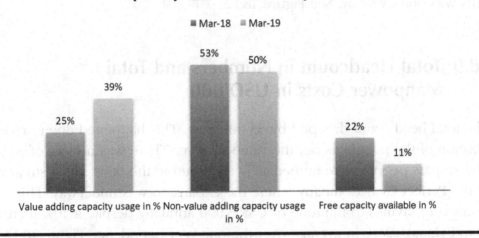

Figure 18.11 Capacity Status for Manpower.

and machines and how well they were using it. The manpower value adding capacity usage went up from 25% to 39%. The non-value adding capacity usage in manpower dropped by 3% and 11% capacity was freed for future usage and bringing in the contract jobs within the plant. See Figure 18.11.

The machine capacity usage went up from 44% to 66%. This was made possible by a drop of 22% of the non-value adding capacity usage by reducing the breakdowns, long changeovers, waiting for material and inspection. A 50% increase in the capacity usage from 44% to 66% is like adding half

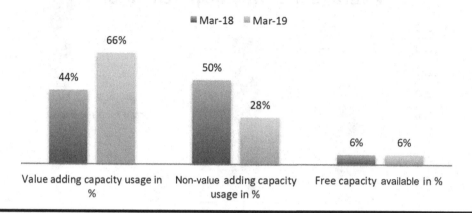

Figure 18.12   Capacity Status for Machines.

the plant in the company without investment in machines and manpower. This was praiseworthy. See Figure 18.12.

18.9 Total Headcount in Numbers and Total Manpower Costs in USD'000

The total head count dropped by 53 numbers. This happened due to reorganization of the people as per the value streams. There was no loss of jobs. The surplus people were immediately absorbed in the other value streams of the Perfect Gear Company where the expansion was underway. This resulted in savings to the tune of US$53,000 annually despite a 10% increase of individual salary in average over the one-year period. See Figure 18.13 and Figure 18.4.

18.10 Annual Sales Revenues

There was a 10% increase in average product sales price from March 2018 to March 2019. Due to increased turnover and reduced conversions costs the annual sales revenue went up from 40 million to 66 million USD, a rise of 65%. This was well recognized by the company and teams were suitably rewarded. See Figure 18.15.

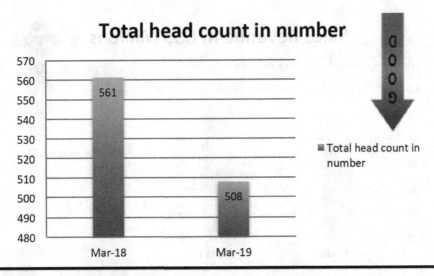

Figure 18.13   Total Headcount in Number.

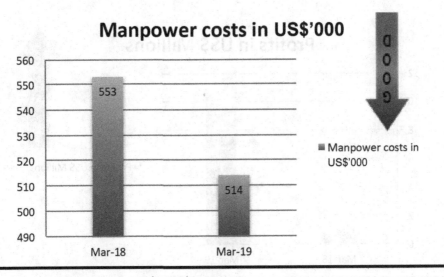

Figure 18.14   Manpower Costs in US$'000.

18.11 Annual Profits in US$ Millions and Percentage Terms

Annual profits in percentage went up from 5% to 17% of the sales value.

In absolute terms the profits jumped from two million to 11.3 million USD, a rise of 5.6 times. See Figure 18.16.

Perfect Gear Company's lean and kaizen journey was a success story and laudable. The teams were fortunate to be part of this company where

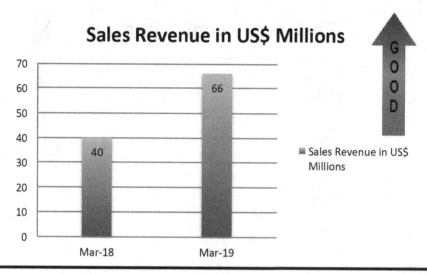

Figure 18.15   Annual Sales Revenue in US$ Millions.

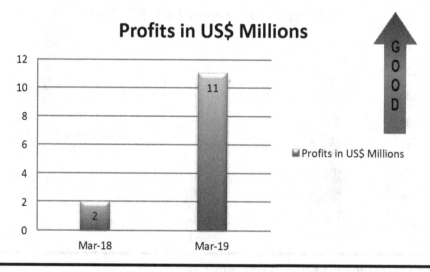

Figure 18.16   Annual Profits in US$ Millions.

the management took the decision to go ahead with phase three simultaneous implementation of lean production system, daily management system and lean accounting system spanning over 24 months. This ultimate success was the result of the coordinated quality work and efforts of the teams. The teams were dedicated and hard working and remained tenacious at the same time. There was an all around motivation to take this journey forward.

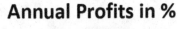

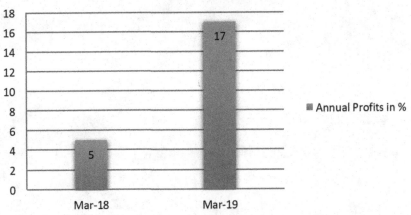

Figure 18.17 Annual Profits in Percentage.

Both the CEO and the CFO stood behind the team in good as well as tough times.

And the kaizen and lean journey continues.

Key Takeaways

1. The key purposes of continual improvement for successful implementation of the lean production system, daily management system and lean accounting system in two lines:
   There are four purposes of improvement: easier, better, faster and cheaper. These four goals appear in the order of priority.

   – Shigeo Shingo

2. A company must implement the lean production system, daily management and lean accounting *simultaneously* to come out of the sticky situation. Lean accounting is the *missing link* that has been ignored too long.

3. The company will become the *'lean cost producer'* with best on time delivery of the quality products and services to the customers than its competition and together with its happy employees.

4. 'Healthy financial statements on *first of every month* and *product costing at the touch of computer button as it is shipped*' are the next best achievements.

Index

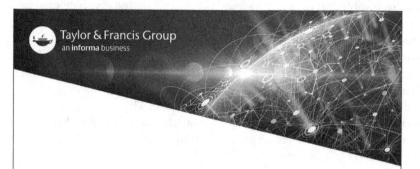

Printed in the United States
by Baker & Taylor Publisher Services

Printed in the United States
by Baker & Taylor Publisher Services